The Kurdish National Movement in Turkey

This book provides an interpretive and critical analysis of Kurdish identity, nationalism and the Kurdish national movement in Turkey since the 1960s. By raising issues and questions relating to Kurdish political identity and highlighting the ideological specificity, diversity and the transformation of Kurdish nationalism, it develops a new empirical dimension to the study of the Kurds in Turkey.

Cengiz Gunes applies an innovative theoretical approach to the analysis of an impressively large volume of primary sources and data drawn from books and magazines published by Kurdish activists, political parties and groups. The analysis focuses on the specific demands articulated by the Kurdish national movement and looks at Kurdish nationalism at a specific level by disaggregating the nationalist discourse, showing variations over time and across different Kurdish nationalist organisations. Situating contemporary Kurdish political identity and its political manifestations within a historical framework, the author examines the historical and structural conditions that gave rise to it and influenced its evolution since the 1960s. The analysis also encompasses an account of the organisational growth and evolution of the Kurdish national movement, including the political parties and groups that were active in the period.

Bringing the study of the organisational development and growth of the Kurdish national movement in Turkey up to date, this book will be an important reference for students and scholars of Middle Eastern politics, social movements, nationalism and conflict.

Cengiz Gunes holds a PhD in Politics from the University of Essex, UK. His main research interests are in Identity and Nationalism, Democratic Theory and Post-structuralist Political Theory.

Exeter studies in ethno politics
Series Editor: Gareth Stansfield
University of Exeter, UK

Unrecognized States in the International System
Edited by Nina Caspersen and Gareth Stansfield

The Kurdish National Movement in Turkey
From protest to resistance
Cengiz Gunes

The Kurdish National Movement in Turkey

From protest to resistance

Cengiz Gunes

LONDON AND NEW YORK

First published 2012
by Routledge
2 Park Square, Milton Park, Abingdon, Oxfordshire OX14 4RN

Simultaneously published in the USA and Canada
by Routledge
711 Third Avenue, New York, NY 10017

First issued in paperback 2014

Routledge is an imprint of the Taylor & Francis Group, an informa business

© 2012 Cengiz Gunes

The right of Cengiz Gunes to be identified as author of this work has been
asserted by him in accordance with sections 77 and 78 of the Copyright,
Designs and Patents Act 1988.

All rights reserved. No part of this book may be reprinted or reproduced or
utilised in any form or by any electronic, mechanical, or other means, now
known or hereafter invented, including photocopying and recording, or in
any information storage or retrieval system, without permission in writing
from the publishers.

Trademark notice: Product or corporate names may be trademarks or
registered trademarks, and are used only for identification and explanation
without intent to infringe.

British Library Cataloguing in Publication Data
A catalogue record for this book is available from the British Library

Library of Congress Cataloging in Publication Data
Gunes, Cengiz.
    The Kurdish national movement in Turkey: from protest to resistance/
    Cengiz Gunes.
    p. cm. – (Exeter studies in ethno politics)
    Includes bibliographical references and index.
    1. Kurds–Turkey–Politics and government–20th century.
    2. Kurds–History–Autonomy and independence movements.
    3. Kurdistan–History–Autonomy and independence movements.
    4. Nationalism–Turkey–History–20th century. 5. Government,
    Resistance to–Turkey–History. 6. Kurds–Turkey–Government relations.
    7. Partiya Karkerên Kurdistanê. I. Title.
    DS59.K86G855 2011

    320.5409566′7–dc23

ISBN 978-0-415-68047-9 (hbk)
ISBN 978-1-138-89841-7 (pbk)
ISBN 978-0-203-18086-0 (ebk)

Typeset in Times
by Wearset Ltd, Boldon, Tyne and Wear

Contents

Acknowledgements	viii
Abbreviations	x

Introduction: the Kurdish question in Turkey   1

1 Deconstructing Kurdish identity and nationalism in academic discourses   8

Introduction 8
The Kurds and the Kurdish question in Turkey: conflict analysis
   and political history literature 9
The Kurdish movement and the PKK as a case study 16
Conclusion 23

2 Understanding Kurdish identity and nationalism in Turkey   25

Discourse theoretical account of identity formation 27
Understanding Kurdish nationalist discourse: hegemony, myth and
   radical democracy 31
Methodology and sources 37

3 The organic intellectuals and the re-emergence of Kurdish political activism in the 1960s   49

Introduction 49
Kurdish organic intellectuals and the public discussion of the
   'Eastern question' 50
Organised dissent and mass protest: the TKDP, the TİP and the
   'meetings of the East' 57
Conclusion 64

vi *Contents*

4 The emergence of the Kurdish socialist movement   65

Introduction 65
The signs of separation: establishment of the DDKO 66
The fragmentation of the Kurdish socialist movement 74
Conclusion 80

5 The Kurdish national liberation discourse   81

Introduction 81
Accounting for Kurdistan's fragmentation: 'colonialism'
  and 'feudalism' 83
Contestation and the PKK's hegemony 91
Conclusion 100

**6 'Becoming a Kurd': the 'national liberation' war and mass
   mobilisation**   101

Introduction 101
Fighting for Kurdistan: the 'war of liberation' and mass
  mobilisation 103
The sedimentation of the PKK's discourse during the 1980s and
  1990s 112
Conclusion 122

**7 Dislocations and the PKK's turn to democracy
   (1992–present)**   124

Introduction 124
Dislocations and the emergence of democratic discourse as the
  alternative (1992–1999) 126
The PKK's democratic discourse (1999–present) 135
Conclusion 150

**8 Contesting democracy and pluralism: the pro-Kurdish
   political parties in Turkey**   152

Introduction 152
Searching for 'inclusion' and 'recognition': the HEP and
  the emergence of Kurdish parliamentary opposition
  (1990–1994) 155
Rebuilding the pro-Kurdish democracy movement 164
Conclusion 174

Contents vii

**Conclusion: democracy, pluralism and Kurdish subjectivity
in (post)national Turkey**   176

Summary of findings: beyond essentialism 177
*Opportunities, difficulties and challenges for the Kurdish national
    movement in Turkey 180*

Notes   186
Bibliography   212
Index   230

Acknowledgements

The research that forms the basis of this book was carried out at the Ideology and Discourse Analysis (IDA) Programme, Department of Government, the University of Essex, and the supportive environment there equipped me with the knowledge and skills to fulfil my ambition to study the contemporary Kurdish national movement in Turkey. I am thankful to the members of the IDA programme: Aletta Norval, David Howarth, Jason Glynos and Ernesto Laclau for their guidance and support. I have benefited immensely from Ernesto Laclau and Chantal Mouffe's *Hegemony and Socialist Strategy*, and their theorisation of Radical Democracy has been the inspiration behind this book. I am most grateful to my supervisor, Aletta Norval for her feedback and support throughout my doctoral studies. She has been an excellent supervisor. I am also grateful to David Howarth, Yasemin Soysal, Jason Glynos and Ephraim Nimni, for their feedback on my research. Thanks are also due to the department's PhD administrator, Mrs Jackie Pells, for answering many of my enquiries and being helpful, and to the Government Department for providing me with the Postgraduate Research Scholarship that has significantly eased the financial pressures of doing a PhD. I am grateful to my family's encouragement and support throughout my studies. I thank my sisters, Hatice, Tulay and Makbule, and my brother Medo, for reading earlier drafts. I owe a large debt to my good friends Fesih Eren and Yu Tsai Hung (Evin), for their support and kindly lending me many useful books on Kurdish politics; Karen Karapetyan, for his useful feedback and encouragement at the early stages of my research; Hasan Eren, for sharing his observations of Kurdish politics in Turkey; Derya Bayır and Prakash Shah, for their continuous support, numerous conversations and providing me the space to explore and discuss, in a more informal context, some of the ideas developed in the book. I am grateful to the staff at the Kurdish Library in Stockholm, the International Institute of Social History in Amsterdam, the British Library in London and the National Library (*Milli Kütüphane*) in Ankara for making my life a lot easier by helping me to obtain the essential primary sources that I used in my research. Thanks are also due to the staff at ROJ TV, to Hozan Seyitxan and Hozan Şemdin – two members of the *Koma Berxwedan* music group – and to Rotînda Yetkiner for sharing their knowledge and experience of Kurdish music and culture. I am grateful to my editors at Routledge, Joe Golding and Suzanne

Richardson, and Gareth Stansfield – the editor of the series 'Exeter Studies in Ethno Politics' – for their helpfulness and efficiency in overseeing the production of my book. Finally, I am grateful for the support of many Kurdish political activists and ordinary people that I have had the pleasure of meeting and befriending during my research. They are too many to mention individually, and their kindness and generosity has never stopped surprising me.

Abbreviations

ADYÖD	*Ankara Demokratik Yüksek Öğrenim Derneği* (Ankara Democratic Higher Education Association)
AKP	*Adalet Ve Kalkınma Partisi* (Justice and Development Party)
ARGK	*Artêşa Rizgariya Gelê Kurdistan* (Kurdistan People's Liberation Army)
BDP	*Barış ve Demokrasi Partisi* (Peace and Democracy Party)
CHP	*Cumhuriyet Halk Partisi* (Republican People's Party)
DDKD	*Devrimci Demokratik Kültür Dernekleri* (Revolutionary Democratic Cultural Associations)
DDKO	*Devrimci Doğu Kültür Ocakları* (Revolutionary Cultural Hearths of the East)
DEHAP	*Demokratik Halk Partisi* (Democratic People's Party)
DEP	*Demokrasi Partisi* (Democracy Party)
DP	*Demokrat Parti* (Democrat Party)
DTH	*Demokratik Toplum Hareketi* (Democratic Society Movement)
DTP	*Demokratik Toplum Partisi* (Democratic Society Party)
ECHR	European Court of Human Rights
EMEP	*Emek Partisi* (Labour Party)
ERNK	*Eniya Rizgariya Netewa Kurdistan* (The National Liberation Front of Kurdistan)
FKF	*Fikir Kulüpleri Federasyonu* (Federation of Thought Clubs)
HADEP	*Halkın Demokrasi Partisi* (People's Democracy Party)
HEP	*Halkın Emek Partisi* (People's Labour Party)
HÎK	*Herekata Îslamiya Kurdistanê* (Islamic Movement of Kurdistan)
HPG	*Hêzên Parastina Gel* (People's Defence Forces)
HRFT	Human Rights Foundation of Turkey
HRK	*Hêzên Rizgariya Kurdistan* (Kurdistan's Liberation Forces)
İHD	*İnsan Hakları Derneği* (Human Rights Association)
KAB	*Kürdistan Aleviler Birliği* (Union of Alevis of Kurdistan)
KADEK	*Kongreya Azadî û Demokrasiya Kurdistanê* (Kurdistan Freedom and Democracy Congress)
KCK	*Koma Civakan Kurdistan* (The Council of Communities of Kurdistan)

Abbreviations xi

KDP	Kurdistan Democrat Party (Iraq)
KİP	*Kürdistan İşçi Partisi* (Kurdistan Workers' Party)
KKK	*Koma Komalan Kurdistan* (The Council of Associations of Kurdistan)
KNK	*Kongreya Netawa Kurdistan* (Kurdistan National Congress)
Kongra-Gel	*Kongra Gelê Kurdistan* (People's Congress of Kurdistan)
Kon-Kurd	The Federation of Kurdish Associations in Europe
KPSK	*Komaleya Partizanen Sor an Kurdistan* (Union of Kurdistan's Red Partisans)
KUK	*Kürdistan Ulusal Kurtuluşcuları* (National Liberationists of Kurdistan)
MGK	*Milli Güvenlik Kurulu* (National Security Council)
MHP	*Milliyetçi Hareket Partisi* (Nationalist Action Party)
MKM	*Navenda Çanda Mezopatamya* (Mesopotamian Cultural Centre)
NDR	National Democratic Revolution
OHAL	*Olağanüstü Hal Bölge Valiliği* (Governorship of the Region Under Emergency Rule)
ÖDP	Freedom and Solidarity Party
PAJK	*Partiya Azadiya Jin a Kurdistan* (Freedom Party of Women of Kurdistan)
PÇDK	*Partiya Çareseriya Demokratik a Kurdistan* (Kurdistan Democratic Solution Party – Iraqi Kurdistan)
PJA	*Partiya Jina Azad* (Party of Free Women)
PJAK	*Partiya Jiyana Azad a Kurdistanê* (Party of Free Life – Iranian Kurdistan)
PKK	*Partiya Karkerên Kurdistan* (Kurdistan Workers' Party)
PSK	*Partiya Sosyalista Kurdistan* (Socialist Party of Kurdistan)
PSSK	*Peşmergeyan Sor en Şoreşa Kurdistane* (Red Peshmergas of Kurdistan's Revolution)
PUK	Patriotic Union of Kurdistan – Iraq
PWD	Patriotic and Democratic Party of Kurdistan
SHP	*Sosyaldemokrat Halkçı Parti* (Social Democratic Populist Party)
SR	Socialist Revolution
TAK	*Tayrêbazên Azadîya Kurdistan* (Liberation Falcons of Kurdistan)
TİHV	*Türkiye İnsan Hakları Vakfı* (Human Rights Association of Turkey)
TİİKP	*Türkiye İhtilalci İşçi Köylü Partisi* (Revolutionary Party of Workers and Peasants of Turkey)
TİP	*Türkiye İşci Partisi* (Workers' Party of Turkey)
TKDP	*Türkiye Kürdistan Demokrat Partisi* (Kurdistan Democrat Party of Turkey)
TKSP	*Türkiye Kürdistanı Sosyalist Partisi* (Socialist Party of Turkish Kurdistan)
UDG	*Ulusal Demokratik Güçbirliği* (Union of National Democratic Forces)

xii   *Abbreviations*

YEK   *Yekîtiya Êzîdiyan Kurdistan* (Union of Yezidis of Kurdistan)
YJA Star   *Yekitiyen Jinen Azad STAR*
YJWK   *Yekîtiya Jinên Welatparêzên Kurdistan* (Union of Patriotic
             Women of Kurdistan)
YKWK   *Yekîtiya Karkerên Welatparêzên Kurdistan* (Union of Patriotic
             Workers of Kurdistan)
YTP   *Yeni Türkiye Partisi* (New Turkey Party)
YXK   *Yekîtiya Xortên Şoreşgerên Welatparêzên Kurdistan* (Union of
             Revolutionary Youth of Kurdistan)

The KİP and the PKK both have the same names when translated into English. However, they are two separate organisations. The full name for the KİP originates from Turkish and the full name for the PKK, from Kurdish.

Introduction
The Kurdish question in Turkey

The re-emergence of Kurdish nationalism in Turkey from the 1960s onwards and, more specifically, the subsequent conflict has become a significant political problem that Turkey found particularly difficult to deal with constructively. The Kurds' early attempts during the 1960s and 1970s to seek a remedy through legitimate channels and by raising their demands democratically were suppressed, leading them to seek other avenues to address their demands. The most vital expression of the Kurdish question in Turkey has been the guerrilla insurgency by the Kurdistan Workers' Party (Partiya Karkerên Kurdistan, PKK) and the conflict that started in 1984 and this has had major social, political and economic consequences, including significant loss of life. The limited recognition of Kurdish identity and cultural rights in the past decade indicates that the Kurdish challenge has succeeded in bringing about a discussion on the need to re-conceptualise the uniform Turkish national identity. The significant reduction in the military activities of the PKK since the withdrawal of its guerrillas and the declaration of a permanent ceasefire in August 1999 has significantly contributed to this change in Turkey's Kurdish policy. Overall however, the Kurdish question remains still without a permanent solution and the conflict is ongoing, with periods of relative tranquillity followed by intensification of antagonisms and escalation of violence.

The consolidation of the democratic regime in Turkey is closely linked to the successful institution of a pluralist democratic framework that is capable of including representation from the country's significant Kurdish minority. The Kurds constitute the majority of the population in the 'South-East' and the 'East' Anatolian regions; however, due to internal displacements during the 1920s and 1930s, and during the 1990s as part of the counteroffensive against the PKK, and due to voluntary migration during the 1960s and 1970s, currently they are dispersed and it is quite common to find them residing in almost all major towns and cities in Turkey.[1] Additionally, since the 1980s there has been a steady increase in the Kurdish refugee communities in many of the West European countries. Whereas the exact number of the Kurds is unknown, their population is estimated to be between 15 and 20 million constituting roughly 20 to 28 per cent of Turkey's population.[2] Hence, the position of the sizeable Kurdish minority within the Turkish society, the linguistic and cultural oppression that they

2   Introduction

were subjected to, and their challenge during the past 40 years to the sedimented 'Turkish' identity that foreclosed the possibility of any other national identification, continues to be a major social and political issue for Turkey and it clearly shows the weaknesses and limitations of Turkish democracy.

The construction of the political system in Turkey as a unitary and highly centralised republic, the definition of the national identity as exclusively Turkish and such that it prohibited the public expression of minority cultural differences was the result of the oppressive practices that Turkish nationalists pursued in the first half of the twentieth century to annihilate their political opponents, rather than the superiority or better suitability of the republican model to Turkey's reality. The reconstruction of the post-Ottoman political space in the Middle East into highly authoritarian nation states followed the failure of attempts to reform the Ottoman Empire and its *ancien regime* in the mid nineteenth century. As an attempt to modernise and westernise the Empire, the Ottoman reformers formulated the doctrine of Ottomanism as a 'supranational ideology'.[3] This doctrine proposed a uniform conception of Ottoman citizenship to replace the previous legal designations used for the subjects of the Empire under the *millet* system, which granted the Christian, Jewish and Muslim communities extensive powers to exercise self-rule. Hence, the political reforms sought to centralise the Empire and integrate the Christian and non-Turkish nations and ethnic groups, and resulted in the abolishment of local autonomy and all the associated privileges that the Kurds became accustomed to, which incited a series of Kurdish rebellions during the nineteenth century.[4]

A significant development during the end of the nineteenth century was the development of nationalism among Muslim nations and the establishment of the Ottoman Committee of Union and Progress (CUP) in 1889.[5] The CUP played a leading role in the Young Turk revolution of 1908. Initially, 'under the banner of "Liberty, Equality, Fraternity, and Justice"', the revolution offered hope that a 'constitutional monarchy founded on the rule of law' and parliamentary democracy will replace the absolutist monarchy.[6] However, instead of the institutionalisation of a new form of citizenship that respected pluralism and fostered fraternal relations among the Empire's many nations, the subsequent regime instituted by the CUP resulted in further centralisation and the reversal of the recognition of religious and cultural differences that the minorities enjoyed under the Ottoman *millet* system and that to a lesser extent the nineteenth century Ottoman reformers were keen to maintain.[7] Although support for Ottomanism among the non-Turkish and non-Muslim deputies of the re-instituted Ottoman Parliament remained strong, from 1909 onwards it became clearer that it was losing its appeal among the Turkish deputies as a more exclusive and aggressive form of Turkish nationalism started to dominate the CUP. Following the proclamation of the republic, the Turkish republican nationalism or *Kemalism* became the official state ideology and the guiding principle behind the widespread socio-political reforms.[8] However, instead of creating the desired homogenous Turkish nation, the strict application of Kemalist policies resulted in Kurdish nationalist backlash and conflict.

Introduction   3

Although the Kurdish Question has acquired the centre stage in the political debate in Turkey only in the past three decades, it has been a perennial feature of the country's politics throughout the twentieth century. The transformation of a multinational empire to a nation state required comprehensive social and political reforms, which were introduced by the nationalist elite in the early years of the republic and carried out with an uncompromising zeal to build the 'westernised', 'secular' and 'homogenous' Turkish nation. Hence, in stark contrast to the Ottoman Empire, Turkey adopted a completely different attitude to ethnocultural difference and diversity with a policy of integration through assimilation of what remained of the Empire's minorities forced through in a top-down fashion.[9] The widespread destruction that the Armenian and Greek communities experienced during World War I and the years that immediately followed it had significantly altered the demographics of the new republic and left the Kurds as the main non-Turkish national group in Turkey.[10] Consequently, the modernisation and assimilation policies the state pursued from the 1920s and 1930s onwards brought the Kurds into conflict with the authorities. The Kurdish demands for the recognition of their national and cultural rights were brutally suppressed. The subsequent demands by the Kurds for the constitutional recognition of their identity and rights has continuously been rejected by the state and the Kemalist regime on the basis that such demands promote 'separatism', and contradict the uniform conception of national identity and citizenship and the principle of the 'indivisible unity of the nation and the state' that the constitution has been set out to defend.

However, the rise of the contemporary Kurdish national movement in Turkey since the 1960s has provided a sterner challenge for the Kemalist regime. With the rise of Leftist, Islamist and Turkish nationalist oppositional movements in the same period, Turkey has been experiencing widespread social and political polarisation especially since the 1980s. A number of political proposals have been put forward by different political groups during the 1990s and the 2000s to overcome the political polarisation, reform the republican institutions and build a new overarching 'common identity' in Turkey. One such proposal by President Turgut Özal during the early 1990s attempted to re-conceptualise the national identity to make it more sensitive to cultural differences while at the same time emphasising the communalities such as the Islamic and the Ottoman heritage.[11] As steps towards raising the democratic standards in Turkey and to meet the EU membership criteria, the current Justice and Development Party (*Adalet Ve Kalkınma Partisi*, AKP) government have also been carrying out political reforms that have resulted in the limited recognition of Kurdish identity and demands. Again, the Islamic and Ottoman heritage is emphasised as the basis of the new common identity. As an alternative – and as I elaborate on in greater detail in my research – the pro-Kurdish democratic movement has been formulating a radical democratic political project to construct a democratic and plural society and institute a new framework to manage diversity and pluralism in Turkey.

4 *Introduction*

The research question

The main questions that my research seeks to answer relate to Kurdish political identity and the ideological specificity, diversity and transformation of Kurdish nationalism in Turkey. I draw on the post-Marxist discourse theory and discourse analysis framework, as articulated in the seminal works of Laclau and Mouffe, amongst others, to conduct my research.[12] As I elaborate in greater detail in Chapter 2, this framework allows me to offer a holistic approach to, and an extensive account of, the contemporary Kurdish national movement in Turkey since the 1960s. I analyse an extensive amount of primary sources that the Kurdish activists and political groups and parties have published in this period. My choice and analysis of the primary sources and data, including a discussion of selection criteria and the geographic spread and availability of the sources, is discussed under the 'Methodology and Sources' section also in Chapter 2.

As I discuss in greater detail in Chapter 1, the academic discussions of Kurdish identity converge around two dominant positions: either they assume an ethnicist, pre-given and essentialist conception of Kurdish identity, such as Hassanpour (2003) and Izady (1992),[13] or the validity of the Kurds' claim to be a 'nation' is questioned on the basis that they do not meet the necessary 'objective' conditions for nationhood, such as White (2000) and Kirişci and Winrow (1997).[14] Although questions of Kurdish identity, such as whether the Kurds are a 'nation' or not, are highly political, by occupying the position of an 'objective' truth-teller, academics provide a technical answer that is deemed devoid of any political concerns. Instead of situating my research within one of the existing approaches, that is, either trace the evolution of an essentialist Kurdish identity, or try to determine the status of the Kurds by engaging in questions about whether they are a 'nation', I utilise the discourse theory framework to transcend the existing polarities. By essentialist conception of identity I mean any account of political identity that treats identity as pre-given and posits the claim that it contains a stable authentic core that has remained the same throughout the time.[15] Against such a claim, as Chapter 2 explores more fully, discourse theorists highlight that all forms of identity are contingent and constructed within political discourse.

From the 1960s onwards Kurdish political activists started to challenge, once again, Kemalism and the set of relations of identity and difference instituted by it. The Kemalist understanding of Kurdish identity – or the denial of Kurdishness – was inverted by an alternative understanding of Kurdish identity and political subjectivity that instituted a new set of relations of identity and difference in its place. I analyse the discourses of the Kurdish activists and political organisations during the 1960s and early 1970s to provide the background to the emergence of the 'national liberation discourse' during the mid 1970s. It is important to note here that the discussions and elaborations that I offer of 'national liberation' are confined specifically to the Kurdish context in Turkey and do not attempt to posit general claims. The play of identity and difference takes place on two separate levels: one, on the level of Kurdish nation and national identity, and two, on the level of the organisations that contest the

Introduction 5

Kurdish identity. I reflect this in my analysis by highlighting the political and ideological debates that took place among numerous Kurdish political parties and groups during the 1970s. My analysis of the post-1980 period pays special attention to the discourses of the PKK as it has been the hegemonic force in Kurdish resistance in Turkey.

It is now accepted by many, especially by the Kurdish national movement, that any possible solution of the Kurdish question involves the deepening of democracy in civil society, respect for cultural and national diversity, and the further development of, and changes to, the democratic institutions in Turkey. The pro-Kurdish representation in Turkish politics dates back to 1990 and there is vast political experience at the local as well as the national level, which can shed important light on the experience of democracy in Turkey. By analysing the discourses of the pro-Kurdish political parties that existed since 1990 and focusing on the articulation of Kurdish rights and demands within the discourse of democracy, my research develops insights into the nature of democracy that is proposed and how will it be developed as well as highlighting the possible problems or setbacks for democracy in Turkey. This allows me to draw substantial conclusions about the deepening of democracy in Turkey, including the role the Kurds will play in this process, and my analysis offers normative and critical purchase for democratic theory in general and radical democracy in particular. Hence, the political challenge formulated by Kurdish nationalism against the Kemalist regime raises the following interesting questions, which are the central questions that this book examines:

- How was the category of 'Kurd' produced and reproduced within the two discourses deployed by the Kurdish nationalists? In particular, how are *difference* and Kurdish subjectivity being constructed within each discourse?
- What kind of political project is proposed by the Kurdish National Movement? How has it changed over time?
- What is the relationship between the assertion of Kurdish identity and the official Turkish (Kemalist) identity?
- Why and how did the discourse of democracy replace the previous 'secessionist' discourse of national liberation?
- What is the character of this discourse of democracy? How or to what extent does it address questions of pluralism, both within and outside the Kurdish community?
- To what extent has this discourse of democracy challenged the dominant conceptions of democracy in Turkish society at large?

By answering these questions, I delineate the way in which Kurdish nationalist discourse transformed a previously dormant ethnic identity into a dynamic political identity by:

- fostering a new understanding of Kurdish identity;
- transcending the given identity of the 'Kurd' as the 'other' of the 'Kemalist' identity by challenging it and proposing to change it;

6   *Introduction*

- stabilising Kurdish identity by redefinition and reconfiguration of 'being Kurdish';
- tackling the Turkish hegemony and representation of the Kurds within the dominant order through constructing and presenting its own notions of Kurdish community and citizenship.

Outline of the book

In order to elaborate on the research question in greater detail, Chapter 1 critically engages with the literature on the rise of Kurdish nationalism in Turkey to show its limitations and draw out the important questions and issues that are not addressed in the existing literature but find an answer in this book. In Chapter 2, I discuss more fully the theoretical and methodological resources that I draw upon in conducting this research. To highlight the organisational growth and evolution of the Kurdish national movement and provide an account of the political parties and groups that have been active in the period, the analysis of the empirical material is spread over six chapters with each chapter examining a particular period and a relevant set of issues and questions. This enables me to give the overall picture of the Kurdish national movement in Turkey, and the background to its emergence, evolution and transformation.

Chapter 3 explores the emergence of Kurdish political activism in the 1960s by examining the discourses and activities of the Kurdish activist intellectuals. It elaborates on the political context within which the debate on the 'Eastern question' was taking place, including the trials of the leading Kurdish activists, which played a significant role in raising the awareness of the Kurdish question in Turkey. It analyses the contents of the magazines that they published and the public debate that they generated. Initially during the 1960s, most of the Kurdish activists took part in the activities of the Workers' Party of Turkey (*Türkiye İşci Partisi*, TİP), and the Kurdish demands for equality and socio-economic development were articulated as part of broader demands for equality and socialism in Turkey. Additionally, we witness the emergence of an autonomist movement in the form of the Kurdistan Democrat Party of Turkey (*Türkiye Kürdistan Demokrat Partisi*, TKDP). The activities of the Kurdish intellectuals found a strong resonance among the Kurdish population and succeeded in mobilising a considerable number during the 'Meetings of the East' in the late 1960s. Then on, however, the Kurdish activists started to demand the establishment of separate Kurdish political organisations and founded the Revolutionary Cultural Hearths of the East (*Devrimci Doğu Kültür Ocakları*, DDKO). This gradually led to the Kurds' separation from the Turkish left-wing movement and the emergence of the Kurdish socialist movement in the early 1970s, which is examined in Chapter 4. Additionally, I provide an account of the numerous Kurdish socialist groups and political parties that came into being in the 1970s, and the articulation of Kurdish identity and demands within the Marxist discourse, which resulted in the constitution of the Kurdish national liberation discourse during the mid 1970s.

Introduction 7

Chapter 5 elaborates on the Kurdish national liberation discourse more fully and gives an account of the process of ideological condensation of the discourse. In particular, the problematisation of the national fragmentation and oppression that the Kurds suffered as a result of Kurdistan's division and disunity, and of the economic exploitation that the Kurdish working class and the peasantry experienced, is discussed. It also highlights the construction and deployment of the *Newroz* myth in political discourse as a myth of origin to construct and represent an ethnicist conception of Kurdish identity. The political practices that the national liberation discourse fostered, and the PKK's organisational growth during the 1980s and 1990s, are discussed in Chapter 6. Specific attention is paid to the PKK's construction and deployment of a contemporary myth of resistance to mobilise the Kurds during the 1980s and 1990s. The PKK's reinvigoration of Kurdish culture and music is also discussed in relation to the role it played in the Kurds' mass mobilisation.

Chapter 7 gives an account of the numerous dislocations that the PKK experienced together with the political practices that they fostered, such as the attempts to find a peaceful solution through ceasefires and the strategic transformation towards democracy. An account of the PKK's difficulties, how it has been attempting to overcome them via political renewal and an evaluation of its democratic discourse since 1999 are provided to show the rearticulation of the Kurdish question and the construction and representation of Kurdish identity and difference within it. Chapter 8 provides an account of the pro-Kurdish democratic movement in Turkey since its emergence in 1990. It focuses on the discourses and activities of the main pro-Kurdish political parties, their attempts to build a broader pro-democracy movement in Turkey, and their proposals for political reconciliation through democratisation and institution of a plural and participatory democratic framework.

1 Deconstructing Kurdish identity and nationalism in academic discourses

Introduction

The lack of academic institutions to coordinate and fund research into Kurdish history and society meant that surprisingly little research about the Kurds was carried out until the 1980s.[1] For many years the denial of the existence of a separate Kurdish 'nation' was pursued as an official policy and the Kurds were described as 'Mountain Turks'; in this way, the state restricted the scope of studies on all aspects of Kurdish society and culture. Unsatisfied with such restrictions, the state sponsored, produced and disseminated research, which had the aim of proving the 'Turkishness' of the 'Kurds' and was used to justify their forced assimilation.[2] Additionally, academic debate and research on the Kurds was suppressed as a result of the hegemonic representation of the Kurdish question in the state's discourse as a case of 'reactionary politics', 'separatism' or 'terrorism'.[3] This classified research on the Kurds as undesirable and created barriers for researchers by preventing them from questioning the 'official' representation of the Kurds in the state and popular media discourses or from engaging with the pertinent questions of Kurdish identity.[4] From the 1960s onwards, the state's discourse on the Kurds and the Kurdish question started to face a challenge from Kurdish activists.[5] Such a political critique was supplemented by ethnographic research carried out by sociologist İsmail Beşikci, who has been the main proponent of the critical studies of the Kurds in Turkey.[6]

The gradual emergence of the Kurdish national movement and the increase in Kurdish political activism in Turkey from the 1980s onwards witnessed a corresponding increase in books and articles on the Kurds and Kurdish nationalism. Overall these studies address a diverse range of issues and focus on different periods and aspects of Kurdish society and politics. Whereas the overwhelming number of these studies focuses on the historical origins and development of Kurdish nationalism in the Middle East,[7] with the intensification of the conflict between the PKK and the Turkish army and the security forces during the 1990s, numerous conflict analyses and political history accounts of Kurdish nationalism in Turkey have also been published.[8] This is unsurprising given that with the intensification of the conflict during the 1980s and 1990s, the Kurdish question acquired a central stage in Turkish politics, and had a huge impact on Turkey's

Deconstructing Kurdish identity and nationalism 9

domestic politics and on her relations with the European and Middle Eastern states. More recently studies that have a narrower focus on the PKK and the contemporary Kurdish national movement in Turkey have also been published.[9] However, in comparison with conflict and political violence, the Kurdish democratic and legal form of political engagement in Turkey has received relatively little attention. This chapter analyses the current literature to see how the issues and questions raised by my research – namely those pertaining to Kurdish nationalist ideology, and identity and mobilisation – are addressed.

The Kurds and the Kurdish question in Turkey: conflict analysis and political history literature

Predominantly the political history literature focuses on the re-emergence and evolution of Kurdish nationalism from the 1960s onwards and the conflict between the PKK and Turkey during the 1980s and 1990s. The causal explanation provided by the political history accounts, such as Taspinar (2005), McDowall (2000) and Van Bruinessen (2000), highlight the significance of the social and economic changes that took place in the Kurdish society as a result of the modernisation process in Turkey – in particular increased urbanisation, higher levels of educational attainment and increased contact with the wider world during the 1960s and 1970s. Similarly, the conflict analysis literature as exemplified in the works of Gürbey (1996; 2000), Kirişci and Winrow (1997), Barkey and Fuller (1998), Gunter (1990; 2008) and Ibrahim (2000) examine the conflict between the PKK and Turkey within a historical framework. They trace its origins and evolution and highlight the contributing social, political and economic factors, such as economic backwardness, underdevelopment and migration.

The discussion of Kurdish political activism during the 1960s in the political history and conflict analysis accounts designates a significant role to the new generation of activists and mentions the activities they have engaged in, especially the publication of magazines. However, this descriptive account does not examine the contents of the magazines that Kurdish intellectuals published.[10] Not only would such an analysis appropriately provide detail on the specificity of the demands that Kurdish activists were raising during the 1960s, but it would also draw attention to their conceptualisation of Kurdish identity and difference, and the cultural and political issues that they discussed in their magazines. By shedding light on how the Kurdish issue and demands were constituted in the discourses of the new Kurdish activist, such an analysis – as provided in this book – would allow us to formulate a better understanding of the process of self-reflection and self-understanding during the 1960s that the Kurdish intellectuals fostered among the Kurds, which in later years led to the re-conceptualisation and re-interpretation of Kurdish identity and its articulation through the discourse of Marxism.

The main focus of conflict analysis and political history accounts is the conflict and the evolution of the Kurdish national movement from the 1970s

10 *Deconstructing Kurdish identity and nationalism*

onwards. In particular, the PKK's hegemony over the Kurdish resistance is discussed; for example, Van Bruinessen cites the PKK's relations with other political groups and states in the Middle East, such as Syria, as a significant factor.[11] Conversely, Taspinar argues that what enhanced the PKK's appeal amongst the Kurds was the state's excessive and often indiscriminate use of force and repression, which was most acute during the military rule between 1980 and 1983, and included the use of indiscriminate violence against ordinary people and widespread torture against activists.[12] Barkey and Fuller, on the other hand, attribute the PKK's dominance to its ability to fight the Turkish military and survive against the efforts to eradicate it. It is argued that the PKK exploited and benefited from the existing tribal rivalries and established and maintained 'a broad infrastructure that facilitates its recruitment campaign'.[13] Bozarslan (2000) also draws attention to the role that the 'state's coercion' played in the PKK's use of violence. He argues that the construction of the Kurds and the Kurdish identity demands as a threat to national security made the integration of Kurdish demands into the Turkish political arena difficult.[14]

Although an overview of Kurdish politics in Turkey since the 1970s is provided in the political history and conflict analysis literature, the ideological specificity of Kurdish nationalism and the demands articulated by the Kurdish national movement have received insufficient attention. This is because the above-mentioned studies do not incorporate into their analysis the vast amount of primary sources and political and ideological literature produced and disseminated by the Kurdish movement. In fact, there is either very little or only superficial discussion on the ideology and discourses of the Kurdish national movement. The lack of sustained attention on ideology and discourses of the Kurdish movement creates certain barriers to understanding the nature of the conflict and antagonism between the Kurds and Turkey. For example, the discussions provided by Gürbey (1996), Taspinar (2005) and Barkey and Fuller (1998) accept the form of antagonism between the Kurds and Turkey as *given* and draw attention to the conditions that made antagonism possible. They describe the subjection of the Kurds to state violence and persecution that made them react and oppose such practices. However, none of them focus on *how* the Kurds interpreted or saw their experience as *oppression* and how they proposed to challenge it.[15] More specifically, they do not elaborate on *how* the relations of oppression were constructed within the discourses of the leading political groups and how this construction of antagonisms, in a particular way, implicates Kurdish identity in Turkey. Although most Kurds would have been victims of indiscriminate state violence, especially during political crises and military rule, many chose assimilation instead of resistance, whilst others chose to support Turkish left or Islamist groups. Hence, there were other avenues that could and were used to channel Kurdish discontent but the following relevant questions are not discussed in political history and conflict analysis literature: How did the Kurds interpret and formulate the solution to their oppression? And what made the Kurdish identity and demands articulated by the Kurdish national movement *more appealing* than the alternatives?

Deconstructing Kurdish identity and nationalism 11

Ideology and identity

As stated above, in general there is insufficient discussion of the ideology and discourses of the Kurdish national movement. In fact, the specificity and ideological diversity of Kurdish nationalism in Turkey are ignored and the issues of identity, especially how Kurdish identity is constructed within the hegemonic discourses that have been articulating Kurdish national demands, are not raised. For example, scholars often refer to the PKK as a Kurdish nationalist organisation without clarifying what is presupposed by this definition and without examining the key demands the PKK articulates. Such a characterisation creates confusion particularly when the PKK's national liberation discourse is analysed. Barkey and Fuller set out to determine whether the PKK is a 'nationalist' or a 'socialist' organisation. They state:

> The PKK's program mirrored the slogans of the extreme Left: Kurdistan with all four of its segments, controlled by Turkey, Iraq, Iran and Syria, represented the weakest link in "capitalism's chain" and the fight against imperialism was a fight to save Kurdistan's natural resources from exploitation.[16]

Despite acknowledging the PKK's socialist credentials and the influence of the 'extreme left', in discussing the PKK's discursive transformation, they argue:

> In fact, *behind the left-wing rhetoric*, the PKK had always been a nationalist movement. Its promise to save the exploited of the Middle East notwithstanding, its very formation represented a break with the Turkish Left and abandonment of the 'common struggle'.... Hence, its assumption of a nationalistic image is in fact not just in keeping with the times but also *a return to its real self*.[17]

Furthermore, Barkey and Fuller state: 'Although the PKK is primarily a nationalist organisation, it would be wrong to assume that it has completely abandoned the political Left. Its discourse is that of a national liberation movement dedicated to the construction of a socialist state.'[18] We do not know what Barkey and Fuller mean by 'nationalist movement' as they do not offer any definition but they presuppose that a national movement cannot use 'left wing rhetoric' or it cannot remain nationalist if it does so. As I argue in Chapter 2, it is very difficult to define a movement as 'primarily nationalist' because nationalism is strongly connected to other political ideologies and nationalist movements are involved in some other aspect of political demands. This is evident in the Kurdish case because since the creation of Turkey, Kurdish national demands were articulated within various discourses; initially, within the Islamist-conservative discourse (the early 1920s), as a modernist discourse (1920s and 1930s), underdevelopment (1960s), Marxist-Leninism (1970s and 1980s), and, finally, democracy (1990 onwards). Therefore, it is possible to articulate Kurdish national demands within a Marxist or socialist discourse and doing so would not mean that claims of social equality, as traditionally articulated by Marxism or socialism, are

12 *Deconstructing Kurdish identity and nationalism*

diminished; however, such an articulation changes the meaning of Kurdishness by altering the nature of the national demands. Also, instead of interpreting the PKK's ideological and discursive changes as a 'return to its real self', focusing on how the articulation of Kurdish demands within different political projects conceptualises Kurdish identity in a specific way would help us towards a better understanding of the contemporary Kurdish political identity.

The discussion of the ideology and discourses of the PKK provided in White (2000) also suffers from similar limitations and simplifications. Without making *any* attempt to understand the ideological complexity of the PKK and the key claims that it has been articulating over the years, he argues: 'The PKK claims to be Marxist and Leninist, but its ideology, strategy and tactics are a mixture of Stalinism and nationalism.'[19] Furthermore, in his discussion of the PKK's strategy and tactics, he again makes the connection to 'Stalinism':

> In theory, the PKK remains formally wedded to a Stalinistic two-stage theory of revolutionary strategy, in which the first stage is the achievement of a united democratic and independent Kurdistan (including the current Kurdish regions of Turkey, Iran, Iraq and Syria), via a 'national democratic revolution'.[20]

White's assertion is a serious simplification of the PKK's discourse as it does not seek to understand the specific claims and demands articulated by it. The specific articulation of Kurdish rights and demands and what conceptions of Kurdish identity emerge within the discourse of the PKK do not feature in his account. Hence, White's account fails to provide a sufficient discussion on the processes of identity formation and does not discuss the contours of the contemporary Kurdish political identity as has been constructed within the discourse of the PKK or other Kurdish organisations.

The debates on Kurdish identity in the political history and conflict analysis literature converge around two dominant positions: they either deploy an ethnicist and subjective conception of Kurdish nation and national identity, or they question the claim that the Kurds are a nation. Izady (1992) is a good example of the former and he reconstructs the entire history of the Kurds and Kurdistan dating far back to the ancient period, covering geography, history, language, culture, economy and national identity. He defines the Kurds rather generally as 'a multi-lingual, multi-religious, multi-racial nation, but with a unified, independent, and identifiable history and culture'.[21] Furthermore, he treats the category 'Kurd' as something that has always existed and has been internally constituted and, consequently, the interpretation of Kurdish identity demands or its representations does not feature in his study. Hassanpour (2003) also deploys a subjective understanding of nation and defines the Kurdish society as 'the population that identifies itself as Kurds' and Kurdish identity as 'the feeling, idea, or experience of belonging to a collective entity called "Kurd"'.[22] He examines the pre-twentieth century historical and literary discourses to trace the expression of this 'distinct' Kurdish identity; however, he does not offer any dis-

Deconstructing Kurdish identity and nationalism 13

cussion of how the Kurdish collective entity is defined or re-interpreted by the Kurdish national movement in the contemporary period.

Conversely, the scholars that question the categorisation of the Kurds as a nation do so on the basis that the Kurds do not meet the necessary 'objective criteria', such as 'a well-defined state', 'a single economy', 'common legal rights and duties for all members' and 'a shared language'.[23] Kirişci and Winrow (1997) argue that 'it would seem inappropriate to allocate to "the Kurds" a particular label ... it would seem that the Kurds are an amalgam of Turkic, Armenian and Assyrian and more dominant Indo-European groupings. The origins of the Kurds are hence somewhat obscure.'[24] White (2000) offers a similar exploration of Kurdish identity and draws attention to the difficulties of achieving 'scholarly unanimity' on 'who the Kurds are' and reviews the academic discussions on the origins of the Kurds and those that seek to *define* them.[25] He highlights the linguistic and religious diversity prevailing in Kurdish society and gives it as evidence that 'there is no single, universally agreed-upon meaning for the term Kurd'.[26] Furthermore, White's account contains some highly controversial claims: 'the so-called "Alevi Kurds" or Kızılbaş of Anatolia are arguably no more Kurdish than another minority people in Anatolia to whom they are closely related, the so-called "Zaza Kurds."'[27] He suggests that the Alevi Kurds and Zaza Kurds have 'a common ancestor in the Dailamites' and they are not Kurdish.[28] Such assertions are ill-advised, highly problematic and difficult to sustain. This is because, generally speaking, the Alevi Kurds consider themselves Kurdish, and the great majority, perhaps 70 per cent, speak *Kurmanci* – the mainstream Kurdish language – making them linguistically and culturally closer to the Kurds rather than the Dailamites.

In fact, White's and Kirişci and Winrow's discussions of Kurdish identity raise an important issue that has faced Kurdish nationalism since its inception, namely the fragmentation of Kurdish society, which is further deepened by religious, linguistic, tribal and regional differences. However, neither White nor Kirişci and Winrow offer any details of the Kurds' identity claims or the conception of Kurdish identity as articulated by the Kurdish national movement. They do not explore the practices that have been important in stabilising the meaning of Kurdishness. Instead they focus on the Kurds' local, regional, religious and tribal identities (the sub-national identities) rather than *the* Kurdish political identity as has been contested by the Kurdish national movement in Turkey. Every nationalist movement provides their nation's long history depicting their presence in the region and how the nation came into existence. This may include, for example, national myths and important historical events. A discussion of Kurdish nationalist historiography and the myth of origins, and the significance of such beliefs in enhancing the power and appeal of nationalism among the Kurds, are missing in their accounts.

Within the available literature there are some studies that analyse the Kurdish identity in ways that elucidate its specificity or highlight the processes at work in its transformation. Vali (2003) provides a theoretical critique of the primordialist and ethnicist theorisation of Kurdish identity and draws our attention to the

14 *Deconstructing Kurdish identity and nationalism*

modern nature of Kurdish nation and national identity.[29] O'Shea (2004) studies the social geography of Kurdistan to sketch the Kurds' and outsiders' perceptions of Kurdistan in a historical context. She draws attention to how the Kurds have used national mythologies and maps to construct and maintain group unity and a sense of belonging.[30] Hirschler (2001) studies the Kurdish nationalist historiography in Turkey during the 1990s.[31] Van Bruinessen (1998) examines the impact of the standardisation of Kurmanci Kurdish undertaken by Kurdish institutions in Western Europe.[32] Uçarlar (2009) provides a detailed and original study of the Kurdish linguistic rights in Turkey and important contributions that the exiled Kurdish intellectuals and writers made to the development of Kurdish language and literature.[33] Watts (2004) looks at the activities of the Kurdish transnational cultural, political and legal organisations and networks in Western Europe and assesses their impact.[34] Aksoy (1998) offers an extensive and historical account of the mythical origins of the *Newroz* festival.[35] In contrast, Aydın (2005) offers a more systematic examination of the Kurdish nationalists' construction of the myth of origin and resistance around the legend of Kawa and their appropriation of the *Newroz* festival as a Kurdish national festival.[36] Çağlayan (2007) examines the discourses of the Kurdish national movement in Turkey to account for the discursive construction of women's identity.[37] Gündoğan (2007) studies the evolution of the discourses deployed by the Kurdish national movement through examining the defences that the Kurdish political activists provided in Turkish courts from the 1920s onwards and specifically with reference to his own defence prepared for the *Kawa* movement during the early 1980s.[38] While these accounts provide important reflections on the discursive constructions of Kurdish identity and the process that played a key role in its stabilisation, they do not offer a systematic and comprehensive analysis of Kurdish nationalist discourse, including a detailed analysis of the reasons behind why the myth of Kurdish society resurfaced in Turkey during the 1970s and the subsequent mass mobilisation during the 1980s and 1990s.

The pro-Kurdish democratic politics

Kurdish national demands and claims, in addition to the radical and violent manifestation epitomised by the PKK, have also been articulated through the legal channels by various pro-Kurdish political parties since 1990. Although the pro-Kurdish democratic movement emerged in 1990 and it has been a feature of Turkish politics since then, surprisingly very little academic work has been done on Kurdish democratic politics.[39] Of those that exist, the books by Ölmez (1995) and Demir (2005) published in Turkish present a detailed chronological account of the emergence and evolution of the pro-Kurdish democratic movement in Turkey. Without engaging in a detailed discussion, the demands raised by the pro-Kurdish political parties are reflected in both of these studies. However, neither of these studies presents a detailed analysis of the discourses of the pro-Kurdish political parties to highlight their conceptions of democracy in Turkey, their articulation of Kurdish rights and demands and their attempts to form a

Deconstructing Kurdish identity and nationalism 15

wider democratic movement for political change in Turkey. Having served as an MP for the Democracy Party *(Demokrasi Partisi*, DEP) from 1991 to 1993, Alınak (1996) presents an interesting and reflective account of the party's activities. Çağlayan (2007) provides an account of women's mobilisation within the pro-Kurdish political parties since the 1990s and the articulation of women's rights and demands for gender equality in their discourses. However, Çağlayan's sole focus is on the women's mobilisation and the construction of women's political identity within the discourses of the Kurdish national movement.

Watts (1999) gives an account of the emergence of the pro-Kurdish legal political activism in Turkey and the state's attempts to suppress it between 1990 and 1994. By providing an informative insight into the nature of Kurdish activism which shows the complex and shifting nature of the relations between the pro-Kurdish parties, various state actors and other mainstream Turkish political parties, she highlights the difficulties that the pro-Kurdish parties presented for Turkey and the political elite in incorporating the Kurds' demands and dealing with its existence in the national political space. Also, in listing the state's oppressive policies against the People's Labour Party *(Halkın Emek Partisi*, HEP) and limiting the participation of the subsequent pro-Kurdish political parties, she shows 'the contradictions between Turkish nationalism as traditionally implemented by the state and the state's espoused commitment to democratisation.'[40]

Watts (2006) continues the assessment of the pro-Kurdish democratic movement and examines, more specifically, the impact that the participation of pro-Kurdish parties in Turkish politics had on the Kurdish national movement in Turkey in general. She argues that the Kurds' participation in the Turkish political arena helped to 'normalise' Kurdishness in the public realm, led to its consolidation in relatively stable arenas, enhanced the durability of the pro-Kurdish movement in Turkey, and lay 'the groundwork for government reforms approved by the parliament between 2000 and 2004 and loosened restrictions on collective public expressions of Kurdish identity.'[41] She lists Turkey's increased integration with the EU, the desire to maintain democracy, and the regional developments – especially the legitimisation of Kurdish self-rule in Iraqi Kurdistan – as having an impact on the rise of Kurdish electoral contention in Turkey and giving the Kurds the chance to utilise democratic process for their own benefits.[42] The reinvigoration of Kurdish culture and national festivals, such as the *Newroz*, by the pro-Kurdish movement created new opportunities for Kurdish symbolic politics in Turkey, which is defined as 'the use of representation – narratives, symbol, and spectacle – to maintain or transform a power relationship' and which brought about new impetus and durability to the movement as a whole and helped it to delineate Kurdish cultural distinctions.[43]

Although Watts's articles give an overall picture of the difficulty that the Kurds experienced in taking part in a wider movement for democracy in Turkey and draw attention to the public debate that has been taking place in Turkey concerning the legitimacy of pro-Kurdish representation, the account she provides does not include a discussion of the conception of democracy being proposed by the

16 *Deconstructing Kurdish identity and nationalism*

pro-Kurdish movement, how it addresses questions of pluralism – both within and outside the Kurdish community – and to what extent this discourse of democracy has challenged the established notions of democracy and citizenship in Turkey. A comprehensive analysis of the discourses of the pro-Kurdish political parties as carried out in this book is therefore needed to highlight how the Kurdish democratic discourse fosters a new understanding of Kurdish identity in Turkey and how it proposes to change the sedimented 'Turkish' identity through constructing and presenting its own notions of national identity and citizenship in Turkey.

The Kurdish movement and the PKK as a case study

Özcan (2006) and Romano (2006) are the two main case studies published recently on Kurdish nationalism in Turkey.[44] The former analyses the PKK as a movement and the impact it had on Kurdish nationalism in Turkey and explores various aspects, including the PKK's discourses and objectives, how it motivated its members and its internal structure. The latter is a theory driven study that, first, uses the resource mobilisation and rational choice theories to understand how 'people are mobilised into ethnic nationalist organisations', second, examines the 'politico-structural context' within which ethnic nationalist challenges to state authority occur, and, finally, focuses on 'identity politics' to understand 'grievances, interests and goals'.[45] Although an elaborate and extensive account of the PKK as a movement emerges from Romano's study, his focus, in contrast to Özcan, is broader and includes sections on the Kurdish national movements in Iran and Iraq. In this section, I critically review the account provided in these studies of the Kurdish nationalist mobilisation, the Kurdish political identity, the PKK's hegemony and its discursive transformations from the early 1990s onwards.

Mobilisation

Romano's explanation of the re-emergence of Kurdish nationalism in Turkey explores the 'structural conditions' and the 'political opportunity structures', and he highlights the importance of the democratic opening of 1960, economic development, and the urban to rural migration of the Kurds. These factors, in Romano's account, combined to create a 'non-traditional Kurdish nationalist elite' that became the spearhead of the Kurdish movement in Turkey during the 1960s and 1970s.[46] Through education, the Kurds were exposed to the ideas of nationalism and socialism and they participated in the left-wing movement in Turkey because it offered them a platform to express their opposition to the state.[47] Romano emphasises the lack of economic opportunities in his explanation of the political mobilisation of the leading Kurdish activists:

> High unemployment levels left increasing numbers of educated Kurds, who were now aware of the wealth and possibilities around them thanks to modern media and communications, frustrated and in search of options to

Deconstructing Kurdish identity and nationalism 17

better their plight. This stratum of the population would emerge in the 1960s and 1970s as the new elite leadership of many left-wing and Kurdish nationalist movements.[48]

This generalises the claim that the lack of economic opportunities caused the Kurds' radicalisation and their taking up of the cause of Kurdish liberation from the 1960s onwards. The leading Kurdish activists of the 1960s and 1970s, which Romano singles out as playing an important role in the rise of the Kurdish national movement, were either established professionals or students from well-off backgrounds; for example, among the leading Kurdish activists during the 1960s, *Musa Anter* was a prominent intellectual, businessman and journalist; *Naci Kutlay* was a doctor; *Sait Elçi* was an accountant; *Kemal Burkay* was a lawyer. In addition, there were many law, medical or economics students from Turkey's leading universities, who could and did establish themselves in important public and private positions, such as MPs, Senators, even Ministers. Also, the activities that this new Kurdish elite undertook, such as publishing magazines and books, required considerable financial resources to establish and sustain them without the expectation of obtaining large monies from them in the future. In fact, by taking part in Kurdish nationalist activities they would have jeopardised their professional positions and status as engagement in such activities is generally seen as a barrier for advancement in Turkish society. All of this suggests that lack of economic opportunities *did not* play a significant role in mobilising these leading activists.

During the 1960s many Kurdish activists took part in the activities of Turkish left-wing groups and seemed committed to a common socialist programme; however, during the mid 1970s the Kurds withdrew their support from the Turkish left and began to establish specifically Kurdish revolutionary groups and parties. The emergence of so many new Kurdish political organisations is explained through 'political opportunity structures'.[49] After acknowledging that from 'a perspective of political opportunity structures, the emergence of so many new leftist Kurdish nationalist groups is somewhat puzzling', Romano draws attention to the closed nature of the political system vis-à-vis the Kurdish demands during the 1970s, which made it impossible to pursue Kurdish nationalist aspirations within the institutionalised system.[50] Although he rightly highlights the Turkish left's rejection of the demands raised by the Kurds, or its unwillingness to incorporate particularistic Kurdish demands, as being important in influencing the Kurds' decision to establish their separate organisations, his account does not provide *any* detail on the specific demands that the Kurdish activists raised nor does it discuss the Kurdish activists' stated reasons for advocating their separate organisations. Furthermore, Romano neither explains how the position of Kurdish socialists differed from that of Turkish socialists nor provides any discussion of the debates that were taking place during the 1960s and the 1970s within Turkey's socialist movement, which would reveal the numerous ideological and political differences and provide an account for the emergence of the Kurdish national liberation discourse. In fact, the demands Kurdish

18 *Deconstructing Kurdish identity and nationalism*

socialists raised, which became increasingly radical throughout the 1970s, played a significant role in the Kurds' separation from the Turkish left because they could not have been incorporated into the programme of Turkey's socialist movement. The Kurdish question was reformulated as a problem of colonialism and national liberation during the 1970s.

Romano's account of the rise of the PKK focuses on the mobilisation process; in particular, he draws our attention to the effectiveness of strategies, tactics, and resource mobilisation that the PKK deployed which enabled it to develop into a mass movement. By using the already existing networks and exploiting the conflicts between the landlords and peasants – by fighting against landlords in defence of peasants' rights – the PKK's early cadres ('the political entrepreneurs' – defined as 'individuals whose prime motivator is not self-interest and who are not as risk-averse as the general population') enhanced the movement's base and operations and managed to win the sympathy of the peasants.[51] The PKK's strategy to manipulate local politics to its advantage is identified by Romano as the key factor in its success.[52] In addition, the PKK's attacks on the Turkish army and security forces, which showed the limits of the state control, further enhanced its credibility. It is argued that:

> by offering goals that mattered to the people, selective (dis)incentives, astute organisation and coordination, and the establishment of credibility with the local Kurdish population through ideology, self sacrifice, and demonstrative actions against Turkish security forces, the founders of the PKK were able to turn their movement into a mass-based, significant challenge to the state.[53]

Romano's exclusive focus on the mobilisation process analyses the PKK's strategy in isolation by separating it from its ideology and discourse and ignores the articulation of the national demands of the Kurds by the PKK. The PKK's involvement in the peasant–landlord disputes that Romano highlights not only strengthened the peasants' relative position within the dispute but transformed the nature of the dispute. It provided a new understanding of the position of Kurdish peasants that emphasised economic exploitation by Kurdish feudal elites and foreign bourgeoisie, and cultural oppression and forced assimilation, and conferred a new political meaning to their struggle by re-interpreting and articulating their demands as part of the liberation of Kurdistan. This directed peasants' actions against individual landlords and also against the system that allowed for such oppression; the peasants were no longer identified as individuals subjected to exploitative and oppressive practices by the landlords but as part of a class and nation with its own political aims and goals. Hence, the PKK's discourses are not explored by Romano in any meaningful detail to show how the practices of Kurdish feudalism were problematised and how the relations of feudal oppression were constructed.

Furthermore, various other important aspects of the mobilisation of the Kurds by the PKK are missing in Romano's account of political mobilisation. The

Deconstructing Kurdish identity and nationalism 19

discursive construction of the PKK's struggle as the embodiment of the Kurds' struggle and its representation as such within its discourse and through music and various commemorative practices, including the reactivation of the myth of *Newroz* to construct a contemporary myth of resistance that was used extensively to represent its struggle, has not been examined at all by Romano. Similarly, he does not make any attempt to examine Kurdish cultural renewal and development that the PKK has fostered through its affiliate organisations and the role that Kurdish cultural politics played in its mobilisation of the Kurds in both Turkey as well as Europe. An exploration of the PKK's mobilisation of Kurdish women and the Kurdish Diaspora in Europe, which have been two significant aspects of its mobilisation of the Kurds and has significantly contributed to its financial, political and human resources, is *completely* missing in Romano's study. Additionally, the mobilisation of the Kurds by the series of pro-Kurdish political parties in Turkey since 1990 and the role that such a mobilisation played in the Kurds' overall mobilisation does not feature in Romano's account. The separation of the mobilisation process from ideology and discourse hinders Romano from providing a fuller account of the mobilisation as he does not examine the *affect* and *appeal* of the PKK's discourse and why its articulation of Kurdish demands was more convincing to the Kurds, which played a major role in its hegemonic appeal and successful mobilisation of the Kurds. Therefore, Romano's account is unable to provide us with the complete picture of the Kurdish national movement's mobilisation of the Kurds in Turkey and in Europe. Similarly, the reasons behind the PKK's hegemony, the representation of the PKK's struggle through its discourse and in artistic forms, the specific strategies the PKK used to mobilise specific sectors of Kurdish society, and the cultural and political renewal that it fostered, all of which played a central role in the PKK's mobilisation of the Kurds during the 1980s and 1990s, is not examined in any systematic and meaningful manner in Özcan's study.

Ideology and discourse

Özcan states that the PKK's early political objective was the creation of an independent socialist Kurdistan through revolutionary activity, and internally it was organised around the principle of democratic centralism. Its membership involved full-time commitment to the cause and required from its cadres to forego their 'private life' or 'individual initiative'.[54] Starting from the early 1980s, the PKK leader Abdullah Öcalan began to develop and exert his 'charismatic authority' with more force, which according to Özcan was 'an effective source of motivation both within the party organisation and among the Kurdish masses'.[55] However, the narrow focus Özcan deploys and his characterisation of the Kurdish question as an ethnic one, leads him to ignore the general Kurdish question and how it was constructed within the PKK's discourse – even though it is one of the stated principal items under investigation in his study.[56] Özcan reserves a lengthy chapter to the PKK's discourse and ideology. He does not, however, indicate what the key concepts 'discourse' or 'ideology' refer to. As in

20   *Deconstructing Kurdish identity and nationalism*

the case of political history and conflict analysis literature discussed above, this lack of clarity creates difficulties for Özcan because his account of the PKK's discourse and ideology contains various simplifications and confusions. For example, Özcan states that the PKK's programme:

> is a 'Kurdicized' copy of those customary communist parties that undertake a nation's 'national' liberation as an 'initial stage' of the ultimate socialist revolution. The ideology by which the PKK formulates this initiative's aims and objectives is a Middle-Eastern translation of traditional Marxist socialism.[57]

In addition, when discussing the ideological similarities between the PKK and other Kurdish parties that were active in the 1970s, Özcan states, 'The striking point is that the views, diagnoses, proposals, aims and objectives outlined so far are simply a copy of all the other fellow political initiatives' programmes claiming to undertake Kurdish national and social emancipation.'[58]

This characterisation of the PKK's national liberation discourse as a *copy* of communist and other Kurdish parties' programmes simply ignores the process that led first to the individuation of the national liberation discourse during the early 1970s and second to its articulation by the PKK from the late 1970s onwards. Even if there were *significant* similarities in the key texts published by the Kurdish parties – this is not surprising since the discourse of national liberation was hegemonic and most Kurdish political parties and groups were committed, in varying degrees, to Kurdish liberation and socialism – nevertheless, significant differences remained over strategy and in practice, and there was a vibrant debate during the late 1970s between the Kurdish organisations concerning such issues. Hence, the main limitation of Özcan's study is that his discussion of the PKK's discourses only provides a review of the key PKK publications and Öcalan's numerous books to show *how* its aims and objectives evolved since its establishment. The subsequent discussion is *not* targeted towards understanding the specificity of Kurdish national demands articulated by the PKK or the conception of Kurdish identity that emerges from it. Furthermore, his account does not offer *any* discussion of the conception of the Kurdish nation in the PKK's discourse, including the construction of the *Newroz* as a 'myth of origin', which enabled the PKK to conceptualise and 'imagine' the unity of the Kurdish nation in its political discourse.

Özcan examines how the PKK changed its policies regarding Kurdish rights and demands by stressing the shift in emphasis from 'independent, united and democratic Kurdistan' to a much more elusive term 'free Kurdistan' and argues 'the united-independent Kurdistan almost withered away towards the late 1980s'.[59] He also traces the 'mutation' of the Marxist element in the PKK's discourse and how gradually the ideas of the PKK's leader Öcalan replaced Marxism as emphasis was shifting towards concepts such as 'humanisation', 'socialisation', 'human emancipation' and 'freed personality'. Based on an analysis of Öcalan's speeches, he sketches how the PKK totally retreated from

Deconstructing Kurdish identity and nationalism 21

socialism and Marxism, which after the collapse of the Soviet Union and the Eastern Block became an ideological guide as opposed to an all-encompassing ideology.[60] This mutation, he argues, took a new turn with Öcalan's legal defences which proclaimed the new strategy and which turned into the PKK's new political programme. In its current discourse the emphasis is on concepts such as 'Democratic Republic', 'Free Togetherness' and 'Democratic Solution'. A democratic solution to the Kurdish issue within the current borders of Turkey is proposed.[61]

Özcan's discussion of the causes behind such significant changes in the PKK's discourse is rather elusive. He states: 'As the struggle progresses, trans-formations, alterations, modifications and metamorphoses occur due to the simultaneous rise of mass participation and confrontations.'[62] Although Özcan discusses Öcalan's analysis of Soviet Socialism and how its collapse is inter-preted, he does it on the basis of the development of Öcalan's cult of personality. This attempt does *not* provide a convincing account of the reason behind such a comprehensive discursive change nor does it offer an account of how Kurdish rights and demands are articulated within the discourse of democracy. We need not only to show the scale of these changes, but also how the nature and under-standing of certain elements ('the Kurdish nation', 'socialism', and 'democracy') that are currently being articulated in its discourse have changed, and account for why such changes have been taking place, including the internal and external dislocations that the movement faced.

In Romano's study the ideology and discourses of the PKK are dealt within his discussion of 'Kurdish identities and cultural tool kits in Turkey' and consti-tutes an important part of his study. He defines the concept of cultural tool kits as 'generalised attitudes and ideas within a given population' and directs his focus on 'cultural frames that have become prevalent within the population over time, and not through conscious strategic efforts of the organised groups we are examining'.[63] From the onset, Romano's discussion of cultural framing strat-egies deployed by the PKK seems useful in reflecting its broad claims and objec-tives. Romano states that the PKK's 'framing efforts and ideology fused a modified Marxist-Leninist discourse with Kurdish nationalism and a focus on human rights abuses committed against the Kurds. Depending on the audience, one or all three of these elements would be stressed.'[64]

Romano states that in order to mobilise the Kurds against the state and politi-cise Kurdish identity the PKK used the oppression of the Kurds in its framing strategy.[65] Additionally, he mentions that the PKK used 'national Kurdish myths of common ancestry and past differentiated from that of other groups in the area' to enhance its nationalist claims.[66] However, there is not *any* discussion of how the deployment of myths of common ancestry in the PKK's discourse enhanced its claims for the Kurdish nation; for example, rooting the Kurds within a spe-cific territory, constructing and representing Kurdish difference, and stabilising Kurdish identity and the meaning of Kurdishness. The concept of 'cultural tool kits' that Romano uses to analyse the Kurdish movement simplifies the PKK's discourse and is unable to highlight the specificity of Kurdish identity and

22 Deconstructing Kurdish identity and nationalism

demands articulated within it. Therefore, it cannot be an adequate substitute to the concept of *discourse* – which is discussed more fully in Chapter 2 – that discourse theory provides. In particular, Romano does not address questions of 'change' and 'continuity' in the discourses of the PKK in a systematic manner and does not offer an account of the PKK's 'national liberation' and 'democratic' discourse and the various stages involved in their constitution and ideological condensation.

Additionally, Romano evades the specificity of Kurdish nationalist ideology and avoids discussing the nature of the Kurdish national demands as constructed within the PKK's discourse. For example, he does not show *what* happens to the Kurdish national claims and demands when they are articulated with the discourse of Marxist-Leninism, or *how* Kurdish nationalism 'modifies' Marxist-Leninism. To explain the changes in the PKK's discourse from 1993 onwards, Romano focuses on the *changes in the political opportunity structures*, especially the emergence of an elite in Turkey (including President Turgut Özal) that was willing to find a solution to the problem, and the PKK's need to 'improve its image and reach out to more allies'. He argues that increasingly the PKK framed Kurdish grievances within the human rights discourse and the Kurdish demands as demands for democracy and minority rights, and intensified its attempts to shed its 'terrorist image'.[67] Romano's classification of the changes that the PKK has been undergoing as changes from one strategy to another seems problematic because the transformation in the PKK's strategy are much more comprehensive and redefined the aims and objectives of the Kurdish national movement and the political project that it has undertaken. Romano's account also does not offer the underlying reasons for such profound changes but only speculates on the intentions and the interests that the PKK might have had in formulating its strategy.

The lack of sustained focus on the discourses of the PKK prevents Romano from capturing the conception of Kurdish identity that emerges in the PKK's discourse. Although his account of Kurdish identity politics is designed to explicate why both 'Kurdish ethnic nationalist dissent arose in Turkey, as well as the values, aims, and objectives of Kurds in the country', his characterisation of Kurdish identity in Turkey, however, is unclear.[68] Throughout the study he interchangeably uses 'ethnic nationalist', 'nationalist', 'ethnic' and 'politicised ethnicity' to describe the Kurdish identity. He highlights the existence of a higher form of Kurdish identity (politicised ethnicity) and argues that this existed among Kurds for the past few centuries despite the various religious, tribal and linguistic divisions.[69] He also acknowledges the difficulties that these various divisions created for Kurdish nationalism in extending its appeal to all Kurds, especially during the 1920s and 1930s, when despite numerous attempts Kurdish nationalists failed to generate a sense of 'politicised ethnic identity'.[70] These divisions, he argues, have been superseded with the rise of the PKK as its challenge to Turkey brought a higher level, politicised Kurdish identity, to the forefront of many people's consciousness.[71] This assertion acknowledges a process at work that generates identity and the role that nationalist movements play in cultivating identity; however, as discussed above Romano only focuses on the

Deconstructing Kurdish identity and nationalism 23

mobilisation process and does not discuss how the PKK and Kurdish nationalists in the past sought to overcome these deep divisions by representing the image of a homogenous Kurdish nation, including the myth of origin and common ancestry that he mentions.

Furthermore, similar to the political history accounts discussed above, Romano's discussion of Kurdish identity is limited to the identities that Kurds' acquired over time rather than the Kurdish identity represented or contested by the Kurdish national movement. Consequently, he refrains from engaging in a discussion about the Kurdish discourses on identity and Kurdish nationalist historiography as formulated by Kurdish activists during the 1960s and 1970s and by the PKK during the 1980s and 1990s. In fact, a serious limitation of Romano's study is that he uses *hardly any* primary sources published by the Kurdish activists and political groups during the 1960s and the 1970s or those published by the PKK from the 1980s onwards. This creates serious obstacles for Romano to understand the Kurdish identity as he does not engage at all with the Kurdish movement's discourses on identity. Hence, a range of questions concerning Kurdish identity arises but remains unanswered. Questions such as: What did/does Kurdishness, or being Kurdish, mean to the Kurds? What does the Kurdish identity entail? How, amidst all these divisions, did the PKK manage to foster or construct and represent an overarching Kurdish national identity? How is the existence of diverse Kurdish identities accounted for by the Kurdish nationalists?

Conclusion

As the discussion above has shown, the literature on the rise of Kurdish nationalism in Turkey provides a causal explanation and ignores a number of pertinent issues; in particular, there is insufficient focus on the nature of the demands that the Kurdish national movement has been articulating and more broadly on its ideology and discourses. Important questions about the Kurdish activists' separation from the Turkish socialist movement during the late 1960s and 1970s, the Kurds' contestation of their identity, and the process of self-reflection, self-understanding and re-interpretation of Kurdish identity that such a contestation generated, are evaded. The literature also fails to provide a detailed account of how the Kurds interpreted their oppression in Turkey and formulated their challenge against it or how they constructed their own notion of Kurdish society and what it entailed. Additionally, the existing studies either evade or inadequately explain the important issues concerning the nature of the Kurdish political identity in Turkey; specifically, they either treat the Kurdish identity as given and the continuation of an identity that has been in existence for a long period, or deploy a superficial approach to understanding Kurdish identity that focuses only on the cultural identities that the Kurds acquired over the centuries rather than the contemporary Kurdish political identity constituted by the contemporary Kurdish national movement. In particular, a range of questions concerning the mass mobilisation of the Kurds by the PKK during the 1980s and 1990s, its hegemony

24 *Deconstructing Kurdish identity and nationalism*

over the Kurdish national movement, its discursive transformation, the specificity of the national demands articulated in its discourse, and the representation of its struggle in the political discourse and other artistic forms, which significantly enhanced its appeal, remain unexplored. Moreover, while important aspects of the pro-Kurdish democratic movement have been highlighted in some of the existing literature on the subject, these studies do not engage with several significant issues, and a comprehensive analysis of the pro-Kurdish democratic discourse is yet to be carried out. Specifically, the political proposals it has been putting forward to change the existing notions of democracy and citizenship in Turkey and what kind of a political challenge it has been offering – as discussed in this book – need to be brought to the centre of the analysis.

2 Understanding Kurdish identity and nationalism in Turkey

As the critical review conducted of the existing literature in Chapter 1 revealed, the analyses of the contemporary Kurdish political identity, and ideology and discourses of the Kurdish national movement in general, and the PKK in particular, that the existing literature provides, were found wanting. In this chapter, I discuss the theoretical and methodological framework that I utilise in my research to provide a more informed understanding of Kurdish identity, nationalism and mass mobilisation in Turkey. The theoretical and methodological framework I outline here focuses on the study of nationalism as a discourse and seeks to highlight its specificity and particularity by emphasising its ideological nature and the particular elements that it articulates. The existing studies that apply a similar framework stress that 'individual nationalisms always contain a very particular "content" that aims to define the general culture and values of the "national" people and which, in turn, is related to the construction and deployment of such values within political ideological discourse'.[1] Nationalism, in this sense, is seen as a 'quintessentially homogenizing, differentiating, or classifying discourse' and 'one that aims its appeal at people presumed to have certain things in common as against people thought not to have any mutual connections'.[2] Focusing our analysis to uncover, specify and highlight the particular 'content' of nationalism would enable us to understand nationalism 'at a more narrow and specific level'.[3] This draws out the particular national claims articulated by an individual nationalism, which is of huge significance because nationalism is a 'variegated phenomenon ... always caught up in the process of specifying and defining particularity'.[4] Focusing on the key national claims that are articulated within nationalist discourse, which in turn specifies the content and character of nationalism, and defines the national community in a particular way by conferring a specific meaning and identity onto it, would reveal the full meaning that nationalism takes in 'specific conjunctures, particular moments of political or social practice'.[5] The exploration of the content of nationalism would highlight its ideological nature:

> the ways in which nationalism operates as a specific kind of ideological discourse – a discourse that is not merely responding to events and extraneous social forces but one that is actively involved in the process of interpreting

26 *Kurdish identity and nationalism in Turkey*

such events by defining and constructing the people of a 'pre-existing' or projected national community.[6]

Therefore, as Finlayson argues, 'We do not see nationalist movements that are purely and simply nationalist but rather movements involved in some other aspect of political demands – hence the hyphenated nature of many nationalist movements.'[7] This means that 'nationalism is always linked to other political ideologies. It is through association with nation that these political ideologies are legitimated.'[8]

The ideological nature of nationalism is also stressed in Freeden (1998), which assesses the claim of whether nationalism can be seen as a distinct ideology or not.[9] Freeden rejects the claim that nationalism is a comprehensive ideology because its 'conceptual structure is incapable of providing on its own a solution to questions of social justice, distribution of resources and conflict management which mainstream ideologies address'.[10] Instead he draws attention to a strong link between nationalism and other 'host' ideologies and to the distinctions made in the literature of variants of nationalism ('liberal', 'radically illiberal', 'moderate', 'aggressive'), and characterises nationalism as oscillating between a 'thin-centred ideology' – defined as an ideology that 'severs itself from wider ideational contexts, by deliberate removal and replacement of concepts' – and a component of other ideologies, such as liberalism and conservatism.[11]

By placing identity central to political struggle, Verdery (1996) also develops a framework that seeks to uncover 'how ideas about nation and identity are produced and reproduced as central elements in a political struggle'.[12] Such an approach does not treat nationalism as either political or cultural, but defines it, as 'the political utilization of the symbol nation through discourse and political activity, as well as the sentiment that draws people into responding to this symbol's use'.[13] Nation works as a symbol because first, its meaning is 'ambiguous' – hence it can be interpreted in different ways by different political actors – and second, 'its use evokes sentiments and dispositions that have been formed in relation to it throughout decades of so-called nation building'.[14] Nation is seen as a social construct the meaning of which 'shifts with the changing balance of social forces'.[15]

Therefore, focusing on Kurdish nationalism as a discourse and conducting a comprehensive examination of the emergence and individuation of the hegemonic discourses articulating Kurdish identity enables me to provide an account of identity formation and explore the issues of hegemony, mass mobilisation and political transformation. This framework is used to develop a new empirical dimension to the study of Kurdish nationalism and identity in Turkey. Laclau and Mouffe's discourse theory is highly applicable and suitable for this study, as it offers a rich theoretical repertoire and a valuable framework that allows me to conduct a critical analysis of the contemporary Kurdish political identity by situating it within a historical framework that examines the historical and structural conditions that gave rise to it and influenced its evolution since the 1960s. It comprises 'a novel fusion of recent developments in Marxist, post-structuralist,

Kurdish identity and nationalism in Turkey 27

post-analytical and psychoanalytical theory' and 'investigates the way social practices systematically form the identities of subjects and objects by articulating together a series of contingent signifying elements available in a discursive field'.[16] Discourse theorists emphasise that 'Issues of identity formation, the production of novel ideologies, the logic of social movements and structuring of societies by a plurality of social imaginaries are central objects of investigation for discourse theory.'[17] Before I offer some preliminary elaborations of the discourses of the Kurdish national movement to draw out the important issues that I analyse in the rest of this book, I discuss the nature of social and political identities and highlight the key concepts that I use in my analysis.

Discourse theoretical account of identity formation

Discourse theoretical accounts of identity formation reject the essentialist notions of social and political identity, and instead treat identity as being *relational* and *contingent*. This is because society, defined as 'an objective and closed system of differences', is impossible due to the radical contingency surrounding any form of objectivity. Laclau states that 'what we [social agents] find is a limited and given situation in which objectivity is *partially* constituted and *partially* threatened'.[18] This is due to the 'symbolic' and overdetermined nature of social relations, which 'implies that they lack an ultimate literality which would reduce them to necessary moments of an immanent law'.[19] In fact, due to radical contingency permeating social objectivity, social identities are unable to achieve full closure or complete stability or fixity: 'what we get is a field of simply relational identities which never manage to constitute themselves fully, since relations do not form a closed system'.[20] The contingency of identities is revealed through negativity, which symbolises the failure of an identity's constitution.[21] This is significant for the constitution of any identity as it means that identity comes into being through a reference to an 'other' outside of it, which is shown to be opposing the identity of the self, and in relation to which the meaning of the identity of the self is partially fixed.[22] The relationship the self has with the other is negative or antagonistic because the other is a threat and its existence reveals the contingency of the identity of the self. Laclau highlights two important consequences of this: first, that 'the identities and their conditions of existence form an inseparable whole', and, second, the antagonising force is also part of 'the conditions of existence' of that identity as it shows its contingency by blocking its constitution.[23] In Laclau's discussion of antagonism, this relationship is conceived as the 'constitutive outside' and attention is drawn to the role it plays in constituting the identity of the 'inside':

> It is an outside which blocks the identity of the 'inside' (and is, nonetheless, the prerequisite for its constitution at the same time). With antagonism, denial does not originate from the 'inside' of the identity itself but, in its most radical sense, *from outside*; it is thus pure facticity which cannot be referred back to any underlying rationality.[24]

28 *Kurdish identity and nationalism in Turkey*

Antagonism is constitutive in the following sense: the identity of the inside cannot be constituted as it is denied by a force outside of it, and with antagonism it is not the identity of the inside which is expressed but the 'impossibility of its constitution'.[25] On the one hand, we are faced with a situation in which there is always a need to constitute the social in its full unity, but it is a task which is impossible to achieve. On the other, it is the impossibility of constituting the social which makes the constitution of the social possible – since there is always a need to constitute the social in its unity, there will always be an attempt to constitute it. On this account, individuation of identity is not on the basis of 'positive characteristics' or 'essence' that pre-exists identity or determines its construction.[26] Instead, identity comes into being through the articulation of various 'elements' together: 'all identity emerges through the articulation or rearticulation of signifying elements'.[27]

The *delimitation* of identity is achieved through the articulation of various elements together around a 'nodal point', defined as the 'privileged signifiers or reference points ... in a discourse that bind together a particular system of meaning or "chain of signification"'.[28] The construction of nodal points within a discourse is important because through them antagonisms are constructed and identities or meanings are stabilised or partially fixed: 'A principle of articulation is thus needed to stop the play of differences, delimiting identity from *what it is not.*'[29] In *Hegemony and Socialist Strategy*, Laclau and Mouffe define *articulation* as 'any practice establishing a relation among elements such that their identity is modified as a result of the articulatory practice'.[30] The 'structured totality resulting from the articulatory practice' is defined as *discourse* and through the articulatory practice *elements* – which are defined as 'difference that is not discursively articulated' – are transformed into the *moments* of a discourse or the 'differential positions, insofar as they appear articulated within a discourse'.[31] The 'theoretical horizon within which the being of objects is constituted' is defined as the *discursive field* and '*all* objects are objects of discourse, as their meaning depends upon a socially constructed system of rules and significant differences'.[32]

In a more narrow sense, discourse can be seen as 'social and political construction that establishes a system of relations between different objects and practices, while providing (subject) positions with which social agents can identify'.[33] At any given time however, an agent chooses to identify with a particular subject position out of various others or to emphasise hers/his identification with one subject position more than the others. In order to investigate issues concerning how individuals identify with a particular subject position or why they mobilise as a subject, discourse theory utilises the concept of *political subjectivity*. Thorough contextual analyses are needed before we can determine the emergence of new political subjectivities that challenge the existing order. However, on a more general level, discourse theory utilises the concept of *dislocation* – which 'refers to the process by which the contingency of discursive structures is made visible'[34] – in providing an explanation of the emergence of new political subjectivities:

Kurdish identity and nationalism in Turkey 29

Here dislocation can be understood as a moment when the subject's mode of being is experienced as disrupted. In this sense, then, we could say that dislocations are those occasions when a subject is called upon to confront the contingency of social relations more directly then other times.[35]

Dislocations can be conceived of specific events, such as the collapse of communist regimes in Eastern Europe and the Soviet Union, or of more common processes, such as the development of capitalism, the socio-economic modernisation and spread of education. On the specific issue of dislocations and the emergence of new political agents, Laclau states:

We thus have a set of new possibilities for historical action which are the direct result of structural dislocation. The world is less given and must be increasingly constructed. But this is not just a construction of the world, but of social agents who transform themselves and forge new identities as a result.[36]

Hence, given this is the setting within which the constitution of identity takes place, the result is that the social and political identities are always relational and never able to constitute themselves fully. Through articulation of various elements, political movements construct a 'common identity' for various disparate groups, which are brought together via the drawing of *political frontiers* that differentiates between the 'insiders' and 'outsiders'.[37] The constitutive role that antagonism plays in this process of the construction of an identity for the self was highlighted above. Specifically, it plays a significant role in the individuation of identity through externalising an *antagonistic* other. This is achieved through the institution of political frontiers, which play a vital role in the construction of political identities: 'It is through the consolidation or dissolution of political frontiers that discursive formations in general, and social and political identities more specifically, are constructed or fragmented.'[38]

Political frontiers

Focusing on frontiers allows us to understand the delimitation of identity and provides us with an account of why certain elements rather than others act as constitutive characteristics for a group.[39] As well as fulfilling a primary function in the individuation of identity, political frontiers play an important role in the organisation of political space. In *Hegemony and Socialist Strategy*, Laclau and Mouffe use the concept of *political logics* (this is also discussed in the section 'Methodology and Sources' below) to analyse the construction of political frontiers. They propose two types of political logics: the *logic of equivalence*, and the *logic of difference*.[40] The logics of equivalence are said to be predominant if 'political practices entail the construction of new frontiers to challenge old social structures in the name of an ideal or principle (implying a new set of inclusions and exclusions)', and the logics of difference are predominant if 'there is a

30   *Kurdish identity and nationalism in Turkey*

breaking down of those frontiers so as to maintain existing social structures (thus retaining the old distribution of inclusions and exclusions)'.[41] The logics of equivalence foster the development of equivalential identities by creating a polarity between 'them' and 'us' and leads to 'the simplification of political space', whereas the logics of difference tries to weaken the already established divisions and identities by forming a wider political movement or alliance and leads to the 'expansion and increasing complexity' of the political space.[42]

The political logic of equivalence predominated in the discourse of national liberation because it fostered an antagonistic relationship between the Kurds and Turkey and between the Kurdish masses of rural peasants, workers and students and the Kurdish feudal elites. The relations of equivalence were constructed on a national basis as the political practices it fostered had the aim of uniting Kurdistan and constructing a socialist society. Conversely, in the pro-Kurdish democratic discourse and the PKK's democratic discourse, the logics of difference predominate as the aim is to weaken the antagonisms and promote political reconciliation and democracy in Turkey. The emphasis is on the historical unity of the Turkish and Kurdish 'peoples' and more specifically the National Covenant (*Misak-ı-Milli*) of 1920 which envisioned a polity for both the Turks and Kurds within the then Ottoman territories and which mobilised both the Turks and Kurds in the 'War of Liberation' for the defence of those lands. The democratic discourse proposes to form an equivalential chain with other groups in Turkey who also advocate political change and democracy, such as some trade unions, human rights organisations, socialist and feminist groups, the pro-EU liberal groups and so on. It fosters an agonistic relation with the current Kemalist elite that seeks to maintain the exclusionary, authoritarian, homogenising and anti-democratic character of the republic. The separation of the political logics into two does not mean they are mutually exclusive; in fact, in political practice, their operation is simultaneous, though in any given political practice only one of them will predominate.[43]

In 'Frontiers in Question', Norval argues that in discourse theory, especially in Laclau and Mouffe's conceptualisation of political frontiers, there is an overemphasis on the role that negativity plays in the individuation of identity.[44] This, in theoretical terms, leads to privileging the logic of *equivalence* over that of *difference*. Norval argues for the need to separate the process of the individuation of identity from the institution of political frontiers and to provide accounts for each process separately. This is needed because the conflation of the two processes in Laclau and Mouffe's account leads to a sacrifice of the complexity of identity formation and is unable to draw out the full complexity of political frontiers.[45] By drawing on Wittgenstein's discussion of 'family resemblances' and Derrida's discussion of 'iterability', Norval proposes a framework of identity construction that maintains its anti-essentialist position but does not privilege the moment of antagonism or exclusion.[46] In this reformulation the differential dimension of identity is also emphasised, and the multiple forms of the relation between the *self* and the *other* are shown, which is much more complex than the antagonistic friend/enemy distinction that characterises *difference* as *otherness*.

Kurdish identity and nationalism in Turkey 31

In his recent work on populism, Laclau introduces the unit of *demand* to elaborate on the emergence of equivalential logics and provide further explanation to the processes involved in the forging of political identities and movements.[47] Specifically, he looks at 'how isolated demands emerge, and how they start their process of articulation'.[48] According to this theorisation, a *particular* demand can either be absorbed into the existing order by being satisfied in a *differential* manner, or remain unsatisfied. In the case of the latter, a particular demand can be accumulated into an *equivalential chain* with a series of other unfulfilled demands, which are united together on the basis of their negative dimension – the entity that failed to satisfy the demands. The articulation of a particular demand within an equivalential chain transforms the nature of that demand by making it constitutively split: 'on the one hand it is its own particularised self, on the other it points, through equivalential links, to the totality of the other demands ... each demand is actually the tip of the iceberg'.[49]

This equivalential articulation of popular demands establishes an 'internal frontier' within the society and leads to the dichotomisation of the social space and emergence of new political subjectivities.[50] Laclau introduces the concept of the 'empty signifier' to account for the emergence of new political subjectivities and representation of the equivalential chain.[51] The *empty signifier* is defined as the signifier 'of a lack, of an absent totality' and its function is to fill the ultimate impossibility of closure or fixity.[52] However, before a signifier can emerge as the empty signifier and assume the function of representing an equivalential chain, it needs to be 'emptied' of any 'particular, differential signified'.[53] In his discussion of empty signifiers in the context of populism, Laclau states 'representation is only possible if a particular demand, without entirely abandoning its own particularity, starts also functioning as a signifier representing the chain as a totality'.[54] In addition to the concepts and theoretical categories discussed above, my analysis of the two hegemonic discourses of the Kurdish national movement and the mass mobilisation of the Kurds during the 1980s and 1990s will utilise the concepts of *hegemony* and *myth*, and Laclau and Mouffe's theorisation of Radical Democracy, which I discuss in greater detail below.

Understanding Kurdish nationalist discourse: hegemony, myth and radical democracy

The concept of hegemony is drawn from Marxist theorist Antonio Gramsci and refers to 'ethical, moral and political leadership'.[55] To counter the political power of the bourgeoisie, Gramsci argued that the working class needed to institute its own hegemony and achieve internal control over the social classes and the nation. For a class to become hegemonic and achieve power it needs to, in addition to dominating or coercing other classes or groups, provide ideological leadership and struggle, with ideology seen as the means through which one group dominates the others in civil society.[56] In *Hegemony and Socialist Strategy*, Laclau and Mouffe provide reformulations to Gramscian concepts:

32   *Kurdish identity and nationalism in Turkey*

A social and political space relatively unified through the instituting of nodal points and the construction of *tendentially* relational identities, is what Gramsci called a *historical bloc*. The type of link joining the different elements of the historical bloc – not unity in any form of historical a priori, but regularity in dispersion – coincides with our concept of discursive formation. Insofar as we consider the historical bloc from the point of view of the antagonistic terrain in which it is constituted, we will call it *hegemonic formation*.[57]

Crucially however, Laclau and Mouffe untangle the association between a hegemonic force and a fundamental class that Gramsci and other Marxist theorists maintained. According to Norval, in this theorisation hegemony 'becomes a form of social relations in which the unity of a political force is constituted through a process of articulation of elements with no necessary class belonging'.[58] More specifically, hegemony refers to 'the linking together of different identities and political forces into a common project, and the creation of new social orders from a variety of dispersed elements'.[59] A hegemonic articulation of identity is possible because, as discussed above, the social is open and incomplete, and through dislocations and the dislocatory effects of events the contingency of the existing social order is revealed.[60] Through a hegemonic articulation a new set of relations among dispersed elements is established and elements are transformed into the moments of a discourse. Laclau and Mouffe argue that for an articulatory practice to be considered hegemonic, it 'should take place through a confrontation with antagonistic articulatory practices – in other words, that hegemony should emerge in a field criss-crossed by antagonisms and therefore suppose phenomena of equivalence and frontier effects'.[61] In this account neither antagonisms nor division of the social into two opposing sides are pre-given but are the effect of the hegemonic articulation.[62]

The importance of the concept of dislocation in creating the conditions for the emergence of new political subjectivities was emphasised above. An important consequence of dislocations is that *myths* of an alternative social objectivity emerge and challenge the existing social objectivity. Laclau defines myth as a 'space of representation which bears no relation of continuity with the dominant "structural objectivity"' and states that myths emerge as a result of dislocations.[63] Myth fulfils an important function by providing a 'surface on which dislocations and social demands can be inscribed'.[64] Furthermore, a 'myth is constitutive of any possible society' because it allows for the suturing of the dislocated space by constituting 'a new space of representation': 'the effectiveness of myth is essentially hegemonic: it involves forming a new objectivity by means of the rearticulation of the dislocated elements'.[65] The practice of the institution of hegemony – of a practice becoming hegemonic – is explained in Laclau's theorisation by a discussion of the process of sedimentation:

Insofar as an act of institution has been successful, a 'forgetting of the origins' tends to occur; the system of possible alternatives tends to vanish

Kurdish identity and nationalism in Turkey 33

and the traces of the original contingency to fade. In this way, the instituted tends to assume the form of a mere objective presence. This is the moment of sedimentation.[66]

Gradually, during the 1960s and 1970s the myth of Kurdish society resurfaced in Turkey to structure political discourse and as a space to register dislocations. An ethnicist conception of Kurdish identity was deployed in the discourses of the Kurdish intellectuals and political organisations in the period. During the 1960s Kurdish political and economic demands were articulated differentially predominantly within the discourses of the socialist movement as part of diverse demands for equality. However, during the 1970s, we witness an equivalential articulation of Kurdish demands and the construction of the Kurdish national liberation discourse. This was partly because the Turkish socialist movement's construction of antagonisms during the 1970s emphasised the 'anti-imperialism' dimension and ignored the demands for equality that various sections of the society had, including the Kurds. From the 1970s onwards, the construction of the relations of difference – and the representation of the alternative Kurdish society – in the discourses of the newly formed Kurdish political parties and groups were done on the basis of the myth of *Newroz*. The myth allowed the Kurdish national movement to trace the origins of the Kurds to the ancient Medes and reactivated/recreated *Newroz* and the legend of Kawa as the myth of origin.

In fact, there were two competing versions of the Kurdish national liberation discourse during the late 1970s. These two alternatives represent different attempts to suture the dislocated space and represent the Kurdish national demands in Turkey. Specifically, in the discourse of the Socialist Party of Turkish Kurdistan (*Türkiye Kürdistanı Sosyalist Partisi*, TKSP) and the DDKD/ KİP (the Revolutionary Democratic Cultural Associations/Kurdistan Workers Party), the logics of difference predominated as the emphasis was placed on greater cooperation between the Turkish socialist movement and the Kurdish national movement. Conversely, in the discourse of the PKK, the *Kawa*, the *Rizgarî* (Liberation) and the *Ala Rizgarî* (the Flag of Liberation) the logics of equivalence predominated and emphasis was put on unification of Kurdistan and the reconstruction of the Kurdish society. Hence, analysing the contestation of Kurdish identity and demands by a plethora of political parties and groups during the late 1970s and the hegemony of the PKK's national liberation discourse from the early 1980s onwards constitutes an important aspect of this research. My exploration of this issue focuses on why the nodal point 'liberation' in the PKK's national liberation discourse became the 'empty signifier'. Moreover, how and why did the demands of the Kurdish working class and peasantry become synonymous with the Kurdish national demands and start to represent the Kurds' demands for liberation?

In comparison to its rivals, the representation of Kurdish identity and construction of antagonisms in the PKK's discourse were clearer. This was done via establishing a strong association between the Medes and the modern day Kurds

34   *Kurdish identity and nationalism in Turkey*

to invoke a historical 'golden age' of the Kurdish nation to construct an image of their absent fullness, and construct and represent a homogenous notion of Kurdish identity. Furthermore, the PKK reactivated the myth of *Newroz* to construct a contemporary myth of resistance centred primarily on the PKK inmate's resistance in the Diyarbakir Prison during the early 1980s and its ongoing struggle. The PKK's construction of a contemporary myth of Kurdish resistance to represent its struggle and the romanticising of its guerrilla war against the state enhanced its hegemonic appeal by bringing the myth of resistance into reality.

Hence, via an extensive discussion of the PKK's contemporary myth of resistance, my research highlights the factors that added *affect* and *force* to the PKK's national liberation discourse. The construction and deployment of the contemporary myth of resistance in its discourse, including the construction of *exemplars*, is significant for our understanding of the process of the PKK's mass mobilisation of the Kurds and the sedimentation of its national liberation discourse in practice. This is because it was used extensively in the PKK's political discourse as well as other artistic forms, to represent its struggle to the wider Kurdish society as the *embodiment* of Kurdish national struggle, which enhanced its appeal to the masses. During the early 1990s, organising mass gatherings during the *Newroz* festival and other important days in the Kurdish political calendar in many Kurdish cities and towns, especially in Diyarbakir created *Newroz* as the symbol of Kurdish popular resistance.

Additionally, by utilising Laclau and Mouffe's concept of hegemony, I argue that the PKK's success was also due to its ability to articulate the demands of various sectors of the Kurdish society, including students, the newly urbanised Kurdish workers and above all the biggest group, that of the Kurdish peasants, whose experience of dislocations, especially the erosion of their traditional way of life due to the mechanisation of agriculture and the development of capitalism, was much more severe. The suitability of the PKK's national liberation discourse to address the problems experienced by these groups and offer a convincing interpretation of their plight enabled it to hegemonise Kurdish resistance against the state.

However, a myth is essentially incomplete and its content is constantly reconstituted and displaced.[67] Its appeal can recede leading to its dissolution. On this matter, Laclau states that:

> Insofar as a mythical space begins to absorb less social demands, and an increasing number of dislocations that cannot be integrated into that space of representation coexists, the space is, so to speak, re-literalized; its power of metaphorization is reduced, and its dimension of horizon is thus lost.[68]

My research advances the claim that dislocations experienced by the Kurdish national movement – for example, the collapse of the socialist systems in Europe, the military losses suffered by the PKK, political polarisation, the weakening of civil society and political institutions experienced in Turkey as a result of the conflict, the state's mobilisation of Turkish nationalist groups against the

Kurdish identity and nationalism in Turkey   35

Kurds and the PKK, which created a possibility of a 'civil war' between the Turks and Kurds, and the capture of the PKK's leader Abdullah Öcalan – meant that the national liberation discourse deployed no longer corresponded to the realities of the age, and did not resonate with the demands of the Kurds. These factors led to an ideological impasse, limiting its ability to hegemonise and redefine Kurdish identity in Turkey.

Drawing on discourse theory, I analyse both the *availability* and *suitability* of different discourses to fill the gap left by the loss of legitimacy of the national liberation discourse. Existing links with political and human rights organisations in Turkey and in Europe at large, in which democratic rights played a key role, made the discourse of democracy a candidate to fill the gap left by the discourse of national liberation. This also allowed the Kurds to gain support in the national and international arena. Moreover, the shift to a discourse on democracy, I argue, can be attributed to better suitability of democratic discourse to the Kurds' social and political situation. That is, articulating Kurdish subjectivity through reference to democracy is potentially more inclusive of religious and linguistic differences within Kurdish society, hence putting into question a homogenous notion of 'Kurdishness'. In addition, the Kurdish population dispersed around Turkey could also find representation in a democracy movement without having to compromise their position as citizens and residents of Turkey. However, the PKK's attempt to transform itself into a democratic movement has been facing major difficulties. The PKK's discursive transformation and the difficulties associated with it are highlighted in my assessment of the PKK's democratic transformation. The PKK's inability to transcend the antagonistic state of affairs in Turkey is due to the appeal of Turkish nationalism and the hegemonic representation of the Kurdish question in Turkey as a 'threat' and a 'terrorist' or 'security' concern that needs to be dealt with militarily. This hegemonic representation of the Kurdish question in Turkey has been a stumbling block also for the success of the pro-Kurdish democratic movement.

To understand and explain the political challenge offered by a series of the pro-Kurdish political parties to recognise the Kurdish identity and Kurdish cultural rights in Turkey and the difficulties that they experienced in their attempts to institute a new democratic subjectivity in Turkey, my research draws on Laclau and Mouffe's theorisation of 'radical democracy'.[69] Laclau and Mouffe's conception of radical democracy entails a reformulation of the link between socialism and democracy and encapsulates their proposals for a New Left movement in the advanced industrial societies that are characterised by the decline of 'traditional' forms of political identities and the emergence of new antagonisms and political subjects.[70] A radical democratic political project seeks to unify different struggles against oppression to achieve the democratic transformation of the society.

This conception of radical democracy has been further elaborated in Laclau's subsequent writings. In 'Democracy and the Question of Power' Laclau states that 'on the one hand, democracy was the attempt to organise the political space around the *universality* of the community, without hierarchies and distinctions.

36 *Kurdish identity and nationalism in Turkey*

Jacobinism was the name of the earliest and most extreme of these efforts to constitute *one* people'.[71] Turkey's experience of nation building falls within this tradition as it was orchestrated by an elite who attempted to constitute one people (Turkish) out of many heterogeneous elements. The alternative identifications or group interests were denied any space of representation in the homogenised public sphere. The demands raised by the pro-Kurdish political parties for the recognition of the Kurds' identity and cultural differences falls within the alternative tradition of democracy, which in Laclau's words, makes attempts at the 'expansion of the logic of equality to increasingly wider spheres of social relations – social and economic equality, racial equality, gender equality, etc. From this point of view democracy constitutively involves respect for difference.'[72]

Laclau also draws our attention to the 'unilateralization' of any of the two tendencies, which 'leads to a perversion of democracy as a political regime'[73] because it either results in constructing the universality of community around a particular element, or accepting the cultural communities as they are, which can lead to ignoring practices or traditions that are incompatible with the practice or norms of democracy. A radical democratic political project seeks to avoid the pitfalls of the unilateralisation of either tendency by combining both of these traditions and articulating 'diverse forms of subordination' and the political demands of different groups, such as ethnic and racial minorities and women within the working-class struggle. In this way the struggle for equality and freedom is broadened and also unified within a common project. Therefore, at the heart of this conception of democracy is the attempt to 'unite' diverse political struggles to contest the political power at the state level and construct a 'popular position' incorporating different identities and political subjectivities. The equivalential articulation of diverse demands emphasises the construction of 'popular-democratic subjects', which is essential for the success of democracy: 'democracy is grounded only on the existence of a democratic subject, whose emergence depends on the horizontal articulation between equivalential demands. An ensemble of equivalential demands articulated by an empty signifier is what constitutes a "people"'.[74]

By articulating the demands that are ignored and marginalised by the mainstream political parties in Turkey, the pro-Kurdish parties put forward a 'radical democratic' political project that directs its focus to tackling the marginalisation and oppression of the Kurds and other minorities, and seeks to unify principally demands for economic, political and gender equality that the diverse groups in Turkey have, around signifiers such as 'peace', 'democracy' or 'freedom'. As an alternative to the centralised and highly elitist political structure, they propose a new political framework that would develop an open, participatory and plural democratic society in Turkey that respects human rights and ensures peaceful coexistence. To achieve the new proposed framework, the pro-Kurdish political parties put forward measures to change the established political framework and the sedimented conception of citizenship in Turkey to enable the Kurds' cultural difference to be represented and recognised nationally.

Methodology and sources

The methodological framework of discourse theory has been elaborated in detail in the following studies: Glynos and Howarth (2007), Howarth (2000; 2005), Howarth and Stavrakakis (2000).[75] These studies emphasise the 'problem driven' approach (often contrasted with 'method driven' or 'theory driven' approach) that discourse theory deploys and state that the starting point for discourse theoretical research is a 'set of pressing political and ethical problems in the present', which are analysed in detail by examining 'the historical and structural conditions which gave rise to them, while furnishing the means for their critique and transgression'.[76] This method has much in common with Foucault's technique of 'problematisation' which 'synthesised the archaeological and genealogical methods of analysis'.[77] Such a synthesis enables us not only to examine the 'forms' that entities take but also offers an account of 'their contingent emergence and production'.[78]

My research analyses how Kurdish political practices, by proposing and undertaking to build a new political community – a united, socialist and independent Kurdistan in the early years of the movement, and seeking to transform Turkey to a democratic republic at the present – problematised and altered the existing Kemalist 'regime' and its social practices, and the Kurdish 'feudal' social practices.[79] Discourses and political practices that problematised the position of the Kurds in Turkey by seeking to redefine the 'given' Kurdish identity, and change or transform the Kemalist 'regime' and its 'social practices' through either instituting a new political structure, i.e. a separate Kurdish state, or by putting forward proposals to alter the present institutional setup of Turkey to include representation and recognition for the Kurds as a national group within the existing boundaries of Turkey, are defined as 'Kurdish' discourses or political practices. 'Social practices' are defined as 'the ongoing routinised practices of human and societal reproduction'.[80] Whereas, 'political practices' refers to the 'struggles that seek to challenge and transform the existing norms, institutions and practices – perhaps even the regime itself – in the name of an ideal or principle'.[81] The relation between political and social practices is formulated by Glynos and Howarth in the following way: 'Clearly, then, insofar as political movements are successful in challenging norms and institutions in the name of something new, political practices bring about a transformative effect on existing social practices.'[82]

As elaborated by Glynos and Howarth the basic unit of explanation in discourse theoretical research is *logics*. The following definition of logic is provided: '*the logic of a practice comprises the rules or grammar of the practice*, as well as, *the conditions which make the practice both possible and vulnerable*'.[83] Discourse theory proposes and articulates its critical explanation through the use of a 'three-fold typology of logics – social, political and fantasmatic',[84] which are applied 'to characterize and elucidate the transformation, stabilisation, and maintenance of regimes and social practices'.[85] Each of these logics plays an important part in formulating a critical explanation to a problematised phenomenon: 'Since

38 *Kurdish identity and nationalism in Turkey*

all dimensions are to some degree present in a practice or regime, every logic has a role to play in furnishing us with a complete explanatory account.'[86] They do this by addressing the 'what', 'how' and 'why' questions that we ask ourselves in analysing a problematised phenomenon:

> If social logics assist in the process of characterising *what* a practice is, and political logics show *how* it is challenged and defended, then fantasmatic logics can be said to generate reasons for *why* practices are maintained or transformed. All are necessary in any account of a problematized phenomenon and thus mutually implicate one another. It is, however, heuristically helpful sometimes to think of them as picking out different aspects of a critical explanation.[87]

Hence, 'This complex of logics provides us with the theoretical resources to characterize practices and regimes, to account for their dialectical relationship, and to explain how and why they change or resist change.'[88]

Discussions of social logics has the aim of 'characterising a particular social practice or regime' as they 'comprise the substantive grammar or rules of a practice or regime.'[89] Identification of social logics involves (though it need not be, as the analyst can also identify them) the self-interpretations of social actors.[90] Within the context of this study, social logics are applied to characterise the Kemalist regime and its practices and the Kurdish 'feudal' practices that the Kurdish national movement sought to transform. Necessarily, social logics involve the contextual description of a regime and its practices and they are 'always contextual entities, arising in particular historical and political circumstances'.[91] For example, the Kemalist social logics of 'Westernisation' and 'Secularisation', which were argued by the Kemalist elite to be positive necessary steps towards the modernisation of society and catching up with the West, for Kurds, meant assimilation and denial, as the only acceptable identity was the secular Turkish national identity. Hence, the definition of identity in exclusive terms denied the possibility of existence of the other cultural and national identifications, and justified the repressive practices to homogenise Turkey and create the desired Turkish nation. This, amongst other things, led to the following practices: the Turkification of Kurdish geography by changing the popularly known Kurdish names of towns, villages and mountains to Turkish ones and building symbols of Turkish nationalism in Kurdish areas; the enforcement of the Turkish language by forbidding the Kurds from learning and speaking Kurdish; making the Kurdish subject position unavailable by banning the use of terms such as 'Kurdistan' and 'Kurd' and instead popularising derogatory substitutes such as *Doğu* (East) and *Doğulu* (Easterner). Similarly, the sedimented and naturalised practices of 'tribalism' and 'religious orders' that characterised Kurdish 'feudalism' were invoked by the Kurdish national movement for being the root cause of the unequal power relations between big landlords and the masses of landless peasants, and were challenged for justifying the economic exploitation of the latter by the former and for leading to the fragmentation of the Kurdish nation.

Kurdish identity and nationalism in Turkey 39

The political logics, in contrast, help us to understand how 'a social practice or regime *was* instituted or *is being* contested or instituted'.[92] In doing this, they enable us to 'capture those processes of collective mobilisation precipitated by the emergence of the political dimension of social relations, such as the construction, defense, and naturalisations of new frontiers'.[93] Hence, as elaborated above in the subsection 'Political Frontiers', political logics are central to understanding the construction of social antagonisms and drawing political frontiers. As mentioned previously, in discourse theory, the concept of *dislocation* is of prime importance because it reveals the contingency of the existing social order and brings about the conditions that give rise to new political practices and identities.[94] In the case of the Kurds in Turkey, the dislocatory effects of various developments, such as the development of capitalism, mechanisation of agriculture which led to the Kurds' migration to Western Turkey, transformation to multi-party democracy in 1946, the rise of an oppositional left-wing movement during the 1960s, the Kurds' experience of oppression and discrimination and the spread of education in Turkey created the conditions for the emergence and development of a Kurdish movement that began to problematise Kemalist practices, such as forced assimilation and the denial of Kurdishness. This, during the 1970s, led to the emergence of the Kurdish national liberation discourse, which proposed to construct a counter-hegemonic order. The above developments also had a dislocatory effect on Kemalism and led to a loss in its hegemonic appeal in Turkey.

However, not all of the political practices that may come about as a result of a 'dislocation' are able to challenge the established hegemonic order. Inevitably some political practices prove more successful than others. Conversely, not all dislocations result in a challenge to an established social practice as in certain cases the hegemonic order remains intact despite various dislocations. To provide a critical explanation of change and continuity of social practices, that is, account for why in some cases political practices successfully challenge hegemonic regimes and alter the associated social practices, or why the existing social practices are able to contain dislocations, discourse theory relies on fantasmatic logics.[95] Fantasmatic logics capture the reasons behind why a particular political practice as opposed to others is able to challenge the social practices: 'When working in tandem with political logics, fantasmatic logics may be invoked to help explain why certain demands – or responses to demands – succeed in gripping or interpellating a particular constituency.'[96] Therefore, fantasmatic logics 'furnish us with the means to account for the *grip* of an existing or anticipated social practice or regime', which Glynos and Howarth define in the following way: 'What we term the "grip of ideology" thus comprises a myriad of practices through which individuals are turned into subjects with an identity, and through which such identities are sustained and reproduced.'[97]

This is also elaborated in Stavrakakis (2007), which discusses the use of the Lacanian psychoanalytical categories (desire, fantasy and enjoyment (*juissance*)) for political analysis in general and nationalism in particular.[98] Deploying fantasmatic logics to the study of nationalism seeks to uncover the *force* of nationalist

40   *Kurdish identity and nationalism in Turkey*

discourses and ideologies by exploring the identification process to uncover the 'affective bonds' and psychic investment that conditions people's identification with their 'nation' as 'desirable and often irresistible'.[99] The success of a political project depends on its ability to invoke the desire in the subject: 'Almost all political discourses focus on the delivery of the "good life" or a "just society", which are both fictions of a future state in which current limitations thwarting our enjoyment will overcome.'[100] Hence, another significance of fantasy lies in its ability to identify those who are held responsible for the loss of enjoyment. In nationalist discourses typically the 'internal' and the 'external' enemies of the nation are held responsible for blocking it from obtaining its full *juissance*.

Although I do not offer a psychoanalytical reading of Kurdish nationalism in Turkey, my analysis of the PKK's hegemony is informed by the psychoanalytical concepts of 'desire' and 'fantasy'. Specifically, fantasmatic logics are deployed to capture the fantasy dimension of the discourse and account for why the PKK's national liberation discourse managed successfully to 'grip' the Kurds. As I argued above and elaborate on more fully in Chapter 6, the construction of a 'golden age' and a contemporary myth of resistance provided the *fantasmatic dimension* to the PKK's national liberation discourse, which as well as enabling it to conceptualise and represent a homogenous Kurdish nation and bring *naturalness* to its 'existence' and 'unity', invoked the 'fantasy' of Kurdish unity to construct the antagonisms against the Kurds' 'external' and 'internal' enemies who were held responsible for keeping the Kurdish masses under oppression and Kurdistan divided. In the PKK's discourse these enemies prevented the Kurds from achieving their full identity and unity and the PKK managed to unify the Kurds in a common struggle transcending the religious, linguistic and tribal differences making the sedimentation of its national liberation discourse in practice possible. As well as creating and sustaining 'desire' in the Kurds, the fantasmatic dimension added *force* to its discourse to successfully mobilise a significant number of the Kurds.

The selection and analysis of primary sources

Kurdish political activism in Turkey in the period from the early 1960s to April 2011 is the focus of my research. In this period numerous political organisations were active. The Kurdish national movement followed a complex trajectory and fostered the development of interconnected political practices to challenge the existing Kurdish feudal and Kemalist social practices. My problematisation of the existing literature in Chapter 1 emphasised the insufficient attention paid to the discursive constitution of Kurdish national identity, the diversity of Kurdish nationalism and the specificity of Kurdish national demands. The problem driven approach I develop offers an interpretive and critical account of Kurdish identity and nationalism and examines a large amount of primary sources published by Kurdish activists and political organisations. As well as providing an account of the dominant Kurdish political practices that challenged the existing social practices, my research aims to generate a deeper understanding of the historical context within which these practices emerged and developed. Hence, my interpretive account focuses on highlighting the processes and historical and structural conditions that have played a key role in the rise of Kurdish nationalism and its evolution since the 1960s.

I study Kurdish nationalism as an ideology and disaggregate Kurdish nationalist discourse to highlight its specificity and ideological diversity during the past 50 years and to show the variations over time and across different nationalist organisations. The main focus is on the two hegemonic discourses that have been articulating Kurdish national demands in Turkey: the 'national liberation' and the pro-Kurdish 'democratic discourse'. Examining the hegemonic discourses articulating Kurdish identity in Turkey and providing an account of *identity formation* allows me to formulate a better understanding of the contemporary Kurdish identity, including how it has been transforming. Specifically, my analysis focuses on the following key areas: the discursive construction and representation of Kurdish identity and difference, the articulation of Kurdish national demands, and the political imaginary that the Kurdish national movement has been seeking to construct. A close examination of the discourses of the Kurdish national movement highlights the ideological diversity and specificity of Kurdish nationalism.

First, my analysis focuses on the emergence, individuation and transformation of each discourse, and highlights the periods of change and discontinuity, and the articulation of new elements or changes in the emphasis of certain elements. My aim in deploying this approach is to reflect on the Kurds' own problematisation of their position and oppression in Turkey – their self-interpretation of their predicament – and the political proposals that numerous Kurdish political organisations and parties have put forward for its solution. Also, the analysis aims to show the construction and the ideological condensation of each discourse, what aspects of the sedimented social practices they problematised and what particular elements were articulated within each discourse. Second, I analyse the processes that led to each discourse hegemonising Kurdish politics during respective periods. Specifically, I examine the PKK's hegemonic articulation of Kurdish identity, how it managed to hegemonise the Kurdish national movement from the 1980s onwards and account for the transformation in its discourse from 'national liberation' to 'democracy' from the early 1990s onwards. Finally, I highlight the specificity of Kurdish political identity articulated within each discourse.

Reconstructing a comprehensive account of each of the hegemonic discourses (as well as the two competing versions of the national liberation discourse during the 1970s) that have been articulating Kurdish identity in Turkey could only be done by conducting a discourse analysis of a large body of text published in a variety of formats by numerous political actors. Therefore, as well as examining the key texts or documents – such as manifestos or political programmes – belonging to a particular political party or group to give an account of their political discourse, I have also examined political magazines, pamphlets, leaflets, posters, music and TV broadcasts, that were used as outlets to formulate and

42 *Kurdish identity and nationalism in Turkey*

disseminate the discourse to the wider civil society and for the representation of the Kurdish struggle. It is important to examine a variety of sources to give a complete picture of the discourse, and to interrogate issues of contestation and affect more fully in order to explain the mobilisation process in greater detail.

Specifically, the analysis of the primary sources centres on highlighting the political logics of the Kurdish nationalist discourse. As discussed above, the Kurdish national movement problematised and challenged not only the national oppression and exploitation imposed on the Kurds by the ruling Kemalist elite in Turkey but also the exploitation of the Kurdish masses (mainly landless peasants) by the Kurdish 'religious and feudal elites'. I specify the key demands raised by Kurdish activists and political organisations in the period under discussion, their characterisation of the Kurdish question, the proposals they formulated for its solution, their challenge of the existing notions of identity, citizenship and democracy in Turkey, their conceptualisation of pluralism in Turkey as well as in the Kurdish society, and the construction of political frontiers and relations of difference and equivalence. The quotations that I use in my research are drawn mainly from the key political texts of the main organisations or from the political magazines that they published to disseminate their discourse to the wider Kurdish society. A significant part of my research focuses on the national liberation discourse which hegemonised Kurdish politics from the early 1970s until the early 1990s. However, in order to provide a background to its emergence, my analysis of the empirical material starts from the beginning of the 1960s.

The original sources from the period that have survived to the present are rather scarce and the overwhelming number of the sources that I studied for my analysis of the 1960s and 1970s were published in Turkey. Due to legal restrictions the political magazines the Kurdish activists published were not able to continue their existence for a sustained period. Therefore, I analyse the articles written by the leading Kurdish activists that appeared in the political magazine *Dicle-Fırat* in 1962–1963 to examine the discourses of the Kurdish intellectuals and highlight the role that they played in the public debate in Turkey and in raising Kurdish political awareness in the period. The ideas expressed in the articles by the new generation of activist intellectuals who were the main discourse producers in the 1960s, such as Musa Anter, Edip Karahan, Sait Kırmızıtoprak and Sait Elçi, offer an important insight into the way the Kurdish question was framed by leading political activists in the period. The exclusive focus on *Dicle-Fırat* is because it was the longest surviving magazine and subsequently was reprinted in Sweden in 1997. Although it is not possible to determine the exact spread of the distribution of the magazine, given it was published legally in the city of Diyarbakır, it is highly possible that it was distributed to all of the regional urban centres.

For my analysis of the 1960s, I also draw from the memoirs and other reflective accounts that the Kurdish activists published. In particular I focus on the accounts provided by Musa Anter, Naci Kutlay and Kemal Burkay. In my analysis of the second part of the 1960s, I focused on the activities of the TKDP and the TİP as they were the main organisations that attracted Kurdish activists of the period. Court documents and defences that the members of the DDKO submitted to the courts in defence of their activities and movement have also been examined in detail. Many Kurdish political activists who played a significant role in Kurdish political activism during the 1970s, such as Musa Anter, Edip Karahan, Mümtaz Kotan, İbrahim Güçlü, İhsan Aksoy and Mehdi Zana were arrested and tried as part of the DDKO trial. The establishment of the DDKO is significant for it represents a new stage in the separation of Kurdish socialists from the Turkish socialist movement during the late 1960s. This analysis of the primary sources has been supplemented by numerous secondary sources published on Kurdish activism in the 1960s. These include the academic studies that were published on the 'Kurdish question' or 'Eastern question' and that have contributed to the development of national and political awareness among the Kurds, such as Mehmet Emin Bozarslan's *Doğu'nun Sorunları* (The Problems of the East), Ismet Chériff Vanly's *Survey of the National Question of Turkish Kurdistan*, and İsmail Beşikci's *Doğu Mitinglerinin Analizi*.[101]

In the late 1960s and early 1970s, the discourse of the Kurdish political activists started to develop a much more elaborate critique of the political proposals formulated within the Turkish socialist discourse. These early critiques mark the emergence and individuation of the Kurdish socialist discourse and offer significant insights into the debates taking place in Turkey concerning the Kurdish question and socialism. The intention behind analysing the two pamphlets written by Kemal Burkay and published in Europe is to reflect on the reasons behind the Kurdish socialists' separation from the Turkish socialist movement. While it is highly unlikely that these pamphlets were distributed in large numbers to the Kurds in Turkey, they would have been accessed by the leading activists and members of the nascent Kurdish socialist movement. Hence, both the defences of the DDKO members and the two pamphlets published by Burkay are highly reflective of the views and ideas circulating among the new generation of Kurdish activists during the early 1970s, who, in the later years, came to occupy a leading position in the Kurdish movement. In particular, the discourse analysis I conduct highlights the political activists' understanding of the Kurdish identity, their formulation of Kurdish national demands and their critique of the Kemalist regime and of the Turkish socialist discourse. As Chapter 4 highlights, the critiques developed in these early texts have been elaborated and expanded in the numerous political magazines that Kurdish socialists published in the second half of the 1970s. During the 1970s numerous organisations contested Kurdish identity and from the early 1980s onwards the PKK has become the dominant force in Kurdish resistance in Turkey. Moreover, in 1978 and 1979 conflict flared within the Kurdish movement deepening the already existing fragmentation and disunity. Therefore, in addition to analysing the discourse of the political groups and parties, which I discuss below, my account of the 1970s also focuses on the political practices that Kurdish activism generated in the period, and the significant differences, in terms of strategy and ideology, that existed between the groups and parties.

44   *Kurdish identity and nationalism in Turkey*

From the mid 1970s onwards political organisations and groups became the main producers of discourse and primarily their discourse was disseminated to the wider Kurdish society through the political magazines that they have published. Hence, naturally my focus centres on the discourses of the political groups and parties, ideas and proposals formulated in the political magazines that they published in the period. Established in December 1974, the TKSP was the first Kurdish socialist group and the strongest one during the mid 1970s. To disseminate its discourse to the Kurdish population in Turkey, it published a legal monthly magazine, *Özgürlük Yolu* (the Path of Freedom), between June 1975 and January 1979 and fortnightly the bilingual *Roja Welat* (the Day of Homeland) between September 1977 and 1979. While both magazines reserved ample space for the analysis of current affairs, they also published numerous articles conveying the TKSP's discourse. Often the author of these articles was not specified or a pseudonym was used to conceal the author's identity. Numerous such articles in *Özgürlük Yolu* were written by C. Aladağ and Ş. Dicleli, which were the two common pseudonyms used by the founding leader of the TKSP, Kemal Burkay. It is highly possible that the other leading members also contributed to writing and producing the discourse that was disseminated through the *Özgürlük Yolu*; however, as their identity was concealed we are not in a position to give a thorough account of the TKSP's other discourse producers.

The analysis I conduct of such articles published in *Özgürlük Yolu* during the period from 1974 to 1979 highlights the key political demands articulated by the TKSP, its articulation of Kurdish identity and its definition of, and proposal for, the solution of the Kurdish question. Additionally, the party's original political programme drafted in December 1974 has been examined. According to the TKSP sources consulted, *Özgürlük Yolu* managed to achieve a circulation of between 5,000 and 10,000 copies and *Roja Welat* maintained a circulation of between 20,000 and 40,000 copies.[102] However, in contrast to *Özgürlük Yolu*, which managed to survive for nearly four years, the other magazines, such as *Kawa*, *Rizgarî*, *Denge Kawa*, *Jîna Nû* published by other Kurdish political groups managed fewer issues and were published in irregular intervals before the 1980s. There are no statistical records concerning the spread and distribution of these magazines as many were prohibited and their publication and distribution were done secretly. Therefore, it is very difficult to state precisely or to obtain verification figures of how many of these magazines were in circulation, what their exact geographic distribution was and the nature of their readership. However, it is highly likely that their primary readership consisted of the members and sympathisers of each group. Nevertheless, these publications made important contributions to the public discussion of the Kurdish question in Turkey and they offer us important insights into the issues that dominated the agendas of the political groups and parties that were active during the 1970s.

In addition to the TKSP's discourse, my analysis draws from the *Rizgarî* magazine and *Jîna Nû* (KİP/DDKD) to reflect the views of a cross section of the Kurdish political groups and to highlight the political and organisational fragmentation that the Kurdish national movement experienced during the 1970s,

Kurdish identity and nationalism in Turkey 45

which has been the predominant feature of Kurdish politics in the period. The articles published in the *Rizgarî* magazine did not specify an author; however, two of the leading members of the group, Ruşen Arslan and Hatice Yaşar, were stated as the owner and editor of the magazine and it is highly likely that they were the main producers of the group's discourse. Although we cannot determine the precise extent, the other leading members of the group, including Mümtaz Kotan and İbrahim Güçlü, would have played a major role in the production of the *Rizgarî*'s discourse.

A genuine effort was made to locate and obtain the magazines and other primary sources that all the political parties and groups active in the period published; however, it has not been possible. While I examined sufficient material to substantiate the claims I make in this book, the primary sources examined are not exhaustive. This was mainly due to the problem of access as the copies of some magazines, such as *Kawa, Denge Kawa, Ala Rizgarî* and *Tekoşin*, were unavailable at the libraries or other public bodies in Europe and Turkey. Due to the repressive political environment in Turkey, many of these publications were published and distributed illegally. However, the defence that a leading *Kawa* member, Cemil Gündoğan wrote in 1981 and 1982 and submitted to the court in January 1983, and that has been published in 2007, which presents a detailed summary of its ideas, has been used in my research as broadly reflective of the movement's political objectives.

In contrast to its rivals, the group that came to be known as the PKK did not, in the early years, disseminate its political discourse via a political magazine. Its members' agitation activities and the propagation of discourse orally through the members' personal contacts were the predominant forms of dissemination of its discourse to civil society. The first occasions it disseminated its discourse to large groups were during the numerous meetings it organised in the Kurdish regions between April and May 1977. These meetings were used as occasions to increase its organisational capacity and recruitment. Soon after its formal establishment as a clandestine political party on 27 November 1978, its political discourse was disseminated through two pamphlets, *Kuruluş Bildirisi* (The Founding Declaration) and *Kürdistan Devriminin Yolu* (The Path of Kurdistan Revolution – Manifesto). These two documents have been chosen for my analysis of the PKK's national liberation discourse during the late 1970s. Additionally, other pamphlets, the political programme of the party and other ideological material, the defences that the leading PKK members submitted to the courts, reports submitted to party conferences and congresses and the books that it published have been examined to offer a comprehensive account of the evolution and transformation of the national liberation discourse during the early 1980s.

The sources of the post-1980 period have been drawn exclusively from the PKK because during the period following the military coup in Turkey, the political activities of the other groups either ceased due to the oppression or were carried out mainly in Europe alone. The PKK has been the hegemonic force from the early 1980s onward. My account focuses on providing an account of the political practices that the PKK activities generated and its organisational

46 *Kurdish identity and nationalism in Turkey*

and military growth during the 1980s. I examine its political magazines, *Serxwebûn* (1982–present) and *Berxwedan* (1982–1995), to cover the dissemination of the PKK's political discourse to the wider public and its active members. Although there are no statistics available on the geographic spread of the PKK's political magazines, they were widely distributed in Europe and clandestinely in Turkey. The political discourse disseminated through the magazines was likely to have been disseminated orally during numerous public meetings, demonstrations, speeches and commemoration practices that the PKK organised in Europe. Moreover, it is highly likely that some articles published in either *Serxwebûn* or *Berxwedan* and that conveyed the PKK's contemporary resistance myth were reproduced in Turkey by the pro-Kurdish magazines published in Turkey legally, such as *Özgür Halk*, during the 1990s. Hence, a significant number of sympathisers and supporters in Turkey would have access to the PKK's discourse. Additionally, numerous books were published by the PKK during the 1980s and 1990s to convey its discourse, which have also been examined in my research.

There is much more clarity in terms of the authorship of the PKK's key political texts, and the PKK's leader Abdullah Öcalan is cited as the author in most cases. Although in the early editions of the key texts, such as the Manifesto, Öcalan was not specified as the author, he was acknowledged as the author in the subsequent reprints. Another leading member, Mazlum Doğan was also another significant discourse producer in the PKK's early years and a collection of his articles was published as a book in 1982.[103] However, generally it is difficult to separate Öcalan's political thought from the general political claims made by the PKK and to determine the extent of the contribution the other leading members of the PKK made to its ideological texts and discourses; hence, his political writings are seen as synonymous with PKK's ideology and discourse. In many other political ideological books and the published reports submitted to the party congresses and conferences, Öcalan is acknowledged as the author. Additionally, his articles frequently appeared in the PKK's political magazines. Furthermore, the significant discursive and strategic changes that the PKK undertook in the past decade were initiated by Öcalan through the defences submitted to the State Security Court and the European Court of Human Rights (ECHR). Since his imprisonment in Turkey, other members of the PKK's Central Committee have assumed a more central role in discourse production; however, the defences Öcalan presented to various Turkish and EU courts have been subsequently printed as books and used as the main texts for the dissemination of the PKK's new democratic discourse indicating that he continues to play his role as the main producer of the discourse.

The analysis I have conducted of the political discourse disseminated through magazines and books has been supplemented by examining a variety of other outlets that were used by the PKK to disseminate its discourse. In particular, I examined the songs and music of *Koma Berxwedan* and the posters and public statements that the PKK published. The specific focus on the *Koma Berxwedan* music group is because it was the official band of the PKK and was established to convey the PKK's struggle through the medium of music. It played a significant role in Kurdish cultural renewal and, as my analysis highlights in Chapter 6, it made a major contribution to the sedimentation of the PKK's discourse in practice. Additionally, I analyse the content of Kurdish TV broadcasts to draw out the representation of Kurdistan and Kurdishness, the dissemination of discourse and the representation of Kurdish struggle to the masses.

To supplement my analysis of the primary sources, I draw on Çağlayan's analysis of the construction of gender oppression in the PKK's discourse. Additionally, Gündoğan's study has proved a valuable source of the statements and defences made by political prisoners belonging to the various political groups and organisations. Where possible my analysis is supplemented with secondary literature. In particular, Aydın's analysis of the construction of the myth of *Newroz* as the myth of origin of the Kurdish nation in the discourses of Kurdish political parties has been beneficial to my research. Additionally, the numbers relating to the conflict are drawn from the human rights reports published annually throughout the 1990s by the Human Rights Association of Turkey (*Türkiye İnsan Hakları Vakfı*, TİHV).

I have also used numerous newspaper interviews that the PKK's leader conducted with Turkish and Kurdish journalists during the 1990s. The significance of these interviews is that they gave the PKK a rare opportunity to convey its demands to the Turkish population in general and were conducted in a period in which major discursive shifts towards democracy were introduced. Hence, as well as highlighting the wider media context within which certain aspects of the PKK's discourses were disseminated to the civil society in Turkey, these interviews proved to be valuable resources to trace the PKK's discursive evolution during the early 1990s. The PKK's appropriation of the democratic discourse throughout the late 1990s and the early 2000s has been explained in detail in Chapter 7. My analysis of the process of discursive change that the PKK experienced has drawn from the defences that the captured PKK leader Öcalan submitted to the State Security Court and the European Court of Human Rights. The ideas and proposals formulated in these defences have been used by the PKK to construct a more comprehensive democratic discourse. Significant organisational and discursive changes were introduced by the PKK during various party congresses and conferences throughout the early 2000s. The official reports published following the party congresses and the political programmes of the various organisations established following the PKK's formal abolishment also constituted important primary sources for my research. These sources highlight the construction and condensation of the PKK's democratic discourse in detail.

For the analysis of the discourse of the pro-Kurdish legal political parties in Turkey, I used their party programmes, election literature and statements that the leaders and leading members of the parties made to the media. My analysis focuses on the specific political demands that have been articulated in the pro-Kurdish democratic discourse, highlights the movement's contestation of Kurdish identity and sets out its political challenge of the existing notions of citizenship and democracy in Turkey. Moreover, my analysis of the official records of the Grant National Assembly of Turkey highlights the formulation

48 *Kurdish identity and nationalism in Turkey*

and articulation of specific demands in the pro-Kurdish democratic discourse. Also, I conduct an extensive search of Turkey's national newspapers for the statements that the leading members of the pro-Kurdish movement made and the interviews that they conducted. The leading members of the movement, including numerous MPs, party chairmen and local politicians have been the main producers and disseminators of the discourse and their statements have been selected as reflections of the pro-Kurdish democratic discourse. The analysis of newspaper contents has allowed me to also form an opinion on the extent of the difficulties the pro-Kurdish movement experienced to disseminate its democratic and reconciliation discourse through the mainstream Turkish media to reach the wider society in Turkey. Furthermore, the detailed accounts published in Turkish of the pro-Kurdish movement, such as Demir (2005) and Ölmez (1995) have been used to provide a fuller picture of the activities of the pro-Kurdish political parties that have been taking place in the past 20 years.

3 The organic intellectuals and the re-emergence of Kurdish political activism in the 1960s

Introduction

This chapter focuses on the formative years of the contemporary Kurdish national movement. Starting with the trials of the Kurdish activists, the early 1960s witnessed widespread discussion of the 'Eastern question'. In the late 1960s, during the 'Meetings of the East', Kurdish political activism started to succeed in mobilising large numbers of Kurds. The dislocatory consequences of the development of capitalism in Turkey and the Kurdish regions, the transition to multi-party democracy in 1946 and the spread of education combined during the 1950s and 1960s to create the conditions for the emergence of new oppositional discourses that challenged Kemalism's numerous oppressive practices. In the case of the Kurds, the spread of education resulted in the emergence of a new group of activist intellectuals, who took a leading role in Kurdish cultural and political activism in Turkey. The limited freedoms that the 1961 constitution provided were used by the Kurdish activists to raise their demands and voice some of the Kurdish grievances. In order to draw out the articulation of Kurdish demands and trace the nature of the public debate taking place in Turkey concerning the 'Eastern question', I will first offer an account of the emergence of Kurdish political activism and the articulation of Kurdish demands by the Kurdish 'organic intellectuals' during the 1960s.[1] To illustrate the self-reflections and self-understandings that the Kurdish intellectuals and the wider Kurdish society experienced during the 1960s, I provide an analysis of the contents of the magazines that the Kurdish organic intellectuals published. Second, I provide an account of Kurdish political activism during the second part of the 1960s and analyse the popular expression of Kurdish political and economic demands during the 'Meetings of the East' held in many towns and cities in 1967.

Laclau's discussion of *demands* sets out to describe how individual demands emerge and start their process of articulation. A demand can either be absorbed into the existing order if they are *differentially* satisfied or remain unsatisfied. The socio-economic demands that Kurdish intellectuals started to raise, which in the later years started to strongly resonate with the Kurdish public, were ignored by the successive Turkish governments. In fact, it was highly unlikely and difficult to satisfy such demands because the severe regional socio-economic

50 *Kurdish political activism in the 1960s*

inequality and underdevelopment was the result of years of negligence on the part of the authorities. Hence, reversing the harsh socio-economic conditions that many Kurds faced could have only been achieved with long-term state investment in the infrastructure of the region and a significant policy shift. More importantly the debate that the Kurdish intellectuals generated was not met with a constructive dialogue but with suppression and rejection because their demands were equated with separatism. For many Kurds such an attitude typified the inflexible policy of successive Turkish governments. This causal understanding was reflected in the discourses of the Kurdish organic intellectuals which increasingly questioned the reasons behind regional underdevelopment and inequality, and the neglect the 'East' suffered. They started to argue that the denial of Kurdish identity and the oppression of Kurdish culture were the reasons behind the underdevelopment of the East. Due to legal restrictions it was not possible to use the terms 'Kurd', 'Kurdish' or 'Kurdistan'. Instead, 'East' and 'Easterner' were used as substitutes for 'Kurdistan' and 'Kurdish'. In the second half of the 1960s, Kurdish demands started to be articulated *differentially* as demands for social and economic equality by primarily Kurdish socialists active within the TİP. In addition, the late 1960s also witnessed the emergence of an 'autonomist' Kurdish movement in the form of the TKDP, which was established in 1965 but as I argue below, did not manage to gain much ground in Kurdish politics in Turkey. However, as Chapter 4 elaborates in greater detail neither the TİP nor the other Turkish socialist groups were able to formulate a coherent policy on the Kurdish question and incorporate Kurdish demands into their programme.

Kurdish organic intellectuals and the public discussion of the 'Eastern question'

Particularly important in the context of this research are the activities of the Kurdish organic intellectuals because they played a key role in the public discussion of the Eastern question in Turkey and in the articulation of Kurdish demands in the 1960s. Their number increased throughout the 1940s and 1950s as a result of more Kurds attending the universities in Istanbul and Ankara and other higher education institutions. The interaction among the Kurdish students from various towns in Turkey – as well as from Iran, Iraq and Syria – increased the sense of comradeship among them leading to a greater awareness of their 'common' Kurdish identity and the growth of national consciousness. This process was facilitated by the concentration of Kurdish students within specific dormitories, *Dicle Talebe Yurdu* and *Fırat Talebe Yurdu*, established by a group of Kurdish activists in 1941 and by Musa Anter in 1943 respectively.[2] This new generation of students and activists began to establish contact with the Kurdish activists and intellectuals of the 1920s and 1930s, who were exiled to Western Turkey. The leading members of the new activist intellectuals included Musa Anter, Edip Karahan, Ziya Şerefhanoğlu, Yusuf Azizoğlu, Mehmet Emin Bozarslan, Faik Bucak, Sait Kırmızıtoprak and Sait Elçi. The latter two were

Kurdish political activism in the 1960s 51

involved in the establishment of the TKDP in 1965. Edip Karahan and Musa Anter published the Kurdish political magazines, *Dicle-Fırat* and *Deng*, and Mehmet Emin Bozarslan translated the Kurdish epic *Mem-û-Zîn*. Many more, including Kemal Burkay, Tarık Ziya Ekinci, Mahmut Baksi and Canip Yıldırım, were active within the TİP and subsequently played a leading part in the formation of the 'Eastist' movement during the late 1960s.[3] The re-emergence of Kurdish political activism in Turkey also coincided with the reinvigoration of the Kurdish movement in Iraqi Kurdistan and Kurdish student activism in Europe. From the late 1950s and early 1960s Kurdish political activism in Europe increased with the establishment of the Kurdish Student Society in Europe, which published a magazine 'Kurdistan', and the establishment of the International Society Kurdistan in 1961 in the Netherlands to promote the Kurdish culture and political struggle. Their main activity was the publication of a monthly news magazine 'Kurdish Facts and West-Asian Affairs' between 1961 and 1970 (sometimes irregular), which covered various aspects of Kurdish society, culture and language, and provided news and analysis on the Kurdish struggle and the lives of the Kurds.

Hence, the 1960s witnessed a significant increase in cultural activities, mainly the publication of magazines. Such an increase was facilitated by the new political freedoms and rights that the new constitution – accepted in a referendum in June 1961 that laid the ground for the transition to democracy in October 1961 – granted, including 'freedom of thought, expression, association and publication, as well as other civil liberties'.[4] Moreover, the new constitution accorded more autonomy to the universities and crucially the workers' 'right to strike' was recognised. Such freedoms allowed space for the oppositional groups to express their demands and raise their concerns. Organisations to promote the workers' and peasants' interests were formed; the increase in the numbers of the working class was matched with an increase in radicalisation of the working-class movement during the 1960s.

Public discussion of the Eastern question

In the late 1950s and early 1960s there were various high-profile events, such as the arrest and trial of Kurdish activists, which drew attention to the Kurdish question in Turkey and led to a dynamic discussion in the media. Increasingly, these discussions started to highlight the oppressive nature of the relations between the Kurds and Turkey and focused on the Kurds experience of discrimination. Numerous cases brought against Kurdish writer Musa Anter for his columns in *İleri Yurt* newspaper, in particular the court case brought against *İleri Yurt* for publishing Musa Anter's Kurdish poem, *Qimil*, on 31 August 1959, generated much public interest. Numerous commentators writing in the national newspapers in Turkey expressed their insatiable anger for the publication of a poem in the Kurdish language.[5] However, this had a reverse effect by politically mobilising many Kurds in support of the newspaper and Musa Anter; specifically, many Kurdish students in Western Turkey sent telegraphs of support and

52   Kurdish political activism in the 1960s

many people gathered in front of the court during the trial to show their moral support.[6]

The first major event that drew public attention to the Eastern question came to be known as 'the 49'ers incident' (*49'lar Olayı*) and involved initially 50 Kurdish students and activists (one died during the detention), who were arrested on 17 December 1959 and whose trials lasted until 1967. The arrest of Kurdish students and activists was linked to a government plot to punish a high number of Kurds with a possible death sentence to quell the rising threat of Kurdish nationalism in the region. The government gave 'secret' orders to the National Intelligence Organization (MİT) to prepare a 'Kurdish report', which recommended that between 1,000 and 2,500 Kurds be tried and executed for their separatist activities. The report recommended that the 'suspects' be portrayed as 'separatists' within Turkey and 'communists' in the foreign media.[7] The catalyst used for the arrest was the public statement signed by 102 Kurdish students condemning the remarks made by the Turkish nationalist politician Asım Eren in 1959. In a speech that drew much media attention, Eren advocated revenge attacks on the Kurds in Turkey as retaliation for the Iraqi Kurds' attack against Turkmen in Kirkuk. The arrested Kurdish activists were accused of promoting 'Kurdism' or Kurdish nationalism (*Kürtçülük*) and were prosecuted on charges of 'taking part, with the aid of foreign states, in activities to weaken the unity of the state and separate parts of the territory of the state' and 'taking part in activities to weaken the unity of the nation'.[8] The detainees were released in January 1961 for lack of evidence. Following a protracted legal process the accused were finally acquitted of the charges in 1964. However, this did not mean an end to the case as they were charged with forming an organisation to weaken national feelings.[9] The protracted trial of the '49'ers' and the widespread media coverage generated public interest in the Kurdish issue. This was the most notable incident involving the Kurds in Turkey since the brutal suppression of the Dersim uprising in 1938 and included the above-mentioned well-known Kurdish personalities and activists.

Similar cases of arbitrary arrest and political oppression continued on other occasions during the early 1960s. Soon after the first military coup on 27 May 1960, 485 Kurdish tribal leaders and large land owners were detained and subsequently 55 of them were exiled to Southern and Western Turkey. This was followed by the arrest and detention of 23 Kurdish activists on 29 June 1963.[10] The arrested included various Iraqi Kurds and some of the activists on trial as part of the '49'ers case' such as, Sait Elçi, Medet Serhat, Yaşar Kaya, Musa Anter, Ziya Şerefhanoğlu and Edip Karahan, and they were prosecuted for 'endangering and damaging the unity of the state and taking part in activities to separate parts of the territories under the sovereignty of the state'.[11]

The establishment of the YTP (*Yeni Türkiye Partisi,* New Turkey Party) was also a significant development because numerous Kurdish politicians who were former members of the Democrat Party (*Demokrat Parti,* DP) were among its ranks. The YTP was a centrist political party that opposed political polarisation and argued for the need to protect the individual's freedoms and the democratic

Kurdish political activism in the 1960s 53

norms to institute a stable democracy in Turkey.[12] The commitment to strengthen the democratic regime was combined with a commitment for state intervention in the economy to promote economic growth to address numerous imbalances and inequalities. Whereas, the YTP did not articulate overt Kurdish demands in its political programme, it included numerous Kurds among its ranks and gained widespread support from the Kurds. It managed to obtain 13.73 per cent of the national vote in the 1961 general elections, winning 54 seats in the parliament and serving as a junior coalition partner in the government between 1962 and 1965.[13] The party was in charge of 6 ministries and the Minister of Health, Yusuf Azizoğlu, was a Kurd who made various statements to the media about the disparity between the East and the rest of Turkey and the need for more state investment.[14] Additionally, the need to develop the East was one of its pledges for the 1969 national election.[15] Similar demands for socio-economic equality and the development of the Kurdish region were voiced most noticeably by the Kurdish intellectuals in the magazines that they published.

Advocacy journalism: problematising underdevelopment and inequality in the 'East'

During the 1950s various regional newspapers such as *Dicle Kaynağı* in 1948 for a short period, *Şark Postası* in 1954, and the above-mentioned *İleri Yurt* in 1958–1959 (all in Diyarbakır) were published. The early 1960s witnessed a proliferation of Kurdish political and cultural magazines by the new generation of Kurdish activists. These publications included *Dicle-Fırat (Tigris-Euphrates, 1962–1963), Deng (Voice, 1963), Reya Rast (The True Path), Roja Newe (The New Day, 1963) and Yeni Akış (The New Current) (1966)* and managed to steadily increase the public debate and discussion concerning the Kurds and the Eastern question in Turkey. Additionally, various other publications appeared during the late 1960s: a Kurdish grammar book was published in 1965, a Kurdish-Turkish dictionary (prepared by Musa Anter) in 1967 and a book on Kurdish language in 1968 (by Mehmet Emin Bozarslan); the Kurdish national epic *Mem-û-Zîn* was republished in 1968 in Kurdish origin with Latin scripts with a Turkish translation (both the original Kurdish and the Turkish translation were by Mehmet Emin Bozarslan).[16] Also various other works on Kurdish history were translated and published by Mehmet Emin Bozarslan during the late 1960s, who also wrote a book entitled *Doğu'nun Sorunları* (The Problems of the East) in 1966, which was very popular among the Kurds in Turkey at the time.[17]

In this section, I focus on *Dicle-Fırat* in detail because it was the longest surviving newspaper managing eight issues and it was republished in 1997 in Sweden. Being the main outlet for Kurdish activists to campaign for and raise an awareness of the 'Eastern question', *Dicle-Fırat* aspired to provide a 'voice' to the East by reflecting on the pressing political and socio-economic issues of the region. The editor of the newspaper, Edip Karahan, in the introductory editorial, stated the objectives of *Dicle-Fırat* to be 'to work towards the cultural and economic development of the East, and to address and unite the differences in

54   *Kurdish political activism in the 1960s*

opinion that may arise on the matter'.[18] It sought to offer a platform for discussing the issues in greater detail as well as providing reflections on the regional issues. Hence, primarily articles that focused on the underdevelopment and economic backwardness of the region were published. Additionally, there were various articles on the Kurdish language, literature, poetry, history and the origins of Kurds. The articles on the history and origins of the Kurds were written in an academic style and comprised mainly reviews of academic studies on the history and origins of the Kurds written mostly in English, French and Arabic. They contested the state's claim that the Kurds were *essentially* of Turkish origin and traced Kurdish presence in the region to the ancient past to the 'Karduchis' and 'Gutis' who inhabited the territories near Lake Urmia (Western Iran) and Northern Mesopotamia around the eighth century BC onwards.[19] The link to such groups was also established through language and Kurdish being a distinct language within the Indo-European family of languages was interpreted to indicate that the Kurds had an Indo-European as opposed to Turkic origin.[20] Furthermore, the articles on Kurdish language, literature and poetry, as well as showing the distinctiveness of the Kurdish language, also enhanced the Kurds' understanding of their heritage and culture.

The discourse of the organic intellectuals focused on mainly the economic disparity between the Kurdish regions and rest of Turkey and drew attention to the fact that the existence of widespread inequality meant that the East was widely accepted as a 'zone of deprivation' (*mahrumiyet bölgesi*). This was seen as undermining the unity of the nation and the state's claim to the existence of political equality among all its citizens. The organic intellectuals often repeated the claim that urgent and comprehensive state investment was needed to develop the Eastern regions and address the socio-economic inequality and regional disparity. The reasons for the backwardness of the region were clearly stated as the lack of state investment especially in the areas of education and health infrastructure, and pursuing policies that ignored the social realities of the region.[21] In fact, the underdevelopment of the East was seen as the result of the state's deliberate negligence of the region:

> The East has been neglected for centuries and as a result it became a zone of deprivation. This negligence continued during the republican era. Regardless of their party belonging, every politician, in order to assimilate the people and intellectuals of the East, *systematically and purposefully*, represented the East, to the world and Turkey, as an area full of fanaticism, ignorance and as the enemy of civilisation.[22]

It was argued that the deliberate negligence of the East had the aim of facilitating cultural assimilation of its people as did the economic development policies that the state pursued:

> Development as a whole comprises material and psychological sides. It is not possible to sacrifice one to the other. In the past, the East was neglected

Kurdish political activism in the 1960s 55

so that the Easterners forget their mother tongue and customs and traditions. In our day, politicians and intellectuals, advocate the rapid development of the East. Their aim is the same: to absorb the East.[23]

Furthermore, the state's suppression of any debate and discussion concerning the development of the East was criticised and interpreted as another form of discrimination. Particularly, labelling any regional demands of the East with separatism was singled out and questions were raised on why advocating the development of other regions in Turkey was not seen as separatism but only the development of the East.[24]

The discussion the magazine sought to encourage – in various articles as well as in the editorials – problematised the social and cultural aspects of economic development. Specifically, it was argued that the economic development of the region could not be isolated from its cultural and social development and the state policies were criticised for focusing on solely the material development of the society. In Edip Karahan's words, economic development should not aim at 'the destruction of the language, traditions, and regional differences, in short the ethnic and linguistic presence' of the people of the East.[25] Instead, the need to develop the Kurdish language and culture was seen as essential to economic development. This argument incorporated the critique of the state's assimilation policies and called for the recognition of Kurdish cultural and linguistic differences. However, the critique did not develop into an elaborate critique of Kemalism and its practices but developed as responses to the statements made by Turkish nationalist politicians and writers in the Turkish media that emphasised cultural assimilation as a precondition of development. The nationalist publications such as *Milli Yol* and *Ötüken* published articles regularly that criticised Kurdish society and depicted the Kurds as tribal and backward, and an impediment for Turkey's development. For example, *Milli Yol* went as far as suggesting that the Kurds should be driven out of their lands and replaced by ethnic Turks from Kirghizstan and Kazakhstan.[26] Such views were reiterated by various high-profile politicians. For example, the former Chief of General Staff and the founder of the Justice Party, Ragıp Gümüşpala, who argued that the state needed to take harsh measures to break the influence of the Kurdish landlords and sheikhs over Kurdish society and intensify its assimilation efforts to cultivate Turkishness in Kurdish regions.[27] In their challenge to such statements – described as 'racist' and 'anti-East' – and to support the Kurds claim for equality, the organic intellectuals criticised the Turkish nationalist interpretation of the principle of 'unity of the nation':

We do not understand why it is seen as a threat, when within the [unity of] Turkish community, the people of a region speak, read and write in their own language? The modern nation cannot be viewed only on the basis of a single language. As there are communities that speak one language, there are others that speak many. Unity within diversity is possible. This unity is not weaker than the unity achieved in communities that speak only one language.[28]

56   Kurdish political activism in the 1960s

In their view, respecting Kurdish cultural differences would make the policies of development and integration more successful. In his article published in the left-wing weekly newspaper *Yön* and reprinted in the April 1963 edition of *Dicle-Fırat*, Sait Kırmızıtoprak – in relation to the 'wrong assumptions concerning the development of the East' – stated that the policy of forced assimilation needs to come to an end if the state wants to integrate the Kurds into Turkish society. The assimilation policies did not produce any of the expected outcomes and the state should allow the use of the Kurdish language to successfully pursue social and economic modernisation, as it would make it easier to convey the state's message to the Kurdish people. Above all, Kırmızıtoprak argued that forbidding the use of the Kurdish language contradicts the principles of political, social and economic equality that socio-economic development aims at achieving. Therefore, the economic development policies needed to take into account cultural and social factors for them to be successful.

Furthermore, Edip Karahan clarifies what he means by the concepts of national unity and togetherness before condemning the various statements that Turkish nationalist media made against the Kurds:

> For us the concepts of [national] unity and togetherness can be explained in the following way: to prevent the domination of one group of citizens by another; equal treatment before the law for every citizen regardless of their race, religion, religious denomination, and language; to punish any action, regardless of the situation it arises from, which harms the unity of the motherland and the brotherly manner that the members of the nation extend towards each other.[29]

This reading interpreted Kemalism as *civic nationalism* capable of accepting Kurdish rights and demands, and made a distinction between Kemalism and the much more exclusive pan-Turanist strands of Turkish nationalism that rejected the Kurds and were seen as the principal 'enemy' of the 'East'.[30] This distinction was elaborated in various articles by Sait Elçi and Sait Kırmızıtoprak, who drew attention to the dangers that this strand of Turkish nationalism (described by them as a form of 'fascism') represented. The need to be alert about the dangers of 'fascism' were echoed in various editorials of the newspaper and also in other articles, which also stress the important role that Kurdish people played in the democratic movement in Turkey since the transition to multi-party democracy in 1946: '...Easterners, with all their power need to support Turkey's democratic forces in their struggle against fascism and fascist anti-democratic laws'.[31] Such a statement is significant in showing the emphasis on the democratic nature of the Kurdish demands that the organic intellectuals articulated. Furthermore, it also shows the drawing of a political frontier that aims at bringing together the Kurds, socialists, workers and the youth in a democratic movement against the Turkish nationalists (described as 'Fascists' and 'Turanists'):

> ...racist fascism, being despotic, aggressive and profiteering by its nature, is an enemy to the people of the East. On this consideration, the Easterners

should be as vigilant about racist fascism as the populist revolutionary intellectuals, the youth and workers, and should contribute their strength to the anti-fascist democratic front.[32]

This characterisation reveals the democratic orientation of many of the Kurdish intellectuals and their shared view that a broader movement for democracy was indispensable to defeat anti-democratic and anti-Kurdish elements, whose rise was observed with much alarm. Being closely associated with Turkey's progressive political forces indicates the Kurdish activists' commitment to a broad democratic movement and achieving their rights and demands within a democratic Turkey. It is also interesting to note that Kurdish demands were conceived as demands for political equality. However, the Kurdish activists' urgency was not shared by many of the other Turkish groups that they identified as their allies, and the task of constructing a broad mass-based democratic movement proved much more difficult and challenging than they anticipated.

Organised dissent and mass protest: the TKDP, the TİP and the 'meetings of the East'

The second half of the 1960s was characterised by the evolution of Kurdish activism towards a more organised form. The reinvigoration of the Kurdish national movement in Iraq had a direct bearing on this development. This is evidenced by the establishment of the TKDP in Turkey advocating a similar autonomist programme as the Kurdistan Democrat Party (KDP) in Iraq. The TKDP was the first clandestine Kurdish political party to be founded in Turkey in the 1960s. However, soon after its establishment the party was marred by internal divisions and in January 1968 many leading members were arrested. Although the TKDP made an explicit mention of 'the Kurdish nation' and the Kurdish demands were clearer, they were formulated as demands for 'equality' and as I argue below the democratic nature of the Kurds' demands was also strongly emphasised. Hence, the clearer emphasis on the Kurdish nation did not result in an equivalential articulation of Kurdish identity in the discourses of the TKDP. Another source of Kurdish activism in the 1960s was the TİP and the socialist movement in general. The Kurdish activists in the TİP made a significant contribution to the debate on the Kurdish question. These debates gradually led to the appropriation of the Marxist discourse by the Kurdish activists and the conceptualisation of the Eastern question as the Kurdish question and in terms of national oppression.

The TKDP and the TİP

The ideas of underdevelopment and need to foster Kurdish cultural development as discussed by the Kurdish intellectuals formed an important part of the political programme of the TKDP. This is perhaps unsurprising as some of the intellectuals such as Sait Elçi and Sait Kırmızıtoprak were involved in founding the

58   Kurdish political activism in the 1960s

party. The extent and details of the activities of the TKDP are not well known and the party never managed to get a strong hold among the Kurds; however, the party managed to organise in a small scale in the urban centres. The party leader Faik Bucak was assassinated in 1966 and the arrest of many of its leading members in January 1968 significantly weakened its ability to formulate a strong challenge. It was further weakened with the division it suffered in 1969 after a leading member Sait Kırmızıtoprak broke off to form the Kurdistan Democrat Party in Turkey which shared the same initials. In 1971, the leaders of both branches of the TKDP died in mysterious circumstances in Iraqi Kurdistan. The party revived briefly during the second half of the 1970s.

The TKDP's programme put forward demands for the recognition of political, economic and cultural rights of the Kurdish people within the territorial integrity of Turkey. It advocated the establishment of a separate Kurdish administrative region within Turkey incorporating the areas in which Kurds form a majority. More specifically, within such a framework, it sought constitutional recognition for Kurdish national identity and the right to be represented in the national assembly and the 'council of ministers'. In terms of cultural rights, it proposed that the Kurdish language be recognised as the official language of the proposed Kurdish administrative region in Turkey to be used in education, and all the obstacles violating the right to publish and broadcast in Kurdish be removed. Additionally, it demanded that the state take a more active role in the economic development of the region by providing land and credit to farmers, increasing job creation in the regional urban areas, increasing credit to small and medium size businesses and investing in Kurdish regions, to bring an end to the regional imbalance and widespread poverty that the Kurdish people suffered.[33]

Furthermore, greater detail about the party's ideas and its articulation of Kurdish identity demands emerge from the defence that one of the leading members of the party, Şakir Epözdemir, presented to the court during the trial in 1968. Above all, the defence criticised the oppression of the Kurds by the state during the republican era and rejected the state's characterisation of the Kurdish issue as 'separatism'. It defended the existence of a 'separate' Kurdish nation and demanded that Kurdish national rights be recognised within the present borders of Turkey.[34] Kurdish rights and demands were framed as minority political, economic and cultural rights, without endangering the territorial integrity of Turkey.[35] The necessity of recognising the national diversity of Turkey was stressed because the Kurds had 'at least the same rights as the Turks over this homeland and are *a principal element of Turkey*'.[36] Hence, the idea of Turkey being a homeland to the Kurds was not rejected, but rather the conception of national identity on a specifically Turkish basis. Furthermore, similar to the discourses of the organic intellectuals, the Kurdish struggle was situated within the greater struggle for equality and a frontier was established against the Turkish 'extreme' nationalists: 'As we have repeatedly stated, we only want equality and fraternity. In opposition to these demands, the chauvinists call us "Kurdists". According to their logic to demand equality and parity between regions is racism, separatism and regionalism.'[37]

Kurdish political activism in the 1960s 59

Another outlet for Kurdish activism during the 1960s was provided by the TİP, which was founded by 12 trade unionists in 1961 as an independent socialist party promoting a parliamentary and evolutionary route to socialism.[38] During the 1960s the Kurds increased their involvement in Turkish left-wing organisations in general and the TİP in particular. The Kurdish activists saw the left as their allies and in particular the TİP's willingness to promote some demands of Kurdish people within the framework of equality and respect for constitutional rights drew many Kurds to them. As expressed by Musa Anter, the Kurds saw the socialists as their closest political allies because at least the socialists were willing to accept some of the Kurdish rights and demands:

> Turkey's other political groups were fascists and shared a common hostility towards the Kurdish question. The Turanists and Kemalists were of the same opinion. At least they [socialists], genuine or not, were saying that 'if we win in the future we will grant your rights.' At least they recognised the existence of our rights that were seized from us.[39]

Specifically, the underdevelopment of the East and the discrimination that the Kurds faced was a concern that the TİP was keen to address. The party programme accepted at its First Congress in February 1964 in Izmir stated:

> Currently, in the eyes of the majority of the citizens and civil servants, the provinces of the East and South-east regions are seen as a 'zone of deprivation'. The public services in this region are nearly non existent. Parallel to the economic backwardness of the region, the citizens there are faced with a backward social and cultural environment. Additionally, those citizens who speak Kurdish or Arabic, or those who belong to the Alevi denomination are faced with discrimination.... These citizens will also benefit from the rights and freedoms as recognised within the constitution.[40]

The TİP's interest in the underdevelopment of the East was also apparent in its support for the 'meetings of the East' (*Doğu Mitingleri*) in the main Kurdish towns and cities in 1967, which is discussed in greater detail below. In addition, various members of the TİP made important contributions to the public debate on the Kurdish question and voiced some of the demands and concerns of the Kurdish people. For example, in 1970, the leader of the TİP, Mehmet Ali Aybar, delivered a speech in the parliament condemning the commando operations that the state carried out in 'the East', which indiscriminately subjected the Kurdish population to violence. He asked the government to account for such actions and bring an end to it because 'this policy of terror, conceived, I assume, as a preventive measure, will inevitably give birth to reactions which will not serve the cause of national unity.'[41] Furthermore, Aybar stated:

> Since the creation of the republic, our compatriots of the East and Southeast have never been treated as equal citizens. Speaking Kurdish, those

60   Kurdish political activism in the 1960s

compatriots are submitted to a special treatment, as third-class citizens, and the present government is not the first one which has carried out such a policy against them. The policy of terror has always existed in the East and South-east, but the problem cannot be solved in this way. The policy of terror will lead us to a situation contrary to the hopes of those who are carrying out those measures.... An end must be put to this policy, so that the compatriots of the East may feel attached to this country and to this national community.[42]

In the 1965 parliamentary elections, the TİP won 2.83 per cent of the national votes and had 15 representatives in the national assembly, three of which were elected from the 'East' in Diyarbakır (Tarık Ziya Ekinci), Şanlıurfa (Behice Boran) and Kars (Adil Kurdel).[43] For a while, the TİP managed to provide effective opposition and raise the demands of the workers and peasants. However, the defeat the TİP suffered in the 1969 elections resulted in a factional struggle for party leadership between the party leader Mehmet Ali Aybar and opposition led by Sadun Aren and Behice Boran. The factional infighting was part of the more general struggle over the strategy of revolution in Turkey, which focused specifically on 'the national question'. This discussion was aided by the translation of Lenin's and Stalin's books on national self-determination and the nationalities question, and primarily two main positions are discernable: the National Democratic Revolution (NDR) thesis and the Socialist Revolution (SR) thesis. From the mid 1960s onwards, the TİP's official strategy of advocating a 'Turkish' and 'Democratic' route to Socialism was challenged by a strategy that 'envisaged a two-phase revolution, the first phase being the NDR and only the second being SR'.[44] This theorisation characterised Turkey as an economically dependent semi-colony of the Western 'imperialism' and a 'national democratic revolution' was needed for Turkey to have its political and economic independence. In the TİP's Fourth Congress held between 29 and 31 October 1970, the two-stage revolutionary strategy was rejected and the proponents were expelled from the party. However, these factional struggles and the disagreement over the strategy plunged the party into crisis, threatening its unity.

Another significant development that took place in the TİP's Fourth Congress was the party's acceptance of the resolution proposed by the Kurdish delegates that recognised the existence of the 'Kurdish people' in the 'East' and drew attention to the oppression that they had been subjected to since the establishment of the republic. The resolution characterised the Kurdish question not only as underdevelopment but also as an ethnic and national one, and reflected the view that the reason the East was underdeveloped was because it was predominantly Kurdish. Furthermore, the party stated its support of the Kurds in their struggle to achieve their democratic demands and constitutional rights.[45] This recognition was significant because it was the first time a legal political party openly acknowledged the existence of the Kurdish people in Turkey and drew attention to their national oppression. However, despite the TİP's recognition of the Kurds and the Kurdish question and the limited articulation of Kurdish

Kurdish political activism in the 1960s 61

rights, in the early 1970s the NDR thesis became dominant in the Turkish socialist movement. This received opposition from the Kurdish activists as it ignored the Kurdish demands and in response the discontented Kurdish activists intensified their critique by raising the issue of Kurds' national oppression and stressing the need to articulate Kurdish national demands as part of the socialist programme. The Kurdish activists started to develop a distinction between the nationalism of the 'oppressed nations' and that of the 'oppressor nations' and argued for the establishment of separate Kurdish revolutionary organisations to solve Kurdistan's national question. Turkish socialists remained generally unreceptive to Kurdish rights and demands because they perceived them as a threat to the unity of the socialist movement and the working class in Turkey. Although this debate started in the late 1960s, it continued throughout the 1970s as numerous articles critical of the Turkish socialist position continued to appear in the magazines published by Kurdish activists during the mid 1970s. Some Kurdish activists continued to remain active within the numerous organisations of the Turkish left until the 1980s; many started to voice the need to establish specifically Kurdish organisations from the late 1960s onwards. The political divisions and the TİP's hesitancy to formulate Kurdish demands within its socialist programme led the Kurdish activists to search for a separate trajectory. This search resulted in the establishment of the DDKO, which is discussed in Chapter 4.

The Eastern meetings[46]

The 'Eastern meetings' are considered to be the pinnacle of Kurdish activism in the late 1960s. Starting on 13 August 1967 in Silvan a series of 'Protest Meetings Against the Backwardness of the East and South-east Anatolia regions' were held in Diyarbakir on 3 September 1967, Siverek on 24 September 1967, Batman on 8 October 1967, Tunceli on 15 October 1967, Ağrı on 22 October 1967 and concluded with a final one in Ankara on 18 November 1967.[47] These meetings were organised by a committee comprising Kurdish activists within the TİP and the TKDP. The activists that took a leading role in the organisation of the meetings were Mehdi Zana, Tarık Ziya Ekinci, Kemal Burkay, Edip Karahan, Sait Elçi and Naci Kutlay, who were active mainly within the TİP. Furthermore, it is claimed by Ali Beyköylü that a group called, *Koma Azadixwazên Kurdistan* (The Group of Freedom Advocates of Kurdistan, KAK) also played a significant role in the organisation of the meetings. It is stated that this group was founded in 1965 or 1966 and published the statement that protested against the anti-Kurdish statements by *Ötüken*.[48] These meetings marked an important juncture for Kurdish activism in Turkey because they mobilised a large number of Kurds, especially those held in Diyarbakir, Silvan, Siverek, and Batman. Moreover, the demands raised by the intellectuals, such as regional inequality, negligence of the East and cultural and political oppression, found a strong resonance among the ordinary people. According to İsmail Beşikci's study of the 'Eastern Meetings', the main demands expressed in the meetings were the demands for the region's economic development and state investment to achieve

62 *Kurdish political activism in the 1960s*

parity with the West – demands epitomised by the banners that read 'Development for the West, exploitation for the East', 'Factories and roads for the West, commandos and gendarme stations for the East', 'We want teachers not gendarmes' and 'We want schools not gendarme stations'. Although these banners contained elaborate critiques of the nature of the state investment in the region, mainly building gendarme stations and prisons, special effort was made to avoid the accusation of 'Kurdism' or 'separatism'. To this effect, various banners read 'We are not separatists. We want equality', 'Easterner! Work hard to achieve your constitutional rights. Demanding rights does not threaten [national] unity' or 'Our aim is to achieve equality and happiness'.[49] It is suggested by various sources that the numerous anti-Kurdish articles in far-right newspapers (also targeting other minorities such as Gypsies), played a significant role in mobilising the Kurds during these meetings.[50] Hence, there was a complex political dimension and background to these meetings.

In a series of articles in the nationalist newspaper *Ötüken*, the 'pan-Turkist' Turkish nationalist Hüseyin Nihal Atsız made offensive and antagonistic statements and threats of expulsion and ethnic cleansing against the Kurds. In an article entitled 'The howl of Red Kurds' published on 16 June 1967, Atsız characterised the Kurds' attempt to raise awareness of the underdevelopment of the East as 'Kurdism', stating that Kurds were not a nation but 'a primitive' branch of the Persians and argued that they lacked any 'culture' or 'history'.[51] Such attacks culminated in an open threat of expulsion:

> Let the Kurds go away from Turkey! But to where? To wherever they like! Let them go to Iran, to Pakistan, to India, to Barzani. Let them ask the United Nations to find them a national home in Africa. Let them go away before the Turkish nation gets angry. The Turkish race is very patient, but when we get angry we are like lions. Let the Kurds ask Armenians about us![52]

These articles generated a strong reaction from the Kurds. In August 1967 a statement entitled 'Who is expelling who: Come to the Arena' undersigned by 19 Kurdish student organisations representing various Kurdish towns and cities was sent to the President and the Prime Minister and distributed to the public.[53] After rejecting the accusations of 'Kurdism' and re-emphasising the Kurds' commitment to Turkey's unity, the statement read 'Neither is there nor will there ever be a force capable of expelling those who have been living in these lands from the ancient times onwards. Those who will be expelled are the dreamers who aim to create conflict among people.'[54] It is important to mention that the statement rejected the characterisation of Kurdish activities as Kurdist and the animosity that the Turkish nationalists sought to create between the people of Turkey. Instead it reiterated the Kurds support for the constitution and obtaining Kurds' constitutional rights. The organising committee of the meetings of the East called on the Kurds to protest against such provocations; for example, a flyer asking people to attend the meeting in Silvan read:

Kurdish political activism in the 1960s 63

The government cheats us every year and leaves us only the crumbs. Brother of the East! ... the fascist pan-Turanists want to expel you from your fatherland because you speak Kurdish and you are a Kurd.... Brother of the East! ... you must give a reply to those who look at you with contempt because of your ethnic origin and your language.... You are at least as honourable as others and your language is as much respectable as the other languages. You must tell the others your language is respectable and that you are an honourable man.[55]

Hence, as well as emphasising the democratic nature of the Kurdish demands, with the opposition to the Turkish nationalists we see the emergence of an antagonistic frontier between the Kurds and the extreme Turkish nationalists. This challenged the attempts by the Turkish nationalists to exclude and target the Kurds and called upon Kurds to defend their rights from what was perceived as the 'fascist' attacks.

Furthermore, during 1969 other similar meetings took place in various towns and cities, such as Hilvan on 27 July 1969, Siverek on 2 August 1969 and Lice on 24 August 1969.[56] These meetings again highlighted the disparity between the East and other regions of Turkey and the neglect shown to the Eastern region throughout the past. However, we see a much more elaborate attempt at raising the issue of national oppression that the Kurds faced throughout the republican era. National oppression was raised within the background of the liberation war in which many Kurds fought alongside the Turks and others against the occupation. For example, speaking at the Hilvan meeting, the Kurdish socialist activist Mehdi Zana, stated:

We know that our eastern Kurdish brothers, whose ancestors have sacrificed their lives in liberation wars in Çanakkale [Dardanelles], Sakarya, etc. are not able to speak in their own language, and their rights to radio broadcasts, publication and education are not given. Why is this?[57]

However, this did not lead to demands for Kurdish separatism or the establishment of 'separate' Kurdish organisations; Kurdish rights and demands were still seen as possible within the existing constitutional framework. This is evident in the speech that another activist, Mehmet Sözer, delivered at the Lice meeting:

We will not be daunted, we will not be intimidated. We will contend until the end for the realisation of our constitutional rights in full. When we achieve our rights we gain our dignity and self respect.... Being Kurdish is not a crime. Speaking Kurdish is not an offence. The article 12 of the constitution is clear. They are preventing us from speaking our language and living our culture.[58]

The Kurds' participation in Turkey's national liberation war during the 1920s was kept emphasised in numerous other speeches, and the Kurds' experience in

64 *Kurdish political activism in the 1960s*

the republican era, which witnessed numerous acts of violence and repression against the Kurds and suppression of their rights, is interpreted, as the above quotations clearly show, as oppression.

Conclusion

This chapter focused on the public discussion of the 'Eastern question' and the articulation of Kurdish demands by the Kurdish organic intellectuals in the 1960s. The analysis of the discourses of the organic intellectuals I provided focused on their problematisation of the underdevelopment of the 'East' and the articulation of specific political and socio-economic demands. The Kurds' experience of oppression and discrimination also received widespread attention in the discourses of organic intellectuals and political activists. In fact, the threats by the pan-Turkist nationalists as well as the state's rejection, arbitrary violence and general repression played a significant role in the mobilisation of the Kurds during the 1960s. Numerous events throughout the 1960s, led to the increase in the discussion of the 'Eastern question' in Turkey. As well as the public discussion, the 1960s also witnessed an increase in Kurdish cultural activities, primarily carried out by the new group of Kurdish activist and organic intellectuals. Initially, large numbers of Kurdish activists participated in the activities of the TİP, and Kurdish rights and demands were conceptualised as part of broader demands for democracy and equality in Turkey.

In the discourses of the Kurdish organic intellectuals, the TKDP and the TİP, Kurdish rights and demands were articulated *differentially* as part of broader demands for equality, democracy and socio-economic development in Turkey. However, in the late 1960s the discourse of the organic intellectuals and political activists took on a more radical character challenging Kemalism and the state's official discourse on Kurdish identity. In particular, the continual description of any Kurdish socio-political and economic demands as 'separatism' by the authorities was challenged. Invoking the Kurds' popular participation in Turkey's 'war of liberation' and highlighting the violation of the Kurds' democratic rights, the Kurdish activists started to openly call for the recognition of their cultural rights. In the late 1960s, as the high number of Kurds attending the 'Meetings of the East' indicates, Kurdish political activism started to attract and mobilise large numbers of the Kurds. The factional infighting that blighted the TİP meant that it was unable to formulate and maintain a coherent policy on the Kurdish issue, which caused discontent among the Kurdish socialists. This resulted in the birth of the Eastist movement in 1969. From then on, Kurdish activists intensified their attempts to establish specifically Kurdish revolutionary organisations.

4 The emergence of the Kurdish socialist movement

Introduction

As the discussion in Chapter 3 revealed, Kurdish political and economic demands were articulated differentially by Kurdish organic intellectuals, the TKDP and the TİP during the 1960s. Primarily, this took place within the context of underdevelopment and regional inequality, and involved an elaborate criticism of the oppressive practices that the state used against the Kurds. However, in the subsequent period, Kurdish identity and demands started to be articulated increasingly on an equivalential basis by the Kurdish socialists whose discourse became much more radical and started to problematise the Kurds' oppression and the violations of their national rights in a more coherent manner. In fact, the increasing emphasis on the ethnic, cultural and political dimensions of the 'Eastern question' in the discourse of the Kurdish 'organic intellectuals' during the 1960s showed the limitations in the ability and willingness of the Turkish socialist movement to articulate Kurdish demands. Gradually the oppression of the Kurds emerged as the main element in the discourse of Kurdish activists who also started to appropriate the Marxist discourse. Such an articulation transformed the 'Eastern question' from being conceptualised as a problem of underdevelopment to the 'Kurdish question' and one of national oppression. Therefore, the empty signifier 'equality' was unable to represent the particularistic Kurdish demands, which during the late 1960s and early 1970s started to become a source of discontent and division between the Kurdish and Turkish socialists.

This discontent increased throughout the late 1960s as the demands articulated by Kurdish organic intellectuals and the younger generation of Kurdish socialists became more radical leading to calls to 'separate' from the Turkish socialist movement onto an independent route. Such calls culminated in the emergence of the Eastist movement and the establishment of the DDKO centres in Istanbul and Ankara in 1969, which were organised legally, had democratic goals and drew support mainly from Kurdish students. The move towards separation and the establishment of specifically Kurdish organisations continued throughout the 1970s and by the mid 1970s numerous Kurdish revolutionary groups were in existence and active in the Kurdish regions. This shift also

66 *The Kurdish socialist movement*

resulted in the construction and deployment of an ethnicist conception of Kurdish identity in the discourses of the Kurdish organisations. The 'myth' of *Newroz* and the legend of Kawa were constructed as the myth of origin of the Kurdish nation and deployed in the discourses of the newly formed Kurdish organisations to construct their own representation of the alternative Kurdish society and to trace the origins of the Kurds to the ancient Medes. Although the discourses of the Kurdish organic intellectuals that I discussed in Chapter 3 made reference to the 'Gutis' and 'Karduchis' as the Kurds' ancestors, they did not establish an explicit link to the Medes nor did they deploy the 'myth of *Newroz*' in their discourse.

The mid 1970s was a key period for the Kurdish national movement as the need to establish Kurdish organisations to solve the Kurds' 'national question' was strengthened. Therefore, the main focus of this chapter is on the issue of separation, the emergence of the Kurdish socialist movement and the radicalisation of the national demands that the newly established organisations articulated. In order to provide a balanced overview of the separation process, in section one I provide an account of the emergence of the DDKO and the activities it engaged in and analyse the defences that its leading members submitted to the court during their trial in 1972. The defences represent the Kurdish activists' earliest attempts at highlighting the Kurds' national oppression and they are highly informative of the position that the Kurdish socialists started to take during the 1970s in relations to the 'nationalities question' in Turkey. I then provide, in section two, an account of the emergence of the Kurdish socialist movement in Turkey and its fragmentation. First, I look at the establishment of numerous Kurdish socialist parties and political groups that started to contest the Kurdish identity and national demands in Turkey from the mid 1970s onwards. In the process of the appropriation of the Marxist discourse, the Kurdish socialists developed a distinction between the nationalism of the 'oppressed nations' and the 'oppressor nations', and defended the view that the Kurds' national unification was a necessary precondition for their transformation into a socialist society. I evaluate the critique of the Turkish socialist discourse that the Kurdish socialist Kemal Burkay developed in the early 1970s to analyse the understanding that emerged at that time of the 'Kurdish question' as the Kurds' national oppression in Turkey and Kurdistan's division and fragmentation. The articulation of Kurdish national demands within the Marxist discourse led to the constitution of the 'National Liberation Discourse' during the mid 1970s, which is analysed in Chapter 5.

The signs of separation: establishment of the DDKO

Divisions and disunity that the socialist movement in Turkey experienced along the NDR-SR axis that I briefly discussed in Chapter 3 and more significantly their hesitation to articulate Kurdish rights and demands were the main source of the Kurds' discontent with the socialist movement in Turkey. The socialist movement was not prepared to deviate greatly from the Kemalist line on the

The Kurdish socialist movement   67

national problem of the minorities in Turkey and was unwilling to accept the Kurdish national demands or make the Kurdish question one of its main concerns. As the reflections by the Kurdish socialists that I analyse below attest to, it was generally thought that the Kurdish question would be fully solved once the socialist transformation took place in Turkey.[1] In fact, the acceptance of the existence of the Kurdish question and the limited articulation of Kurdish demands, as discussed in Chapter 3, were due to the Kurdish activists' attempts to raise the issue within the socialist movement. Even though the socialist movement appeared to voice some Kurdish demands, overall it remained uncommitted to the articulation of Kurdish identity demands that the new generation of Kurdish activists were raising. Talking of his experience within the TİP, the founder of the TKSP Kemal Burkay states:

> Our [Kurdish activists'] difference was due to being Kurdish. We were the ones who put the Kurdish problem on the agenda of the party. The other members of the party only became aware of the problem then. Within the party, due to our shared ideals of socialism and having been in the same fight, there was a sense of trust between us and our Turkish friends. However, among some sections of the party cadres, there was also a certain amount of suspicion felt against the Kurdish question. Most of the Turkish comrades believed that the Kurdish question was something that would find its solution within socialist conditions, and hence there was no need to put it forward in an earlier period. That is, they did not see the importance of opposing the repression the Kurds suffered and proposing, within a democratic programme, a solution to the problem to win the Kurdish people to the side of the revolution.[2]

Such sentiments are echoed by Musa Anter who also argued for the need for the socialist movement in Turkey to articulate Kurdish national demands:

> Against these friends, I was defending the view that the Kurdish problem is Turkey's main problem and if this problem is not taken up from the start, none of the other problems could be solved and the dynamic Kurdish national potential could not be won over.[3]

Therefore, the increasing discursive fragmentation and the inability to formulate a coherent policy on the Kurdish question led to many Kurdish activists becoming increasingly disillusioned with the Turkish socialist movement. As confirmed by the views expressed by another prominent Kurdish activist Naci Kutlay, this started the Kurdish socialists on a separate and independent trajectory:

> The Kurds were active within the youth organisation the Federation of Thought Clubs (*Fikir Kulüpleri Federasyonu*, FKF), the socialist TİP and in the trade unions. Due to not being represented sufficiently within these

68 *The Kurdish socialist movement*

organisations and their democratic rights not being taken seriously enough, they began to voice the need for 'separate organisation'. The liveliest debates happened in the FKF. The Kurdish youth gradually came to the point of separate organisation.[4]

The Kurdish activists' search led them to establish the Eastist movement and the DDKO centres in May 1969 in Ankara and Istanbul. Their establishment represented a major step by the Kurdish activists to break away from the Turkish socialist movement.

The establishment of the DDKO

In the early 1970s the 'nationalities question' in Turkey continued to preoccupy the Kurdish socialist activists as their discourse continued to problematise the economic underdevelopment, exploitation and national oppression that the Kurds in Turkey faced. The DDKO centres were officially independent from each other and engaged in legal activities to fulfil their objectives, which were defined as:

> To bring together the university students and the youth in Turkey's urban centres into a particular cultural study/work; to facilitate the material solidarity and the mutual support among them; to break the racist, chauvinist and fascist conditionings in Turkey; and, to take part in the revolutionary and democratic struggles for brotherhood, equality and happiness of the people.[5]

Five more DDKO centres were established in the towns of Diyarbakir, Batman, Ergani, Silvan and Kozluk during October and November 1970.[6] The members of the DDKO were mainly but not exclusively Kurdish students of left-wing persuasion. As part of its educational activities, the DDKO in Ankara organised 7 seminars in March and May 1970 mainly on the philosophical and theoretical aspects of Marxism, such as on the Idealism–Materialism debate (4 March 1970), on the notion of surplus value (7 March), on socialism (20 May), on culture (15 March) and on Fascism (23 May).[7] In addition to these seminars, the DDKO organised conferences on specific issues relevant to the Kurds, such as the 'Eastern Problem' (12 March) and 'Organisation and the Issues Relevant to the East' (1–2 May 1970), as well as on more general issues, such as 'The Constitution and Political Freedoms' (9 May) and on 'Analysis of Classes and Groups' (17 May).[8] As well as voicing the issues facing the Kurds and sparking a debate on the 'Eastern Issue', such events provided a meeting point for Kurdish students and activists.

A more significant activity of the DDKO was publishing a monthly news bulletin (*DDKO Bülten*) providing news and analysis about important events taking place in Turkey and the world. In total nine bulletins were published between March 1970 and March 1971, providing news on the DDKO activities and analysis of national and regional events, especially those that had direct relevance to the Kurds. Specifically the second and fourth issues of the bulletin drew

The Kurdish socialist movement   69

attention to the cases and instances of arbitrary arrest of Kurdish or socialist activists, violence against Kurdish civilians – especially during the 'commando operations' taking place in the East and South-east of Turkey – and the violation of the political freedoms as enshrined in the constitution. On this matter, the bulletins published letters from people subjected to violence and news items on specific acts of brutality by state officials. Numerous instances of cultural assimilation during the population count and census were reported, such as the refusal of the state official to record 'Kurdish' as the mother tongue despite the requests of the people. Their mother tongue was recorded as Turkish whether they knew any Turkish or not. Additionally, analysis concerning the underdevelopment of the East was taken up in the same spirit of advocacy journalism with bulletins continuing to problematise the underdevelopment by drawing attention to the role political oppression played in the capital flight to the West of Turkey, which increased the poverty and reduced the living standards of the people living in the East.[9] The coverage of the Kurds in the Turkish media also featured frequently as well as substantial articles about the TİP's resolution on the Kurdish issue. Although not much information on the circulation of the news bulletin is available, given that the DDKO centres were located in various towns and cities in the region, it is likely to have been disseminated widely. More importantly, however, it gave an opportunity to the Kurdish activists to voice popular demands and concerns.

Furthermore, the DDKO published many press releases that sought to inform the general public on the issues that were prevalent in the East, especially the state's oppressive practices but also specific events and developments in which the Kurds were implicated. The increasing use of the anti-imperialist rhetoric in these statements and the expression of support for national liberation struggles elsewhere are indicative of the radicalisation of the Kurdish socialist activists in Turkey and their appropriation of the Marxist discourse. The military coup in March 1971 intensified political oppression and brought an abrupt end to the DDKO and the 'legal democratic' form of Kurdish politics exemplified by it. The leading members of the DDKO were charged with 'finding or taking part in the activities of an organisation to destroy and weaken national feelings'.[10] The trials of the members of the DDKO began in December 1971 and the decision on the case was reached on 11 December 1972. The activists submitted two separate joint defences challenging the claims made in the indictment.

Problematising denial and assimilation: the defences of the DDKO activists

Much of the collective defence of the DDKO activists involved responding to specific comments and assertions made in the court indictment and as such were designed to engage with specific issues such as the origins of the Kurds or the status of the Kurdish language. Contrary to the view propagated by the military court that saw Kurds as essentially of Turkish origin and the Kurdish language as an amalgam of words from Persian, Turkish and Arabic, the DDKO members

70 *The Kurdish socialist movement*

argued that the Kurds' origins were not Turkic but Indo-European and traced the origins of the Kurdish people as far back as to the Karduchis (*c*.2000 BC) and the Medes.[11] It was argued that the Kurdish presence in the region pre-dated the arrival of Turks in Anatolia: 'Before the Turkish arrival in Anatolia, the Kurds were living in Eastern Anatolia; the area in the vicinity of Lake Van is the real homeland of the Kurds.'[12] The defence drew from numerous sources in Western languages as well as in Arabic and Persian in making this statement. The existence of the Kurds was seen as 'an objective and sociological reality' and the evolution of Kurdish society within a historical background since the medieval period was presented.[13] Furthermore, attention was drawn to the existence of the autonomous Kurdish Emirates within the Ottoman Empire. In fact, it was argued, as evidenced in various statements and telegraphs of Mustafa Kemal, the existence of the Kurds and their national rights and demands were recognised by the Turkish national movement even during the 'War of Liberation'.[14] In addition, the defence included detailed study of the Kurdish language (syntax, phonetic structure, vocabulary) to refute the claim that the Kurdish language was 'primitive' and a mixture of other languages.[15] It drew attention to the existence of a classical Kurdish literature, which attested to the fact that the Kurdish language has been a medium of communication for a long period, and despite the linguistic oppression, it has maintained its distinctiveness.

Therefore, the DDKO activists argued that the claims made in the indictment about the Kurdish identity as being essentially Turkish were *ideological*, formulated after the proclamation of the republic in 1923:

> The objective existence of the Kurdish nation, its democratic constitutional rights, its language and culture were rejected and a forceful period of assimilation started.... Especially after 1925, universities and political institutions, including the Turkish Hearths, cultivated the view that the Kurds are of Turkish origin and sought to impose this view on the masses.[16]

It also stated that the erosion of Kurdish autonomy and the denial of Kurdish identity were due to Turkish nationalism's restrictive and oppressive attitude to cultural and national difference, which was challenged by the Kurds in a series of uprisings during the 1920s and 1930s, despite resulting in increased state brutality and oppression. The oppression of the Kurds continued unabated even during the democratic era. The defences reiterated the view that the Kurdish region was neglected deliberately and its underdevelopment was the result of state policy:

> The political power and the ruling classes did not make the necessary investments in the region. This has prevented the emergence and the development of capitalist relations of production and has maintained the existence of feudal structure. The maintenance of feudal structure is the main reason for backwardness of the Eastern Anatolia and as long as they remain in place, the region would necessarily be backward.[17]

The Kurdish socialist movement 71

Although an elaborated Marxist analysis of Kurdish society and the problem of underdevelopment and fragmentation of Kurdistan were not presented in the defences, the radicalism of the analysis is apparent in the way that the problem of underdevelopment was characterised. It stated that the problem of underdevelopment had political, economic, sociological and ideological dimensions and can only be solved by a political authority representing the masses, not by the ruling classes. Additionally, the widespread debates taking place within the Marxist movement concerning the nationalities issue was also reflected in the defences with the emphasis on the need to recognise the fraternity and equality of nations within Turkey.[18] Moreover, the state's description of Kurdish demands for equal treatment, the respect and recognition of their democratic, human and cultural rights as Kurdism, and characterisation of Kurdism as a form of minority racism, also received a sustained critique from the DDKO members. Specifically, the defence rejected the prosecutor's 'deliberate confusion' of Kurdish nationalism or the Kurds' democratic demands with racism and stated:

> A nation, which does not yet have the right to speak its language freely or those who voice the concrete problems of this nation, cannot be 'racist'. The methods, tactics and policies of the ruling classes and the fascist ideology, or the institutions and individuals they nourish, are deliberately dragging the issue to such a complicated and meaningless point.[19]

Such an argument in the subsequent years was developed into a broader distinction between the nationalism of the 'oppressed' nations and the 'oppressor' nations, which received substantial attention in the discourses of the new Kurdish socialist groups throughout the 1970s. Although almost all of the Kurdish activists were detained after the coup d'état on 12 March 1971, some of them – such as Kemal Burkay – managed to escape to Europe, which gave them an opportunity to establish links with the Kurdish activists there as well as publish their views on the Kurdish national problem and critiques of the Turkish socialist discourse and movement.

The Kurdish 'national question'

The first broad critique of the Turkish socialist discourse appeared in two pamphlets published in Europe in 1973 and 1974. One pamphlet was published under a pseudonym Hıdır Murat and the other was a publication of the 'Hevra – the Organisation of Revolutionary Kurds in Europe'; however, the authorship of both these pamphlets was later attributed to Kemal Burkay.[20] Ideas expressed in these pamphlets elaborated on the nature of the Kurdish struggle and the correct revolutionary strategy for Turkey. In particular, Burkay criticised the NDR thesis and rejected the characterisation of Turkey as a 'semi-colony'.[21] Burkay argued that, with the exception of Turkish Kurdistan, capitalist economic relations prevailed in Turkey and the proposal for a new national democratic revolution in Turkey completely ignored the 'Kurdish question' as it treated the Kurds as part of the Turkish nation:

72   *The Kurdish socialist movement*

Anyone examining the conditions of Turkey needs to consider this: there are two nations in Turkey and Turkish Kurdistan constitutes one third of the country. Whoever does not appraise this reality cannot outline a correct strategy and revolutionary programme for Turkey. Mr Belli's [Turkish Marxist ideologue and proponent of the NDR thesis] main fault lies in there and he is not alone. Ignoring the reality of Kurdistan and the oppression of the Kurdish nation is the main reason behind their theoretical defects.[22]

Specifying the 'reality of Kurdistan' led to examining the social, cultural and economic aspects of oppression that the Kurds were subjected to, and according to Burkay the region was kept backward in economic and cultural terms to stifle Kurdish national consciousness and the Kurds' struggle for their democratic rights:

Turkish governments have prevented and delayed, in economic and cultural terms, the nation-building process of the Kurdish people. Their freedom has been subjected to bloody suppression and terror. Force is used to keep Turkish Kurdistan under control and to suppress the Kurdish people's democratic revolution. The Turkish bourgeois governments reduced Kurdistan to the status of a colony.[23]

Burkay drew attention to the uniqueness of the Kurdish national question and defined the Kurds as a 'dependent nation', whose country was:

divided by the combined efforts of the imperialist, racist and feudal reactionary forces and which has been forced to live under the yoke. Because of this, in Kurdistan, the feudal relations have not been defeated and a bourgeois democratic revolution has not occurred. Therefore, the main contradiction for the Kurdish people is national.[24]

Highlighting the political motives behind Kurdistan's underdevelopment enabled Kurdish activists, such as Burkay, to counter the narrow characterisation of the Kurdish question as economic underdevelopment, and raised the oppression of the Kurds and the national aspect. The views expressed by Burkay in the above quote were shared by many Kurdish activists and increasingly they began to see the Kurdish question as a national one from the late 1960s onwards. In these pamphlets, Burkay invoked Lenin's support for the national self-determination of the nations and argued that it was an 'absolute' and 'unconditional' right that every nation possessed.[25] Furthermore, the need to make a distinction between different nationalist movements was raised: 'The ideology known as nationalism, or the national question, should not be looked at as an abstract concept. It should be assessed within its time and conditions.'[26] Burkay refuted the claim that each and every manifestation of nationalism was necessarily reactionary:

The Kurdish socialist movement   73

Consequently, when determining the characteristics of national ideology in each instance, we need to look at the purpose it is used for. If this ideology assists or is used for the purpose of making a society progress and become free, then it can be revolutionary. If it is used for suppression of other classes or nations, or for a policy of aggression and exploitation, then it is reactionary.[27]

The need to understand the specific role nationalism played in each context was an answer to the Turkish socialists that Burkay was challenging, who classified Kurdish nationalism as serving the same reactionary purpose as Turkish nationalism and treated the nationalities issue in Turkey as a conflict between two different 'chauvinisms'. In reality, as Burkay was keen to highlight, there were significant differences between Kurdish and Turkish nationalisms:

> Turkish nationalism is a weapon used by the Turkish bourgeoisie to keep the Kurdish nation under the yoke and at the same time to disguise its exploitation of the working class, the peasants and the middle classes. For this reason it is chauvinist and racist. As for the Kurdish national movement, being the expression of the Kurdish people's self-defence and struggle for freedom against the Turkish, Arab and Persian chauvinisms, it does not assert the claims of being a superior race; it demands concessions/autonomy for Kurdish people and does not want to place other nations under the yoke.[28]

Separating and distinguishing nationalism of the oppressed nations from that of oppressor nations enabled Burkay to highlight the nature of the actual demands that the Kurdish national movement was raising and the problems it was addressing. According to Burkay, since the fundamental contradiction in the Kurdish case was 'national', at the first instance a national democratic revolution was needed to unify the nation, bring an end to feudal relations and lead to the development of capitalism in Kurdistan. Kurdish nationalism was defended as progressive because it would pave the way to the development of capitalist relations in the region and by doing so would prepare the Kurdish society to the socialist stage. The discussion presented in the two pamphlets is highly relevant because it offers a reflection of the views of the Kurdish activists during the first half of the 1970s. However, Burkay's emphasis on the need for a Kurdish national democratic revolution – separate from a socialist revolution in Turkey – to solve Kurdistan's national problem did not mean he envisioned a complete separation between the Kurdish national movement and Turkish socialist movement. In fact, their close cooperation and unity was possible and needed because both movements had common interests and shared goals:

> The Turkish nation wants to establish a democratic government. The Kurdish nation wants to achieve the same for itself. The Kurds want all forms of national oppression to be lifted, their national rights to be recognised and have equal rights with the Turks.[29]

74 *The Kurdish socialist movement*

Moreover, Kurds' national self-determination could be achieved via closer collaboration with the socialist movement in Turkey. Kurdish national aspirations could be realised while remaining part of Turkey as equal partners within their own regional republic. Greater cooperation between the revolutionary movements would be the most productive strategy as it would increase the likelihood of both revolutions.[30]

It is important to note that a rare occasion on which the Turkish socialists defended the Kurds' national rights came about during the collective defence that the Revolutionary Party of Workers and Peasants of Turkey (*Türkiye İhtilalci İşçi Köylü Partisi*, TİİKP) submitted to the military court at their trial in June and July 1974. In the TİİKP's defence, the Kurdish question was also formulated around the idea of national self-determination and a wider sociopolitical and historical analysis of the Kurdish society was provided. Specifically, attention was drawn to the national oppression that the state carried out against the Kurds and all the associated discriminatory practices, including widespread economic inequality. The Kurds were characterised as one of the 'oldest nations' of the Middle East and attention was drawn to their rich cultural and linguistic heritage. The significant aspect of the TİİKP's defence was that it recognised the Kurds' right for self-determination, including political separation. However, it advocated the voluntary unity of both nations within a democratic people's republic in Turkey that would provide equal rights and freedoms to both nations.[31] Such a characterisation of the Kurdish issue was only an exception and the majority of the Turkish socialist movement remained critical of the Kurdish demands because they were seen as divisive of the common struggle for socialism in Turkey.[32] In fact, in the late 1970s, the TİİKP started to pursue a policy of complete rejection of the Kurdish demands. Throughout the 1970s the distance between the Kurdish national movement and the Turkish socialist movement widened, and both movements experienced fragmentation.

The fragmentation of the Kurdish socialist movement

The period between 1974 and 1980 witnessed a significant increase in Kurdish political activism mostly by the newly established socialist groups. The discourse of the Kurdish socialists in the second half of the 1970s became much more condensed and started to stress 'national oppression', 'colonialism' and 'national liberation', and was disseminated widely in the political magazines of the Kurdish political groups and clandestine political parties. The main activities that the new groups involved were publishing political magazines to disseminate their ideas. This provided a platform to express their views and engage with the Turkish left-wing groups in ideological and theoretical discussions to illuminate their political position. Also, the magazines published polemical articles in which a particular group presented a critique of either another Kurdish group or the Turkish socialist groups concerning the Kurdish national issue. *Özgürlük Yolu* managed to survive for nearly 4 years, but most of the magazines, such as *Kawa, Rizgarî, Denge Kawa, Jîna Nû* (KİP/DDKD) managed far fewer issues and were published in irregular intervals before the 1980s. These publications made important contributions to the public discussion of the Kurdish issue in Turkey.

In these debates, specifically the Turkish socialists' 'ambiguous' stance on the Kurdish question and their failure to adequately address the Kurds' national oppression received an avid critique. Similar arguments made by Burkay concerning the nationalism of the oppressed nations that I discussed above were repeated and elaborated on by the new groups. In their discussion of the 'nationalities issue', the Turkish socialists equated nationalism with the bourgeois nationalisms in nineteenth century Europe and saw it as closely tied to capitalism and the bourgeoisie's desire to create and protect 'its' national market. The Kurdish groups, on the other hand, drew from national movements in the colonial and Third World contexts and emphasised the 'national oppression' that the Kurds were subjected to in Turkey. To counter the Turkish socialist claim that bundled each and every manifestation of nationalism together, the Kurdish groups argued that the practice of nationalism in the anti-colonial case revealed that there were significant differences between each nationalist manifestation and movement.

For example, an article published in the daily newspaper *Cumhuriyet* (Republic) on 28 January 1976 by İlhan Selçuk likened *Mustafa Barzani*, the leader of the Kurdish movement in Iraq, to the Turkish ultra-nationalist leader *Alparslan Türkeş*. As a response to this the *Rizgarî* evoked the distinction between the nationalism of the oppressor nations – seen as a reactionary force in the hands of the bourgeoisie used to justify the exploitation of the masses – and the nationalism of the oppressed nations, which articulated the demands of the oppressed people and, as in the case of colonies, took an anti-imperialist character. On the basis of such an analogy, the *Rizgarî* argued:

> People who struggle to obtain their seized national democratic rights cannot be seen as equivalent to those who advocate or justify the continuation of such a seizure. Those who colonise an area or a nation and those who oppose colonialism are not the same.[33]

Nationalism, therefore, in a colonial context – as it was argued by the Kurdish socialist groups and political parties to be the case in Kurdistan – was revolutionary because it struggled against 'national oppression' and 'colonial exploitation'. This claim was used by the Kurdish groups to articulate national demands without being branded in negative terms. The Kurdish national demands were seen as *complementary* to the proletarian revolutionary position, and the difference in opinion that existed between the Turkish and Kurdish socialists was explained by the Turkish socialist movements' 'nationalist values and social chauvinism that have tainted and that harm the socialist movement'.[34] In fact, the Turkish socialist movement's failure to acknowledge and defend Kurdish rights led to the Kurdish groups developing an increasingly fierce critique branding the Turkish socialist movement as 'social chauvinist' for continuing to treat the

76   *The Kurdish socialist movement*

Kurds as part of the Turkish nation and more importantly not recognising the national oppression that the Kurds were subjected to:

> The programme that social chauvinism put forward in the name of the vanguard of the proletarian revolution is filled with opportunist suggestions that either approach the struggle of the Kurdish people in a pragmatic way, or try to paralyse its anti-colonialist potential.[35]

The Kurdish groups stressed that each country's specific conditions needed to be examined in order to formulate the appropriate revolutionary strategy and the situation that Kurdistan found itself in necessitated that it organised its revolution separately. As I discuss more fully in Chapter 5, analysing Kurdistan's specific conditions led to the characterisation of Kurdistan as a colony. Therefore, the debate that Kurdish socialists took part in with the Turkish socialists is informative of the construction and individuation of the national liberation discourse as well as offering helpful insights into its evolution during the late 1970s.

The new Kurdish groups and parties traced their origins to the 'Eastist Movement' and claimed to be mainly pro-Soviet Union and Marxist-Leninist. However, the Soviet Union's support for the Baathist regime in Iraq during the Kurdish uprising in the early 1970s caused disappointment among some Kurdish socialists, who began to support the 'independent' line advocated by the Chinese Communist Party or the Albanian Labour Party. The existence of numerous groups and their proliferation in such a short period clearly indicates the fragmentation and division of the Kurdish movement as a whole. This prevented it from organising a credible challenge to the state during the 1970s. Issues around strategy and tactics as well as the groups' differing attitude towards the Soviet Union or the Kurdish movement in Iraq contributed to their fragmentation. Also, the division and fragmentation is, to a certain extent, a reflection of the division and fragmentation that the Turkish socialist movement experienced during the 1970s.

The popularity of socialist ideas among the Kurdish activists in Turkey can be attributed to numerous factors: first, the participation of a high number of the Kurds in the Turkish socialist movement meant that the Kurdish activists were already familiar with Marxism and in a position to appropriate it for the Kurdish national question. Second, the defeat that the KDP suffered in 1975 against the Baathist regime in Iraq discredited, in the eyes of many Kurdish activists in Turkey, the 'conservative' brand of Kurdish nationalism and convinced many that reliance on the support of the 'imperialist' forces was bound to fail. Hence, it created a new space for a movement seeking to articulate Kurdish rights and demands within the Marxist discourse. Third, the popularity of the socialist movements around the world, especially the successful anti-imperialist struggles in Africa and Asia, showed the validity and applicability of Marxism-Leninism as an ideology for the oppressed nations. The popularity of socialist ideas among the Kurdish activists is especially recognisable in the ideological evolution of the formerly conservative TKDP whose members founded the left-wing orien-

The Kurdish socialist movement 77

tated KUK (*Kürdistan Ulusal Kurtuluşçuları*, National Liberationists of Kurdistan), the KİP/DDKD and the *Kawa* groups in the mid 1970s. Finally, the fact that the demands of the most populous section of Kurdish society – the landless peasantry whose living conditions deteriorated as a result of capitalist development and the mechanisation of agriculture – could be reflected and articulated by a socialist discourse enhanced the suitability of the national liberation discourse.

The discourses of Kurdish organic intellectuals and the DDKO activists emphasised the Kurds' distinct and non-Turkic origin and drew links to ancient groups in the Middle East such as the *Gutis* and *Karduchis*. Increasingly from the mid 1970s onwards, the Kurdish socialist groups started to deploy the legend of Kawa and the myth of *Newroz* in their discourse to construct Kurdish difference and political subjectivity. Specifically, *Newroz* provided the Kurdish movement with a myth of origin that was deployed to differentiate and specify a separate Kurdish identity and provided a narrative of the Kurds' emergence as a nation. The utilisation of the myth of *Newroz* was an important and new development because neither the discourses of the DDKO nor the TKDP mentioned *Newroz* or the legend of Kawa. Traditionally, *Newroz* has been celebrated across the Middle East on 21 March, which coincides with the spring equinox, as a New Year festival and its historical or mythological origins are often traced back to the ancient period.[36] The Kurdish nationalist attempts to construct the myth of origin around the *Newroz* festival as a national festival dates back to the early twentieth century. This is despite the fact that *Newroz* being traditionally celebrated by Kurds for many centuries as their new year (*Sersal*), which is confirmed by the existence of various sources within the classical Kurdish literature that mention the celebration of *Newroz*.[37] Although the construction of the myth of origin was started by the early Kurdish nationalists during the early twentieth century and went through various stages, by the 1970s the Kurdish national movements in Iran and Iraq had already established an association between the *Newroz* festival and the legend of Kawa.[38] The myth of *Newroz* as told by contemporary Kurdish nationalists narrates the overthrow of the Assyrian King Dehak by a popular uprising led by Kawa the Blacksmith (*Kawayi Hesinkar*), who, on 21 March 612 BC led an uprising by the Medes and defeated the Assyrian Empire, killed Dehak and liberated the Medes – the ancestors of Kurds – from long-suffering oppression and tyranny. To inform the people of his victory, Kawa lighted a bonfire on top of a mountain. In the discourses of the new socialist groups, *Newroz* was constructed to symbolise the Kurds' long struggle for freedom. The practice of lighting a bonfire is recreated during each *Newroz* celebration in the contemporary period.

The political groups and parties[39]

The first Kurdish socialist group to be established by the TİP's Kurdish members (known as the 'Easterner's Group') in December 1974 was the TKSP. It was one of the strongest groups during the mid 1970s. It published a legal monthly magazine, *Özgürlük Yolu* (the Path of Freedom), between June 1975 and January

78 The Kurdish socialist movement

1979 and fortnightly the bilingual *Roja Welat* (the Day of Homeland) between September 1977 and 1979 to spread and propagate its ideas, and expand its organisational base among the masses. In 1977, one of its members, Mehdi Zana, was elected as the Mayor of Diyarbakir as an independent candidate, which shows the strength of the appeal of the Kurdish movement in the region. In 1979 some members of the TKSP separated to form *Kurdistan Halk Partisi* (Kurdistan People's Party) and in 1986 to form *Tevgera Sosyalista Kurdistan* (Kurdistan Socialist Movement). These two parties did not manage to establish a popular base or maintain their existence. In 1992, during its Third Congress, the TKSP changed its name to *Partiya Sosyalista Kurdistan* (Socialist Party of Kurdistan, PSK).

Another group, the *Rizgarî* (Liberation) movement, also traced its origins to the 'Eastist movement' and saw itself as the continuation of the DDKO. The leading members of the DDKO established a publishing house, *Komal Yayınevi* in 1975 to publish books on Kurdish history, politics and culture, including a collection of articles by the Kurdish activist Edip Karahan and books on Kurdish society in Turkey by the Turkish sociologist İsmail Beşikci. In March 1976, the same group started to publish the *Rizgarî* magazine, which managed numerous issues before the military coup of 1980. Subsequently, the activists around the magazine evolved into a political group.[40] Towards the end of 1978, advocators of a more 'forceful' strategy separated from the *Rizgarî* group to found *Ala Rizgarî*, which emphasised the need to develop a revolutionary party organised on the basis of the principle of democratic centralism.[41]

One more outlet for Kurdish political activism was provided by the Revolutionary Democratic Cultural Associations *(Devrimci Demokratik Kültür Dernekleri*, DDKD) which were legal centres established in 1974 in numerous towns and cities in Turkey, including Diyarbakir, Ankara and Istanbul and represented a cross section of Kurdish activists, including the students and former members of the TKDP which began its revival in 1975. Three groups, *Kawa*, the KİP/DDKD and the KUK emerged from the DDKD movement.[42] The first group to separate was the *Kawa* movement, which was founded in 1976 as a Maoist revolutionary group, and in 1977 the KUK was formed by the socialist wing of the TKDP, and the remaining members of the group organised under the name of the KİP/DDKD and were popularly known as the Revolutionary Democrats *(Devrimci Demokratlar)*. The *Kawa* movement was divided in 1978 and another group, *Denge Kawa*, entered the Kurdish political scene. None of these groups were able to survive the effects of the military coup. There were other smaller groups such as *Beş Parçacılar* (Five Partists) and *Tekoşin* (Struggle) which were formed by Kurdish activists from the *Kurtuluş* and the *Halkın Kurtuluşu* movements in 1976 and 1978 respectively.[43] Furthermore, there existed other cultural and political associations linked to various groups in many Kurdish towns and cities as well as in Istanbul and Ankara, such as *Devrimci Halk Kültür Dernekleri* (The Revolutionary People's Cultural Association) and *Anti-Sömürgeci Demokratik Kültür Dernekleri* (Anti-Colonialist Democratic Cultural Associations).

The group that would later become known as the PKK also had a notable presence in the region during the late 1970s. The group emerged as a political/

The Kurdish socialist movement 79

ideological group in the early 1970s in Ankara within the left-wing university circles. The leading group members were active within the ADYÖD (*Ankara Demokratik Yüksek Öğrenim Derneği*, Ankara Democratic Higher Education Association) in 1974 and 1975. By the end of 1975 the group moved most of its cadres to the Kurdish regions to expand its efforts to build the group's support base there. Initially it was organised within the small groups in the towns of Ağrı, Kars, Tunceli and G.Antep. During a series of meetings held secretly in Kars, Bingöl, Diyarbakır, Elazığ and G.Antep during the period April to May in 1977, the group's ideas and political programme were shared with a larger group of sympathisers. The documents relating to the group's activities during the mid 1970s were published subsequently in 1999.[44] Additionally, numerous interviews with the PKK's leading members, during which the movement's early years were discussed, have also been published.[45]

From 1978 onwards the group's discourse and political demands for the Kurds became much clearer. The group's attempts to organise in the Kurdish regions created friction and conflict with other Kurdish groups and the Turkish left groups. A group member, Aydın Gül, was killed by *Halkın Kurtuluşu* in 1977. This was followed by the murder of a leading member of the group, Haki Karer, by *Tekoşin* on 18 May 1977 in Gaziantep. As a response *Tekoşin*'s leader Alattin Kaplan was killed by the PKK on 1 May 1978. In May 1978 in the town of Hilvan a leading group member Halil Çavgun was attacked and killed by the pro-state *Süleymanlar* tribe. As a response the group took part in an organised resistance in which a significant proportion of the town-people were mobilised to defeat the *Süleymanlar* tribe. The group intensified its efforts to build its organisational capacity and increase its recruitment. In 1978 two of its earliest brochures were published: *Kuruluş Bildirisi* (The Founding Declaration) in October and *Kürdistan Devriminin Yolu* (The Path of Kurdistan Revolution) in November. It held its First Congress on 27 November 1978 in a village near Urfa during which the decision to transform itself into a clandestine political party was taken. However, it was not until 27 April 1979 that the name 'PKK' was first used formally in the Founding Declaration. On 1 July 1979 the central committee of the party took the decision to relocate to Lebanon and built its organisation there. In order to publicise its establishment as a party, the PKK attacked the pro-state Bucak tribe in Siverek on 30 July 1979. Overall this attack proved costly as two of its leading members, Cuma Tak and Salih Kandal, were killed.

Despite the overall division and fragmentation that the Kurdish movement experienced during the late 1970s, there was an attempt by some Kurdish groups to form a union of forces. To this end, the Union of National Democratic Forces (*Ulusal Demokratik Güçbirliği*, UDG) was formed by the TKSP, the KUK and the KİP/DDKD in February 1980 as a common platform for advocating Kurdish demands and rights and a first step towards a wider national democratic front.[46] However, this attempt reached a premature end shortly after the public declaration of the UDG. Perhaps the military coup of 12 September 1980 caught the Kurdish movement (as well as the socialist movement in Turkey) at a time of disarray and inflicted the most fatal damage that it intended. Although prior to

80 *The Kurdish socialist movement*

the military coup a considerable number of Kurdish political activists managed to escape Turkey, many more were captured by the state's security forces and incarcerated in various prisons in the Eastern and South-eastern towns, mainly in the notorious Diyarbakir Prison, which was the site of horrific torture to subdue the inmates.[47]

Conclusion

This chapter offered the background to the emergence of the Kurdish National Liberation discourse that hegemonised Kurdish resistance in Turkey during the 1980s and early 1990s. The above analysis examined the emergence of the Kurdish socialist movement in Turkey and its fragmentation. First, the Kurdish socialist activists' separation from the Turkish socialist movement and the establishment of their own organisations was examined in detail. The establishment of the DDKO and its activities, including the defences that its members submitted to the military court for their trial, were analysed to show the radicalisation of the Kurdish demands. Kurdish activists' participation in the socialist movement in Turkey meant that they were in a position to appropriate the Marxist discourse for the Kurdish national question. The Marxist discourse was highly suitable for the articulation of Kurdish national demands as it was able to reflect the demands of the Kurdish masses, which consisted of peasants and the newly emerging working class. Additionally, the defeat that the Iraqi Kurdish movement suffered in 1975 meant that the conservative autonomist brand of Kurdish nationalism that the TKDP represented lost its credibility and opened the possibility for the articulation of Kurdish national demands within the socialist discourse and also the construction of the Kurdish national liberation discourse.

Second, this chapter focused on the Kurdish activists' appropriation of the Marxist discourse. The critiques of the Turkish socialist discourse that the Kurdish activists presented were examined to show the radicalisation of the demands raised by the Kurdish socialists. Their discourse focused on the 'Kurdish question' and increasingly emphasised the Kurds' national oppression, the denial of their identity and their forced assimilation. It was argued that such an emphasis gradually brought 'Kurdistan' and 'the Kurdish people' into the foreground of the political debate and made the nodal point in the discourse. The Turkish socialists' rejection of Kurdish demands strengthened the opinion among the Kurdish socialists that separation from the Turkish socialist movement and the establishment of the Kurdish revolutionary groups and clandestine parties was necessary. Additionally, by providing an account of the emergence of numerous political groups that were active in the 1970s, the organisational development of the Kurdish movement was discussed. Many of the groups deployed the myth of *Newroz* and the legend of Kawa as a narrative of Kurds' origin and resistance, which was discussed briefly to offer a description of the Kurdish identity that the Kurdish political groups contested and to show how the nascent Kurdish movement attempted to conceptualise and represent a 'homogenous' Kurdish society and Kurdistan's unity.

5 The Kurdish national liberation discourse

> Protest is when I say this does not please me.
> Resistance is when I ensure what does not please me occurs no more.[1]
> A desperate disease requires a dangerous remedy.[2]

Introduction

This chapter continues my assessment of the public discussion of the Kurdish question with an exploration of the articulation of Kurdish identity and national demands within the national liberation discourse. Starting from the mid 1970s onwards, the national liberation discourse started to hegemonise Kurdish politics in Turkey and principally articulated the elements of 'socialism', 'revolution', 'colonialism' and 'oppression' around the nodal point 'Kurdistan' and the 'Kurdish people'. The political and ideological debates that took place within the Kurdish movement and between the Kurdish groups and the Turkish left-wing groups during the 1970s and early 1980s led to the ideological condensation of the national liberation discourse. Specifically, it characterised Kurdistan's relations with Turkey on the basis of 'colonialism', and Kurdistan was seen as an international and inter-state colony. It perceived the Kurds' existence as a nation to be in danger as they were forcefully assimilated into the Turkish, Arab and Persian nations and put forward the proposal that Kurdistan's national unification could only be achieved under the leadership of a revolutionary movement led by the working class. It, therefore, represents a greater level of problematisation of the Kurds' national oppression and their socio-economic marginalisation in the Middle East, and marks the beginning of the delineation and separation of a Kurdish 'subject position' emphasising the need to liberate Kurdistan from exploitation and colonialism.

First, this chapter sketches the origins and development of the national liberation discourse during the late 1970s and the early 1980s. It includes an account of the discourses of the TKSP, the *Rizgarî*, the DDKD, the *Kawa* and the PKK, which were the influential groups during the 1970s. It analyses the magazines and periodicals that the above-mentioned groups published to provide an account of the articulation of Kurdish national demands within the national liberation discourse. Specifically, the elements that were articulated within the national

82 *Kurdish national liberation discourse*

liberation discourse, its definition and characterisation of the Kurdish question, the construction of the antagonistic relations within it and how it challenged the hegemonic representation of the Kurds in Turkey by defining its own notion of Kurdish society are analysed. As discussed in Chapter 2, the discourse theoretical account of identity formation emphasises the contingency of social relations and the role antagonism plays in the individuation of political identity. Identities are delimited via the institution of political frontiers that identifies and constructs an antagonistic 'other'. The national liberation discourse constructed a complex set of antagonistic relations not only against the ruling Kemalist elite in Turkey on the national basis but also against the Kurdish feudal elites on the basis of class. Hence, the political practices that the national liberation discourse fostered sought to end the national oppression besieged on the Kurds by the nation states that ruled Kurdistan as well as the prevalent oppression and exploitation of the Kurdish masses by the feudal elites.

Second, the analysis focuses on the issue of contestation over Kurdish identity in Turkey by examining the ideological and political debates over strategy that took place within the Kurdish movement during the 1970s. The plurality of groups undertaking Kurdistan's national liberation meant that the debate over strategy and tactics during the late 1970s was a lively one. Two positions were discernable differentiated mainly on the basis of strategy and tactics of the Kurdistan revolution. The position advocated by the TKSP and the KİP/DDKD emphasised the need for greater cooperation between the Turkish socialist movement and the Kurdish national movement. The position typified by the discourse of the PKK, the *Rizgarî*, the *Ala Rizgarî* and the *Kawa* movements emphasised the need for separation and the logics of equivalence predominated. These two alternatives were responses by the nascent Kurdish movement to the dislocations that Turkey and the Kurdish society were experiencing. However, as shown below, numerous groups oscillated between the two positions and gradually the idea of armed resistance gained widespread acceptance in the late 1970s. Hence, the issue of violence and how the need for violent resistance was justified is also explored in this chapter. The move towards radicalisation, the prevalence of violence and the PKK's hegemony of the Kurdish resistance from the late 1970s onwards is the final issue that is examined in this chapter.

In the conflict analysis and political history accounts of Kurdish nationalism in Turkey that Chapter 1 examined, the impact of the 1980 military coup and the widespread suppression that followed it in the early 1980s is given as the cause of the move towards radicalism. The account presented here of the contestation over Kurdish identity in Turkey between different groups and political parties as well as between the two alternative versions of the national liberation discourse focuses on the political logics and the construction of political frontiers in each version of the national liberation discourse. The analysis searches for 'clues' to the PKK's hegemony by exploring the fantasmatic dimensions of its discourse; specifically, the representation of Kurdish society in the PKK's discourse, the institution of the political frontiers and the construction of the antagonistic relations is examined. It argues that invoking the Median Empire as the 'golden age'

Kurdish national liberation discourse 83

of the Kurdish nation in its discourse enabled the PKK to conceive of a homogenous Kurdish nation, which was used to construct the fantasy of Kurdish
unity. This was in turn used to construct antagonistic relations against the Kurds'
'internal' and 'external' enemies, and mobilise the Kurds.

Accounting for Kurdistan's fragmentation: 'colonialism' and 'feudalism'

The distinction that the Kurdish socialist groups and political parties made
between the nationalism of the 'oppressed nations' and the 'oppressor nations'
in the magazines they published enabled them to problematise the practices of
Kemalism and Kurdish feudalism with more rigour. This led to the emergence of
the claim that a national democratic revolution in Kurdistan was needed to overcome the two main barriers in front of Kurdistan's unity and independent development. The Kemalist denial and oppression of Kurdish identity and the
oppression of the masses by the Kurdish feudal elites were problematised in the
national liberation discourse to construct a complex set of antagonistic relations.
This characterisation highlighted the *intrinsic* antagonistic nature of the relations
between Turkish nationalism and the Kurdish people, and between the Kurdish
revolutionary movement and the Kurdish feudal classes who also contributed to
Kurdistan's division and fragmentation. Furthermore, identifying feudal fragmentation and colonial division as the main barriers in front of Kurdistan's
national unification meant that both the national and democratic aspects of
Kurdistan's revolution were emphasised, albeit in varying degrees, by each political group or party. The problem at hand was not only the linguistic and cultural
oppression of the Kurds and the denial of their identity but also the capitalist
exploitation of Kurdistan and the oppression of the masses by the feudal classes.
Moreover, a strong link was established in the national liberation discourse
between the practices of colonialism and the continuation of feudalism.

Kurdistan: the inter-state colony

As the discussion of the two pamphlets by Burkay that I discussed in Chapter 4
showed, the Kurds were seen as a 'dependent nation' deprived of their unity and
independence by 'the combined efforts of the imperialist, racist and feudal reactionary forces'.[3] In the later discussions by the Kurdish groups this characterisation was radicalised by describing Kurdistan as a 'colony'. The use of the myth
of origin constructed around the legend of Kawa and the festival of *Newroz*
enabled the Kurdish movement to 'imagine' and represent Kurdistan's unity as a
country, which became fragmented as a result of the imperialist division and
feudal fragmentation. In numerous sources published by the Kurdish groups,
Kurdistan was described as a key region in the Middle East, which had a wealth
of natural resources, notably rich oil reserves.[4] Colonialism in Kurdistan
was theorised by the PKK, the *Rizgarî*, the TKSP and the *Kawa* and their analysis focused on the political and economic appropriation and subjugation of

84 *Kurdish national liberation discourse*

Kurdistan mainly by the countries that ruled it as well as the role that 'imperialist' forces played in this division. While the PKK traced the origin of colonialism – or external domination – as far back as the defeat of the Median Empire around 550 BC – and argued that throughout its history, Kurdistan suffered one form of external domination after another – in the discourses of other socialist groups and political parties the emphasis was placed on the late Ottoman and the Republican era.

The role that Britain and France played in Kurdistan's colonisation was highlighted by providing a discussion of the Lausanne Treaty of 1923, which settled the current borders of the Middle East, and which was described as the 'imperialist division of Kurdistan'. According to the *Rizgarî*, this division and colonisation of Kurdistan came about as a direct result of the combined efforts of the British and French 'imperialists', Turkish nationalists and the Persian Monarchists.[5] Moreover, the fact that the colonisation of each part of Kurdistan was by a separate power meant that Kurdistan was a 'common' or an 'international colony'.[6] Both Britain and France played a vital role in the division and colonisation of Kurdistan via their involvement in the establishment of Iraq and Syria respectively. This was emphasised by most groups: for example, the PKK drew attention to Britain's special interests in the oil reserves in the Iraqi Kurdistan. The *Kawa* group, in their defence submitted to the court, stated, 'at Lausanne, in the company of wolves, Kurdistan was divided into four parts and left a fragmented country. This fragmentation played a negative role in terms of national development and unification.'[7]

Hence, the 'colonialist' division of Kurdistan was presented as one of the main reasons behind Kurdistan's fragmentation and lack of national unity. As a result of the division of Kurdistan, each part was forcefully separated from the other. Moreover, any attempts by the Kurds to achieve national unification were forcefully oppressed by the countries that ruled Kurdistan with the support of the imperialist forces. Following this division, colonialism occurred with each force colonising the part of Kurdistan that they controlled and taking over all its natural resources.[8] This was formulated by the PKK in the following way:

> In political terms, Kurdistan is under the rule of four colonialist states that are tied to imperialism. Each state, in the light of its interests and the interests of the international monopolies, plays the central role in developing colonialism in the part it keeps under its rule.[9]

A similar argument about colonialism being a major barrier to Kurdistan's development was also echoed by the TKSP, who drew attention to the continuation of feudal economic relations and their role in Kurdistan's colonisation:

> Through its development in Turkey during the past 50 years, capitalism, even if in an evolutionary way, has overcome feudalism to become hegemonic. In Kurdistan, however, the feudal structure continues to exist. This situation inevitably created the Turkish bourgeoisie's colonialist mechanism

Kurdish national liberation discourse 85

in Kurdistan. Kurdistan's raw materials (especially oil, copper, iron, chrome, and coal) are being exploited; Kurdistan is the region that provides the cheap workforce for the west [of Turkey]; the capital accumulated in this region is flowing to the west; and, Kurdistan became a very suitable market for the bourgeoisie to introduce its products.[10]

The analysis of colonialism was effective in explaining not only the economic and political marginalisation of the Kurds but also their national division and fragmentation. Although the main discussion evolved around the economic aspects – the economic relations between Kurdistan and the states that ruled it, which were characterised as exploitative and to satisfy their national interests and the interests of the international monopolies – colonialism had important social, political and cultural aspects that were closely linked to it. Specifically, the discourses of the groups highlighted the political and social consequences of economic exploitation, such as forced assimilation and linguistic oppression. For that reason, capitalist and industrial development in Kurdistan was managed by the Turkish bourgeoisie in such a way that facilitated its policy of national destruction of the Kurds through forced assimilation. The development of capitalism in Kurdistan neither followed a natural course nor was independent but served only the interests of the colonisers and responded to their economic needs. The PKK's analysis argued that the capitalist development in Kurdistan was accelerated, especially after the 1960s, to annihilate Kurdish national consciousness:

> We cannot expect such a capitalist development to be national. Even the smallest independent economic development in Kurdistan is not possible under the capitalist development managed by the cooperation of the international monopolies, the Turkish bourgeoisie, and their local agents, the Kurdish feudal elements. Economic independence could only develop in an environment where there are no external imperialist interventions and internally there is political unity. In Kurdistan these conditions have not developed for centuries, and, in the present environment, can only develop after the victory of the national liberation struggle.[11]

In fact, what has been taking place in Kurdistan with the development of capitalism has been the development of Turkish nation building that endangers the existence of the Kurdish nation:

> In Kurdistan, under the advancing Turkish colonialism, national destruction instead of national consolidation is the case. The Turkish bourgeoisie is playing a destructive role over the national elements in Kurdistan, and in their place, it tries to impose Turkish nationalism.[12]

Similar statements highlighting the dangers that the development of 'Turkish' capitalism, and with it Turkish nation building, presented to the Kurds was

86 Kurdish national liberation discourse

re-emphasised in the PKK's other key publications. In *Kurdistan Ulusal Kurtuluş Problemi ve Çözüm Yolu* this is expressed in the following way: 'In Kurdistan, under such foreign economic, social and political advancement, the Kurdish national values are facing destruction; instead, the national values of the dominant nations are being imposed through forceful assimilation.'[13] As well as presenting the colonialist division of Kurdistan as the reason behind the Kurds' national fragmentation, the role Kurdish feudalism played in the continuation of this process was highlighted. This was because the Kurdish feudal classes were actively involved in Kurdistan's exploitation and acted as agents for colonialists and imperialists. In fact the two were linked and feudalism was kept intact to facilitate Kurdistan's exploitation.

Kurdish feudalism

The national liberation discourse put forward the view that the feudal structures in Kurdish society were allowed to continue because they facilitated the economic exploitation of Kurdistan; they were upheld deliberately to prevent the development of national consciousness and the independent political development of the Kurdish nation. Generally speaking, the groups and political parties defined Kurdistan as a semi-feudal country with feudalism being described as a main source of fragmentation and a constant obstacle to the development of the national consciousness. For example, according to the TKSP the continuation of the feudal structure was 'not only a barrier to the development of [capitalist] productive forces but also to the development of the national movement, and the two are connected'.[14] This was because under the normal conditions of socio-economic modernisation and the development of the productive forces, feudal fragmentation would have been replaced with a higher form of social organisation, such as the nation. However, in Kurdistan the development of capitalist productive forces and national unification was stagnated to facilitate colonialist exploitation.[15] The TKSP presented the following analysis on the matter:

> The main local obstacle blocking the democratic struggle of the masses in the East is the feudal and tribal structure and the feudal traditionalist ideology built upon these structures. Without changing the feudal productive relations, the tribal structure and defeating the grip of the feudal ideology over the masses, it is very difficult for the society to take the important forward steps.[16]

The prevalence of feudal relations in Kurdistan and the destructive effect that they had on Kurdish national development needed to be taken into account, and their presence raised important issues concerning the nature of the Kurdish national problem and the conditions of the revolution in Kurdistan. It was for this reason that the Kurdish socialists put forward their proposals to organise separately and independently from the revolutionary movement in Turkey. Since the conditions prevailing in Kurdish society and the nature of the problems that

Kurdish national liberation discourse 87

they faced radically differed from the ones present in Turkish society, the Kurdish socialists needed to pursue their own revolutionary activity to achieve Kurdistan's national liberation. This was formulated by the *Rizgari* as the Kurds mobilising their own cadres and dynamics for their own national democratic struggle to achieve their right to 'national self-determination':

> To solve the Kurdish people's different and specific problems, it is essential to descend from the universal to the specific and apply the scientific world view to the concrete problems of this nation. This solution is the national-democratic programme for the Kurdish people's liberation.[17]

Such sentiments were reflected by the TKSP, who also emphasised the national oppression that the Kurds were subjected to:

> Quite evidently, the conditions of the Kurdish and Turkish societies are different. The Turkish society has established a national state, and capitalism is dominant in their country. The Kurdish nation has not achieved its national independence and is under national oppression – besides, this oppression is being applied by the Turkish ruling classes – and it has the structure of a semi feudal society. These differences alter the nature, aims and alliances of the revolution.[18]

Hence, due to the specific conditions that Kurdistan faced, 'a national democratic revolution' was needed:

> Consequently, the democratisation of the region does not only mean that the feudal exploitation and oppression will come to an end. It also means that the racist discriminatory policies and chauvinist oppression that the ruling classes in Turkey apply to the people of the region will also end.[19]

The feudal class's negative influence and oppression over the whole society was something that needed to be eliminated. Therefore the national liberation discourse constructed a strong link between feudalism and colonial exploitation and Kurdistan's national liberation needed to overcome both barriers to succeed in achieving national unification. This complex situation meant that a national revolution was needed to overthrow the external domination of Kurdistan and the internal oppression of the masses. The two were linked because in addition to the deliberate attempts to destroy the Kurdish nation, a policy to stifle the Kurdish national dynamics was pursued to facilitate assimilation through upholding the feudal relations in Kurdistan. From the mid 1970s onwards, the national liberation discourse was the hegemonic discourse articulating Kurdish identity and demands. Hence, in varying degrees Kurdish political parties and groups were committed to both socialism and Kurdistan's liberation. However, differences remained in terms of the level of ideological condensation of the discourse and the strategy and the tactics of the revolution.

88 *Kurdish national liberation discourse*

Kurdistan's national democratic revolution

The description of the aims and objectives of the Kurdistan revolution provided by the *Kawa* group – which was broadly reflective of many of the other group's positions – stated that 'this revolution aims to eliminate imperialism, colonialism and its derivatives fragmentation and feudalism to establish people's democratic rule'.[20] Equally, the PKK's manifesto stated that the specific conditions that Kurdistan faced required the revolution, in the first instance, to evolve in a national direction as national oppression was the most prevalent issue facing Kurdish society:

> Kurdistan's revolution is a revolution of a country where the problem of national oppression was never solved, on the contrary, it continues to grow.... Throughout history national oppression has been developing and in our day it is carried out by capitalist Turkish colonialists. This necessitates that the first stage of Kurdistan's revolution must be to develop towards a national direction. Without solving national oppression none of the other problems of the country will be solved.[21]

Similarly, the national component of the revolution was emphasised by the TKSP stating that due to Kurdistan's specific conditions:

> ...all three stages of revolution remain in front of nations that have semi-feudal structures and experience the continuation of colonial oppression. Such nations, without overcoming colonial oppression and fulfilling the requirements of democratic revolution, cannot arrive at the higher stage of revolution, that is, the socialist stage. What is in front of these nations, in historical terms, is a national democratic revolution. For this reason the *national* component plays an important role in the revolutionary struggle of such nations.[22]

As the discussions concerning feudalism suggest, the democratic component of the revolution was also significant. Moreover, a strong link was established between the existence of feudalism and colonialism, closely connecting both the national and democratic components of Kurdistan's revolution. For example, in this holistic approach to Kurdistan's revolution adopted by the PKK the national element meant that the main antagonistic relations were constructed against the Kemalist regime, whereas the democratic element constructed the antagonistic relations with the Kurdish feudal classes:

> First of all the revolution in Kurdistan targets Turkish colonialism. It is Turkish colonialism that has seized political independence; that continues to fulfil its function of annihilating the Kurdish language, history and culture, and destroying and pillaging Kurdistan's productive forces. This colonialism is externally supported by the imperialists and internally by the feudal comprador classes. These three forces, which are connected together

Kurdish national liberation discourse 89

through close economic ties, constitute the targets of Kurdistan's revolution.[23]

Although both the national and feudal elements were emphasised by all the groups and political parties, not all emphasised both elements equally or with the same force. In contrast to the PKK and the TKSP, the *Rizgarî* – which formulated its solution to the Kurdish problem around the idea of the 'Anti-Colonialist Democratic Struggle' – stressed the national element of the revolution much more than the feudal one. By drawing attention to Kemalism's antagonistic attitude towards the Kurds, *Rizgarî* constructed the antagonistic relations on the national basis:

> Kemalism is a racist ideology. It is very rare to find the equivalents of this type of racism in the world. In order to seize the national-democratic rights of the Kurdish people it developed the argument that "there isn't a Kurdish nation, everyone is a Turk and they are very happy to be Turkish". To implement this it deployed all of the state's resources. What they do to people who refuse this denial or who advocate its opposite is tyranny. It is oppression. Yet, nowhere in the world has the existence of a nation been denied and its national rights seized upon.[24]

Moreover, since Kurdistan's feudal classes were incorporated into the Turkish system and took part in the perpetuation of the Kurds' oppression, the national liberation discourse formulated that the Kurdish working class was the only force capable of attaining the country's national liberation. According to the PKK, as the experience of the Kurdish national movement in Iraq demonstrated, political organisations such as the Kurdistan Democrat Party (KDP), in which the feudal elements dominated, only formulated autonomist political programmes that served their narrow class interest rather than the interests of the whole nation.[25] This meant that only the proletariat was in a position to lead Kurdistan's national liberation movement and only it could formulate a political programme that was 'the expression of the interests and hopes of all the people of Kurdistan'.[26] Additionally, the articulation of Kurdish national demands within the discourse of Marxism meant that not only national oppression but also economic exploitation was problematised. Kurdistan's national liberation was seen as part of a broader move towards social and economic emancipation that a socialist transformation promised. This meant that true emancipation could only be achieved by the proletariat and when it accomplished all the stages of Kurdistan's revolution.

A revolution led by the working class in Kurdistan was seen as possible because the theoretical resources that the Kurdish movement drew from purported, according to the *Kawa* group, that:

> In national questions, under the hegemony of the proletariat, a national liberation movement gradually moves from a democratic popular revolution to

90 *Kurdish national liberation discourse*

socialism and then to communism. The most important aspect of this theory is that it perceives colonies or semi-colonies as units that can realise their own revolutions.[27]

Furthermore, a revolution in an economically backward region was conceivable because through colonialism Kurdistan had established links with the developed capitalist system and the development of capitalism in Turkey produced a Kurdish working class who could lead the national liberation struggle. According to the PKK, the conditions for a revolution in Kurdistan were ripe because:

> In the imperialist era, the development of objective conditions for the revolution in a colonised country exists because the country is part of the imperialist chain. As a result it has experienced capitalist development and there exists, first of all, the proletariat and other modern classes.[28]

It was perceived that the working class and the peasantry, in alliance, will play a leading role in the revolution, with their primary allies being the youth, the intellectual stratum, the urban petty bourgeoisie and other national elements.[29] Similarly, the TKSP singled out the working class of Kurdistan as the main actor to carry out the national liberation: 'The success of the national democratic revolution, which is the next step that the Kurdish nation needs to take, is conditional upon stimulating all progressive patriotic forces of Kurdish society, and activating the national forces.' The patriotic force was defined as the urban and rural workers.[30]

Being divided between four states raised the further problem of the leadership of parts, as the defeat of the Iraqi Kurdish movement created a void. Although each part of Kurdistan maintained a strong link to the other parts, it was proposed by the TKSP that due to their internal specificity, each part needed to organise its own revolution separately. Given that Kurdistan was forcefully divided without the consent of the Kurds, the unity of Kurdistan was something that the revolutionary organisations in each part needed to work towards.[31] The PKK on the other hand, proposed that one part of Kurdistan needed to lead the revolution and re-unify the whole of Kurdistan. The only part that could achieve the unity of Kurdistan was the revolutionary movement in Kurdistan in Turkey:

> Only the struggle in Centre-North-West Kurdistan [Kurdistan in Turkey] can lead the Kurdistan national liberation movement. This is because this part represents more than half the area and population of Kurdistan and more importantly it is the area where the new social forces have broken the backward old social structure and are the most developed.[32]

Furthermore, both the *Kawa* and the PKK accepted the principle of 'Independent, United and Democratic Kurdistan'.[33] Although not elaborated on in detail, the *Rizgarî* group also advocated a similar line. However, as I argue below, on the question of independence or federalism, the TKSP's position was less discernable.

Kurdish national liberation discourse 91

The PKK relocated to Lebanon in 1980 where it rebuilt its organisational structure and intensified its attempts to develop its fighting force. From the early 1980s onwards the PKK has been the hegemonic force in Kurdish resistance in Turkey. The other groups resurfaced in Europe during the early 1980s and their attempts to form a closer alliance and a common front in Europe failed to mount a serious challenge to the PKK's hegemony.[34] In fact, only the TKSP, through its affiliate community organisation, KOMKAR, in Europe, managed to maintain a meaningful existence. I now turn to sketching the differences between the groups on the issue of revolutionary strategy and tactics and on the general orientation of the national movement.

Contestation and the PKK's hegemony

On the basis of a group's radicalism (the national element) and their position on the need to transform the social relations in Kurdistan (the democratic element), and the issue of alliances and the method of revolution, overall two predominant positions can be discerned. In the strategy that the TKSP and the KİP/DDKD advocated, the logics of difference predominated because it emphasised the need to forge a strong alliance between the Kurdish revolutionary groups and the Turkish socialist movement to overthrow the domination by the Turkish bourgeoisie and the Kurdish feudal classes. In the revolutionary strategy advocated by the PKK, the *Kawa* and the *Ala Rizgarî* movements, the logics of equivalence predominated as it advocated continuous revolution through a protracted people's war and emphasised the antagonistic nature of the relations between the Kurds and the Kemalist regime. In this section, I provide a comparison between the TKSP and the PKK in terms of revolutionary strategy because their respective strategies were broadly representative of the positions of the other Kurdish groups, and also both had the most comprehensive and condensed discourses. Specifically, I examine the discussions over the strategy of the revolution and the institution of new political frontiers to represent the alternative society that the Kurdish national movement contested and on the basis of which the antagonistic relations were constructed. I provide an account of the political practices in the early 1980s to highlight how the PKK's credibility increased in the eyes of many people.

Strategy of the revolution

The practice of national liberation often involved armed struggle but a clear revolutionary strategy was not articulated from the onset. However, violence within the Kurdish movement in the late 1970s and the state's increasing repression from 1979 onwards and especially during the military coup in 1980 created a difficult environment to conduct any sort of legal politics and made violent resistance and armed struggle the dominant practice. Although the PKK is usually seen as the main advocator of violence as political practice, the necessity of armed struggle was part of the general debate that took place within the

92 Kurdish national liberation discourse

Kurdish national movement. This is evident in the establishment of the *Ala Rizgarî*, which proposed the need for a political party organised according to the principle of democratic centralism and which advocated armed struggle. The establishment of armed groups in 1980 affiliated to various groups within the *Kawa* movement, such as the PSSK (*Peşmergeyan Sor en Şoreşa Kurdistane* – Red Peshmergas of Kurdistan's Revolution) and the KPSK (*Komaleya Partizanen Sor an Kurdistan* – Union of Kurdistan's Red Partisans) is also indicative of the inclination towards political violence.[35] These developments indicate that the preference for the use of violence as a revolutionary strategy started to gain ground within the Kurdish movement.

In comparison to other groups, the need for violent resistance as a revolutionary strategy was discussed more extensively and in a systematic way by the PKK. Given the conditions, armed struggle was seen as necessary and the only effective means to achieve national liberation. The PKK's manifesto stated that the 'revolutionary force must be as organised and concentrated as the reactionary force' to displace the reactionary force because it was highly unlikely that a forceful organisation, such as a state, would give up its power voluntarily or abolish itself.[36] Therefore, what was envisaged was a forceful overthrow of the oppressive colonialist regime in military, political and economic terms; in fact, national liberation could only be achieved through a protracted 'people's war'.[37] Although the PKK's manifesto stressed a long and protracted period of military engagement through guerrilla warfare to bring about a popular revolt, the details of its strategy were further elaborated on during its efforts to re-group and rebuild the party abroad in the early 1980s, during its First Conference in July 1981 and the Second Congress in August 1982. On both of these occasions the need to expand on the strategy and tactics of the revolution and the practical issues associated with the application of the strategy were emphasised. To this end the PKK published a number of books in the early 1980s, such as *Kürdistanda Zorun Rolü* (The Role of Force in Kurdistan), *Kürdistan Ulusal Kurtuluş Problemi ve Çözüm Yolu* (Kurdistan's National Liberation Problem and Its Solution).[38] These publications set out the steps to develop the PKK into a fully operational armed movement.

The military and political struggle were seen as inseparable for it was 'impossible to have revolutionary practice without the revolutionary theory and it is also clear that a revolutionary theory and programme without the corresponding revolutionary practice signifies nothing'.[39] The guerrilla struggle was seen as the first stage of a wider rebellion of the masses and as a tool that will accelerate political development.[40] Hence, the PKK deployed a developmental guerrilla strategy in which, initially, small units of guerrillas would carry out attacks against military targets to weaken the army's authority in the region and incite a popular rebellion. In the final phase of the war, the people's army supported by the popular uprising of the masses would overthrow the rule of the state and establish the people's rule. In this sense the revolution was to be uninterrupted in which the party (the PKK) would organise the masses in a national democratic front and achieve revolutionary change through the military activities of a people's army and popular uprising.[41] Broadly speaking the *Kawa* movement also advocated a similar strategy as did the *Ala Rizgarî* group, which proposed the need for a proletarian party organised throughout all parts of Kurdistan and according to the principles of democratic centralism. In a similar way to the PKK it also advocated continuous revolution, protracted people's war and a national popular front. However, the discourse of neither group was as condensed as the PKK's.

In contrast, the TKSP's revolutionary strategy was a highly open-ended one which, upon further reflection, seems ambiguous. The TKSP's programme summarised its revolutionary strategy in the following way:

> The historical developments may present the solution to Kurdistan's national problem to us in the following two forms:
>
> 1 The Kurdish nation, mainly by its own means and without waiting for a revolutionary movement in Turkey, starts its national liberation war and succeeds;
> 2 A revolutionary movement led by the working class of Turkey as a whole, including the working class of Kurdistan, overthrows the rule of the reactionary bourgeoisie and the landlords to establish the democratic rule of the people and to recognise the Kurdish people's right to national self-determination.
>
> Our party, knowing that the historical developments may present one or the other possibilities, is open to both and prepares itself accordingly.[42]

The party programme also stated that should the conditions require an uprising the party will be at the forefront.[43] Additionally, while not completely ruling out armed struggle, the main activities that the TKSP took part in involved organising the masses and mass action to achieve revolutionary change. In practical terms however, this led to the TKSP oscillating between the two and unable to present a clear position: while it did not rule out violence as a strategy, it never resorted to it. Moreover, the TKSP preferred a two-stage revolutionary strategy as opposed to an uninterrupted one. It stated that the construction of a socialist society in Kurdistan was the ultimate aim of the party, but given the conditions what was needed in the first instance was a national democratic revolution to overthrow colonial oppression, achieve national liberation and destroy the feudal structure to democratise the country.[44]

A closer examination of the TKSP's strategy also reveals that by emphasising the anti-colonial and anti-feudal aspects of Kurdistan's revolution, the TKSP drew a frontier between the 'the progressive patriotic forces who were on the side of national liberation and democracy, and the colonialist administration, the local feudal forces and others agents'.[45] Additionally, it frequently emphasised the alliance between the Turkish socialist movement and the Kurdish national movement in which the workers and the revolutionary forces of both Turkey and Kurdistan were united under a common 'anti-imperialist' and 'anti-fascist' programme:

94 *Kurdish national liberation discourse*

In Turkey the struggle against fascism and imperialism is the common struggle of both peoples. For this reason, it is absolutely necessary that the revolutionary and democratic forces of the Kurdish people – if possible in the form of a Kurdistan National Democratic Front – take part in any future Anti-Imperialist and Democratic Front.[46]

In practice, however, the articulation of Kurdish demands within an equivalential chain represented by a signifier such as 'anti-imperialism' that had clear and different meanings to Turkish socialists created difficulties for the TKSP to clearly represent the Kurdish demands within it. This is because the representation of Kurdish demands by the empty signifier 'anti-imperialism' was unable to clearly represent the national demands in a complex political space. Similar problems were faced by the KİP/DDKD – who also preferred mass action as a strategy and took part in elections to bring about change – in its discussion concerning construction of a common platform of socialist and democratic forces in Turkey and the Kurdish national movement. For example, the election proclamation in which the KİP/DDKD and a Turkish socialist group TSIP cooperated on broadly democratic demands, Kurdish national demands were formulated *only* as minority and human rights demands that ignored addressing the Kurdish issue as formulated by the national liberation discourse.[47]

Also, the partial articulation of Kurdish demands in Turkey within the discourse of socialism during the late 1960s came to an end as the Turkish socialists were not prepared to accept Kurds' particular rights and demands. Therefore, it is highly questionable whether there was any basis for a close cooperation between the Kurdish national movement and the Turkish socialist movement during the late 1970s. Furthermore, the ideological and political debates and discussions between the Kurdish socialists and their Turkish counterparts clearly demonstrated the difficulties that the Turkish socialist movement faced in articulating Kurdish demands as part of an equivalential chain represented by the empty signifier 'equality'. Hence, the TKSP's and the KİP/DDKD's strategy of close cooperation with the Turkish socialist movement on the basis of 'anti-fascism' and 'anti-imperialism' was unable to clearly represent Kurdish national demands. The TKSP and the KİP/DDKD's positions were further weakened by the military coup of 12 September 1980 and the subsequent widespread oppression that followed. This is because the military coup had a devastating effect on the Turkish socialist movement and the Kurdish national movement and ended the possibility of a socialist revolution in Turkey, which reduced the effectiveness of the TKSP's strategy. Therefore, in the case of the TKSP and the KİP/ DDKD, the representation of the Kurdish demands was less clear and they were not able to present a clear strategy for Kurdistan's revolution.

Conversely, constructing the relations of equivalence and political frontiers on a national basis meant that the PKK's national liberation discourse constructed antagonisms more clearly, and 'liberation' emerged as the 'empty signifier' in its discourse. This clarity was maintained during the attempts of various Turkish and Kurdish socialist groups during 1981 to form the Anti-Fascist

Kurdish national liberation discourse   95

United Revolutionary Front (*Faşizme Karşı Birleşik Devrimci Cephe (FKBDC)*). While the PKK proposed the need for a strategic alliance between the Kurdish and Turkish socialist movements, it nevertheless firmly established Kurdistan's national liberation as one of the main aims of such an alliance.[48]

In addition, during the late 1970s and early 1980s the PKK concentrated on publishing key texts, such as the 'Foundation Document' (*Kuruluş Bildirisi*) and its manifesto that clearly articulated its discourse and aims and objectives. In comparison, the discourses of the other political groups were not condensed; for example, it was not very clear, what the *Rizgarî's* 'anti-Colonialist Democratic Struggle' involved, or how it was to be carried out. Similarly, what the KİP/ DDKD or the KUK advocated was not clearly formulated or disseminated to the public. Even though the TKSP was the first Kurdish socialist political party to be established, as well as not clearly articulating its strategy and objectives, its discourse was not as condensed as the PKK's and was disseminated to the public loosely through numerous opinion and commentary articles in *Özgürlük Yolu*.

In fact the differences in terms of revolutionary strategy were a source of friction between the groups. For example, the TKSP's ambiguous revolutionary strategy coupled with the general preference for a strategy of alliance with the Turkish socialist movement, in which Kurdish national rights were not clearly articulated, was interpreted by the *Rizgarî* as sacrificing Kurdish national self-determination.[49] In turn, the TKSP accused the *Rizgarî* of ignoring the feudal oppression that the Kurdish masses suffered.[50] The PKK on the other hand accused the TKSP of being reformist and advocating the petty bourgeois line, which in its view neither provided the correct analysis of Kurdistan's national oppression nor proposed a viable programme for its solution. It was reformist because it believed that revolutionary change could be achieved through mass action and without the need for a people's war. The PKK described the KUK and the KİP/DDKD – due to their links with the TKDP – as 'primitive nationalists' who formulated an autonomist programme that ignored the oppression of the Kurdish masses and who represented the interests of the feudal classes.[51] In contrast, the TKSP accused the PKK of glorifying 'individual terrorism' and criticised its rejection of any form of legal political activism and also the violence it used in its conflict with other Kurdish organisations during the late 1970s.[52] Similarly, the PKK's strategy of a 'protracted people's war' was interpreted as 'adventuresome' by the KİP/DDKD.[53] Its methods were seen as destructive to the Kurdish movement as a whole and a recipe for disaster because, in their analysis, Kurdistan was not ready for a protracted people's war.

Identity and representation

In addition to the clarity of the PKK's discourse in terms of the strategy, aims and objectives of the movement and the representation of Kurdish demands, a clearer conception of identity emerges in the PKK's discourse. In Chapter 4, the use of the myth of *Newroz* in the construction of a new Kurdish political identity was discussed. Although almost all of the groups made reference to the myth of

96   *Kurdish national liberation discourse*

Newroz, its importance for the Kurds' national struggle and as a symbol of rebellion against tyranny, there were variations in the meanings attached to it in each group's discourse. In comparison to other groups or parties, the myth of *Newroz* received more elaboration in the discourses of the PKK. The manifesto emphasised in detailed the importance of the Medes' long and heroic struggle against Assyria for their independence:

> Assyrians were the most destructive imperialists of the period who prevented our ancestors – the Medes – from becoming a people and having a homeland. The Medes by declaring themselves to be 'Aryen' [the people of fire] decided to resist such a ferocious enemy who were a nightmare to every other Middle Eastern people. If they had accepted submission, they would not have become a people but stayed restricted to where they were.... To become a people and have a homeland, the Medes fought against the Assyrians for 300 years and in the course of this fight, they defeated the Assyrians to establish the foundations of the Kurdish people. They called the day of their freedom '*Newroz*' and celebrated their freedom and the freedom of the other Middle Eastern people every year.[54]

Furthermore, a parallel between Kawa the blacksmith and the struggle of the Medes and the PKK and the struggle of the contemporary Kurds against oppression was drawn. Its discourse stressed the need to develop a 'new Median movement' in order to *recreate* the Kurdish national existence in the contemporary era.[55] In later years as the PKK's struggle progressed during the 1980s and 1990s, *Newroz* was *reactivated* to construct a *contemporary* myth of resistance, which centred around the PKK's resistance in Diyarbakir Prison during the early 1980s and its resistance against the state in general. The contemporary myth of *Newroz* – which is analysed in detail in Chapter 6 – was reflected in many songs and disseminated to a wider audience. This enabled the PKK to conceive of the 'fantasy' of the Kurds' unity, construct antagonistic relations with the Kurds' internal and external enemies that prevented them from achieving their unity and added force to its discourse.

In the *Rizgarî's* discourse *Newroz* was described as a day that symbolised 'independence, freedom, and struggle for a nation refusing oppression and liberation'.[56] However, in stark contrast in *Özgürlük Yolu*, it was described as a day for 'struggle against racism'.[57] Instead of constructing Kurdish difference, distinction and the closure of identity, such a description of the *Newroz* myth seeks to emphasise the common bonds between the different nations in the Middle East to create harmony between them. Furthermore, in Burkay's polemic against the PKK, he disputes the association made in the PKK's discourse between the Medes and the modern day Kurds and the construction of the time of the Median Empire as the 'golden age' of the Kurdish nation.[58] The view that the Kurds are the descendants of the Medes dates back to the beginning of the twentieth century, or perhaps earlier, was commonly shared by most Kurdish nationalists and was reflected in the discourses of most political groups. Therefore, it is highly uncharacteristic of a Kurdish socialist to reject it. In fact, the failure to construct the *Newroz* myth as a myth of Kurdish origin and resistance created further difficulties for the TKSP during the late 1970s and early 1980s to clearly represent Kurdish identity and demands in its discourse as it was unable to conceive and represent the Kurds' national unity for it did/could not construct an alternative narrative of identity and origin.

In contrast, the frequent reference to the Medes enabled the PKK to reconstruct the history of the 'Kurdish people' and Kurdistan, as a geographic entity:

> The Kurds, like any other people at the dawn of history, were living in the last phase of primitive communal society.... In this phase many tribes from the Indo-European groups spread from Northern Europe to Asia and Central Europe. The Kurds can be traced to the Medes who originated from the tribes in this group and later migrated and settled in 1000 BC in the area between the lakes of Urmia and Van. The connection between the Kurds and the Medes is certain if we compare their geographic spread, language and historical developments.[59]

The construction in the PKK's discourse of the Median era as the 'golden age' of the Kurdish nation was used to conceive of the 'fantasy' of Kurdish national unity; its achievement or recreation being the main task of the national liberation struggle.[60] This clear representation of Kurdish identity and national demands enabled the PKK to construct and represent an image of a homogenous Kurdish nation and conceive of the unity of Kurdistan to transcend the various fragmentations experienced by the Kurdish nation. Furthermore, it allowed the PKK to present the long history and evolution of the Kurdish nation through time, which not only strengthened its nationalist claims, but also located the Kurds' liberation struggle within a longer time frame. In the defence submitted to the military court, the *Kawa* group also drew attention to the Kurds' long presence in the region and made reference to the myth of resistance:

> The Kurds who have been living in the same mountainous area from the earliest period in history, based on the conditions of the time, continued their existence either as an independent state or under the rule of an occupying nation. Their long resistance struggle waged against occupations and invasions throughout time has been transformed into a historical tradition.[61]

Although an ethnicist conception dominated the discussions of Kurdish identity, the national liberation discourse cannot be viewed narrowly as only seeking to construct an ethnicist conception of Kurdish identity. The main issue it problematised was Kurdistan's colonisation and exploitation. Kurdistan as a country, including its numerous minorities, was the nodal point in the national liberation discourse. For example, the *Kawa* group's defence stated: 'What we are referring to is the problem of independence and freedom of the people of Kurdistan.

98 Kurdish national liberation discourse

That is, the people of Kurdistan inclusive of various nations and minorities.'[62] Similarly, the PKK stated: 'The Kurdistan revolution, will destroy the oppression and exploitation beset on minorities, and will create the conditions for their free development.'[63]

Kurdish political activism in the early 1980s

Turkey was ruled by a military regime after the coup d'etat on 12 September 1980 until 1983. As stated in Chapter 4 most of the Kurdish political activists were arrested and incarcerated in numerous prisons. Hence, in the early 1980s, prisons – especially the Diyarbakir Prison – were the main site of resistance and Kurdish political activism. To protest against endemic torture and oppression, and the violation of their basic human rights, prisoners organised a hunger strike in Diyarbakir Prison in December 1980 led mainly by the PKK members and sympathisers.[64] The resistance of the PKK members in Diyarbakir Prison continued throughout 1981 and 1982 and culminated in the suicide of Mazlum Doğan on the night of 21 March 1982, the self-immolation of four other PKK members (Eşref Anyık, Ferhad Kutay, Necmi Öner, Mahmut Zengin) on 18 May 1982 and the death fast that began on 14 July 1982 in which the PKK's four senior cadres, Kemal Pir (7 September), Mehmet Hayri Durmuş (12 September), Akif Yılmaz (15 September) and Ali Çiçek (17 September) died.[65]

Furthermore, during the PKK trials in 1981, the central committee members Kemal Pir, Mazlum Doğan and Mehmet Hayri Durmuş defended their involvement in the PKK and the movement's struggle for Kurdistan's national liberation and socialism.[66] Specifically, the description of the PKK as a 'gang' by the state prosecutors and the use of names such as *Apocular* (literally 'the followers of Apo', with Apo being a shortened name for Abdullah Öcalan) and UKO (National Liberation Army) was challenged. It was argued that these were used deliberately to confuse people and deride the movement and its popular base. Similar to the defences of the DDKO, the Kurds' existence as a separate nation and their distinct history was defended in the PKK members' court defences. Defending the movement and its objectives in front of the military court that was conducting the trial meant that the resistance in the prisons was transferred into the courtrooms.[67] The dedicated resistance by the prisoners and the defence of the movement in the courts enhanced the PKK's credibility in the eyes of the many ordinary Kurdish people.[68] Moreover, as I discuss in Chapter 6, its resistance in the Diyarbakir Prison provided the PKK with an important symbolic resource as it enabled it to construct a contemporary myth of resistance, which became the cornerstones of its discourse and practice throughout the 1980s and 1990s, and was used to distinguish itself as the only and true representative of Kurdish resistance. The construction of this new myth of resistance enhanced the PKK's credibility in the eyes of many Kurds and was given as the evidence for its strong conviction in Kurdistan's liberation, which – even during very harsh conditions – it was prepared to defend. The Governor of the Diyarbakir Prison, army captain Esat Oktay Yıldıran, who was credited with the harsh

Kurdish national liberation discourse 99

treatment of the inmates was assassinated by a PKK militant on 22 October 1988 in Istanbul. In contrast, the other main groups, such as the KUK, the TKSP, the KİP/DDKD and the *Rizgarî* either short-circuited the political dimension of the trials by presenting their group as only a periodical (as was the case with the *Rizgarî*) or not defending the movement at all.[69] Some of the members of the *Kawa* movement also defended their group and challenged the assertions made in the indictment.

A significant number of PKK members relocated to Syria and Lebanon in 1979 and 1980 and established the organisation's bases there. Its relocation to Lebanon presented it with an opportunity during the early 1980s to form close links with the Palestinian organisations and established its guerrilla training camps. Also, starting in the early 1980s it started to build a strong presence in Europe, mainly in Germany, through a network of community organisations. In subsequent years the PKK concentrated its efforts to build the revolutionary party. Specifically, efforts were concentrated on rebuilding and re-organising the central unit of the party, ideological and military training of the party cadres to become professional revolutionaries and constructing an information network to communicate party ideals to the masses. In practical terms this led to the establishment of a publishing house and a monthly newspaper in Europe, a party school and guerrilla training camp (Helwe camp) to train the party members, and preparatory steps were taken to establish the National Liberation Front to coordinate political activities and organise amongst the masses.[70] The PKK's Second Congress also emphasised the need to build the PKK's activities in Europe, which would have fostered the organisational links and alliances with working-class and socialist movements there. More importantly, it would have given the PKK an opportunity to organise amongst the Kurdish communities in Europe and provide much needed financial and human resources. Hence, throughout the 1980s, the PKK gradually established a network of cultural and community organisations located in numerous major European cities. Through these centres and in a relatively safe environment, the PKK organised amongst the Kurdish communities to build its mass base and popular support. The efforts in Europe as well as in Lebanon and Syria provided the PKK with the necessary organisational and financial networks to begin its guerrilla war.

Additionally, the PKK's Second Congress held in 1982 stressed the need to take practical steps towards enhancing its military capabilities. An important development at this stage began when the PKK decided to move some of its forces to Iraqi Kurdistan and establish a guerrilla training camp near the border with Turkey. In 1982 the PKK started to form good relations with the Kurdistan Democrat Party (KDP), which in 1983 was formalised as an alliance agreement that facilitated the PKK's movement in Iraqi Kurdistan.[71] The alliance agreement was made public in 1983; broadly, it emphasised that the Kurdish national movement needed to take an anti-imperialist and anti-capitalist orientation and that both parties were committed to fostering good relations among the Kurdish political groups in the region.[72] The proximity to the Turkish border allowed the PKK to start its preparations for the guerrilla war by sending units to Turkey to map

100 *Kurdish national liberation discourse*

the terrain, identifying areas where the military bases and stations were located, drawing possible routes that the guerrillas could use, identifying hide-out places and, more importantly, establishing links with the local population.

Conclusion

Overall this chapter provided an account of the national liberation discourse, the definition and solution of the Kurdish question emerging in the discourse of the Kurdish revolutionary groups. The critique that Kurdish socialists developed of the Turkish socialist discourse lessened the Kemalist influence over the socialist discourse and created the possibility of articulating the Kurdish national demands within the Marxist discourse. The construction of difference and Kurdish subjectivity within the discourse of national liberation, and the political practices promoted by it, are the two main issues that have been examined in this chapter. The national liberation discourse perceived the Kurds' existence as a nation to be in danger as their national values were being destroyed and they were forcefully assimilated into Turkish, Arab and Persian nations. It proposed that Kurdistan's colonial exploitation and national fragmentation could only be achieved by a revolutionary movement led by the working class. Due to the specific conditions prevailing in Kurdistan and the prevalence of national oppression from the onset the revolution needed to take a national democratic character to unify Kurdistan, but its eventual aim remained the transformation of Kurdistan into a socialist society. The characterisation of the Kurdish issue as one of national liberation established a complex set of antagonisms with principally the states that ruled Kurdistan and the Kurdish feudal elites being held responsible for Kurdistan's backwardness and national fragmentation.

The discussions revealed that overall there were two different revolutionary strategies: one, reform-oriented strategy advocating mass action and alliance with Turkey's socialist movement; two, a revolutionary strategy involving a popular rebellion to overthrow the colonialist rule. The discourses and the representation of the Kurdish demands in each of the national liberation discourses were analysed to search for the clues of the PKK's subsequent hegemony of the Kurdish resistance in Turkey. The clarity of the PKK's discourse and the construction of antagonistic relations (internal and external enemies) as well as the credibility it gained as a result of its practice in Diyarbakir Prison made its discourse more affective. Attention was drawn to the differences in the deployment of the myth in each discourse and how *Newroz* was reactivated by the PKK to construct an ethnicist conception of the Kurdish nation and a new myth of resistance, which is explored more fully in the next chapter. Additionally, relocating to Lebanon presented the PKK with the opportunity to organise as a military movement. Its presence in Europe created opportunities in terms of financial and human resources.

6 'Becoming a Kurd'

The 'national liberation' war and mass mobilisation

Nothing is more valuable than independence and freedom.[1]

Berxwedan Jiyana[2]

Introduction

On 15 August 1984, the PKK declared the start of its guerrilla insurgency against the state by raiding two army bases in the towns of Eruh and Şemdinli near the Turkey-Iraq border. In the next decade the scope and depth of the guerrilla war increased significantly and through its widespread political consequences, it brought about the mobilisation of a large number of Kurds in Turkey. In the late 1980s and the early 1990s, as the PKK grew in strength, its guerrilla war started to gather momentum and spread over a large area with attacks occurring frequently. The principal targets of the PKK's political violence were the state's security forces and the village guards. Through its military and political activities, and the media and information network it created, the PKK was able to reach out to many Kurds. In the early 1990s, it evolved into a mass movement with supporters and sympathisers numbering several million drawn from all parts of Kurdistan and the Kurdish communities in Europe. Hence, in the late 1980s and early 1990s, the PKK started to present a powerful political challenge to Turkey's authority in the Kurdish regions. This period represents the peak of the PKK's resistance and is characterised by the heightening of the antagonistic relation between the Kurds and Turkey. Kurdish political activism during the 1980s and 1990s, therefore, raises the following important questions: How did the PKK manage to grow into a mass movement? Why was it successful in its mobilisation of the Kurds? Why and how did it manage to hegemonise Kurdish resistance in Turkey? What accounts for the sedimentation of its discourse in practice?

In this chapter, I analyse the development of the guerrilla war covering the period until the early 1990s, and the corresponding political mobilisation, including the mass protests and popular uprisings. As well as giving an overview of the PKK's military and political activities in the late 1980s and early 1990s, the account presented here allows me to highlight the PKK's organisational development and growth as a movement in Turkey and Europe. The analysis focuses

102   *War and mass mobilisation*

on the escalation of the guerrilla war, the mass mobilisation and popular uprisings (*serhildan*) and the Kurdish cultural renewal that the PKK fostered through the work of Kurdish organisations in Europe. Specifically, the creation of *Eniya Rizgariya Netewa Kurdistan* (the National Liberation Front of Kurdistan, ERNK) allowed the PKK to establish an extensive organisational network in Europe, including numerous representative organisations for specific social or religious groups, which enabled it to mobilise a wider section of Kurdish society. In the PKK's hegemonic articulation of Kurdish identity, the logics of equivalence predominated and the antagonistic relations against the Kemalist regime and the Kurdish feudal classes were fostered. Although I cover the political and the military activities in separate sub-sections, it is difficult to make a clear distinction between the two as they were combined and the military activities served the political development of the movement. Formally, however, there were two separate organisations organising these activities.

The account offered in the first part of the chapter is enhanced by a closer examination, in the second part of the chapter, of the factors that played a significant role in the mobilisation process and account for the PKK's hegemony over the Kurdish resistance in Turkey. Whereas the 1970s – the period discussed in Chapters 4 and 5 – represent the fragmentation of the Kurdish socialist movement, the 1980s and early 1990s represent the PKK's hegemony and the sedimentation of its national liberation discourse in practice. In this process the existence of various affiliated cultural and political organisations in Europe that produced and disseminated its discourse to wider Kurdish communities played a significant role in extending the PKK's appeal to the masses. Furthermore, the cultural organisations offered artistic representation of the PKK's practices of resistance, which as well as making a significant contribution to the reinvigoration of Kurdish culture, also enabled the sedimentation of its discourse.

As discussed in Chapter 2, in Laclau's theorisation the concept of *sedimentation* refers to the process of the institution of hegemony, of a practice becoming hegemonic. When the sedimentation of a discourse or practice takes place, its 'original' contingency or its contingent emergence through acts of repression and exclusion of its alternatives become concealed and less visible to 'assume the form of a mere objective presence'.[3] The concept of hegemony is drawn from Marxist theorist Antonio Gramsci and refers to 'ethical, moral and political leadership'.[4] In order to understand the processes at work in the sedimentation of the discourse in practice, this chapter expands on the previous discussion of the PKK's reactivation of the *Newroz* as a myth of Kurdish resistance to construct a contemporary myth of resistance – centred on the resistance of its members in the Diyarbakir Prison during the early 1980s and its insurgency in general – to represent its struggle as the *embodiment* of the Kurds' long struggle for 'independence' and 'freedom'. The deployment of the contemporary myth of resistance in the discourse enhanced the PKK's appeal and strength, and played a key role in its mobilisation of the Kurds. Specifically, the romanticising of its guerrilla war against the Turkish army and the state security forces enhanced its hegemonic appeal by bringing the myth of resistance into reality. Overall, this

War and mass mobilisation   103

analytical account is utilised to explore the appeal and *force* of the PKK's national liberation discourse and account for its *sedimentation* in practice.

Fighting for Kurdistan: the 'war of liberation' and mass mobilisation

As discussed in Chapter 5, the military practices that the PKK undertook became the focal point in its struggle in the early 1980s. While its First Conference and Second Congress held in 1981 and 1982 respectively emphasised the need to maintain strong connections with the masses, the initial efforts were concentrated on building the guerrilla forces and the party's central structure.[5] Initially during the late 1970s, the PKK's use of violence was sporadic and against the Kurdish tribal leaders and other Kurdish groups with whom it had enduring disagreements. From 1984 onwards, however, the nature of the campaign changed significantly with the Turkish army and the state's security forces becoming the main targets of the PKK's attacks. The better trained, equipped and organised guerrillas started to fight the army and security forces in coordinated attacks predominantly in the rural areas. These military practices had, in the long run, the aim of inciting a popular national rebellion that would lead to the overthrow of Turkish rule and the liberation of Kurdistan. Therefore, guerrilla insurgency and political violence was accepted as the fundamental form of the movement's political strategy and its key importance lay in its ability to cause extensive political developments and harness mass support in a short period of time.

The efforts during the early 1980s to rebuild the party's central organisation and command structure also emphasised the need to create a popular national liberation front. To this end, the outline and programme of the National Liberation Front was published by the PKK as a key publication in 1982.[6] The fragmentations in terms of religion, language and tribe were seen as the main internal reasons that impeded the development of a national movement and its success, and the primary objective of the National Liberation Front was to forge and achieve the political unity of the masses. More specifically, the objectives of the National Liberation Front were described in the following way:

> The National Liberation Front will protect and develop the national values of the people, destroy all forms of tribal and sectarian fragmentation to achieve national unity, organise the people's economic, social, political and cultural life, and is the only form of unity that directs the people's power in the service of the national liberation. The Front will play its historical role by achieving national unity for the first time in Kurdistan's history.[7]

However, mass support for the movement was seen as something that would grow with the development of the military struggle: 'In fact, our armed struggle is a method that will lead us to the organisation of the masses. The guerrilla struggle has mostly a political aim, that is, it is a type of struggle that has the function of organising the front.'[8] Indeed, the growth of the PKK's military

104   War and mass mobilisation

activities generated the outcome it intended. During the early 1990s, the PKK evolved into a transnational mass movement that organised political activities in Turkey as well as many other European countries. In Turkey numerous popular uprisings (*serhildan*) took place between 1990 and 1993 in many towns across the Kurdish region in which ordinary Kurds demanded the recognition of Kurdish identity and openly showed their support for the PKK.

The guerrilla war and the escalation of the conflict (1984–1992)

The long anticipated guerrilla war began with two concurrent attacks against the Turkish security forces on 15 August 1984. Initially the PKK's armed forces were organised within the HRK (*Hêzên Rizgariya Kurdistan*, Kurdistan's Liberation Forces). At the onset, the HRK consisted of three armed units – named after the dates of the PKK member's significant acts of resistance in the Diyarbakir Prison: 21 March, 18 May and 14 July.[9] However, during 1985 and 1986, the PKK found it difficult to sustain the initial hype generated by its attacks in 1984. As well as the lack of experience on its part, this difficulty was caused by the actions that the state took to prevent the development of the PKK's guerrilla campaign. The state increased the number of its forces and security operations and resorted to various strict measures. Although martial law was declared Turkey-wide after the coup on 12 September 1980 and lasted until 1983, in majority Kurdish areas it was frequently used from 1978 onwards.[10] In 1987, military rule became a permanent feature with the declaration of emergency rule and the creation of the *Olağanüstü Hal Bölge Valiliği* (OHAL, Governorship of the Region Under Emergency Rule) to administer the emergency rule. The OHAL covered the following provinces: Batman, Bingöl, Diyarbakır, Elazığ, Hakkari, Mardin, Siirt, Şırnak, Tunceli and Van, and it exerted considerable authority, including 'exiling' persons or whole settlements. As part of increasing the number of the security personnel in the Kurdish areas, in 1985 the village guards were assembled as a pro-state 'Kurdish' militia responsible for the security of the rural settlements and to fight against the PKK.

Consequently, the development of its military capacity was the main point of discussion in the PKK's Third Congress held in October 1986 during which a number of significant decisions were taken. One of these was the re-organisation of the HRK into the ARGK (*Artêşa Rizgariya Gelê Kurdistan,* Kurdistan People's Liberation Army) the short-term objectives of which were specified to be:

> In the next four years, the aim is to form a guerrilla army, a people's army. It will have wide capacity and the establishment of the units will be in accordance with the real attributes of military units. We have the possibility to achieve this and it is our fundamental task. All other party activities, that is, all the ideological–political developments will have the aim of enriching and strengthening this fundamental form of struggle; the essence of our activities abroad will also serve the development of the armed struggle and

War and mass mobilisation 105

it is connected to it. All the activities – from cultural activities to external relations – that we will carry out, in the final instance, will emerge from the people's war and from strengthening the fundamental form of struggle.[11]

The numbers of the ARGK guerrillas together with the resources that the PKK had at its disposal were significantly short of achieving such ambitious objectives. Subsequently, the PKK resorted to radical measures in order to increase its recruitment and to this end the Third Congress also recommended a conscription law that made joining the ARGK compulsory:

> We will take our society into a guerrilla war. According to this stage, from now on, the recruitment of peasants into the fighting units needs to take place not on the voluntary basis but on the basis of a compulsory conscription law. We need to propose this and invite our masses to take on the military tasks. That is to say, a compulsory conscription law is likely to be increasingly more useful.[12]

As a result, during the late 1980s, the numbers of the ARGK guerrillas increased significantly, which allowed it to build its presence in the region. In fact it is highly unlikely that the PKK would have managed to recruit large numbers without compulsory conscription, especially during the critical early years of its guerrilla war. During the late 1980s, this led to a gradual increase in the number of attacks against the Turkish security forces and the village guards as well as widening of the area within which they occurred. The mountainous terrain alongside the Turkey-Iraq border provided many hiding places for the guerrillas to shelter and was particularly suitable for the successful execution of the guerrilla war. The guerrillas were able to connect with local populations and establish local militias (*milis*), who provided important logistic support and also helped coordinate the PKK's activities when needed. Predominantly, the targets of the guerrillas were the state security forces and the village guards. The main form of military activity by the ARGK consisted of raids on gendarme stations and other forms of military installations nearby the borders with Iraq and Iran, raids on gendarme and army stations in rural areas, ambushes, road checks, raids on villages where the village guards were located and sabotage against economic facilities or state institutions in the Kurdish regions.

Throughout 1987 the number of attacks carried out by the ARGK increased significantly. In two of its official monthly magazines, *Serxwebûn* (Independence) and *Berxwedan* (Resistance), both published in Germany, the PKK provided regular updates on the evolving conflict. Although the number of casualties in the conflict quoted by the PKK and the state differed significantly – with a tendency on each side to show the other's losses higher – the reports from both sides of the conflict clearly show the increase in both the attacks and the intensity of the conflict during the late 1980s and early 1990s. For example, according to the statistics provided in *Berxwedan* in March 1987, the ARGK raids and ambushes in numerous locations in Eruh, Uludere, Eğil, Ceylanpınar, Nusaybin,

106   War and mass mobilisation

Cizre and Doğubeyazıt resulted in the death of more than 40 security forces and village guards.[13] Similarly, in April 1987 according to *Berxwedan*, the Milli Gendarme Station in Şırnak was completely destroyed by an ARGK attack.[14] Also, some of the attacks were large scale and as reported in May 1987 in *Berxwedan*, on 24 April 1987, the guerrillas ambushed a commando unit which resulted in the death of 63 security forces, including one major and two first lieutenants. In May 1987 a military vehicle was blown-up by a mine resulting in the death of 20 soldiers.[15]

From 1987 onwards the ARGK raids on towns also increased significantly. Raids on Tunceli, Karakoçan, Uludere and Hozat were reported in *Berxwedan* to have taken place during July and August 1987. The towns were kept under the control of the guerrillas for up to three or four hours during which PKK propaganda was carried out.[16]

Therefore, as a result of the higher numbers recruited and the development of the guerrilla war, the PKK's guerrilla activities increased significantly during the late 1980s. According to the *Berxwedan* magazine, from August 1989 to August 1990, the ARGK was involved in 314 incidents (including raids, skirmish and sabotage). These incidents resulted in the death of nearly 1,500 security personnel, including the village guards.[17] Raiding of towns increased significantly during 1990 and 1991 and included the following towns: Cizre, Şırnak, Çukurca, Nusaybin, Tunceli and Bingöl. Such raids clearly show the significant growth in the PKK's military capacity.[18]

The guerrillas were organised at various levels from small squads to teams comprising a number of squads to larger units equivalent of battalions. In an interview with a Turkish journalist in September 1989, the PKK leader Abdullah Öcalan, without specifying the numbers, argued that the PKK forces in the 'Botan Province' alone equalled the number in a military brigade, roughly 4,000–5,000 guerrillas.[19] Although mainly hit and run tactics were deployed, the Turkish army's numerous large-scale operations against the guerrillas and other forms of 'hot pursuits' during the early 1990s resulted in large-scale skirmishes that lasted a few days or even weeks. Therefore, the early 1990s were exceptional years in terms of the level of violence with attacks becoming much more frequent and widespread. The areas in which the guerrilla attacks were carried out also became widespread. The guerrillas were organised extensively in many areas though the main conflict zones were the border areas primarily comprising the provinces of Hakkari, Şırnak and Siirt (the mountainous areas that Kurds popularly refer to as *Botan*). The PKK's units were organised within regions referred to by their popular Kurdish names. In addition to the *Botan* region or province (*eyalet*), the guerrillas were initially organised in five other provinces: *Serhad* (Kars, Ağrı, parts of Van, Bingöl and Erzurum), *Dersim* (Muş, Tunceli, Elazığ, Sivas and parts of Bingöl, Erzurum and Erzincan), *Mardin* (roughly the Mardin Province), *Diyarbakir–Bingöl–Garzan* province (comprising the Diyarbakir province and parts of Bingöl and Muş) and *Güney-Batı* (the South-West) province (comprising K.Maras, Malatya, Adıyaman, Urfa and G.Antep).[20] During the early 1990s, as the guerrilla war extended, more provinces were created: *Riha* (Urfa province), *Garzan* province was separated from *Diyarbakir*, *Koçgiri* province separated from *Dersim*, *Erzurum* province from *Serhad*, and *Zağros* province was created comprising the areas of Van and Hakkari. During the mid 1990s, PKK activities expanded into a wider area extending towards Southern Turkey to Hatay and Antakya and towards the Black Sea region in North-East Turkey. The Turkish army and the security forces found it very difficult to eliminate the PKK's presence in the region despite its numerous military campaigns and large-scale operations. From 1992 onwards, every year during autumn the army carried out cross-border operations supported by air strikes against the PKK. Of these, the 1992 operation, which I discuss at length in Chapter 7, caused the most losses to the PKK. On 21 March 1995, the Turkish army again attacked the PKK bases in Iraqi Kurdistan with 35,000 soldiers. Additionally, there were numerous smaller operations throughout the 1990s against specific PKK targets.

Overall, the guerrilla war proved very practical and the PKK grew in strength and size in a short space of time. Being the only Kurdish organisation that challenged the state put the PKK in the leading position to hegemonise Kurdish resistance in Turkey. Unlike the other Kurdish political groups – who either ceased to exist or relocated to Europe – the PKK managed to maintain its guerrillas in the region and increased its recruitment throughout the 1980s and early 1990s. Its Turkish socialist rivals, who also drew considerable support especially from the Alevi Kurds, also began to experience major difficulties during the late 1980s once the signs of the difficulties in the Soviet Union became much more apparent. Consequently, the rival oppositional political groups/movements in Turkey that the Kurds supported lost their appeal, which created opportunities for the PKK to mobilise a wider section of Kurdish society. Having a presence in the region presented the PKK with the opportunity to reach out to many Kurdish rural populations and through its political work it managed to win support and cooperation from many villagers. The PKK's popularity also increased because of the state's harsh and heavy-handed approach towards civilian Kurds. The state's antagonistic and oppressive practices allowed the PKK to galvanise public opinion. The animosity that the Kurds felt towards the Kemalist regime was widespread and many popular grievances started to be expressed when the PKK's insurgency began.

On a more general level, the PKK's mass mobilisation of the Kurds was facilitated by the rapid social change that the Kurdish society in Turkey experienced during the period between the 1960s and 1980s, which lessened the influence of the feudal classes and the 'grip' of traditional identities and values. This created the need as well as the opportunity for the construction of a new Kurdish identity with the PKK's national liberation discourse filling the void. Various other factors have also contributed to the development of the PKK. For example, the Iran-Iraq war (1980–1988) and the Gulf crises during 1990 and 1991 played important roles because the loss of state authority in Iraqi Kurdistan allowed the PKK to expand its bases there, train an increased number of its guerrillas and create more opportunities for it to manoeuvre and organise.[21] The Kurdish

108 *War and mass mobilisation*

refugee crises in August 1988 and in 1991, the latter following the failed uprising in Iraqi Kurdistan during which many Iraqi Kurds fled to Turkey, drew ample attention to the Kurds in the media. The initial lack of interest by the Turkish authorities and the major outbreaks of food poisoning amongst the refugees demonstrated the state's discriminatory attitude towards the Kurds.[22] These events made the Kurds more visible in Turkey because most of the refugees went there, and it brought about renewed feelings of pan-Kurdism increasing the understanding and interaction between the Kurds of Iraq and the Kurds of Turkey. To many Kurds in Turkey the refugee crises were poignant symbols of the oppression and persecution that the Kurds faced in the entire Middle East.

Due to the early success the PKK had in mobilising the Kurds, in its Fourth Congress, held in 1990, it hinted at the establishment of a popular government and the creation of 'liberated zones'. The increase in the number of popular uprisings and more avid popular support shown throughout 1990 and 1991 encouraged the PKK to emphasise the need to develop the people's army to take the war to a higher level. Furthermore, in numerous articles that appeared in *Berxwedan* and *Serxwebûn* during 1990 and 1991, the PKK emphasised the importance of the people's army and the guerrillas in leading the masses in a popular uprising that would result in the overthrow of the state's rule. The September 1991 edition of the *Serxwebûn* magazine declared the PKK's intention to establish the '*Botan-Behdinan* War Government'.[23] In Europe elections were held in November 1992 for the Kurdistan National Assembly, which was established to offer representation to all the Kurdish groups from Turkey. During the spring of 1993, the elected delegates met in areas under the control of the PKK guerrillas in Iraqi Kurdistan to engage in meetings and draw up laws for a future Kurdish state. However, the Assembly was not active in the later years and joined the Kurdistan Parliament in Exile upon the latter's foundation in 1994. The sudden success that the PKK enjoyed in the conflict and mobilising of the Kurds meant that the conflict was to both deepen and widen, and that the PKK was to not only wage a 'hit and run' war but engage in the defence of the liberated zones. As Chapter 7 discusses, this created problems for the PKK as its guerrilla army was neither equipped nor trained to fight a regular war.

According to the Human Rights Foundation of Turkey (HRFT) numerous attacks against civilians also took place during the conflict. Whereas it is impossible to ascertain how many of these were carried out by the PKK because the Turkish security forces and counter-guerrilla units were also responsible, attacks against civilian family members of the village guards were usually considered to have been carried out by the PKK. According to the HRFT report for the year 1992, 189 civilians were killed in that year during such attacks by the PKK, 34 of them being children.[24] The corresponding numbers for 1993 were 406 and 107 respectively.[25]

War and mass mobilisation 109

The National Liberation Front: political mobilisation, serhildan and mass protests

In March 1985, ERNK was established to carry out political development and mobilisation of the masses. Even though ERNK members began to infiltrate Turkey from the mid 1980s onwards, its activities remained weak until the late 1980s.[26] The PKK's Third Congress stressed the importance of developing the activities of the National Liberation Front:

> The issue of the [national liberation] front – which is closely connected to the military struggle and influences it as well as being influenced by it – is the other main issue that forms the basis of our party's practice. To the masses it represents not the military but the political orientation and organisation.[27]

From the mid 1980s onwards much more effort was placed on developing ERNK and consequently its activities, as well as the organisational network, grew rapidly throughout the late 1980s and early 1990s:

> On this matter, we have very comprehensive and intensive tasks. These include the tasks of organising the peasantry, the youth, the women's section, the tradesmen, the workers, the people who are abroad, even the old people, the mosques, and developing organisations that take the character-istics of different national and religious denominations as their basis.[28]

ERNK was legally organised through a network of community and cultural centres in Europe. The importance of organising among the Kurdish communit-ies in Europe was emphasised as early as 1982 in the political report submitted by the central committee to the First Conference.[29] Overall, the European activ-ities of the PKK were significant as they allowed it to draw the support of the Kurds in Europe and the funding it collected enabled it to finance and expand its guerrilla activities in Kurdistan. Throughout the 1980s and 1990s the Kurdish population in Europe increased steadily, many of whom made regular donations to the PKK.[30] The absence of legal restrictions placed on Kurdish identity and culture in Europe enabled ERNK to organise legally and establish a network of cultural and community organisations that played a pivotal role in the mobilisa-tion of Kurds in Europe. The PKK's activities in Europe constituted a significant part of its political mobilisation. Throughout the late 1980s and early 1990s, in many cities in Europe, ERNK organised numerous events such as rallies and demonstrations, meetings, protests, hunger strikes, music festivals, cultural activ-ities and festivals, the *Newroz* celebrations and events to commemorate the PKK martyrs, etc. Such events attracted large crowds, built the PKK's support base and helped raise public awareness of the Kurds' struggle. For example, the Kurdistan peace festivals and rallies that began to be held every year from 1993 onwards were attended by large crowds of 50,000–100,000 drawn from various

110   War and mass mobilisation

European countries. Also, such events made valuable contributions to the PKK's stream of income through the sale of tickets, food, books, music CDs and so on.

Within ERNK's organisation in Europe, there were numerous sub-organisations established to represent different segments of Kurdish society. Initially, three main sub-organisations were established in August 1987: the Union of Patriotic Workers of Kurdistan (*Yekîtiya Karkerên Welatparêzên Kurdistan* (YKWK)), the Union of Patriotic Women of Kurdistan (*Yekîtiya Jinên Welatparêzên Kurdistan* (YJWK)), and the Union of Revolutionary Youth of Kurdistan (*Yekîtiya Xortên Şoreşgerên Welatparêzên Kurdistan* (YXK)), which was later renamed as *Yekîtiya Ciwanên Kurd* (the Union of Kurdish Youth).[31] In 1993, more organisations representative of the religious groups were established. These included the *Herekata Îslamiya Kurdistanê* (the Islamic Movement of Kurdistan, HÎK), the Union of Alevis of Kurdistan (*Kürdistan Aleviler Birliği, KAB*) and the Union of Yezidis of Kurdistan (*Yekîtiya Êzîdiyan Kurdistan*), which were established to provide representation to the Muslim, Alevi and Yezidi religious communities respectively. The existence of such representative organisations enabled the PKK to articulate their specific demands within its discourse in a chain of equivalence as part of Kurdish political demands and transcend the religious and tribal divisions and fragmentation, which in turn enabled it to evolve into a mass movement.

Additionally, the PKK's publication house *Weşanên Serxwebûn* was established in Germany and both *Serxwebûn* (1982–present) and *Berxwedan* (1985–1995) were published there and distributed in most European countries. The PKK's presence in Europe enabled it to establish institutions that produced and disseminated its discourse. Also, through its activities in Europe, ERNK established links with socialist and working-class parties as well as human rights organisations that gave the PKK leverage in a diplomatic sense to put pressure on Turkey.[32] As the second part of this chapter discusses, being in Europe offered space and opportunity for cultural development by enabling the Kurds to establish their own institutions that engaged in and fostered cultural revival.

From 1990 onwards, the popular expression of Kurdish identity demands and open support for the PKK became much more commonplace in Turkey as Kurdish political activism evolved into a vocal social movement. This was demonstrated in a number of *serhildan* (popular uprisings) between 1990 and 1993, in which large numbers of ordinary Kurds participated and who often fought with the police and the gendarmeries. Furthermore, numerous mass rallies, shop closures and other forms of protest, such as school boycotts were organised during the *Newroz* and other significant days for the PKK such as 15 August and 27 November, especially in Diyarbakır, Batman, Şırnak and Siirt. Additionally, many people attended the funerals of the PKK guerrillas, which became a political act in itself. In the early 1990s, Kurds in Turkey became much more visible and actively voiced their demands for the recognition of their identity.

The first instance of *serhildan* occurred in the town of Nusaybin on 15 March 1990 after the funeral of *Kamuran Dündar*, an ARGK guerrilla who was killed in a skirmish near Nusaybin. On the day of the funeral, students boycotted

War and mass mobilisation   111

schools and the shops remained closed all day. After the burial the people marched towards the centre of the town shouting slogans. However, the march was forcefully stopped by the security forces, who opened fire on the people, wounded 20 and arrested 500.[33] Following this incident, the PKK asked the people to participate in large numbers to show their support during the 'Week of National Heroism'. This was the week between 21 and 28 March and was declared during the PKK's Third Congress to commemorate the death of two of its leading members: Mazlum Doğan on 21 March and Mahsun Korkmaz, who was a commander of the HRK (*Hêzên Rizgariya Kurdistan*, Kurdistan's Liberation Forces) and died in combat on 28 March.[34] This call for protest coincided with the *Newroz* celebrations; many people took part in the protests. Furthermore, the PKK's Second National Conference held in May 1990 took the decision to organise resistance at the national level.[35]

Another case of s*erhildan* took place in Diyarbakir on 10 July 1991 during the funeral procession of Vedat Aydın, who was a prominent human rights activist, chairman of the Diyarbakir Branch of the HEP and was murdered on 5 July 1991 in an extrajudicial killing. The coffin was covered with an ERNK flag and pro-Kurdish speeches condemning the murder and similar violent practices against civilians were made during the funeral. Prior to the murder of Vedat Aydın, there were numerous acts of violence committed against Kurdish civilians, such as executions of civilians and bombing of cars of pro-Kurdish activists, the offices of the Human Rights Association in Diyarbakir and the pro-PKK magazine *Özgür Halk*. The funeral attracted a large crowd and throughout the procession the crowd shouted pro-PKK slogans (such as '*Biji Kurdistan*' (long live Kurdistan), '*Biji PKK*' (long live PKK), '*Kürdistan Faşisme Mezar olacak*' (Kurdistan will be the graveyard of fascism), '*Gerilla Vuruyor Kürdistanı Kuruyor*' (the guerrillas are fighting to establish Kurdistan)).[36] In response, the security forces opened fire randomly at the people attending the ceremony, the result of which was seven people killed.[37]

Similar protests that attracted large crowds continued to take place in the region. The 1992 *Newroz* celebrations across the Kurdish region was another occasion on which Kurds demanded recognition of their identity. The celebrations also resulted in clashes between the security forces and the protestors with a large number of civilian casualties. In Cizre the police opened fire on the people attending the *Newroz* celebrations, which resulted in the death of 24 people and wounding of 60.[38] Similarly, in Şırnak, the protest turned violent with 38 people dead and 120 wounded.[39] From 1993 onwards mass *Newroz* celebrations became much more common and took place in many towns and cities across the majority Kurdish regions in Turkey. Occasionally, the *Newroz* celebrations witnessed violent clashes between the Kurds and the security forces. However, the atrocities of the 1992 *Newroz* were not repeated. The *Newroz* celebrations became events where the people openly showed their support of the PKK and the Kurdish struggle.

112 *War and mass mobilisation*

The sedimentation of the PKK's discourse during the 1980s and 1990s

The favourable conditions that presented the PKK with various opportunities to mobilise the Kurds and establish institutions in Europe that produced and disseminated the PKK's discourse to the wider Kurdish community were an important factor in the PKK's growth and sedimentation of its discourse. The existence of numerous political and cultural organisations in Europe meant that the PKK was able to connect with many Kurdish people there. A significant development that the PKK fostered was the Kurdish cultural renewal and revival, which, as briefly discussed above, initially took place in Europe. However, following the easing of the use of the Kurdish language in public in 1991, Kurdish cultural activities started to take place in Turkey as well. Having a base in Europe created opportunities for the PKK to establish institutions that were able to promote Kurdish cultural development and renewal. Primarily music and folk dancing constituted the basis of the PKK's cultural renewal, which meant that the new Kurdish popular culture was easily accessible to many people. Moreover, another significance of music was that it served as a medium through which the PKK's struggle was represented. In fact, music constituted an important medium for the construction, dissemination and narration of the PKK's contemporary myth of resistance that played a key role in the sedimentation of the PKK's national liberation discourse in practice and its embodiment as the Kurds' national struggle. Additionally, the contemporary myth of resistance was disseminated through a myriad of commemoration practices, which also strengthened the PKK's appeal and sedimented its discourse. In addition to the cultural and community organisations that were established by the PKK, there were various other Kurdish organisations and independent artists/musicians in Turkey as well as Europe whose work made a significant contribution to Kurdish linguistic and cultural development and renewal.

Kurdish cultural politics

Initially, the PKK's cultural activities were comprised of the music group *Koma Berxwedan* (The Resistance Group), which was formed in 1981 in Germany to communicate the struggle through music to the Kurds in Europe. Furthermore, the members of the group took a leading role in the establishment, also in Germany, of the PKK's cultural organisation *Hunerkom* (Association of Artists) in 1983 that had the aim of promoting Kurdish cultural development and revival. Initially *Hunerkom*'s activities were carried out within cultural and community centres in Germany, France and the Netherlands. Following the quantitative increase in activities and the increase in the Kurdish communities in other European countries, the cultural activities spread as well as becoming more professional. In 1994, the *Hunerkom* took the name 'Kurdish Academy of Culture and Arts' (*Kürt Kültür ve Sanat Akademisi*). Music constituted a significant aspect of Kurdish cultural renewal and development and was an important medium

War and mass mobilisation 113

through which to communicate the PKK's struggle as the songs the newly-formed groups sang narrated the resistance practices that the PKK engaged in starting in the early 1980s onwards. In fact, *Koma Berxwedan* established itself as the main vehicle for conveying the resistance music and it became a permanent feature of Kurdish struggle. Although primarily it organised performances and musical activities in Europe, its cassettes and CDs managed to secretly reach Kurds in Turkey.

In 1991, after the easing of restrictions on the use of the Kurdish language in public, another significant Kurdish cultural centre, the *Navenda Çanda Mezopatamya* (Mesopotamian Cultural Centre, MKM) was established in Istanbul with the similar aim of promoting Kurdish cultural development and renewal. Within the MKM and its associated branches that were established during the 1990s in other major cities in Turkey, the following music groups were established: *Koma Çiya, Koma Azad, Koma Mizgîn, Koma Asman, Koma Amed, Agirê Jiyan, Koma Rewşen, Koma Şirvan* and *Koma Rojhilat*.[40] The songs and music of these groups featured similar themes of resistance to those used in the music of *Koma Berxwedan*. In addition to these groups there were numerous independent musicians such as Şivan Perwer, Ciwan Haco, Nizammettin Arıç, Hozan Dilgeş, Aram Tigran, etc. who also produced Kurdish resistance, popular and folk music.

Another important aspect of the PKK's cultural activities in Europe that the *Hunerkom* organised was the popularisation of Kurdish folk dancing. Almost every Kurdish cultural centre in Europe organised numerous classes for folk dancing, making it a significant activity that many ordinary Kurdish people took part in. From 1987 onwards, *Hunerkom* began to organise *Mîhrîcan* as an annual Kurdish cultural festival, which featured performances and contests that various folk dancing groups representing numerous areas in Kurdistan took part in. These festivals were important in increasing the interaction between the Kurds from various areas and promoting cultural integration and understanding. Similarly, musical performances were given in numerous cultural and musical events that ERNK organised in various cities in Europe, which offered an environment for the Kurds to consume their culture in.

The development of a popular Kurdish culture was fostered and accompanied by the revival of the Kurdish language. In this process the Paris based *Institute Kurde* – established in 1983 independently of the PKK to promote the study and research into Kurdish language and history – played a significant role. A similar language institute, *Enstîtuya Kurdî*, which was established in Istanbul in 1992, also played an important role by carrying out research and undertaking academic studies into Kurdish history and language.[41] In particular, the study of Kurdish culture and history became more widespread, research into the standardisation of the Kurmanci Kurdish language was carried out and numerous Kurdish written texts were produced. The Kurdish Kurmanci language as used by the Kurds from Turkey has been written in the Latin alphabet since the late 1920s. The alphabet and the written standard were developed by the Kurdish intellectual Mir Celaded Bedirxan, who published the periodical Hawar in Damascus and Beirut between

114   War and mass mobilisation

1932 and 1943. Bedirxan also wrote a grammar book and Kurdish–French dictionary amongst numerous other literary works.[42] In addition, Kurdish language teaching was offered in the above-mentioned institutes and in community centres in many cities in Europe, which contributed to a general rise in Kurdish national consciousness. Furthermore, the translations of Kurdish classical literature during the 1960s and more during the 1970s and 1980s also increased knowledge about the Kurdish culture. This was followed by the emergence of a new generation of Kurdish writers such as Cegerxwîn (a pseudonym meaning 'the bleeding heart' used by the socialist poet Sheikmous Hasan, who died in Sweden in 1984), fiction writer Mehmet Uzun (died in 2007) and the famous Kurdish film director Yılmaz Güney (died in 1985). The availability of novels and poetry in the Kurdish language increased its use and helped its reinvigoration. The social realist cinema of Yılmaz Güney on the other hand brought Kurdish society into existence in the realm of cinema.[43]

Additionally, the existence of a pro-Kurdish media network made the dissemination of the national liberation discourse and the PKK's struggle to the wider Kurdish populations possible. Through its official publications, *Serxwebûn* and *Berxwedan*, and the publication of numerous books and other magazines, the PKK was able to connect with many Kurds, disseminate its discourse and also provide its version of events concerning the conflict. From June 1992 onwards, a pro-Kurdish daily newspaper, *Özgür Gündem* (Free Agenda) began to be published in Turkey and provided extensive coverage of the conflict, including interviews with Öcalan and statements from the pro-Kurdish parties. This newspaper challenged the official account of the conflict presented in the mainstream Turkish media. The pro-Kurdish media network in Turkey included a monthly political magazine (*Özgür Halk*) from 1990, a Kurdish language weekly newspaper *Azadiya Welat* (The Freedom of Homeland) from February 1994 and a satellite TV station, Med TV, broadcast from Europe to the Middle East, North Africa and Europe from March 1994. The media network and the TV station made significant contributions to fostering greater understanding of the Kurdish issues and increased integration and interaction among the Kurds.

The establishment of a Kurdish language satellite TV station in Europe was the most significant development and the main outlet for the representation of Kurdish culture and national life. In 1995 the Med TV increased its broadcast from six to 18 hours. Its TV studios were located in Belgium but initially the licence was taken from the British Independent Television Commission (ITC). However, Med TV's licence was withdrawn in 1999 and from July 1999 to February 2004 Medya TV broadcast in the Kurdish language. Currently ROJ TV is the main Kurdish language channel that broadcasts under a licence from Denmark; it was established in March 2004. In total, ROJ TV broadcasts to 78 countries in the Middle East, North Africa, Europe and the former republics of the Soviet Union. In addition to the above, there are other Kurdish language TV channels from Iraqi Kurdistan. The most important contribution that Kurdish satellite TV channels have been making is that they have popularised the use of the Kurdish language. *Kurmanci* Kurdish is the main language of broadcast and it is used in almost 70 per cent (69.66 per cent) of the programmes. Additionally, other Kurdish languages such as Zazaki (2.1 per cent), Sorani (8.95 per cent), Hawremani (1.91 per cent) as well as languages spoken by Kurds or in Kurdistan such as Assyrian (0.48 per cent), Arabic (2.86 per cent), Turkish (13.81 per cent) and Persian (0.23 per cent) are used in broadcasting.[44] By broadcasting programmes and documentaries on Kurdish culture, history and geography, Kurdish language TV programmes have become a valuable source of information on Kurdish culture. Overall, the content of the broadcast displays images of Kurdistan, its nature and mountains and the map of Kurdistan and it includes numerous informative programmes, such as *Welate me Kurdistan* (Our Country Kurdistan) and documentaries on the regions, cities and towns of Kurdistan that give information about Kurdish history and geography. Kurdish language TV broadcasts many informative programmes about Kurdish religious communities, such as documentary programmes about Alevi and Yezidi beliefs as well as programmes about their religious festivals. Also, political programmes, live coverage of events such as the main Kurdish festivals and *Newroz* have been regular features of the broadcasts.[45]

Turkey has protested to the countries that granted the licences to the Kurdish TV stations on the basis that there is a link between the PKK and these TV channels. As discussed above, on many occasions the Kurdish TV stations were shut down. This however, has not managed to completely close them down as new Kurdish TV channels were established to replace the closed ones. Having a powerful mass communication outlet such as a TV station has presented the Kurdish national movement with an important opportunity to transmit programmes about Kurdish culture and popularise the use of Kurdish language, which strengthens among the Kurds a sense of belonging to a Kurdish community. By displaying various national symbols, such as the map and flag of Kurdistan and reciting the Kurdish national anthem, Kurdish television stations are able to construct and represent a sense of national unity among the Kurds, which is significant in stabilising the meaning of Kurdishness.

The 'heroes' of Kurdistan: construction of exemplarity and the PKK's contemporary myth of resistance

In Chapter 4, the construction of *Newroz* as a myth of origin in the discourses of the Kurdish socialist groups to differentiate and specify Kurdish identity and national history was discussed. This myth traced the Kurds' origins back to the Medes and constructed an ethnicist conception of Kurdish identity. In Chapter 5, the deployment of the myth in the PKK's discourse, especially the construction of the Median Empire as the 'golden age' of the Kurdish nation, was discussed. This was significant not only for conceiving of the unity and homogeneity of the Kurdish nation but also for the cultivation of the 'fantasy' of Kurdish unity. The myth of *Newroz* as a symbol of the triumph of the struggle of the Medes was used to construct a benchmark, as something that needed to be recreated and emulated by the contemporary Kurdish national movement. In the later years,

116 *War and mass mobilisation*

during the 1980s and 1990s, the PKK reactivated the myth of *Newroz* to construct a contemporary myth of resistance based on the PKK's resistance in the Diyarbakir Prison during the early 1980s. The *Newroz* festival became the most significant day in Kurdish political activism in Turkey and during the 1990s large crowds were attracted to celebrate and protest on 21 March. Such public celebrations and mass protest enhanced *Newroz* as the day of national resistance with many individual acts of resistance and self-sacrifice taking place then, allowing the PKK to describe and represent such acts as part of Kurdistan's long struggle for freedom. Moreover, such a reference situated the PKK's struggle in a longer timeline and allowed it to represent it as the embodiment of the Kurds' national struggle. As the PKK's struggle progressed, its guerrilla war ('of liberation and national revival') and struggle in general, and the *serhildan* became constituent parts of its contemporary myth of resistance.

The resistance in the Diyarbakir Prison has been a mainstay in the PKK's discourse and as stated earlier, the key events started with the suicide of Mazlum Doğan on 21 March 1982 to protest ongoing torture and oppression. The resistance continued with the self-immolations of four other members on 18 May 1982 and culminated in the death fast that started on 14 July 1982 and resulted in the death of four more leading members in September 1982. Initially, the main emphasis in the PKK's representation of the events was on torture and oppression of political prisoners and Doğan's death was described in *Serxwebûn* as part of a concerted effort by the Kemalist regime to annihilate all Kurdish political prisoners.[46] However, the statement commemorating the first anniversary of his death, distributed on 21 March 1983, described him as the 'Contemporary Kawa' and his suicide as an act of resistance.[47] In subsequent articles published to commemorate the resistance, the significance of the actions of the leading members became the focal point and their resistance was described as a 'conscious political action':

> Since entering the conscious stage of their life, they have taken part at a leadership level in our people's national and social liberation struggle. The prison resistance was conscious political action by people who, if needed, were prepared to consciously sacrifice their life for the sake of developing our struggle. Their actions have created the true measures of our people's national and social liberation struggle under the leadership of the proletariat, and have become *the spirit of our struggle*. It is its steering and sheltering force and it has left an ineradicable effect that will pull our people into continuous action and organise them.[48]

The historical importance and significance of the resistance in Diyarbakir Prison for the Kurds' struggle and their survival as a nation was also emphasised and the resistance was defined as the beginning of a new era:

> To attain an honourable status, human decency, stand on our feet and say a few words or a few sentences in that period of history, we needed to resist.

On behalf of a nation and for a section of humanity they said the most significant few words. However, these were such words that if not spoken then our party and our nation would have perished. It would have not made much sense to talk about the other values.[49]

The significance of the resistance lay in the fact that the PKK inmates did not accept the authority of the state despite continuous unimaginable torture and attempts at subjugation. Their resistance to oppression, the defence of the Kurdish struggle under even the harshest conditions, and sacrificing their own lives to defeat the submission imposed on the Kurds has been interpreted by the PKK as the 'spirit of its struggle'.[50] With the start of the guerrilla war on 15 August 1984 resistance took a new dimension with the 'national liberation war' becoming the centre of the contemporary myth of resistance. The start of the guerrilla war was described as the 'leap of 15 August' (*15 Ağustos Atılımı*) and the PKK's activities from 1984 onwards provided ample material to build on the myth of resistance. With the start of the guerrilla war, resistance was something that took place in practice on a daily basis.[51] The guerrillas who lost their lives in the war were described as 'heroes and martyrs of national resistance' and extensive obituaries were published in the PKK's magazines detailing their bravery and heroism.[52]

In addition to guerrilla war that elevated resistance practices to a new level, acts of self-immolation were repeated in the early 1990s and were represented as examples of 'exceptional acts of resistance'. This started with Zekiye Alkan – who was a medical student at the Dicle University in Diyarbakir – setting herself alight on the city walls on 21 March 1990. Similarly Rahşan Demirel set herself alight in Izmir in 1992 and 'Berivan' and 'Ronahi', pseudonyms used by Nilgün Yıldırım and Bedriye Taş respectively, repeated the same practice in Germany in 1994.[53] These self-immolations were described as sacred acts of resistance and sacrifice for the sake of the nation's freedom, with *Newroz* being the day on which these acts of sacrifice and heroism occurred. The crucial difference was that, however, in the early 1990s women were the main performers of the self-immolations and 'heroic' acts of 'sacrifice'. Additionally, the 'heroic acts' and 'sacrifices' by women guerrillas also started to acquire a central stage in the representation of the PKK's contemporary myth of resistance. Of these, the death of Gülnaz Karataş (Beritan) on 25 October 1992 – who, upon realising that it was impossible to escape the attack by the KDP peshmergas during the PKK's war with the Iraqi Kurds, threw herself off a mountain cliff to avoid being taken hostage – received sustained emphasis.[54] Beritan's action was represented as an act of utmost heroism and dedication to the struggle and was used extensively by the PKK as the embodiment of its spirit of resistance. Similarly, Zeynep Kınacı (Zilan), who carried out the first suicide attack against Turkish troops in Tunceli, has also been represented as the embodiment of the PKK's spirit of resistance.

The representation of resistance practices in the PKK's discourse constitutes its members who carried out the numerous acts of resistance as 'exemplars'. Drawing on Conant's discussion of exemplars in the work of Nietzsche, Norval

118   War and mass mobilisation

argues that 'the role of the exemplar is to "unsettle us"'[55] and create an impersonal feeling of shame. The issue of shame is discussed in detail by Norval (2007) and its significance lies in its ability to provoke 'a distance from (former) self, and the need to work towards a further self'.[56] The importance of exemplars for politics is that their presence 'acts as a *call*, as a reminder of another self, and another state of things, capturing ... the possibility of another self, another way of doing things'.[57] During the commemoration events of the practices of resistance and in the statements published on their anniversary, these individual acts of resistance and sacrifice are described as the catalyst of a prolonged period of active resistance. For example, the suicide of Mazlum Doğan is described as the event that activated the resistance in the Diyarbakir Prison and the PKK's guerrilla war. Similarly, the self-immolation by Zekiye Alkan is described by the PKK as the catalyst of a prolonged period of active resistance and s*erhildan* in the urban centres of the region in which many ordinary Kurds took part.[58] Although it is highly unlikely that a strong causal connection, as emphasised in the PKK's discourse, was present, the importance of such a claim is that the individuals and their resistance practices are constructed as 'exemplary' of the PKK's resistance and their actions are used to motivate others to take part in resistance.

Above all, the constitution of the exemplars in the PKK's discourse and the commemoration practices associated with their 'heroic resistance' had the aim of motivating ordinary Kurds to perform such acts of heroism and self-sacrifice for the movement and the Kurdish struggle. The resistance of the leading members has been discussed widely in numerous articles published in the *Serxwebûn* and *Berxwedan* throughout the 1980s and 1990s, as well as during meetings and public gatherings that took place on the anniversary of these events to commemorate their resistance. The story of their resistance was narrated and disseminated widely in countless commemoration events and practices held for the leading members of the PKK's resistance and the earliest martyrs of its struggle. It is a standard practice to display pictures of the leading figures as well as the early martyrs of the PKK – especially Mazlum Doğan and others who died in the Resistance in Diyarbakir Prison, and Mahsun Korkmaz, who was the first commander of the PKK's military forces and died in March 1986 – in the Kurdish community centres across Europe. Extensive obituaries of the PKK's early martyrs as well as of other guerrillas frequently appear in the PKK's publications. Remembrance ceremonies were organised in the Kurdish community centres run by ERNK. Commemoration practices, especially the obituaries and life stories of the guerrillas in *Serxwebûn* and *Berxwedan* magazines romanticised guerrilla life. As mentioned earlier, in Turkey during the 1990s the burial ceremonies of PKK guerrillas were events that were popularly attended.

The representation of resistance was not confined to only political discourse but other artistic forms, such as music and poetry, were used to convey the significance of resistance in Diyarbakir Prison. The artistic reconstructions of the acts of resistance appeared in numerous posters. A poem entitled '*Ben İnsandım*' (I was a Human Being) by a high ranking PKK member, Ali Haydar Kaytan,

War and mass mobilisation   119

narrates the life and struggle of Haki Karer, who was killed on 18 May 1977 and is seen as the PKK's first martyr.[59] Moreover, as mentioned above, the stories of resistance practices were narrated in the music of *Koma Berxwedan* from the early 1980s onwards, and in the other groups later on during the 1990s. In fact, the contemporary myth of resistance constituted the centre of Kurdish cultural revival as the PKK's resistance was the main theme that the resistance music by *Koma Berxwedan* and many other groups and musicians narrated. In the early years the resistance was depicted as a celebration or *Dilan* in many popular songs.[60]

Songs commemorating specific events such as the PKK's establishment on 27 November 1978, the start of its war on 15 August, the resistance in Diyarbakir Prison, the PKK's attacks on landlords in Hilvan, songs that 'glorify' the guerrilla war, songs about the *serhildan* in Diyarbakir in 1991 and *Newroz*, and songs that commemorated the resistance and sacrifices of the PKK's countless 'heroes' and 'heroines' all featured frequently in the resistance music. For example, a popular song by Hozan Dilgeş, *Li Mêrdine Li Bagoke*, narrates the story of a battle that took place between the ARGK and the Turkish army at the Bagok Mountain near the town of Nusaybin in Mardin Province on 1 April 1988. During the attack a small group of the PKK guerrillas, mainly new recruits, were encircled by a numerically far superior group of Turkish soldiers and village guards. Despite the numerical and technical disadvantages and the encirclement, the guerrillas decided to fight against the Turkish soldiers.[61] This was one of the most extensive attacks against the PKK that the army conducted, and despite the heavy losses that the PKK suffered it is considered as one of its epic battles. In a similar manner to the discussion of the heroic acts carried out by the PKK's early members in the prison, the song emphasises the heroism and self-sacrifice of the guerrillas that fought and died in the battle.

In addition, international socialist songs and anthems were sung in the Kurdish language, such as the *Internationale,* broadening the repertoire of Kurdish resistance music. Music played a significant role in the sedimentation of the PKK's national liberation discourse in practice by narrating the story of the PKK's struggle and resistance through a medium that was accessible to many people. The cultural representation of the struggle, through music, enabled the PKK to reach out to wider Kurdish communities. The resistance music used and recreated popular folk melodies that many Kurdish people were familiar with and that were used in folk dancing, which added a performative aspect to the commemoration practices.

As mentioned above, during the early 1990s women started to be the performers of resistance acts and acquire a central stage in the PKK's contemporary myth of resistance. From the 1980s onwards, with the gradual increase in the activities of the Kurdish national movement, more and more Kurdish women started to engage in politics. Particularly, women participated in large numbers in numerous *serhildan* and took an active role in the activities of the legal Kurdish political parties as well as in the PKK.[62] Hence, it is unsurprising that women came to the forefront of the resistance from the early 1990s onwards and

120   *War and mass mobilisation*

increasingly began to be constituted as 'exemplars'. In fact, one of the most significant developments that the PKK initiated, especially in the early 1990s, was the mobilisation of women as a new political actor and this had a significant impact on the PKK's overall mobilisation. Not only did the mobilisation of women significantly increase the PKK's overall support base and fighting force, the presence of a significant number of women guerrillas within the ARGK ranks lessened the appeal and force of traditional values, such as male domination in society, and brought about an 'aspect change' that enabled the sedimentation of the PKK's discourse in practice by helping to engrave the ideas of equality and freedom in society, both of which were elements articulated in the PKK's discourse.[63]

Çağlayan (2007) highlights the discursive strategies that the PKK deployed in mobilising women and challenging the prevailing notion of women's position within Kurdish society. During the 1980s, the PKK's discourse untangled the dominant interpretation of 'honour' as the protection of women's chastity and the purity of her body by articulating it more broadly as the defence of Kurdistan's land.[64] By attempting to free men from the burden of defending their 'honour', this rearticulation of 'honour' had the mobilisation of men as its prime objective. However, from the early 1990s onwards there was a major shift in the PKK's discourse as it started to construct a new women's identity, which increasingly identified women with acts of *heroic* resistance and sacrifice for the nation.[65] The conclusions that Çağlayan draws from interviews she conducted with numerous Kurdish activist women reflect the view that meeting the PKK's women guerrillas or seeing their images in PKK publications created a feeling of empowerment, which in turn created, in some cases, a strong desire to join the PKK's ranks.[66] The novelty of the experience of seeing a woman guerrilla, in many cases, would have likely caused an initial feeling of unsettlement. Discussing her initial experience of meeting the PKK's women guerrillas and the appeal it created for the movement, Medya Beytüşşebap – a PKK woman guerrilla – states:

> The first woman guerrilla I saw among them was comrade Dicle Kobani. After seeing these friends and despite being young I fell in love with the PKK. I was so confused; I told myself I needed to go, to join the party. The PKK was pulling me like a magnet. After seeing the women comrades, life became unbearable for me; my life at home started to become meaningless.[67]

Another significance of women's participation and presence in the guerrilla ranks and the active role that they played in resistance, including being the performers of 'heroic acts' of resistance, was that it created 'shame' among men and prompted them into taking action. In relation to the experience of Aysel Çürükkaya in the PKK, Aliza Marcus states: 'Men on the other hand were shamed into action when they realized that women were fighting.'[68] The existence of other high-profile Kurdish women politicians, such as Leyla Zana, and the active role they played in the struggle created the experience of shame in men prompting them to act because in a traditional and male dominated society such activities were seen as the duties of men.

The PKK's contemporary myth of resistance was used extensively in the mobilisation process, and the images of the PKK's early martyrs and the pictures of its women fighters were widely used in PKK publications. Overall, the importance of the new myth of resistance for the PKK's mobilisation of the Kurds was that it added *force* to the PKK's discourse and enhanced its widespread credibility among the Kurds. The guerrilla war and the popular resistance that the PKK organised recreated the myth of resistance in practice, which created the possibility of the fulfilment of the 'fantasy' of Kurdish unity. The guerrilla war was significant as it meant that resistance was something that occurred on a daily basis; it convinced many that the PKK was capable of achieving Kurdish independence, and in so doing it added *force* to the PKK's discourse. This enabled the PKK to represent its struggle as part of the Kurds' long struggle for freedom and this helped the sedimentation of the national liberation discourse. By representing and interpreting its activities in light of the contemporary resistance myth, the PKK was able to define its struggle as the embodiment of the Kurds' struggle for freedom.

To complement the military and security operations that the army carried out to contain the PKK's insurgency, which is discussed more fully in Chapter 7, the state discourse contested the PKK's representation of its struggle as the embodiment of the Kurds' national struggle by representing it as 'terrorism' and as only a 'security threat'. In fact, this representation was used extensively in the state discourse and the mainstream media to cultivate Turkish nationalist fantasmatic logics. Additionally, in order to weaken the fantasmatic logics of the PKK's discourse from the early 1990s onwards, the state contested the *Newroz* myth by attempting to construct it as *essentially* a Turkish festival.[69] In contrast to the popular spelling by the Kurdish nationalists, state documents and officials referred to it as *Nevruz* and began to officially celebrate it from 1991 onwards as a spring festival. The official celebrations were used as occasions to Turkify '*Newroz*' and depoliticise its Kurdish context. As Yanik describes, one aim of this move was to thwart the growing western pressure on Turkey to lift the bans on Kurdish culture. The official celebration of *Nevruz* was cited as evidence that the barriers to Kurdish culture in Turkey, as its western allies and numerous human rights organisations often mentioned, did not exist. Also, the celebrations were used to strengthen Turkey's ties with the Turkic world and the central Asian republics where *Newroz* was recognised as a public holiday. However, the primary aim of the recognition and contestation of the *Newroz* myth was to weaken the appeal of the PKK's resistance myth. In addition, during the early 1990s the state continuously emphasised *Newroz* as a symbol of unity and peace in order to create some kind of harmony between the Kurds and Turks and reduce the polarisation caused by the conflict. Subsequently – as discussed in Chapter 7 – during the 2000s, the *Newroz* celebrations organised by the pro-Kurdish political parties also sought to rebrand *Newroz* as a peace festival.

122 *War and mass mobilisation*

Hence, there is a shift from the use of *Newroz* to achieve closure of identity by emphasising Kurdish difference and distinction, to openness to the other cultures, and as a common symbol to achieve peace and harmony.

Conclusion

The period studied in this chapter witnessed significant changes and transformations. Above all, the PKK's political and military activities throughout the 1980s and the early 1990s led to the mobilisation of a large number of Kurds in Turkey as well as in Europe. The continuation and increase of political violence during the late 1980s and early 1990s caused a corresponding increase in Kurdish political mobilisation. From the early 1990s onwards it started to acquire the characteristics of a mass mobilisation with popularly attended demonstrations, protests and uprisings frequently taking place. The account of mobilisation that is provided in the first section drew out the main aspects of the mass mobilisation of the Kurds and highlighted the organisational growth of the PKK during the late 1980s and early 1990s. Specifically, the important role that the PKK's forceful practices played in the mass mobilisation of the Kurds was emphasised, such as the compulsory conscription law that it introduced to recruit the youth into its fighting forces, which significantly increased recruitment to its military forces.

The PKK established a well-organised network of community organisations and cultural centres in Europe. The Kurds in Europe played an important role by providing financial support to the PKK and establishing the information and organisational network that established links with socialist and human rights groups and harnessed diplomatic support. Additionally, the existence in Europe of institutions that played a key role in Kurdish cultural renewal meant that the restrictions that applied in Turkey were no longer able to suppress Kurdish cultural production and dissemination and presented the PKK with the opportunity to project Kurdish culture publicly. Kurdish cultural revival constituted a significant aspect of the PKK's mobilisation. Kurdish culture was revived and made available to many people in a variety of contexts making it part of people's daily life. The fact that music and folk dancing constituted the key components of Kurdish cultural renewal meant that Kurdish culture became accessible to a wide section of Kurdish society again, and the Kurds could easily access and relate to it. Severe oppression of Kurdish culture had left many Kurds 'alien' to their own culture, and music and folk dancing remained the most viable form of Kurdish cultural consumption in Turkey. Through mass communication the alternative Kurdish identity was represented. Images and symbols of Kurdistan, such as maps and flags created a sense of a unified homeland for the Kurds and helped the Kurds feel part of the Kurdish 'imagined community'.[70] The Kurds utilised technological advances and developments in communication to disseminate their culture and language.

The PKK reactivated *Newroz* as a myth of Kurdish national resistance to construct a contemporary myth of resistance. This was deployed in its discourse to enhance its appeal and add force to its discourse. The significance of the contemporary myth of resistance was that it constituted the performers of resistance practices as exemplars. Initially, the myth was constructed around the performers of the PKK's early resistance practices in the Diyarbakir Prison. Later on, exemplars were broadened and included women. Many of the heroic acts of resistance were committed on 21 March – the *Newroz* festival – and, during the early 1990s, the organising of mass gatherings during the *Newroz* festivals and other important days in the Kurdish political calendar in many Kurdish cities and towns, especially in Diyarbakir, created *Newroz* as the symbol of Kurdish popular resistance. The significance of the construction of *Newroz* as a contemporary myth of resistance lay in the fact that it enabled the sedimentation of the PKK's discourse by constructing it as representative of the Kurdish struggle in Turkey. Additionally, the mobilisation of women by the PKK and its effect on the sedimentation of the PKK's discourse was discussed. It was argued that women's mobilisation helped to embed the notions of 'freedom' and 'equality' in practice and brought about an aspect change, which in turn reduced the grip of traditional identities and religion and brought the liberation and Kurdish struggle for freedom to the foreground.

7 Dislocations and the PKK's turn to democracy (1992–present)

Introduction

As discussed in the previous chapter, the guerrilla insurgency intensified throughout the late 1980s and early 1990s. However, from 1992 onwards, the PKK started to face significant military difficulties and was unable to take the insurgency to the next stage, which was a national popular uprising. Consequently, it started to concede that the revolutionary overthrow of the Turkish rule through a popular uprising and the construction of a 'united', 'socialist' and 'independent' Kurdistan were no longer achievable and realistic. In subsequent years throughout the 1990s, as part of its attempts to formulate a political solution to the conflict, the PKK began appropriating democratic discourse. The clearest indications of change were given when it declared a unilateral ceasefire in March 1993 in an attempt to find a lasting political solution to the conflict. In 1995 and 1998 it declared two more unilateral ceasefires. Such proposals for reconciliation evolved into, from 1999 onwards, a strategic transformation, and the PKK started to construct a comprehensive democratic discourse, which significantly altered the movement's long-term objectives and its political demands for the Kurds. This transformation coincided with the arrest and subsequent imprisonment of Öcalan in February 1999. As a sign of its commitment to democracy and preference for peaceful means, the PKK declared a permanent ceasefire in August 1999 and started to pull its guerrilla forces from inside Turkey back to PKK bases in Iraqi Kurdistan. Such moves were later followed by the formal abolishment of the PKK and the establishment of *Kongreya Azadî û Demokrasiya Kurdistanê* (Kurdistan Freedom and Democracy Congress, KADEK) in April 2002, and *Kongra Gelê Kurdistan* (People's Congress of Kurdistan, *Kongra-Gel*) in November 2003, which represents major ruptures with the past. In providing an account of the PKK's discursive transformation, this chapter enquires into the conditions that brought it about as well as the events that shaped its course. Therefore, the first section principally raises the following questions: Why did the PKK find it necessary to change? How and why did the discourse of democracy replace the previous national liberation discourse? In the second section the following questions are explored: What does the transformation to a democratic movement do to Kurdish identity demands

The PKK's turn to democracy (1992–present)   125

and their representation? And, how does such a transformation change and alter the political project that the PKK seeks to develop?

As discussed earlier, discourse theory emphasises the role of 'dislocations' in bringing about the conditions that give rise to the emergence and development of new political practices. Of dislocations, Laclau states 'If on the one hand they threaten identities, on the other, they are the foundation on which new identities are constituted.'[1] They do this by revealing the contingency of the existing social order.[2] So far, in Chapters 3 and 4, the effects that various dislocations had on bringing about the emergence and development of the Kurdish national movement during the 1960s and 1970s were discussed. This chapter attempts to explain the PKK's above-discussed discursive transformation and the construction of its democratic discourse by examining the principal dislocations that the PKK experienced during the early 1990s. These include the collapse of the Soviet Union and the communist block in the late 1980s, the military losses the PKK started to experience in the early 1990s, and the alarming rise in Turkish nationalism, which created the possibility of a civil war in Turkey. The combined effect of these dislocations weakened the PKK's position and caused a loss of legitimacy of its discourse leading to an ideological impasse limiting its ability to hegemonise and redefine Kurdish identity in Turkey. Specifically, the dislocations meant that the national liberation discourse no longer corresponded to the realities of the age and did not resonate with the demands of the Kurds. The PKK was no longer able to maintain the fantasy of Kurdish unity that it had successfully cultivated throughout the late 1980s and early 1990s, which added *force* to its discourse. Consequently, during the early 1990s the PKK started to introduce numerous new elements into its discourse to contain these dislocations. Subsequently, it began formulating proposals to find a peaceful solution through ceasefires and strategic transformation.

The account provided of the PKK's discursive transformation analyses the *availability* and *suitability* of different discourses that could have filled the gap left by the fragmentation of the national liberation discourse. It highlights various political and international developments that facilitated the appropriation of the democratic discourse and discusses the sociological and political factors that made it more suitable for articulating Kurdish rights and demands in Turkey. The PKK's democratic discourse introduces a new set of equivalential logics that emphasises coexistence and political reconciliation and, therefore, brings about major modifications to the antagonism between the Kurds and Turkey. The term 'political reconciliation' refers to a process that will 'transform a relation of enmity into one of civic friendship'.[3] The PKK's peace proposals and its democratic discourse, more fully, emphasise the need for dialogue and negotiations between the warring parties to end the conflict and solve the political problems that gave rise to the conflict and the issues connected to it, through political means. Also, these discursive transformations resulted in the pluralisation of the demands that the PKK articulates and the democratic discourse articulates Kurdish cultural and linguistic demands as part of a set of other democratic demands, including environmental sustainability and gender equality. The

126 *The PKK's turn to democracy (1992–present)*

apparent difficulties that the PKK has been experiencing in its ongoing transformation from a resistance movement that used political violence into a democratic movement that advocates peaceful political transformation will also be explored.

Dislocations and the emergence of democratic discourse as the alternative (1992–1999)

The PKK's discursive changes in the early 1990s were a response to the wider political developments in the region and the world, such as the collapse of the communist block during the late 1980s. Rather than abandoning its commitment to the construction of a socialist society, the initial shifts involved modifications and reformulations. Additionally, discursive shifts were introduced as part of attempts aimed at facilitating reconciliation, such as the declaration of unilateral ceasefires. In the early 1990s, it became clearer that the PKK's commitment to an independent Kurdistan was weakening with other forms of governmental arrangements also seen as viable alternatives to independence. From then on, more emphasis started to be placed on the development of legitimate and representative Kurdish national institutions. The appropriation of the democratic discourse was aided with the global turn towards democracy after the collapse of the communist regimes in Eastern Europe. However, while initiating these changes and formulating proposals for political reconciliation, the PKK also maintained its commitment to leading the insurgency to the next level. Hence, the discursive changes until the late 1990s did not follow a clear pattern. In fact, the mid 1990s was a period of search for an alternative discourse and as the second and third declarations of the unilateral ceasefires indicated, time and again, democracy emerged as *the* alternative. On the practical level, however, the changing international conditions and the dynamics, the difficulties that the PKK experienced in developing the guerrilla war into a popular uprising and the capture of the PKK's leader Öcalan in February 1999, have meant that the previous position and the revolutionary strategy were no longer viable, which created the need to construct a more comprehensive democratic discourse. Therefore, the period between 1992 and 1999, which is the focus of this section, is characterised by the PKK's difficulty in constructing a democratic discourse and dissociating itself from the practices shaped by being a military organisation.

The fragmentation of the national liberation discourse

The historical changes introduced in the Soviet Union during the Gorbachev era ended with the demise of the socialist regimes in Eastern Europe. The main premise of the PKK's national liberation discourse was to construct, through a protracted liberation war, the working-class hegemony in a united, independent and socialist Kurdistan. The collapse of socialism had major repercussions for the PKK because it meant that the socialist discourse and the socialist system that it sought to recreate were no longer available and effectively ended the

The PKK's turn to democracy (1992–present)   127

likelihood of a 'socialist Kurdistan'. Therefore, it reduced the appeal of the PKK's national liberation discourse, which limited its ability to hegemonise the Kurdish resistance in Turkey. The PKK's initial response during the early 1990s was to continue its commitment to socialism and revolution while at the same time becoming critical of the Soviet Union. Even though the PKK's objective of a revolution through a popular uprising was reminiscent of Maoism more than the Soviet style Marxist-Leninism, prior to the late 1980s the PKK was keen to be seen as close to the Soviet Union and stated Marxist-Leninism to be its guiding principle. Therefore, the critical position vis-à-vis the Soviet Union represents a major rupture in its ideological orientation. The dissociation with socialism continued throughout the early 1990s, resulting, in 1995, in the replacement of the 'hammer and sickle' in the PKK's party flag with a torch.

Retaining the core socialist 'values' while keeping a distance from a political regime that had failed was achieved by developing a distinction between 'experienced' socialism and 'scientific' socialism.[4] In the latter, socialism was seen as a 'science' of society as opposed to a particular system of economic production or distribution.[5] This distinction allowed the PKK to construct a *new* socialist discourse, the central tenets of which were the ideas and the theorisation by its leader Abdullah Öcalan. The new theorisation primarily introduced the concepts of 'freedom' and 'emancipation' to problematise aspects of 'personal freedom' and 'human emancipation' and sought to recreate the PKK as a 'humanisation movement' whose objective was to create a new 'freed' socialist personality for the Kurds.[6] A free person was defined as someone who had purified her/himself of the effects of any form of 'dogmatism' and 'fanaticism', and someone who could apply self-discipline and restrain to their 'individual motives'.[7] The free individual would be created via 'socialisation' and their development was seen as the precondition of transformation into a socialist society.[8]

However, this move proved to be an interim measure as alongside such concepts the PKK increasingly stressed the need for political reconciliation and peace which enabled it to appropriate democracy as an element into its discourse. This was done mainly in a series of interviews that Abdullah Öcalan had with the Turkish media in which he stressed the need to develop democracy in Turkey and the urgency of the political solution. For example, in an interview with Doğu Perinçek published in the weekly magazine *2000'e Doğru* in 1990 (also published as a book in 1993), Öcalan highlighted the possibility of a negotiated political settlement on the basis of equality and unity.[9] Furthermore, in an interview with the Kurdish journalist Hasan Bildirici that was serialised in the *Özgür Gündem* newspaper in June 1992, Öcalan reiterated his willingness to engage in a dialogue by stating that he was prepared to 'go' to the Turkish Parliament or even speak with the Chief of Staff of the Turkish army if it would lead to political reconciliation.[10] In such proposals the attempt to uncouple 'independence' from 'separatism' was made; for example, in an interview with Turkish journalist Oral Çalışlar in 1993, Öcalan suggested that it was possible for different nations to maintain their independent status within a single political community: 'Instead of separation, I give more importance to terms such as

128   *The PKK's turn to democracy (1992–present)*

"independence", "freedom" and "union based on equality". People can be independent within the same state.'[11]

In the early 1990s, the PKK increased its efforts to establish and develop Kurdish national representative organisations in Europe that would provide democratic representation to the Kurds in the international arena. The establishment of the Kurdistan Parliament in Exile in 1994 was the highlight of such efforts and although the PKK took an active part in its establishment, numerous other Kurdish organisations and parties as well as numerous leading intellectuals and independent political figures took part in its establishment and activities. The activities of the Kurdistan Parliament in Exile caused numerous diplomatic problems between the countries that provided it a venue to convene, such as the Netherlands, Spain (the Basque Country), Russia and Turkey. It evolved into the Kurdistan National Congress (*Kongreya Netawa Kurdistan*, KNK) in 1999, which aspires to be a broader representative organisation for Kurds from all parts of Kurdistan. The KNK continues its diplomacy activities in Europe from its headquarters in Brussels and continues to inform the European public about the situation of the Kurds in Turkey and other parts of the Middle East. Additionally, in 1994 an umbrella organisation, Kon-Kurd (The Federation of Kurdish Associations in Europe) was established in Belgium. As a representative organisation of Kurdish community organisations in Europe, it advocates Kurdish cultural and political rights as well as organising many Kurdish political activities in Europe.

The development of such Kurdish national institutions enabled the Kurds to form and develop stronger relations with the European Left, who have remained perceptive to Turkey's democratisation and granting the Kurds their democratic rights.[12] The establishment of Kurdish national representative organisations is indicative of the availability of an autonomist discourse or a nationalist discourse in which equivalential logics predominated, but the demands for social equality and emancipation did not feature as strongly as the PKK's national liberation discourse. This, however, was not pursued and it was unlikely that it would have led to the reduction in antagonisms if it had been chosen. In fact, the legitimate representation that the Kurds found in the international arena via such representative organisations allowed the wider Kurdish movement the space to develop relations and links with European political and civil society organisations that fostered democratic practices and the appropriation of the democratic discourse. Therefore, the existence of such national representative organisations played an important role in the shift to the democratic discourse because the realisation of the Kurdish democratic demands played a key role in their activities.

As discussed in Chapter 6, during the early 1990s the PKK was keen to show its acceptance of the religious diversity within Kurdish society. In particular, it increasingly showed its willingness to embrace positive aspects of Islam. For example, in an article published in *Berxwedan*, Öcalan described Prophet Mohammed as a great revolutionary and the advent of Islam as the biggest revolution that history has witnessed. He argued that concepts such as 'justice', 'equality' and 'freedom' play a big role in Islam.[13] The PKK's appropriation of

The PKK's turn to democracy (1992–present)   129

some elements of Islam into its discourse was a pragmatic move on its part as it coincided with the growth of the Islamist movement in Turkey during the late 1980s and early 1990s. The Islamist leaning Welfare Party (*Refah Partisi*) managed to generate strong support from the Kurds and increased its votes in the Kurdish regions throughout the 1990s. During the 1995 general election, it managed to win more than 30 MPs from the regions predominantly populated by the Kurds, which established it as the main rival to the pro-Kurdish People's Democracy Party (*Halkın Demokrasi Partisi*, HADEP).[14] The strength of the Welfare Party showed the force of the appeal of Islam and its potential to mobilise the Kurds.[15] In fact, emphasising the Kurds' Islamic heritage provides an alternative myth to the myth of origin of Kurdish society as has been constructed by the Kurdish nationalists throughout the twentieth century, which invokes the pre-Islamic Median period as the 'golden age' of the Kurdish nation. Furthermore, the Islamist discourse challenged the PKK's socialist and secular rhetoric and the fact that women were widely part of the PKK's organisational set-up. Such a challenge would have likely resonated with the sentiments popularly held among many Kurds in whose lives Islam continued to play a significant role. Another factor that would have influenced the PKK's appropriation of Islam was the emergence of the *Hizbullah* movement in Turkey during the early 1990s. Although the origins of the *Hizbullah* are quite difficult to trace as very little of its written sources or documents survive, it is generally believed that it had close links with the Turkish security establishment. This is because its main activities involved attacks against the PKK mainly in urban centres in Diyarbakir and Batman and because the security forces tolerated its activities.[16]

The PKK reacted to the Islamic challenge by becoming more sensitive towards Islamic values, and it incorporated certain Islamic elements into its discourse. The creation of the Islamic Movement of Kurdistan within ERNK was mentioned earlier, and this is indicative of the PKK's acceptance and tolerance of Islamic values. However, the PKK's appropriation of certain elements of Islam did not mean that it acquired an Islamist political agenda. Rather, it began to show more tolerance and acceptance of Islamic social practices in order to prevent the loss of popular support as a result of the rise of political Islam during the 1990s. The PKK has been sensitive to the cultural representation and development of both the Alevi and Yezidi Kurds and promoted acceptance and tolerance of the religious diversity that exists in Kurdish society. Concerning the Alevi community, the PKK was keen to point out the widespread oppression, marginalisation and discrimination that the Alevis historically suffered in Turkey.[17] Additionally, the PKK was also tolerant of the linguistic diversity that prevails within the Kurds. Tolerance and acceptance of religious and linguistic diversity reflect the PKK's strategy to articulate the demands of various sections of Kurdish society in order to mobilise them. Nevertheless, this enabled the PKK to emphasise the democratic nature of the Kurdish demands and meant that the democratic discourse was much more suitable for articulating Kurdish demands.

130   *The PKK's turn to democracy (1992–present)*

The counter-violence, the military losses and the impasse

The initial favourable conditions for the growth of the PKK as an organisation and its guerrilla operations started to change during the early 1990s; specifically, its relations with the Iraqi Kurdish political parties became increasingly strained and the conflict with the Turkish army broadened to a wider area making it difficult to sustain. The PKK's success during the late 1980s and early 1990s in the battlefield meant that large areas were directly under its control and certain areas acquired a central importance for its military operations. This meant that the nature of the war was to change as the guerrillas were to engage in the defence of the 'liberated zones'. From the early 1990s onwards, the Turkish army started to carry out 'hot pursuits' and cross-border operations against the PKK camps and hideouts, increasingly using air power to support its ground troops. The guerrillas had very little protection against such large-scale attacks and high-tech weapons, especially the combat helicopters.

The most significant military losses experienced by the PKK were during the autumn of 1992 in Iraqi Kurdistan when it was attacked on three separate fronts by the *pêshmerge* forces of the KDP and the PUK (Patriotic Union of Kurdistan – Iraq), and the Turkish army. Turkey was keen to stop the PKK's use of Iraqi Kurdistan as a base and pressurised the KDP to act against the PKK. The PKK's presence in the region began to concern the KDP also because of its anti-feudal rhetoric. Initial attacks started by the KDP on 4 October 1992, and the PUK forces attacked the PKK bases on 7 October 1992; this was followed by a major cross-border offensive by the Turkish army starting on 22 October 1992 and involving 5,000 soldiers and 400 village guards. Throughout the attacks the Turkish warplanes bombed the PKK bases in the Hakurk and Haftanin areas. The PKK forces in the Hakurk area, under the command of Osman Öcalan – the brother of the PKK leader Abdullah Öcalan – did not put up a resistance and accepted to relocate to Zele. The forces in Haftanin responded to attacks but suffered heavy losses. After a war lasting 45 days in the autumn of 1992, the PKK had to agree to the KDP's demands and reduce its presence in the KDP controlled areas of Iraqi Kurdistan, with many PKK guerrillas crossing into Iran.[18]

As part of its combat against the PKK, the state took widespread measures against Kurdish civilians, facilitated by the Anti-Terror legislation (3713 Numbered Law) passed on 12 April 1991.[19] From the late 1980s onwards, the state forcefully evacuated and burned down the villages that were perceived as being pro-PKK or those who refused to take part in the village guard scheme. Although formally the village guard scheme was voluntary and some Kurdish tribes took part in them voluntarily, those who refused became victims of intimidation and widespread oppression. This ranged from barring the villagers from using the grazing lands to food embargoes and coercing the people to leave. Those who refused were forcefully evacuated and their homes were burnt down. The primary motive was to stop the PKK's logistical support and limit the possibility of the conflict evolving into an armed popular uprising. The most widespread village evacuations occurred in Şırnak province. According to the Human Rights

The PKK's turn to democracy (1992–present) 131

Foundation of Turkey, in 1990, 109 villages and many hamlets were completely destroyed in the majority Kurdish areas. This practice became much more commonplace between 1991 and 1995, with nearly 2,000 villages destroyed by the end of 1994.[20] Between two and three million people were internally displaced by the end of 1994; they mainly moved to regional centres such as Diyarbakir and Van and to urban centres in Western Turkey and on the Mediterranean coast, examples of the latter being Adana and Mersin.[21]

Indiscriminate attacks as part of the general intimidation of the Kurds by the state security forces in the towns and cities of South-East Turkey increased significantly during the early 1990s. As discussed in Chapter 6, the early 1990s witnessed ordinary Kurds becoming politically more assertive of their support for the PKK. Such occasions gave the state the opportunity to apply indiscriminate violence against civilians; for example, the *Newroz* celebrations in 1992 left 94 people dead and many more wounded.[22] Such attacks were perhaps indicative of the level of violence against the Kurds during the second half of 1992 and 1993. One of the better known of such attacks took place in the town of Şırnak on 18 August 1992 and lasted for two days with the city cut off from the outside world until 21 August. As a response to the PKK's attack targeting state buildings, the security forces opened random fire at the town's houses and businesses.[23] The attack caused widespread destruction to the town with many buildings turned into debris. Similar attacks took place during the second half of 1992 in the following towns: Çukurca, Musabey, Kulp, Cizre, Hakkari, İdil, Diyadin, Yüksekova and Silopi. As a result of such attacks 41 civilians were killed and many more wounded.[24] In October 1993 the town of Lice located in Diyarbakir province was attacked, with the security forces randomly firing at the town and houses. The town's communication with the outside was cut off from 14 to 23 October and the attacks left 30 people dead and nearly 100 people wounded.[25] Above all, these attacks had the motive of intimidating Kurds into submission and disciplining them into not engaging in any form of pro-Kurdish and pro-PKK activities.

Another aspect of the state's combat against PKK activities involved murdering PKK sympathisers and civilian Kurds. Primarily, the shadowy organisations such as the counter guerrillas (*kontras*) and *Jitem* (Gendarmerie Intelligence and Counter Terrorism) units and the *Hizbullah* were used in such attacks.[26] The victims included prominent figures such as the president of the HEP Diyarbakir branch, Vedat Aydın, the prominent Kurdish intellectual Musa Anter and the DEP MP for Adıyaman Province, Mehmet Sincar, who were killed on 5 July 1991, 21 September 1992 and 6 September 1993 respectively. Kurdish businessmen Behcet Cantürk (15 January 1994) and Savaş Buldan, Hacı Karay and Adnan Yıldırım (4 June 1994) were also murdered by unknown assailants.[27] However, most of the victims were ordinary Kurds. During 1992, a total of 360 murders by unknown assailants were reported, 267 of which were pro-PKK activists.[28] Such murders increased to 467 in 1993 and 423 in 1994, with most being committed in Diyarbakir, Batman, Nusaybin, Silvan and Midyat regions.[29] In addition, widespread and systematic torture was commonplace in the region

132 *The PKK's turn to democracy (1992–present)*

and applied to people arrested for alleged links to the PKK. According to the Human Rights Foundation of Turkey, in 1992, 11,300 people were arrested accused of aiding and abetting the PKK.[30] Furthermore, execution without a trial, murder during the raids and death under detention were also common.[31] From the beginning of June 1990 to the end of 1994 in total 96 people were reported as disappeared after having been detained or abducted by the security forces.[32] The number of those who disappeared after being detained in 1995 alone stood at 43.[33]

The Turkish army's counter-insurgency measures managed to contain the PKK's military activities within the rural areas, and the evacuation of the rural settlements and many villages significantly curtailed the logistical support that the PKK drew from the rural Kurds. Although the PKK was able to continue its activities, the above losses that it suffered in 1992 during the war in Iraqi Kurdistan and within Turkey broke the momentum of the guerrilla war. These losses meant that the strategy of guerrilla war and people's revolution reached a stalemate and became ineffective. Consequently, as discussed below, the need for dialogue to find a political solution to the conflict began to be expressed more openly and frequently. The emphasis on the necessity of a political solution to solve the conflict was in fact a significant shift because previously the guerrilla war was seen as the fundamental form of struggle to achieve the revolutionary overthrow of Turkish rule. However, this shift did not amount to a complete abandonment of the guerrilla war on the PKK's part as it continued to stress that it had the capability to continue the war if a political solution was not found. To this end, it has remained committed to building a people's army, with a target of 50,000 guerrillas being mentioned in June 1994 following the Third National Conference, and 60,000 in the Fifth Congress in 1995.[34] However, such statements did not lead to an overt emphasis on the continuation of the antagonisms between the Kurds and Turkey. Instead emphasis was on political reconciliation and coexistence to reduce the antagonistic nature of Kurdish-Turkish relations.

Additionally, the losses experienced during the guerrilla war prompted a change in military tactics, and with increasing frequency during the mid 1990s, the PKK carried out attacks against Turkish military targets in the urban centres. Of these, the explosions targeting the students from the military school in Tuzla railway station on 12 February 1994 and at the arms factory in Kırıkkale on 3 July 1997 had major political impact. Suicide bombers started to be used by the PKK against the military targets with the first attack carried out by Zeynep Kınacı (*Zilan*) against the Turkish soldiers on 30 June 1996 in the town of Tunceli during a flag ceremony.[35] Furthermore, in this period attacks or threat of attacks against tourism facilities were used with increasing frequency. These were carried out as part of the PKK's well-publicised 'Boycott Turkish Tourism' campaigns from 1993 onwards throughout Europe to discourage European tourism to Turkey, which constituted an important economic resource. On 22 June 1994, the PKK bombed two Turkish resorts causing 17 people to be injured.[36] On various other occasions, the PKK guerrillas kidnapped Western tourists for short periods; however, deadly attacks against tourists were not carried out as the PKK indicated in its warnings.[37]

The PKK's turn to democracy (1992–present) 133

The conflict as a whole and the PKK's attacks in Western Turkey caused a corresponding rise in Turkish nationalism and led to a general political fragmentation in Turkey during the 1990s. The representation of the PKK and the conflict *strictly* as a security concern and terrorism issue in the state's discourse gained widespread acceptance in Turkey and resonated among the public causing an incremental rise in a more extreme form of Turkish nationalism and leading to the state's mobilisation of Turkish nationalist groups and criminal gangs against the PKK and the Kurds. There were numerous attacks against Kurdish civilians in Turkey, including mob violence and attempts to lynch individuals, which created an atmosphere of Turkish–Kurdish civil war. The PKK's attacks in Western Turkey put the lives of civilians in greater danger, which meant that the conflict could have easily evolved into the whole of Turkey. Hence, the political polarisation in Turkey limited the PKK's ability to reach out to Kurds in Western Turkey as support for Kurdish rights and demands would have made many people targets of violence and less likely to support the PKK. The mobilisation of Turkish nationalists coupled with the heavy-handed approach that the state took in dealing with the urban based mass participation in pro-Kurdish and pro-PKK events demonstrated the possibility of major loss of life if the conflict was to accelerate. Thus, as a way out of the military impasse, to overcome the various difficulties it had been experiencing and the likelihood of a backlash and civil war that would have made many civilian Kurds the target of mass violence from the state and Turkish nationalists, the PKK started to take measures to lessen the antagonistic state of affairs and find a political solution.

The PKK's unilateral ceasefires and the search for a political solution (1993–1998)

The clearest move on the part of the PKK to formulate a political solution to the conflict came on 17 March 1993 when, in a press conference attended by numerous leading Kurdish politicians including the current President of Iraq and the leader of the PUK Jalal Talabani, Öcalan announced a unilateral ceasefire for 25 days starting on 20 March 1993. The ceasefire was declared to facilitate a political solution to the Kurdish question and Öcalan suggested that it could turn into a permanent ceasefire should Turkey respond favourably and show its willingness to solve the issue peacefully by recognising the Kurds' democratic rights and identity.[38] The ceasefire was extended on 15 April 1993 for another month. However, soon after the extension numerous events took place in Turkey that signalled the end of the ceasefire. On 17 April 1993 President Turgut Özal – who was thought to be instrumental in the brokering of a ceasefire – died unexpectedly. On 19 May 1993, the Turkish army carried out an attack against the PKK guerrillas near the Kulp district of Diyarbakir province which left 13 guerrillas dead.[39] The ceasefire came to an acrimonious end when a group of PKK guerrillas killed 33 unarmed and discharged soldiers on 24 May 1993 during a road check on the Elazığ–Bingöl highway.[40] The period following the end of the ceasefire witnessed the escalation of the conflict and the death of many people,

134   *The PKK's turn to democracy (1992–present)*

including those killed as a result of extrajudicial killings. This escalation started with the election of Tansu Çiller as the Prime Minister in June 1993 leading to the continuation of the oppressive practices and antagonisms becoming much more acute.

To reduce the tensions and to give the new government a chance to formulate its policy concerning a peaceful solution to the Kurdish question (elections were scheduled for 24 December 1995), the PKK declared a second unilateral ceasefire in December 1995. The ceasefire was declared as part of the ceasefire between the PKK and the KDP to end the new conflict that had erupted between the two parties in August 1995. Despite the ceasefire not being taken seriously by the new government, not creating the atmosphere of optimism as was the case with the first ceasefire, and the Turkish army continuing its attacks against PKK targets and Kurdish civilians (destroying villages, depopulation, murders by unknown assailants, etc.), the PKK refrained from carrying out attacks until August 1996. Additionally, in the eight months that the ceasefire was adhered to, there were various campaigns supported by human rights organisations, political parties and trade unions that sought to encourage support for dialogue and peace. Throughout 1996, the campaign '*Barış için 1 milyon imza*' (One million signatures for peace) was carried out and the signatures were submitted to the Turkish National Assembly in 1997. On 28 January 1996, the conference 'Together for Peace' was organised in Istanbul by numerous NGOs.[41] Furthermore, on 21 April 1996 'The Peace Train' was organised by the Human Rights Association (*İnsan Hakları Derneği*, İHD) that started from Istanbul with stops in numerous cities before arriving in Diyarbakir where it was greeted by 20,000 people.[42] Such civilian initiatives did not manage to sway the momentum towards peace and reconciliation and thus change the attitude of the newly elected government.

On 7 May 1996, an attempt to assassinate Öcalan was carried out with a bomb blast at the house that Öcalan was staying in, in Damascus.[43] This was followed in June 1996 by a large-scale operation in Iraqi Kurdistan by the Turkish army involving 40,000 soldiers.[44] On 16 August 1996, the PKK declared the ceasefire to be practically over while stressing that although the political solution was inevitable, the war needed to continue until both parties declared their intention to commit to ceasefire and dialogue.[45] In much a similar fashion as in previous years, the guerrilla war continued with the Turkish army conducting large-scale operations against the PKK in Iraqi Kurdistan and in the rural and mountainous zones in Turkey. These operations often resulted in large clashes between the guerrillas and the Turkish soldiers and the loss of life on both sides.

On 1 September 1998 (World Peace Day), the PKK declared another unilateral ceasefire, again aimed at facilitating dialogue and building a platform for peace. It was suggested by the PKK that the ceasefire came about as a result of Turkey's requests, including indirect requests from the Turkish army to find a peaceful solution to the conflict. However, contrary to the PKK's expectation, soon after the ceasefire declaration large numbers of Turkish armed forces were moved to the border with Syria and the army commanders issued threats to

The PKK's turn to democracy (1992–present) 135

invade Syria if it continued to shelter the PKK leader and its forces. In October 1998 Öcalan left Syria and arrived in Russia; then he moved to Italy where he was arrested on 12 November 1998. He managed to stay in Italy until the end of January 1999 but his attempts to remain there on a permanent basis failed. His attempts to stay in Greece, Russia and numerous other countries (Holland, South Africa, Switzerland) all failed and on 15 February 1999 he was kidnapped on his way from the Greek Embassy in Nairobi to the airport.[46] His capture had a euphoric effect in Turkey, and it was described as the event of the century. Initially, the PKK responded by carrying out attacks using petrol bombs in urban centres but such attacks did not develop into a concerted campaign of violence in Western Turkey.[47]

Subsequently, Öcalan was tried and sentenced to capital punishment, which, as a result of diplomatic pressure and fear that it could aggravate the conflict into a full civil war, was changed to life imprisonment. Öcalan has been kept in solitary confinement on the island of İmralı in the Marmara Sea.[48] He used his defence in court to develop and formulate his vision of a political solution to the Kurdish issue in Turkey and to this effect put forward a number of solutions. These formulations precipitated significant discursive changes on the part of the PKK as it began to construct a comprehensive democratic discourse. A significant act that the PKK undertook soon after the trial of Öcalan was to declare a permanent ceasefire and withdraw all its forces from Turkey. Whereas before, the ceasefire was declared to pave the way towards a dialogue and political solution, on this occasion, the permanence of the ceasefire was emphasised. Furthermore, the PKK intensified its attempts to find a peaceful solution by organising numerous campaigns in Turkey and in Europe and surrendering two groups of guerrillas to Turkey as a sign of goodwill.

The PKK's democratic discourse (1999–present)

The chain of events that started with Öcalan's declaration of the PKK's third unilateral ceasefire in September 1998 and ended with his imprisonment in June 1999 significantly accelerated the process of transformation in the PKK. Between 1999 and 2001, the PKK's appropriation of the democratic discourse continued and paved the way for a more comprehensive and deeper 'strategic transformation'. However, the PKK's turn to democracy has faced various difficulties mainly due to being an organisation that used violence to achieve its political objectives and having a highly centralised organisational structure. Consequently, to overcome such difficulties and successfully transform itself into a democratic movement, it initiated wide-ranging organisational changes from 2002 onwards. The political pressure mounting over the PKK as a result of the changing international situation, especially the 'war on terror' that followed the 9/11 attacks on the USA, further complicated this transition as both of the succeeding organisations, the KADEK and the *Kongra-Gel*, have been added to the list of the proscribed organisations in Europe and the US.[49] This has been used as a pretext by Turkey to attack the PKK and marginalise its activities in Europe.

136 *The PKK's turn to democracy (1992–present)*

Before discussing the contents of the PKK's democratic discourse and its organisational evolution since 1999, and to situate the process of change and transformation, this section will first give an overview of Öcalan's defences. This is necessary because the proposals that Öcalan put forward in his defence to the courts have been taken as the basis of the discursive changes and the new strategy that the PKK formulated in subsequent years. Rather than providing a detailed account, however, a summary of his ideas concerning the solution to the Kurdish question in Turkey is provided.

Öcalan's new paradigm: the 'democratic unity' thesis

The ideas that Öcalan put forward in his trial in 1999 have been elaborated and expanded on in later years in the defences submitted to the European Court of Human Rights in 2001 and 2004.[50] Collectively, the defences focus on the democratic solution to the Kurdish question and draw upon a diverse number of radical intellectual traditions including 'the libertarian social ecologist Murray Bookchin, feminist political theorists, leftist Foucauldians and critical Marxists'.[51] Overall, they constitute an analysis of the history of the Middle East and seek to offer a way out of the current stalemate characterised by religious and ideological dogmatism, patriarchy, class-oppression and highly centralised state formation in the region. The 'democratic civilisation' that Öcalan's defences aspire to construct in the region aims for a radical transformation of the whole of the Middle East through the development of pluralist democracy and civil society: 'Women's liberation and the empowerment of minorities can help establish pluralist federative structures, which can provide the framework for the resolution of social, ethnic and religious conflicts.'[52]

Öcalan's solution to the Kurdish question in Turkey is conceived in the light of his decentralised and democratised vision of the Middle East. The development and deepening of democracy is seen as the central component of a lasting solution to the Kurdish question. Forms of regional autonomy or federalism are deemed unsuitable because the Kurdish population is geographically dispersed in Turkey, and therefore such solutions cannot adequately address the demands of all Kurds, especially the demands of those in Western Turkey.[53] Furthermore, the past attempts to solve the Kurdish question by using force – via suppression and denial on the part of Turkey and rebellion on the part of the Kurds – have proved unsuccessful and deepened the problem. Citing the peculiarity and the deep-rooted nature of the relations between the Kurds and Turks, including their historical alliance that resulted in the establishment of the republic, Öcalan argued that a solution within the democratic system is the only viable choice:

> The democratic solution, in general as well as in the case of the Kurdish problem, is the only choice; separation is neither possible nor required. The interests of the Kurds lie in the democratic unity of Turkey. If the democratic solution is applied correctly, it is likely to be more successful than autonomy and federation. The practice is progressing in this way.[54]

Öcalan reiterates that throughout the republican era the Kurds were excluded from participating in politics, and their existence as a separate nation was denied. The early Kurdish rebellions during the 1920s played a negative role in shaping Turkish–Kurdish relations and the antagonistic state of affairs and were used as pretext by the Turkish nationalist elite to apply its policy of forced assimilation.[55] From then on, legitimate Kurdish demands were oppressed, and the Kurds were not given any chance to express their demands through legal political avenues. This gave rise to violence as being the predominant method that the Kurds used to challenge the state's oppression and assimilation. However, the current democratic era offers realisable opportunities for the peaceful solution of the Kurdish question.[56] Öcalan argues that every concerned party needs to channel their efforts to the development of the democratic solution:

> My efforts, if I get an opportunity after this, will be to completely stop the armed conflict, pull the PKK into the legal political space and unite it with the democratic system.... Concerning the Kurdish problem, which has deep historical roots and is now the responsibility of all the social sectors, and as a last word in my defence, I would like to close the era of separation, rebellion, suppression and denial to start the development of democratic unity, peace and brotherhood.[57]

In order to strengthen his proposals, Öcalan makes extensive reference to Atatürk's early speeches concerning the acceptance of Kurdish rights and demands.[58] Such references are in fact used to argue that the proposed democratic solution does not run contrary to the founding principles of the republic. Additionally, Öcalan argues that the proposed democratic solution and granting Kurds' their cultural and political rights do not challenge Turkey's national unity and territorial integrity as claimed by Turkish nationalists.[59] This is because a nation defined in territorial terms ('the nation of Turkey' as opposed to 'the Turkish nation') can contain within itself numerous cultural and language differences and allow for their equal development. Hence, coexistence of the Turks, Kurds and other minorities in the same polity is possible if the republic is democratised and reconstructed to allow each group their cultural and linguistic rights.

Strategic and organisational transformation

The above briefly-outlined reconciliatory stance that Öcalan introduced at his trial and maintained throughout the time of his imprisonment was met with acceptance by the PKK. In fact, Öcalan's proposals for democratic reconciliation have been taken as the basis of the PKK's comprehensive strategic and organisational transformations. Although in August 1999, soon after Öcalan's trial ended, the PKK took reconciliatory measures by declaring a permanent ceasefire and withdrawing its forces, the process of appropriation of the discourse of democracy lasted considerably longer. In this respect, the PKK's Seventh Congress

138 *The PKK's turn to democracy (1992–present)*

held in December 1999 and its Sixth National Conference held in August 2001 were significant events in the transformation process, which discussed various theoretical, political and organisational issues in detail and shaped the new democratic strategy the movement adopted. The new strategy focuses on the political struggle and the construction of a broader 'anti-oligarchic' democratic movement as the fundamental form – as opposed to the use of force and violence – and emphasises the transformation of the system within to achieve widespread political, economic and social change in Turkey.[60] The PKK is seen as an integral part of this broad 'anti-oligarchic' movement and its transformation into a mass-based democratic socialist party is envisioned. The primary aims and objectives of the movement are defined as the initiation of a peace process and democratic solution to the Kurdish question, the democratic transformation and democratisation of society, and the advancement of individual rights and freedoms.[61]

In particular, the Central Committee report submitted to the PKK's Seventh Congress emphasised the 'changed' global environment – which is characterised by the peaceful resolution of conflicts through democracy and the development of supranational political communities that foster cooperation and coexistence – as being an important factor in the movement's democratic transformation.[62] It stressed that in the democratic era, class struggles, national conflicts and various other societal problems, find their solutions without the need for, or use of, violence:

> ...without any doubt this era is one of democracy and freedom. The stage that awaits us will be filled with struggles emerging from contradictions based on differences pertaining to class, gender, environment and development, and with the aim of furthering democracy and freedom.[63]

In the current era, finding a democratic and peaceful solution to the Kurdish question remains a real possibility. Therefore, promoting political reconciliation and a democratic solution to the Kurdish question, to unblock the current deadlock and open-up the possibilities for further democratisation in Turkey, are placed at the centre of the PKK's strategy.[64] However, in addition to the strategic transformation to recreate the PKK as a movement capable of providing constructive solutions to the various social and political problems facing Turkey and Kurdish society, organisational change and renewal of the movement were identified as necessary. As part of its new strategy, in May 2000, the PKK reorganised its guerrilla forces into a 'defence force' with the HPG (*Hêzên Parastina Gel*, People's Defence Forces) replacing the ARGK. While it stated that the use of violence in the past was necessary to break the hegemony of Turkish nationalism and the traditional Kurdish classes over the masses, in the current era, political means were the fundamental form of struggle. The concept of 'legitimate defence' was introduced to characterise the new military strategy, which maintained the PKK's capacity to carry out an armed campaign should the democratic political solution fail or the movement come under attack.

The PKK's turn to democracy (1992–present) 139

Furthermore, keeping the military capacity was seen as necessary for self-defence and to ensure the long-term safety and existence of the movement because the region continued to remain unstable, and the possibility of attacks against the PKK were highly likely.[65] Nevertheless, the PKK emphasised that political organisation and mobilisation of the masses, in which 'popular uprisings' and 'civil disobedience' played a key role, were accepted as the principal form of struggle.

The PKK's initial formulations of its new strategy and discourse articulated Kurdish identity and demands around the nodal point of 'democracy'. It redefined the form of struggle as 'national democratic' and identified its principal objectives as finding a peaceful resolution to the Kurdish question through transforming Turkey into a 'democratic republic':

> Henceforth, the period of peace and democratic transformation that the PKK started and seeks to develop at the strategic level has commenced, which aims to eliminate the blockage and impasse in Turkey, pave the way for the democratic transformation and – following the great revolutionary democratic struggle – achieve Turkey's democratic re-foundation. In this way, the oligarchic structure of the republic will be transformed to realise the democratic re-foundation and create the democratic republic.[66]

This strategy represents a significant ideological shift on the part of the PKK because instead of the equivalential articulation of Kurdish demands on a national basis, the new democratic discourse articulates Kurdish demands *differentially* as part of broader political demands for equality and democracy in Turkey. However, it introduces a new set of equivalential logics on the basis of democracy and freedom that seeks to build a broad pro-democratic movement to challenge the numerous forms of inequality, discrimination and oppression. It draws boundaries between the historically dominant classes in Turkey (described as the 'oligarchy') and various other groups, including the lower middle classes, the labour movement, the Kurds and other minorities, and women.[67] The creation of an equivalential chain of demands and an anti-oligarchic mass-based democratic movement is seen as vital to Turkey's democratic refoundation:

> . . . to counter this oligarchy, what is needed is a movement that will develop and realise the re-foundation on the basis of democratic liberation and democratic republic to rescue the broad masses – workers, civil servants, women, the peasantry and the middle classes – from oppression and exploitation.[68]

According to the PKK's analysis, the demands for political change and democratisation in Turkey are shared by numerous other domestic political actors, such as the liberal circles and the labour movement, as well as international powers, especially the USA and the EU.[69] Although the existence of a wide range of allies aids the process of democratisation, given that there are differences in the

140 *The PKK's turn to democracy (1992–present)*

nature of democratisation and change that each political actor demands, the construction of a pro-democratic movement to drive the democratisation process and articulate the demands of the masses in Turkey is of key importance. Despite the fact that the need for change is felt by the existing 'oligarchic' system, the impetus for change can only come from the pro-democratic forces and their participation in the political system.[70]

To complement such strategic moves and reorganise the movement to make it capable of developing and implementing the new strategy, the PKK introduced a process of organisational change and renewal.[71] In April 2002, during its Eighth Congress, the PKK formally abolished itself and established the KADEK, the founding declaration of which stated that the new formation was necessary alongside the new strategy. In particular, the 'repetitions' experienced by the guerrilla war and the changing international order, which created the possibility of democratic change and development in Turkey, were cited as significant in its formation.[72] The KADEK's programme, in line with the new strategy that the PKK adopted in its Seventh Congress, conceptualised the solution to the Kurdish question within the development of democracy and as the equal and free development of the Kurdish people in the region: 'The solution to the Kurdish question, before anything else, involves making the Kurdish society democratic and free and progressing on such a basis to reach the era of democratic civilisation.'[73] The democratisation programme ('democratic liberation') that the KADEK put forward comprised two dimensions: first, the democratisation of the state and society in Turkey, Iran, Iraq and Syria, and second, the democratic solution to the Kurdish national question.[74] Therefore, the solution to the Kurdish question was envisaged through systemic change across the countries in the Middle East that have a Kurdish population and without the need to alter the existing state system:

> KADEK's solution to the Kurdish question is based on the democratic transformation of the existing states within their present boundaries and without aiming at their overthrow. In line with this view, it first calls upon the Republic of Turkey and all the other concerned states, which have left the Kurdish question without a solution and envisage denial and destruction, to overcome such outworn policies and accept the rights of the Kurdish people that have been recognised by international norms. The abolishment of the death penalty, the recognition of the right to education and broadcasting in Kurdish, conducting politics through democratic channels and participation in government are the matters that will pave the way for the realisation of the democratic solution.[75]

However, in each state the democratic solution needs to be developed separately taking into consideration their particularities. In Turkey, specifically, the KADEK proposed a solution that accepted the citizenship of Turkey as a 'common identity' while developing democratic standards and respecting language and cultural freedoms in all spheres of life.[76] As an alternative to the

The PKK's turn to democracy (1992–present) 141

present state system in the region, the KADEK proposed the construction of the Democratic Middle Eastern Union as a long-term objective. Furthermore, the need for cooperation and reconciliation was emphasised in the KADEK's programme: 'KADEK accepts, as a fundamental principle, to work in a union and cooperate with the democratic and progressive forces of the whole of the Middle East against all forms of reactionism and to create a new Middle East.'[77]

The KADEK's existence was relatively short lived – in November 2003 it too abolished itself and made way for the *Kongra-Gel*. The stated reason for the establishment of the *Kongra-Gel* was that the KADEK continued to be strongly associated with, and was seen as an extension of, the PKK, which made it difficult to fulfil its role and extend its appeal.[78] Furthermore, the movement itself was in need of wide-ranging democratisation to change the hierarchical Leninist party structure it had inherited from the PKK, which the KADEK was unable to achieve. In terms of the political programme, however, there is a remarkable degree of similarity between the KADEK and the *Kongra-Gel* as both of the organisations support the democratic solution to the Kurdish question. The main differences, however, are that the *Kongra-Gel* included more civilian Kurdish politicians, and the former DEP MP Zübeyir Aydar was elected as its leader. This was seen as a necessary step to internalise democracy within the organisation and decentralise the movement.

The organisational changes continued in 2005 with the re-establishment of the PKK and the establishment of *Koma Komalan Kurdistan* (The Council of Associations of Kurdistan, KKK), which later took the name *Koma Civakan Kurdistan* (KCK, which can be translated literally as 'The Council of Communities of Kurdistan', but in the organisation's public statements that appeared in English it is translated as 'Democratic Communities of Kurdistan'). These organisations were established to put into practice the 'democratic confederalism' proposals that Öcalan formulated in his defence to the ECHR in 2004. Both the PKK's and KCK's solutions to the Kurdish question in the Middle East are conceived in terms of decentralised federal polities. This is proposed as an alternative institutional framework to the current state system in the Middle East and as a system that is most suitable for the present era of 'democratic civilisation' as it would overcome the current stalemate by developing a fairer and freer society in the region in which values of gender equality and environmental sustainability can take root.[79] Moreover, by creating a loosely united confederal entity the new proposed political structure would neither challenge the established and internationally recognised boundaries nor resort to nationalism or establishing a nation state. The Kurds would coexist in a greater Middle Eastern Union in cooperation with neighbouring nations and on a voluntary basis.[80] Additionally, two political parties, the PÇDK (*Partiya Çareseriya Demokratik a Kurdistan*, Kurdistan Democratic Solution Party – Iraqi Kurdistan) and the PJAK (*Partiya Jiyana Azad a Kurdistanê*, Party of Free Life – Iranian Kurdistan) were established in 2002 and 2004 respectively.

142 *The PKK's turn to democracy (1992–present)*

Assessing the PKK's democratic transformation

The most significant change that has occurred as a consequence of the PKK's turn to democracy has been the differential articulation of Kurdish national demands as part of numerous other democratic demands. As discussed above, this differential articulation has brought about major modifications to the way the antagonistic relations between the Kurds and Turkey are discursively constructed. In the discourses of the organisations that came into existence following the PKK's democratic transformation, namely the KADEK and the *Kongra-Gel*, Kurdish national demands have been rearticulated as demands for the recognition of cultural and linguistic rights, without putting forward a proposal to construct a Kurdish nation state. Instead, Kurdistan's national unity has been conceived within the Democratic Union of the Middle East and a civic and a pluralist model of citizenship based on territory – 'citizenship of Turkey' – is proposed as a common identity. The attainment of Kurdish language and cultural rights and the establishment and development of cultural institutions that will foster Kurdish cultural renewal have been the main focus of the KADEK's discourse.[81] An end to the denial of Kurdish national identity and to cultural domination of the Kurds by nations within the existing states by the removal of existing barriers that prevent the development of Kurdish language and culture were demanded.[82] More specifically, for such demands to be realised, the constitutional recognition and protection of Kurdish identity, the creation of an environment in which Kurdish language and culture could develop freely, legal guarantees on education in the Kurdish language and the establishment of Kurdish cultural organisations that would develop education in the Kurdish language were the particular demands raised in the KADEK's political programme. Additionally, particular steps aimed at ending the conflict, such as dismantling the village guard scheme, facilitating the return of the internally displaced persons to their pre-conflict settlements and rebuilding the regional economy were put forward as essential steps that would bring a sense of normality to the region.[83]

Similarly, the demands for the constitutional recognition of Kurdish identity and legal guarantees to protect it, the recognition of Kurdish culture and language and the provision of education in Kurdish, were raised by the *Kongra-Gel*.[84] It demands that the same status that is given to the Turkish language and culture be given to the Kurdish language and culture in Turkey.[85] The political programme of the re-established PKK frames Kurdish demands as the constitutional recognition of Kurdish identity and the recognition of the Kurds as a national and cultural entity that have collective political rights.[86] Similarly, the development of Kurdish language and its free use in the media are among the key demands that are articulated.[87] Furthermore, KCK's peace declaration made in December 2008 to quell the rising political violence, which is discussed below, summarised its demands for the Kurds within a seven point list that overall characterised them as demands for minority rights in Turkey. Alongside the proposals for the peaceful resolution of the conflict and political reconciliation, the declaration emphasised the constitutional recognition and protection of Kurdish identity, the removal of obstacles preventing the free development of Kurdish culture and language and the recognition of Kurdish language as an official language in the majority Kurdish areas.[88] Also, in the PKK's Tenth Congress, held in September 2008, the commitment to a democratic solution to the conflict and attaining Kurdish rights through widespread democratisation in the region has been emphasised.[89]

Another major change that the democratic transformation has cultivated is the pluralisation in the demands that the PKK and other organisations subsequently established to represent the Kurdish movement have been articulating. In addition to the Kurdish cultural demands discussed above, the democratic discourse articulates demands for gender equality, environmental sustainability and cultural and religious pluralism. The articulation of women's liberation and the demands for gender equality have become key elements in the democratic discourse. As discussed in Chapter 6, the mobilisation of women has had a significant impact on Kurdish society, and during the early 1990s, the PKK began constructing a new 'liberated' identity for Kurdish women. Following the shift to democratic discourse, the organisation of a separate and autonomous women's movement has been identified as an urgent task. For example, the KADEK's political programme highlighted the development and organisation of the women's movement, as a key social movement in the twenty-first century, as one of its primary objectives.[90] Women have been identified as a key social and political group that will lead the democratic development and renewal in the region and the democratisation of the society.[91] Consequently, steps have been taken to establish the women's movement as an autonomous organisation within the national movement. This led to the establishment of a women's party, *Partiya Jina Azad* (Party of Free Women, PJA) in 2000, which changed its name to *Partiya Azadiya Jin a Kurdistan* (PAJK, Freedom Party of Women of Kurdistan) in 2004. Additionally, there is a women's armed group *Yekitiyen Jinen Azad STAR* (YJA Star) operating as part of the HPG. Whilst the mobilisation of women has been a significant new development, women occupy high positions within the PKK hierarchy and their mass participation in politics has contributed significantly to the spread of notions of gender equality in Kurdish society, the organisational autonomy of the women's movement has not been achieved. The organisations listed above continue to remain an integrated part of the overall Kurdish national movement, which makes challenging the multifarious practices of gendered forms of oppression in the Kurdish society difficult. The missing organisational autonomy places barriers on the attempts by the women's movement to develop a feminist critique that problematises gender oppression and places women's liberation at the centre of its political discourse. Additionally, it may limit its ability to form links with wider feminist groups in Turkey as well as in Europe that can strengthen the Kurdish women's movement and the attempts to promote women's rights within Kurdish society.[92]

The democratic discourse articulates the need for the recognition of cultural and religious diversity within Kurdish society and the wider Middle East. For

144 *The PKK's turn to democracy (1992–present)*

this reason, the KADEK and subsequent organisations that have been established articulate demands for the recognition of various national and ethnic minorities in the region, their right to free association and organisation and the promotion of their cultural development in their discourse.[93] Moreover, the right to the association and organisation of various religious and faith groups in society and the freedom to practice their religion are seen as essential for promoting tolerance and cultural pluralism.[94] Similarly, the existence of a strong civil society and the promotion of new civil society organisations, as well as of political parties that represent the interests of different sections of society, are seen as a central aspect of the democratisation of the region.[95] Additionally, the new democratic discourse articulates concerns for environmental destruction, and consequently 'ecology' is articulated as an element in the discourse. It proposes a new radical rethinking of the established norms that govern the present relations between humans and their environment to overcome the impending economic, moral, social and environmental crises in the world. Although, Öcalan's defences and the PKK's new democratic discourse have been drawing on the ideas developed and strongly associated with the radical democratic tradition, it was not until recent times that the new political project which was undertaken is described explicitly as 'radical democracy'.[96] Moreover, this emphasis is strengthened in Öcalan's recent theorisation, which focuses on the systemic level and is seen as part of a radical democratic alternative capable of unlocking the current global economic and political crises.[97]

The comprehensive discursive transformations and organisational changes discussed above have initially been followed with a degree of suspicion at the grass-roots level. Also, the fact that many organisational changes have been taking place in the past ten years is also difficult to understand. In comparison to the national liberation discourse, the formulations of the strategy concerning violence and Kurdish rights in the current democratic discourse is ambiguous as it contains various new elements. Although articulating Kurdish rights differentially and raising demands for the recognition of Kurds' cultural identity and difference without resorting to separatism corresponds to popular Kurdish demands, the formulation of proposals that aim to radically transform the existing highly authoritarian state system in the region is highly unlikely to succeed in the present environment in the Middle East. Furthermore, it is difficult to explain the significant emphasis put on certain elements articulated in the PKK's discourse, such as 'ecology' and environmental sustainability, as it does not correspond to the popularly held demands of the Kurdish population. Moreover, Öcalan's increasing reference in his numerous 'interview notes' (prepared and disseminated by his legal representatives) to Atatürk and Öcalan's discrediting of the Kurds' early attempts to challenge the Kemalist regime have further created confusion and general apathy among many Kurds.

Additionally, while achieving democratisation of Turkey is a key objective in the PKK's discourse, it is highly difficult to measure its acceptance of democratic norms and practices and their application in its internal affairs and its relations with other organisations. In October 2004, some high ranking PKK

The PKK's turn to democracy (1992–present)   145

members, including Osman Öcalan, Kani Yılmaz, Nizamettin Taş, Sabri Tori, 14 other cadres and 40 guerrillas, left the KADEK and established the Patriotic and Democratic Party of Kurdistan (PWD). This was seen as a result of the deep seated disagreement within the PKK. However, both Kani Yılmaz and Sabri Tori were killed by a car bomb in Northern Iraq in February 2006, which was widely accredited to the PKK despite it never claiming formal responsibility.[98] Whereas the murders of the two former members are clear examples of the continuity of the use or threat of violence, such a practice is not very common and numerous former high ranking PKK activists who left the movement have not been targeted. Furthermore, given the imminent military dangers facing the movement in a hostile environment and the lack of a political process that will lead to the recognition of the PKK as a legitimate political actor by allowing it to participate in formal political processes, it is perhaps unsurprising that violent practices and the capacity for violence remain, which makes the transformation into a committed democratic movement more difficult.

However, democratisation and political reconciliation have remained central objectives of the PKK's democratic discourse despite the fact that they have not resulted in any reciprocal action from Turkey, as discussed in greater detail below. As stated earlier, 'political reconciliation' refers to a process that will transform a relationship characterised by antagonism into one characterised by 'civic friendship'.[99] Two interconnected dimensions emerge in the proposals for political reconciliation formulated by the PKK during its unilateral ceasefires and, more systematically, in its democratic discourse: first, a negotiated end to the conflict and measures taken to address the horrors and traumas of the conflict, and second, to address the causes behind the conflict by the recognition of Kurdish identity and political demands in Turkey. In contrast, the decrease in violence during the past decade in Turkey has been seen as the defeat of the PKK, and successive governments rejected proposals for political reconciliation and dialogue. They have continued to pursue a policy to contain and defeat the PKK militarily. Given the continuation of the attempt by the Turkish army to destroy the PKK and given that violence continues to remain a feature of Kurdish politics in Turkey, what are the prospects of political reconciliation starting and achieving long lasting peace and institutionalising a new political framework to recognise Kurdish cultural identity and national rights in Turkey?

The prospects for political reconciliation

Given that Kurdish rights and demands are articulated within the discourse of democracy and as national cultural demands, a new political framework that takes the existing polity in Turkey as its basis but recognises the existence of the Kurds as a national group and accords them their national cultural rights can satisfy popular Kurdish political demands in Turkey. Furthermore, given the territorial dispersion of the Kurds in Turkey and their integration into Turkish society, a new framework based on the 'National cultural autonomy' model as elaborated in Nimni (2005) seems particularly suitable because it can provide an

146 *The PKK's turn to democracy (1992–present)*

effective method to accommodate Kurdish demands within Turkey.[100] Given that within such a framework cultural autonomy would be accorded on the basis of the 'personality principle' and would not be confined to a particular territory, the geographically dispersed Kurds around Turkey could enjoy Kurdish cultural rights and maintain and develop their identity and culture without endangering their status of 'citizens' and 'residents' of Turkey.[101] However, prior to any discussion of possible models that will provide suitable solutions to accommodating Kurdish demands in Turkey a major shift in the way the Kurdish question is represented in the political discourses in Turkey is needed. The developments that Turkey has witnessed in the past decade concerning the peaceful and political solution to the conflict and accommodating Kurdish national demands have not been very encouraging, and the multifaceted difficulties that hinder the development of political reconciliation in Turkey have become much more visible.

As expected, the PKK's turn to democracy has resulted in a significant reduction in violence in the past decade with a sense of normalisation returning to the region. Additionally, the prospects of EU membership and the accession process has proved to be a major source of motivation for Turkey to raise the country's democratic standards and recognise cultural pluralism, which has resulted in the limited recognition of Kurdish identity and demands. The reduction in violence led, on 30 July 2002, to the bringing of an end to emergency rule in the provinces of Hakkari and Tunceli, and on 30 November 2002 in the last two remaining provinces of Diyarbakir and Şırnak.[102] The legal reforms carried out by successive governments since 2001 as steps to meeting the EU membership criteria – including uplifting capital punishment, allowing limited use of Kurdish language in radio and TV, teaching Kurdish in private institutions and the establishment of a predominantly Kurdish language TV station in January 2009 within the state's broadcasting organisation TRT (Radio and Television Corporation of Turkey) – have contributed positively to the creation of an environment of optimism. In fact, such reforms can be interpreted as signs that the state's policy concerning the Kurdish question is changing. Whereas these changes are seen as steps in the right direction by the PKK and the Kurds in general, the need to follow such changes with more comprehensive legal reforms that will meet the Kurds' national cultural demands and institute a plural and participatory democratic framework are often emphasised.

Furthermore, the announcements made by the government in August 2009 of their preparation of a 'Democratic Initiative' that will accelerate the process of political reform and offer greater recognition of Kurdish cultural rights offered hope of a new era in Kurdish politics in Turkey. However, the rejection by the main opposition political parties of the government's attempts to generate a political will and national consensus that are needed to carry out widespread constitutional reforms and grant the Kurdish minority more rights and freedoms have significantly hampered the progress towards political reconciliation. In fact, the Turkish nationalists' unequivocal rejections show the strength and appeal of Turkish nationalism and its hegemonic representation of the Kurdish question as strictly a 'security concern' and 'terrorism'; such a representation has been a main barrier to political reconciliation. Subsequently, the leaflet prepared to disseminate the 'Democratic Initiative' to the public in Turkey described it as 'The National Oneness and Brotherhood Project' (*Milli Birlik ve Kardeşlik Projesi*), which proposes to defend the unitary structure of the state and the indivisibility of the national community in Turkey.[103] Additionally, despite emphasising that one of the project's key objectives was to be the lifting of restrictions on learning, teaching and broadcasting in other languages spoken in Turkey, the possibility of education in mother tongue is firmly rejected.[104]

The limited recognition of Kurdish identity and rights granted to the Kurds throughout the past decade conceives of Kurdish demands as narrow ethnic demands and falls short of full linguistic rights. Additionally, the recognition does not extend to the political sphere as dialogue with the PKK or any other political organisation, including the democratically elected pro-Kurdish representation in the parliament, has so far been rejected. Initially, the PKK responded to the government's initiative by sending a 'peace group' of 34 people in October 2010 that included eight PKK militants. The group was arrested but released without being charged; however, on 17 June 2010, 10 members were charged with being 'members of the PKK' and 'carrying out PKK propaganda'.[105] Furthermore, the commencement in October 2010 of the trial of the 151 Kurdish political activists accused of being members of KCK was interpreted by the PKK as a sign of the government's insincerity in solving the conflict through political means.[106] Overall, the government's 'democratic initiative' has been interpreted by the PKK as an attempt to marginalise the Kurdish national movement and depoliticise Kurdish identity. This is because, in line with the continuation of the security discourse, the leaflet emphasises the elimination of the PKK in the region as a key objective.[107]

Given that the possibility of a negotiated agreement that would result in the disarmament of the PKK is weak, a large-scale military operation that will result in a significant intensification of the conflict may be attempted by the Turkish army to achieve its objective. The government's approach continues to see the Kurdish question within the parameters of security and does not seek to engage with the PKK or respond to its key demand for political reconciliation. The success of any democratic initiative to end the conflict rests on Turkey's ability to generate a national consensus to recognise and accommodate Kurdish national demands and rights, such as education in the Kurdish language, the constitutional recognition of Kurdish identity and the extension of broadcast rights. Additionally, a host of other related significant issues, such as the issue of internal displacement and widespread violence against Kurdish civilians during the 1990s in which the state security forces played a key role, including the extrajudicial murders during the 1990s of an estimated 17,500 people, need to be fully investigated before the horrors and traumas of the conflict can heal.

Due to the lack of any dialogue with the Kurdish representative organisations, the use of violence by the PKK has not been totally eliminated, which creates further complications for political reconciliation. The continued threat that the

148   *The PKK's turn to democracy (1992–present)*

PKK guerrillas pose and their sporadic attacks against the Turkish security forces enhances the association in the popular Turkish mind between Kurdish demands and 'separatism' and 'terrorism'. Such a representation plays a significant role in representing Kurdish demands as 'illegitimate', which has been a major barrier preventing the development of a process of political reconciliation and full recognition of Kurdish identity in Turkey. From May 2004 onwards, citing the lack of any dialogue and initiative to find a peaceful solution to the conflict and the continuation of the PKK leader's solitary confinement, the HPG declared its permanent ceasefire to be over. Subsequently, this resulted in the acceleration of the conflict, and the HPG started to carry out various attacks against Turkish military targets inside Turkey. The Turkish army's use of chemical weapons to kill 14 guerrillas in the Muş province on 26 March 2006 followed an escalation in HPG attacks in the second half of 2006.[108] In particular, during late March and early April 2006, the reaction in Diyarbakir to the news that the guerrillas had been killed by chemical attacks was widespread unrest and popular riots reminiscent of the popular uprisings of the early 1990s.[109] Following Öcalan's call for a ceasefire via his solicitors in September 2006, the PKK declared a unilateral ceasefire on 1 October 2006.[110] Even though the ceasefire significantly reduced the surge in violence, in October 2007 a new wave of violence started. On 17 October 2007, the Turkish parliament passed a resolution giving the army authority to conduct a military incursion into Iraq to attack the PKK bases.[111] The PKK responded by carrying out a large-scale attack in Hakkari on 21 October during which 12 soldiers were killed, many more injured and eight more were taken as hostages.[112] The hostages were subsequently released unharmed on 4 November 2007.[113]

The escalation of violence continued despite the 'peace declaration' made by the KCK Governing Council on 1 December 2007.[114] The conflict escalated further when the Turkish army carried out a large-scale cross-border military incursion to destroy the PKK bases in the Qandil Mountains in Iraq on 21 February 2007. Under intense international pressure, the incursions were cut short without the stated objectives being met, and the troops were withdrawn on 29 February 2008.[115] The Turkish military claimed that 240 guerrillas were killed during the incursion.[116] However, a buoyant PKK claimed that its losses were far fewer than the army claimed and the sudden withdrawal – despite the previous indications by the army that a long-term presence in the Kurdistan Region was envisaged – was interpreted as a significant moral victory, which according to the PKK confirmed that a military solution to the Kurdish question was no longer viable.[117] Prior and subsequent to the land incursion, the Turkish army carried out numerous air strikes against PKK targets in Iraq. Another significant development in the conflict during 2008 was the attacks on the Aktütün military patrol station on 3 October, which caused the death of 17 soldiers and injury to 20.[118] The lack of protection accorded to the military station despite the knowledge that it was frequently targeted by the PKK led to the army being criticised in the media and losing its previously unquestioned credibility.[119] Subsequently, the PKK declared unilateral ceasefire to reiterate its commitment to the political

The PKK's turn to democracy (1992–present)   149

struggle and peace. This has been re-enforced in the PKK's declaration of a unilateral ceasefire during the local elections in 2009 and its subsequent extension until September 2009.[120] However, on 7 December 2009 an attack in the Tokat province of Central Turkey, which resulted in the death of seven soldiers, was carried out by the PKK. In a statement published on 10 December, the PKK accepted responsibility for the attack and cited the continuation of the harsh prison conditions that Öcalan had been experiencing, as the reason for carrying out the attack.[121] Furthermore, a new wave of violent political protests in the main Kurdish towns in Turkey followed the closure of the pro-Kurdish Democratic Society Party on 11 December 2009, which is discussed in greater detail in Chapter 8. Sporadic violence and PKK attacks continued throughout 2010. The attack on 19 June 2010 in Şemdinli that killed 11 soldiers led to the PM Erdogan reacting that Turkey had to 'annihilate' the PKK.[122]

In the past decade, attacks in tourist resorts and urban centres of Western Turkey that the PKK started to deploy in the mid 1990s also continued to occur after the ceasefire was called off. The TAK (*Tayrêbazên Azadiya Kurdistan,* Liberation Falcons of Kurdistan), which has been widely described as having close links to the PKK, took responsibility for many of these attacks.[123] Of these, a bomb exploded on a bus on 16 July 2005 in Kuşadası resulting in the death of five people including two Britons.[124] On 28 August 2008, a series of bombs exploded in the tourist resorts of Marmaris and Antalya on the Mediterranean coast, which again caused fatalities.[125] Such attacks have created various difficulties for the PKK because they have re-enforced the association in the media and the state discourse of the Kurds with terrorism, which maintains the marginalisation and exclusion of the Kurdish movement in general and creates major difficulties for the PKK in its attempts to transform itself into a legal political movement. For example, placing the blame on the PKK for the bombing in the district of Güngören in July 2008 – despite the PKK's unambiguous denial of involvement, the lack of any evidence and the condemnation of the attacks by numerous Kurdish organisations – has been used by the media to re-enforce the hegemonic representation of the Kurdish question as 'terrorism'.

However, in addition to the violence, peaceful and political forms of political participation and protest have also been taking place. Peaceful meetings and demonstrations in numerous towns and cities in the Kurdish regions in support of Kurdish rights and demands that have attracted large crowds, most notably the *Newroz* festivals, have been occurring quite frequently in recent years. Additionally, various new civil society organisations have been active in raising Kurdish identity demands through peaceful protests. In particular, the Kurdish language pressure group *TZP Kurdi,* as well as numerous human rights and women rights organisations that campaign on diverse issues, has been actively present in raising Kurdish demands. Another type of protest that has been becoming more widespread over the past few years has been protests in which mainly Kurdish youths have been taking part and which have quite frequently resulted in violent clashes with the police. Although democratic forms of protest and the emergence of numerous civil society organisations strengthens

150 *The PKK's turn to democracy (1992–present)*

democratic norms by offering the Kurds new means to engage with politics and participate in raising their demands, the frequent violent clashes between Kurdish youth and the Turkish security forces is indicative of the possibility of a new wave of political protest that entails a certain degree of violence and contains within itself the possibility of the eruption of a new wave of violence in a larger form in the urban centres of the majority Kurdish regions. The security forces' heavy-handed approach in dealing with youth protests, prosecuting the youths under the Anti-Terror laws and punishing them severely can exacerbate the situation and increase the violent potential that youth protests contain.[126]

Conclusion

The principal dislocations that the PKK experienced as a result of international developments, and the military losses it suffered, have been the main factors behind its appropriation of the democratic discourse from the early 1990s onwards and its strategic transformation during the late 1990s. The collapse of the socialist regimes diminished the likelihood of constructing a united and socialist Kurdistan, which was the key premise of the national liberation discourse. During the mid 1990s, the Turkish army's operations succeeded in containing the guerrilla operations within the Kurdish countryside and shielding the masses from the political effects of the latter. Furthermore, the forced evacuations and depopulation of rural settlements in the Kurdish region meant that the PKK was unable to get essential logistic support. Thus, the guerrilla strategy that the PKK used very successfully for its political mobilisation during the late 1980s and early 1990s started to be less effective in terms of generating a popular uprising. The PKK responded to the military stalemate by deploying different methods, such as attacks or threat of attacks against tourists in Western Turkey and the use of suicide bombing. This, however, created the danger of the conflict spreading to the whole of Turkey and evolving into a civil war.

During the 1990s, the PKK increasingly appropriated the discourse of democracy and attempted to initiate a process of political reconciliation by offering unilateral ceasefires on three occasions. In fact, the PKK's inability during the mid 1990s to construct a comprehensive democratic discourse resulted in the premature ending of its numerous unilateral ceasefires, prolonged the conflict and created major barriers to initiating a process of political reconciliation. Öcalan's capture in 1999 precipitated the subsequent discursive and organisational transformation. The new democratic discourse that the PKK started to construct emphasised Turkish-Kurdish historical unity and articulated Kurdish demands differentially as part of an equivalential chain of broader democratic demands. The key demands currently articulated in the PKK's democratic discourse are the transformation of Turkey into a 'democratic republic', the constitutional recognition of Kurdish identity and the democratisation of society to enable the free development of Kurdish language and culture. Hence, we have been witnessing a pluralisation in the demands that the PKK has been articulating. As expected, the democratic transformation has significantly lessened the antagonistic state of relations in Turkey. However, the PKK's attempts to transform itself into a democratic movement during the 2000s, including establishing numerous new political organisations, have faced further difficulties due to the global context and the 'war against terror', which limited the PKK's political space. The difficult international context meant that the PKK's strategic transformation has not successfully led to its acceptance as a democratic movement advocating political change through non-violent means. From 2005 onwards, the conflict started to flare up once again. However, so far the level of violence has not reached its previous levels and the attacks have not been for a prolonged period.

8 Contesting democracy and pluralism

The pro-Kurdish political parties in Turkey

> From the day we stepped into the parliament until now, all we have defended was fraternity, democracy and peace; to stop the spilling blood. If they are considered as crimes, then yes we have committed them. And we will continue to commit them.[1]

Introduction

The Kurdish movement attempted to articulate Kurdish cultural and political demands as part of broader demands for democracy and equality, as discussed in Chapters 3 and 4. However, these attempts were brought to a premature end in the early 1970s. It was only in the late 1970s, when the pro-Kurdish candidates, Edip Solmaz and Mehdi Zana successfully contested and won the 1977 municipal elections in Batman and Diyarbakir respectively, that the Kurdish democratic demands received a new impetus and found a new platform. However, soon afterwards pro-Kurdish political activism and representation at the local level began to experience repression once again: Edip Solmaz was killed in an extrajudicial murder in 1979; Mehdi Zana was arrested in 1980 and imprisoned until 1991 at the Diyarbakir Prison.[2] The severity of repression and the militarisation that Turkey experienced following its third coup d'etat on 12 September 1980 meant that the pro-Kurdish democratic movement was unable to grow. Hence, during the 1980s mainly the centre-right Motherland Party (*Anavatan Partisi*), the centre-left Populist Party (*Halkçı Parti*) and the Social Democratic Populist Party (*Sosyaldemokrat Halkçı Parti*, SHP) dominated electoral politics in the majority Kurdish regions. It was only after 1990 that pro-Kurdish representation and political challenge was able to return. From that point onwards, the pro-Kurdish movement managed to build an institutional base and endure the state's numerous attempts to suppress it. As will be shown below, since 1990 numerous pro-Kurdish political parties have been active in Turkey raising Kurdish demands, challenging the established order in Turkey to recognise Kurdish identity and cultural rights, and putting forward proposals for political reconciliation to end the cycle of violence that started with the PKK's commencement of its guerrilla war in 1984. However, despite their pro-Kurdish inclinations, they have been committed to representing a cross section of political groups in Turkey, and

Pro-Kurdish political parties in Turkey   153

numerous high-profile Turkish socialist politicians took part in the foundation of the first pro-Kurdish HEP.

As discussed in Chapter 2, the pro-Kurdish democratic challenge invokes the alternative tradition of democracy, which seeks to expand the logic of equality to wider spheres of social relations. At the core of pro-Kurdish democratic politics is the attempt to challenge and transform the existing unequal power relations and the political inequality that Kurds have been facing in Turkey that are seen as the root cause of the Kurds' marginalisation. The pro-Kurdish democratic discourse articulates particularistic Kurdish demands as part of broader democratic demands for equality and challenges the Kemalist social and political practices for being incompatible with the practice and norms of democracy. Therefore, the political logics of *difference* predominate as the principal aim has been to weaken the antagonism in Turkey. However, by highlighting the exclusionary, authoritarian, homogenising and anti-democratic character of the republic, and proposing to transform Turkey democratically, pro-Kurdish democratic discourse introduces new equivalential logics. They propose to construct a new common identity that recognises cultural and linguistic difference and pluralism in Turkey.

As emphasised by Norval, questions of political community, the construction of common space, the formation, articulation and universalisation of demands and cultivating 'democratic forms of citizenship' are central to our understanding of modern democracy and democratic practice.[3] The 'decontestation' of the existing notions of citizenship and community that pro-Kurdish democratic discourse attempts problematises the existing logics of universal rights, the construction of universality and the conception of citizenship around Turkish particularity.[4] More specifically, the articulation of Kurdish identity demands within the democratic discourse proposes universal 'national' rights for the Kurds (and other ethnic minorities), which in the current setting in Turkey are only the exclusive privilege of the Turkish nation. However, instead of putting forward proposals to construct a new Kurdish political community to realise such universal rights, the democratic transformation of Turkey to recognise the Kurds' national and democratic rights is the objective. The constant emphasis by a series of pro-Kurdish political parties on being 'a party of Turkey' and claiming to represent the 'whole of Turkey' as opposed to representing only the particularistic Kurdish demands, is an attempt to construct a 'common space'.

The pro-Kurdish democratic movement's challenge and contestation of a new democratic imaginary and to bring about an 'aspect change' offers an interesting case study. It shows the full range of complexities that implicate the construction of new democratic subjectivities and the various processes and difficulties involved in the institution of a pluralist and participatory democratic framework. Laclau's account of the emergence, articulation and universalisation of particularistic demands and interests offers a crucial insight into our understanding of the emergence of a new Kurdish democratic subjectivity in Turkey. As the discussion of 'political frontiers' in Chapter 2 elaborated, Laclau emphasises the significant role that the emergence of a new equivalential chain and the

154 *Pro-Kurdish political parties in Turkey*

equivalential articulation of various particularistic demands play in the construction of new political subjectivities and movements that challenge the existing order. A particular demand among various others emerges as the 'empty signifier' and takes on the challenge of representing the totality of the demands accumulated by the equivalential chain.

The pro-Kurdish democratic discourse seeks to universalise Kurdish demands for equality and democracy in Turkey via an equivalential articulation of various other particularistic demands that workers, women, religious minorities and other ethnic minorities have for equality and democracy. This equivalential articulation of various demands universalises Kurdish demands and also seeks to constitute a democratic subjectivity and counter-hegemonic pro-democracy movement to challenge Turkish nationalist hegemony in Turkey. Hence, 'equality' emerges as the 'empty signifier' in pro-Kurdish democratic discourse and it attempts to represent the equivalential chain of the demands that the pro-democracy movement articulates. The pro-Kurdish challenge does not resemble the antagonistic challenge as exemplified by the PKK's struggle. Instead the key focus has been on lessening the existing relations of antagonism in Turkey and transforming them to relations of 'agonism'. The need to transform an 'antagonistic' relation into 'agonistic' one is argued by Mouffe to be a key feature of democratic politics, given that the antagonistic dimension of social relations is 'ineradicable'.[5] Therefore, a key task of democratic politics is 'to envisage how it is possible to defuse the tendencies to exclusion that are present in every construction of collective identities'.[6]

As this chapter discusses, the contestation of democracy and pluralism by the pro-Kurdish democratic movement in the past two decades is yet to result in the desired 'aspect change' and the institution of a pluralist participatory democratic framework in Turkey. The main difficulty preventing the pro-Kurdish political challenge from succeeding is that the Kurdish demands in the political and popular media discourses in Turkey are represented as separatist and against Turkey's territorial integrity. Hence, they are constructed and represented as 'illegitimate', which prevents the pro-Kurdish democratic movement from extending its appeal to the wider Turkish society and fostering a democratic identity to challenge Turkish nationalist hegemony and its discourse on the Kurdish question.[7] From the onset, the pro-Kurdish democratic movement operated in a highly restricted political space that placed major barriers on the development and institutionalisation of a new political party promoting Kurdish rights and demands through legitimate political channels. It emerged at a time when Kurdish political demands for cultural rights and recognition of their identity were facing serious suppression and nationalist antagonism in Turkey was heightened due to the escalation of the conflict and civil unrest in the South-East region of the country. Additionally, pro-Kurdish proposals for political reconciliation and peace have not reached a wider audience as it could not successfully challenge the hegemonic representation of the Kurdish question. Consequently, due to the nature of the demands articulated in their discourse, they have been seen as part of a wider 'separatist' Kurdish movement and not as

Pro-Kurdish political parties in Turkey   155

legitimate political actors in Turkey, which led to various forms of political suppression.

Therefore, as well as giving an account of the growth of the pro-Kurdish movement, its achievements and contributions to strengthening democracy in Turkey, this chapter also enquires into the difficulties and challenges that it continues to face. In order to elaborate on how the pro-Kurdish movement has challenged the established conception of democracy in Turkey to recognise Kurdish cultural and political demands, this chapter addresses mainly the following questions: What are the characteristics of pro-Kurdish democratic discourse? How, or to what extent, does it address questions of pluralism, both within and outside the Kurdish community? To what extent has its discourse challenged the dominant conceptions of democracy in Turkey? By focusing on the activities of the pro-Kurdish political parties, the analysis highlights the problems that they have been facing, including their difficulties in building a wider pro-democracy movement.

Searching for 'inclusion' and 'recognition': the HEP and the emergence of Kurdish parliamentary opposition (1990–1994)

The HEP's engagement in the formal political process and representative institutions was a significant development. Principally, it articulated demands for the recognition of Kurdish identity and advocated a process of political reconciliation and dialogue to end the increasingly violent conflict between the PKK and the Turkish army. However, the 1982 constitution strictly banned any mention of the existence of the Kurds and incriminated any political party or organisation voicing Kurdish demands in Turkey. Therefore, the political space that the HEP – and following it the DEP – operated in was highly limited. This meant that the political programme and formal expression of demands by the pro-Kurdish parties were highly restricted, and in addition to the formal expression of demands such as the political programme of the party, the actions and speeches of the MPs and other members during public meetings and party congresses were highly scrutinised. This limited their ability to formulate proposals for political reconciliation and challenge the state's sedimented discourse that defined the Kurdish question narrowly as a security concern. Hence, from the onset the HEP found itself in an uneasy position whereby it had to balance the articulation of popular Kurdish political demands with being a legal political party working within the existing constitutional framework which considered the expression of such demands as 'unacceptable'. The pro-Kurdish political parties sought inclusion and accommodation within the democratic system in Turkey while seeking to expand the limits placed on Kurdish identity and culture by campaigning for recognition. This section assesses the early attempts by the HEP and the DEP to promote political reconciliation and recognition of Kurdish demands, and it highlights the problems and difficulties that they experienced.

156   *Pro-Kurdish political parties in Turkey*

The establishment of the HEP

The HEP was established on 7 June 1990 after the centre-left SHP tried to suppress the debate concerning the Kurdish question and political demands by expelling its Kurdish MPs who were at the centre of the debate. In the first election that the SHP contested in 1987, it managed to poll 24 per cent of the national vote and win 99 seats in the parliament to become the main opposition party. The SHP participated in the elections on a platform demanding more democracy in Turkey and limiting the legal and political effects of the 12 September coup and military rule. Consequently, the party successfully drew support from the Kurds, and numerous Kurdish MPs – who in later years became well-known advocates of Kurdish rights in Turkey – were elected, including Ahmet Türk (Mardin), Mahmut Alınak (Kars) and İbrahim Aksoy (Malatya).[8] However, the limit of the SHP's acceptance of the Kurdish rights and demands became evident when it expelled, on 6 February 1989, İbrahim Aksoy for discussing, during a Joint Session of the European Parliament on 19 January 1989, the human rights abuses and the political suppression that the Kurds faced in Turkey.[9] Furthermore, the SHP's Kurdish MPs' attendance at the international conference on the Kurdish question entitled 'The Kurds: Human Rights and Cultural Identity' held on 14–15 October 1989 in Paris was another event that created tension. This was because the SHP banned its members from attending the conference as it would have raised suspicions in Turkey, and despite the ban, several MPs attended the conference, who upon their return were expelled from the party.[10] The expulsion created turmoil in the party with six other MPs and the local leaders of the 12 SHP branches in the predominantly Kurdish cities resigning from the party in protest.[11] In fact it showed the need for a new political movement that would be willing to articulate Kurdish demands and support attempts for political reconciliation.[12]

Consequently, '*Yeni Demokratik Oluşum*' (the New Democratic Formation) was founded by 16 former SHP MPs in December 1989. In the 'Notice of Political Intentions', the group stressed the need to develop a new left-wing movement that would campaign for freedom, pluralism, participation and democracy, and remained committed to representing the marginalised groups and interests in Turkey.[13] They supported broad democratic demands, such as the proposal for a new civilian constitution, the need to have a movement with organic links to the masses and representing their needs. The group vowed to defend 'universal' democratic and human rights values and norms. The aim of the New Democratic Formation was to evolve into a political party.[14] Although Kurdish MPs and other leading Kurdish activists constituted the majority of its members, many Turkish socialist politicians, including Aydın Güven Gürkan, Abdullah Bastürk, Cüneyt Canver, Fehmi Işıklar and Arif Sağ (a popular musician and a leading Alevi community leader) also took a leading role in its activities.[15] However, the predominantly Kurdish support created unease among some of the Turkish politicians, including Gürkan, severing their relations with the movement.[16]

Pro-Kurdish political parties in Turkey 157

On 7 June 1990, the HEP was established as a left-wing democratic mass-based party committed to representing a cross section of social and political groups in Turkey.[17] Its political programme stated that the HEP was a party for:

> The workers, the unemployed, the rural people, the civil servants, the teachers, democrats, the intellectuals of social democratic and socialist persuasion, the small businesses and artisans, the masses who have been subjected to oppression and exploitation and above all everyone who supports democracy.[18]

Specifically, it had two combined objectives: the democratisation of the state and society and formulating a democratic and peaceful solution to the Kurdish conflict in Turkey. The democratic identity that the HEP attempted to institute was seen as key to the development of a democratic and plural Turkey, and the recognition of Kurdish identity and demands in Turkey were necessary steps in the development of a political settlement to end the conflict.

A pluralist and participatory conception of democracy was advocated, which above all sought to place political power and decision making in the hands of the civilian and elected officials. To achieve such a democratic framework and a democratic society in Turkey, the HEP argued that comprehensive political reforms were necessary as they could not have been achieved within the existing constitutional framework, which was drafted by the military junta and accorded a special role to the army-dominated National Security Council (*Milli Güvenlik Kurulu*, MGK). Hence, the HEP proposed a new civilian constitution to be drafted to replace the 1982 constitution. In fact, it was argued that the principles upon which the political system and the constitution were based needed to change to enable the democratisation of the state and society.[19] By taking the principles of human rights, pluralism and participation as its basis, it was stressed that the proposed new constitution should place clear limits on state power to safeguard the fundamental rights and freedoms of the individuals and prevent the likelihood of authoritarian and totalitarian forms of government. More importantly, a free and democratic environment in which all the social sectors and forces were able to participate was seen as essential for the preparation of the new constitution. A democratic regime in Turkey could only be established and its continuation guaranteed if these conditions were met.[20]

In addition to such broad democratic demands, the demands for a political solution to the Kurdish conflict also featured heavily in the HEP's discourse. Articulating Kurdish national rights and demands, however, was a much more complicated matter, due mainly to the legal restrictions and also the likely reaction that it would raise from the mainstream political parties. Whereas the HEP was keen to maintain a critical position to the state's oppressive policy regarding the Kurdish question and the ongoing military operations, which were described as 'oppression' and 'assimilation', the key emphasis in its discourse was on political reconciliation to end the conflict. The Kurdish political demands were articulated *differentially* as part of the HEP's demand for a plural and participatory

158 *Pro-Kurdish political parties in Turkey*

democracy. In fact, a democratic and political solution to the Kurdish question was seen as the main aspect of the development of democracy in Turkey: 'The party accepts that the solution to the Kurdish question is the main component of the establishment of an effective democracy in our country.'[21] It formulated the solution to the Kurdish question within the principles of equality and democracy:

> The party aims at a solution to the Kurdish question within the unity of Turkey by using democratic and peaceful methods, and according to judgements expressed in the Universal Declaration of Human Rights, the European Convention on Human Rights and the Helsinki Final Act.... A feasible democratic and peaceful solution that will benefit every section of our society can only be developed in an environment in which everyone can participate freely.[22]

Hence, the proposed solution was conceptualised within the universal democratic norms and values and it was stated that it needed to be arrived at through open dialogue in a free environment. For this purpose, the creation of a free environment for a debate and discussion of the Kurdish question that all the social and political forces could participate in was stressed to be of paramount importance. To create such an environment, the HEP proposed numerous practical measures. These included lifting the legal restrictions on the discussion of Kurdish identity and demands, granting a general amnesty, abolishing the death penalty and ending the practice of torture and emergency rule in the majority Kurdish regions. Such measures would have led to lessening of the conflict and antagonisms.[23] The HEP's discussion of the Kurdish question also questioned the forceful 'assimilation' of the Kurds throughout the history of the republic and proclaimed to end such policies and seek remedies for their negative effects.[24] For this purpose, one of the main targets of the proposed pluralist participatory democracy in Turkey needed to be ending all forms of 'discrimination on the basis of race, language, religion and ethnic difference' to pave the way for genuine political equality in all spheres between the citizens.[25] Regional economic inequality also featured in the HEP's programme and it proposed that state investment to develop the East and South-East regions and promote regional equality in Turkey was needed.[26] Articulating Kurdish demands within the restricted political space and without endangering the party's existence was a difficult task to accomplish. However, the intensification of the conflict during the early 1990s and the widespread oppression of Kurdish civilians by the state security forces increased the need for, and urgency of, voicing popular Kurdish demands.

The challenge of being a pro-Kurdish 'party of Turkey' and representing the Kurds

Throughout its existence the HEP remained committed to extending its appeal to the wider Turkish society, and it claimed to be a party representing the whole of

Pro-Kurdish political parties in Turkey   159

Turkey; however, it was mainly supported by the Kurds and increasingly seen as a specifically 'Kurdish party'. This had major consequences for it created limitations on the HEP's ability to construct a wider democratic movement for change and political reconciliation in Turkey. In a speech delivered to the First Congress of the HEP on 8 June 1991, Fehmi Işıklar, its chairman, acknowledged the Kurdish connection while stressing its objective to extend its appeal to the wider sections of society:

> We are the party of the most oppressed, exploited and those who are under the most pressure. Despite all our statements, those who describe the People's Labour Party as a 'Kurdish party', in fact, admit a truth or a historical fault, that in this country the Kurds are the most oppressed, exploited and suppressed people. If the People's Labour Party is trusted by the most oppressed and suppressed – and it is accepted as such – then we will be honoured to be also the party of the Kurds.[27]

However, not everyone in the HEP was comfortable with the predominance of the Kurds in the party or with the fact that the solution to the Kurdish conflict was one of the main issues that it campaigned on. As a result, more of the founding socialist members, such as Abdullah Bastürk, Cüneyt Canver and Kenan Sönmez left the party, which in turn strengthened the association between the Kurds and the HEP.[28]

Despite the acrimonious events leading to the expulsion of the Kurdish MPs from the SHP, the relations between the HEP and the SHP continued, and in the parliamentary elections held on 20 October 1991 both parties cooperated. This was partly out of necessity as the HEP was prevented from taking part in the elections for not meeting the requirement of having the party congress six months prior to the election date. Therefore, the HEP candidates contested the elections in the SHP's list. Even though the share of the SHP's vote was reduced to 20.75 per cent and the number of its MPs stood at 88, it performed above the national average in the Kurdish areas with 22 candidates proposed by the HEP winning a seat in parliament.[29] The initial post-election response of the newly elected Kurdish MPs was to continue to stay within the SHP as long as it supported a peaceful solution to the conflict and recognised Kurdish national demands. The election of 22 pro-Kurdish MPs was a unique event in the history of Turkey because for the first time representatives of a party committed to the recognition of Kurdish rights and demands were in Turkey's national assembly. Also, such a representation created a significant opportunity for the Kurds who rejected armed struggle as a method to raise awareness of the Kurdish question and campaigned for peace and political reconciliation.

A major hurdle facing the SHP's pro-Kurdish MPs was the parliamentary oath that they needed to swear in order to inaugurate their position. In fact, their actions were eagerly awaited as taking the oath was seen as the 'Litmus Test' of their commitment to Turkey and of the HEP being a 'party of Turkey'.[30] The difficulty emanated from the text of the oath as it proclaimed to protect the unity of

160   *Pro-Kurdish political parties in Turkey*

the 'Turkish nation' and the continuation of a regime that denied Kurdish identity. A day prior to the ceremony during a press conference, Fehmi Işıklar, the MP for Diyarbakir stated: 'The denial of the Kurdish nation is expressed in this oath. It is against democracy, human rights, peace and the brotherhood of the Turkish and Kurdish people.'[31] Despite having reservations about the text of the oath the Kurdish MPs took the oath; however, Hatip Dicle drew attention to it being a legal requirement, and Leyla Zana added a Kurdish sentence stating that that she took the oath for 'the brotherhood of the Turkish and Kurdish people'.[32]

Also, soon after the election of the 22 HEP candidates as MPs through the SHP list, and as a condition of remaining in the party, they presented a folder comprising 20 'Urgent Demands' to Erdal İnönü, the leader of the SHP.[33] These demands primarily concerned the conflict – such as free discussion of the Kurdish question, lifting emergency rule, terminating the village guards scheme, ending the forceful evacuation of the villages and rebuilding the ones that had been destroyed, ending counter-guerrilla operations, repealing the Anti-Terror law and investigating the extrajudicial murders – as well as those that more specifically targeted the recognition of Kurdish identity and rights in Turkey. These included granting the Kurds cultural rights such as freedom to use the Kurdish language in education and broadcasting. In addition, other democratic demands such as drafting a democratic constitution, workers' rights including the right to strike, and a fair election law, were also included.[34]

For the SHP's Kurdish MPs, the conflict and its consequence, such as the widespread human rights violations carried out against civilian Kurds, especially the extrajudicial murders, the army's widespread oppression of rural Kurds and the village evacuations, created urgency. Although the SHP was at best cautious about the recognition of Kurdish demands, at the same time it remained committed to deepening democracy in Turkey. As the report that the SHP prepared on the Kurdish question in 1992 indicated, it was also prepared to formulate a political solution to the conflict given that the conditions were right.[35] However, for the HEP, the solution to the conflict was an inseparable aspect and feature of the deepening of democracy and democratic consolidation in Turkey.

Zana's and Dicle's actions during the parliamentary oath ceremony were seen by many SHP MPs and the mainstream political parties in Turkey as a provocation and were interpreted as a serious challenge to the principle of national unity as codified in articles two and three of the constitution.[36] Furthermore, the oath ceremony caused uproar in the parliament and strained the relations between the SHP's Kurdish MPs and others, with pressure being put on Dicle and Zana to resign. The open acknowledgement of the Kurds by Zana in the parliament was seen as a clear statement of her and other Kurdish MP's support for separatism and the PKK. They began to be seen as an extension of the PKK and its legal front. Further difficulties for the HEP were created during the Extraordinary Congress held on 15 December 1991 at which Esma Öcalan, the mother of the PKK leader, was a guest and was greeted with much respect and affection by many delegates, including two MPs, Leyla Zana and Sırrı Sakık.[37] This received much criticism and reaction from mainstream Turkish media and politicians,

Pro-Kurdish political parties in Turkey 161

especially given that the SHP was the junior coalition partner in the government and the Kurdish MPs were still within the SHP. Many articles appeared in the Turkish media that interpreted the Kurdish MPs' attendance at the Congress as evidence of their connection to the PKK and their being sympathetic to the Kurdish national movement. In the period following the congress, pressure on the Kurdish MPs to resign from the SHP grew much sterner leading to the resignation of both Leyla Zana and Hatip Dicle on 16 January 1992.[38]

Also, during the first quarter of 1992, it became quite apparent that the coalition government was not willing to pursue policies that would have led to a reduction in violence and create a democratic opening and solution to the conflict. After the initial hesitation, the newly formed coalition government extended emergency rule in the majority Kurdish regions on 27 February 1992. The HEP and the Kurdish MPs were increasingly associated with separatism, and with the conflict being at its apex during the early 1990s, the pro-Kurdish democratic movement was severely oppressed. Hence, the attempts by the pro-Kurdish parliamentary opposition to work within the existing constitutional framework while campaigning to bring an end to the increasingly brutal conflict and for the recognition of Kurdish identity and cultural rights started to face a significant barrier. By 1 April 1992, 18 Kurdish MPs had resigned from the SHP and on 8 July 1992 they joined the HEP.[39]

The HEP's closure and the elimination of pro-Kurdish parliamentary representation

On 22 May 1992, the State Security Court prepared a case for stripping the HEP MP's parliamentary immunity in order to prepare a court case against them. Increasingly, the HEP's attempts to find a solution to the conflict through peaceful and democratic means and its articulation of Kurdish rights attracted negative attention from the mainstream Turkish media, often being presented as clear evidence for its link to the PKK and support for 'terrorism'. On 3 July 1992, the Supreme Court's Attorney General filed a case at the Constitutional Court to close down the HEP.[40] The indictment accused it of engaging in activities to weaken Turkey's territorial and national unity by proposing to change the 'unchangeable' principles of the constitution and for expressing that ethnic, linguistic and cultural groups exist in Turkey. The HEP was closed down by the Constitutional Court on 14 July 1993.[41]

The court case and the reaction that the HEP's MPs got from the mainstream media and political parties in Turkey coincided with the HEP adopting a more radical stance and starting to express more radical Kurdish demands. During the HEP's Second Congress on 19 September 1992, many of the leading members argued that, as an effective step towards ending the conflict, the PKK's engagement in the political process was needed.[42] Also, the establishment of regional parliaments or representative bodies was proposed by the MP Mahmut Alınak as a possible step that could be taken to democratise the state and satisfy Kurdish national demands in Turkey.[43] Moreover, the HEP's new political programme,

162   *Pro-Kurdish political parties in Turkey*

drafted in 1992, was, in comparison to its previous one, much more reflective of Kurdish demands. Although the new programme reiterated the HEP's preferred solution to the conflict to be on the basis of 'free, equal and voluntary union of the Turkish and Kurdish nations', it also stated:

> In the solution of the Kurdish question, the HEP is fully committed to the principle of 'Nations' Right to National Self-Determination'. Within this framework, it declares its total and unconditional support for the proposals of solutions that the [Kurdish] people will develop, such as referendums, federation etc. and that it will do all it can within its power and without any precondition or laying down any conditions.[44]

This was a major shift in the discourse as the national dimension of Kurdish rights and demands were more openly articulated. Moreover, an article that assessed the political developments in 1992 by the deputy leader of the HEP, Mahmut Kılınç, described Kurds as a 'founding element' of the republic and the Kurdish question as a question of 'Kurdish people's freedom'.[45] Similarly, the public statement informing about the commencement of the hunger strike that the HEP MPs started on 12 November 1992 – to protest against the political murders of its members and also against the parliament's 'non-functionality' in terms of representing Kurdish demands – again conceived Kurdish rights and demands in national terms. After presenting numerous instances of denial of the Kurds' national rights and demands, the statement drew attention to the unavoidable need to recognise Kurdish identity and all the associated fundamental rights and freedoms, the denial of which were the root cause of the conflict.[46] The emphasis on Kurdish national rights was indicative of the predominance of the 'Kurdish' equivalential logics in the HEP's discourse in 1992; however, this was balanced by an unequivocal commitment to furthering democracy in Turkey. Moreover, in the early 1990s the HEP took an increasingly more active role in organising Kurdish cultural activities in Turkey. For example, in 1991 it organised the *Newroz* celebration in Istanbul which was attended by 15,000 people.[47]

   To prolong the existence of the pro-Kurdish parliamentary opposition and thwart the dangers that the closure of the HEP would create, the Democracy Party (*Demokrasi Partisi* or DEP) was established on 7 May 1993. Similar to the HEP, the DEP's political programme had the democratisation of the state and society as its principal objective. Specifically, it proposed a peaceful and democratic solution to the Kurdish question and comprehensive constitutional reform to enable Turkey to institute a pluralist democratic regime.[48] The DEP was engaged in a wide range of activities to initiate a process of debate and discussion concerning the Kurdish question. Being the Kurds legitimate representative in Turkish parliament, these occasions also gave the DEP an opportunity to formulate proposals for reconciliation. For example, a 'peace declaration' that the DEP prepared listed a number of proposals that the government needed to take to ensure a peaceful resolution of the Kurdish question. These included the recognition of Kurdish identity and constitutional guarantees to protect it, lifting all

Pro-Kurdish political parties in Turkey 163

the restrictions on the use of the Kurdish language, recognising the Kurds' right to education and radio and TV broadcasts in Kurdish, ending the village guard system and emergency rule in Kurdish areas, repealing the Anti-Terror laws, investigating the extrajudicial murders, rebuilding villages that were destroyed and taking the necessary steps to rebuild the local economy.[49]

The political suppression that the HEP and the DEP experienced prior to their closure marginalised the Kurdish democratic movement and forced them to resort to unconventional methods to draw attention to their plight. Of these, the hunger strike that the HEP MPs took part in to draw attention to the Kurdish demands and the intensification of oppression was discussed above.[50] On 16 April 1993, a delegation comprising six leading members of the HEP, including its chairman Ahmet Türk, visited the PKK headquarters in Lebanon to meet Öcalan and request an extension of the PKK's ceasefire.[51] On 2 August 1993, the DEP started a peace campaign to raise awareness about the conflict and help start a dialogue for peace and reconciliation that was planned to continue until the World Peace Day on 1 September 1993. However, permission for many of the events was not given, and suppression of the DEP activities intensified in this period.

The connection to the PKK was used as a pretext by the state to suppress the pro-Kurdish democratic movement. The Turkish government and the security establishment described both the HEP and the DEP as the 'political wing' of the PKK. This meant that the suppression of the pro-Kurdish movement was done with relatively little domestic opposition. Throughout the early 1990s numerous Kurdish activists connected with the pro-Kurdish political parties were persecuted, including frequent arrests and torture of many activists, murder of some leading members and many grass-roots activists. One of the first high-profile cases was the murder of Vedat Aydın, the HEP's leader in Diyarbakir province in July 1991. On 4 September 1993, the DEP delegation that was conducting a fact-finding mission into the 'murders by unknown assailants' came under armed attack in Batman, which resulted in the death of the MP for Mardin, Mehmet Sincar, and a local party leader. The MP for Batman, Nizamettin Toğuç, and three other people were injured during the attack. Between 1991 and 1994 more than 50 members of the HEP and the DEP were murdered.[52] The DEP's headquarters were bombed on 18 February 1994, which caused the death of one person and injury to 16 people.[53] On 22 February 1994, the Prime Minister, Çiller, accused the DEP MP Hatip Dicle of being a traitor and vowed to uplift parliamentary immunity of the DEP MPs.[54] DEP MPs received similar threats from the Commander of the Turkish Armed Forces, Doğan Güreş.[55] Two sons of the DEP's candidate for municipal elections in the Bağlar district of Diyarbakir were killed on 24 February 1994. Due to the widespread violence and oppression against its candidates and members, the DEP withdrew from the municipal elections scheduled to take place on 27 March 1994.[56]

On 2 March 1994, the parliament lifted the legal immunity of the DEP MPs, which enabled the State Security Court in Ankara to hear the case against them. The DEP was closed down on 16 June 1994.[57] On 17 March 1994, six DEP MPs

164   *Pro-Kurdish political parties in Turkey*

were arrested with two more being arrested on 1 July 1994. The trial ended on 8 August 1994 with Hatip Dicle, Orhan Doğan, Leyla Zana, Ahmet Türk and Selim Sadak receiving 15 year sentences and Sedat Yurtdaş receiving a sentence of seven years and six months. Sırrı Sakık and Mahmut Alınak were released. They appealed to the Supreme Court of Appeals (*Yargıtay*) to reverse the decision of the State Security Court. In the case of Hatip Dicle, Orhan Doğan, Leyla Zana and Selim Sadak the appeal was rejected; however, Ahmet Türk and Sedat Yurtdaş were released.[58] The MPs Mahmut Kılınç, Remzi Kartal, Ali Yiğit, Nizamettin Toğuç, Naif Güneş and Zübeyir Aydar left Turkey for Brussels before the trial began to continue their activities there in exile.[59] The Kurdish political representation in the Turkish Assembly was eliminated in 1994, and subsequently Kurdish political demands were equated with separatism and terrorism, thereby limiting the channels through which they could be raised.

Rebuilding the pro-Kurdish democracy movement

The next decade or so following the closure of the DEP and the elimination of the Kurdish parliamentary opposition was spent by attempts to rebuild the pro-Kurdish democratic movement. The HADEP, established on 11 May 1994, and its 'substitute' the Democratic People's Party (*Demokratik Halk Partisi* or DEHAP), established on 24 October 1997, were the main pro-Kurdish political parties in Turkey in that period. Due to the 10 per cent national election threshold restricting parliamentary representation neither the HADEP nor the DEHAP were able to gain a seat in parliament. However, they both enjoyed some level of success at the local level and more importantly managed to construct a grassroots organisation and a wide-ranging organisational network covering many of the cities in Turkey. Additionally, separate women's and youth's branches were established in the late 1990s, which enabled them to mobilise a wider section of Kurdish society as the participation of women and youth drew a greater number of the Kurds into the movement. Having a strong grass-roots organisation coupled with the fact that the HADEP was able to continue its existence until 2003 – relatively longer compared to its predecessors – meant that the pro-Kurdish movement became much more organised from the mid 1990s onwards. After the general election on 22 July 2007, the pro-Kurdish parliamentary opposition returned with the election of the Democratic Society Party (*Demokratik Toplum Partisi*, DTP) candidates. They stood as independent candidates in order to avoid the 10 per cent national election threshold. The DTP established a political group in the parliament with 21 MPs and remained active until it was closed down by the Constitutional Court on 12 December 2009. Currently, the Peace and Democracy Party (*Barış ve Demokrasi Partisi*, BDP) has taken on the task of Kurdish representation in Turkey.

Pro-Kurdish political parties in Turkey 165

The HADEP and the DEHAP: building the pro-democracy block (1994–2005)

The HADEP was the main avenue of Kurdish political participation in Turkey until its closure in 2003. Being the representative of the pro-Kurdish democratic movement, the discourse and demands articulated by the HADEP were remarkably similar to its predecessors. Political reconciliation through democratisation and the recognition of Kurdish identity and their cultural and political rights in Turkey were its principal objectives.[60] Specifically, as confidence building steps towards finding a peaceful solution to the Kurdish question, the HADEP proposed a general amnesty for political prisoners, the resettlement of the internally displaced people back to their villages, and an investigation into the politically motivated extrajudicial murders and disappearances that took place in the Kurdish towns and cities during the 1990s.[61] Also, similar to the HEP and the DEP, the solution to the Kurdish question was conceived in terms of the democratisation of the state and society in Turkey. It argued that as a first step forward, the creation of an environment that would foster free debate and discussion was needed. In order to create such an environment, the HADEP proposed comprehensive constitutional reform:

> The 1982 constitution is the most significant barrier to democratisation. This constitution needs to be changed completely; a new constitution, which will establish a functional democracy, needs to be prepared in a democratic and free environment in which every social group and force is able to freely participate.[62]

The new constitution needed to foster the development of an open, pluralist and participatory democracy that respected cultural difference and diversity and internalised the universal democratic and human rights norms and values.[63] Moreover, the proposal for the solution of the Kurdish question was conceived within the universal norms and values:

> Concerning the Kurdish question, our party will introduce a just solution based on the principle of equality and in accordance with the contemporary, universal and supra-national legal principles to end all forms of exploitation, oppression and inequality in economic, political and cultural spheres.... Special effort will be placed to eliminate the continuing practices of suppression in the areas of language, culture and education; the barren environment created by the grindstone of assimilation; and the massive inequalities. One of our party's principal objectives is to introduce a just solution to the Kurdish question based on the principle of equality through peaceful and democratic methods.[64]

The HADEP participated in the first general election in 1995 as part of the Labour, Peace and Freedom Block (*Emek, Barış ve Özgürlük Bloku*) that emerged as a movement for democracy and change and included minor socialist

166   Pro-Kurdish political parties in Turkey

parties and democratic political groups in Turkey, obtaining 1.17 million votes (representing 4.17 per cent of the national vote).[65] However, due to the 10 per cent election threshold it was not represented in parliament. Nevertheless, it continued to be the focal point of Kurdish political activities in Turkey. In 1995, the HADEP took part in numerous campaigns to increase the pressure on the government to respond to the ceasefire that the PKK declared to facilitate a lasting solution to the conflict. In particular, it organised or participated in numerous events, including the 'Peace and Democracy Meeting' held in Istanbul on 21 April 1996, which was attended by many people and supported by many NGOs and Trade Unions.[66] Additionally, it participated in many rallies and demonstrations throughout the 1990s. Being the focal point of Kurdish activism created and reinforced the view in Turkey that the HADEP was solely a Kurdish party or represented only particularistic Kurdish demands. This proved to be a barrier in the HADEP's attempts to extend its appeal to the wider Turkish society. Additionally, various specific events caused numerous difficulties for the HADEP and its marginalisation; for example, the 'pulling down' of the Turkish flag during the HADEP's Second Congress, held in Ankara on 23 June 1996, proved detrimental. This event gained widespread coverage in the Turkish media and caused a furore in Turkey with many politicians condemning the incident and using it as an example of the Kurds' 'betrayal' and 'treachery'. It cast a significant doubt on the HADEP's claim to be a 'party of Turkey' as the event was interpreted by many as a clear sign that it did not respect the country's most 'sacred' symbol. Additionally, the polarisation in Turkey caused by the continuation of the conflict between the PKK and Turkey meant that the HADEP was seen as an adversary and its members, as part of the Kurdish movement, as separatists.

The events in Turkey connected with the arrest of the PKK's leader Öcalan in Italy in November 1998 and his eventual capture in February 1999 intensified political oppression against the HADEP. This period witnessed many protests by Kurds and the HADEP supporters against Öcalan's arrest and capture, which created a highly hostile environment in Turkey. The hunger strike that took place under the HADEP's auspices to protest against Öcalan's arrest in Rome resulted in police raids on its branches nationwide and the arrest and detention of more than 700 of its members, including its chairman Murat Bozlak and members of its executive council.[67] On 29 January 1999 the Chief Prosecutor, Vural Savaş submitted a case to the Constitutional Court to close down the HADEP on the grounds that it constituted a threat to Turkey's territorial integrity and that it was engaging in unconstitutional activities.[68] The attempt was not successful in preventing the HADEP from entering the national and municipal elections scheduled for 18 April 1999.[69]

The HADEP managed to continue its existence within such a highly volatile environment and obtained 4.76 and 3.82 per cent in the parliamentary and municipal elections respectively. In total it managed to win the control of 37 towns and cities across the Kurdish region, including the Municipal Councils of Diyarbakir, Ağrı, Bingöl, Hakkari, Siirt, Van and Batman.[70] Despite this success, pressure on the HADEP continued, and on 19 February 2000 its mayors of

Pro-Kurdish political parties in Turkey 167

Diyarbakir, Bingöl and Siirt were arrested, being charged on 23 February with 'aiding and abetting the PKK'.[71] However, they were released on 28 February after intense international pressure.[72] On 23 February 2000, 18 HADEP members including its former chairman Murat Bozlak, and the chairman Ahmet Turan Demir received prison sentences of three years and nine months.[73]

Overall, the HADEP remained active for nearly nine years until its closure in 2003, and as mentioned above it managed to establish a wide organisational network. This occurred amidst continued political oppression with many of its members persecuted and 33 murdered between 1994 and 2002.[74] Although the DEHAP was established in 1997 as a ready substitute in case the HADEP was closed down, it was not until 2003 that it began to take centre stage in Kurdish democratic politics in Turkey. Being part of the pro-Kurdish tradition in Turkey, the DEHAP articulated similar demands for democratisation and political reconciliation in Turkey. Due to the impending court case for the HADEP's closure,[75] the DEHAP contested the 2002 general election under the Labour, Peace and Democracy Block (*Emek, Barış ve Demokrasi Bloku*) winning 6.12 per cent of the votes. While this result represented a nearly 30 per cent increase in the votes of the pro-Kurdish democratic block, it fell short of the level required for parliamentary representation.[76] During the election the pro-democracy coalition articulated democratic demands that other political groups, such as workers, women, Alevis, etc. had for equality and democracy in Turkey.[77] In the 2004 municipal elections, the DEHAP contested again as part of the pro-democracy block under the banner of the Social Democratic People's Party. It won 8.76 per cent of the national vote and increased the number of the councils it held to 54 including the municipality councils of Diyarbakir, Batman, Şırnak and Hakkari.

While the case to close down the DEHAP was being considered by the Constitutional Court, the formation of a new pro-Kurdish political party was on the agenda. The release of the former DEP MPs on 9 June 2004 – who following their release vowed to work towards finding a peaceful solution to the Kurdish question – accelerated the process.[78] The first concrete steps were taken when the former MPs declared the establishment of the Democratic Society Movement (*Demokratik Toplum Hareketi,* DTH) the principal aim of which was to campaign for a pluralist and participatory democracy in Turkey. Specifically, the DTH's political principles were supporting Turkey's EU integration, finding a solution to the 'Kurdish question' without endangering Turkey's territorial unity and through peaceful and democratic means, and campaigning for an inclusive national identity in Turkey that would provide recognition and representation for all the national and cultural minorities and identities in Turkey.[79] The DTP was formally established in November 2005.[80] Although the personnel of the party included many members of the former pro-Kurdish political parties in Turkey, and it certainly represented the pro-Kurdish tradition in Turkey, it was established to represent broader sections of the society and attract other political groups in Turkey that its predecessors had failed. Crucially, therefore, many people took part in its establishment and, according to the DTP sources, in total 300,000 people took part in the meetings and public consultations that the DTH

168   *Pro-Kurdish political parties in Turkey*

organised to elect delegates and the founding members of the party.[81] The DEHAP mayors joined the DTP after its establishment in November 2005.

The permanent ceasefire that the PKK declared in 1999 brought a significant reduction in the conflict and in the violent incidents in the region and created space for the HADEP and the DEHAP to promote reconciliation and a democratic solution to the Kurdish question. The success at the municipal elections gave it an institutional base to promote Kurdish culture and demands. For example, the Diyarbakir Municipality Council started to organise the *Newroz* celebrations legally from the year 2000, which have been attracting large crowds. In the year 2000, it attracted 200,000 people according to the organisers. The organisation of *Newroz* events in the cities of Batman and Van attracted 50,000 and 60,000 people respectively.[82] In 2001, it was reported that nearly 500,000 people attended the *Newroz* in Diyarbakir. In 2002, as well as a large crowd, the *Newroz* organisation in Diyarbakir was attended by many politicians and representatives of socialist political parties and trade unions and by a highly popular Turkish pop music singer, Sezen Aksu, who gave a live performance. As the most potent symbol of Kurdish political identity, *Newroz* acquired the characteristics of a peace festival; it has become an event where Kurdish demands for political reconciliation and democracy are expressed vocally by large crowds. Therefore, being in the centre of Kurdish political activism and channelling it through peaceful means enhances the pro-Kurdish political parties' credibility as the Kurds' legitimate representatives in Turkey.

Furthermore, having an institutional base allowed the pro-Kurdish parties to contest cultural pluralism in Turkey and challenge the homogenising policies of the state. For example, in October 2006 the Sur Municipality – which is located within the Diyarbakir Province and where nearly 75 per cent of the residents speak Kurdish and both Armenian and Assyrian are community languages spoken by the residents of the municipality – adopted the practice of 'multilingualism in local governance' (*Çok Dilli Belediyecilik*) by using, in addition to Turkish, the Kurdish, Armenian and Assyrian languages in the provision of its services and to publish information and leaflets. The decision to use community languages was taken to make local democracy more effective and functional, to increase the participation of the residents, recognise their cultural difference and cultivate respect and tolerance. However, the state responded by suppressing the Municipality's attempt for being unconstitutional and constituting an offence. This led to an investigation by the Ministry of Interior, the dissolving of the assembly of the Municipality and removing the mayor, Abdullah Demirbaş.[83] Even though the practice of multilingual governance at the local level was unable to grow, the attempt to challenge the existing embedded notions of cultural homogeneity and the associated practices showed the possibility of alternative ways of managing cultural difference.

The DTP and the BDP: the re-emergence of Kurdish parliamentary opposition (2005–2011)

The DTP's conception of democracy closely resembled that of its predecessors as it too had the democratisation of the state and society as its main political objective. It proposed to transcend the 'oligarchic' structure of the republic by constructing a democratic society that has achieved internal peace and accepts diversity in Turkey.[84] The democratisation of society and the development of civil society were seen as being of crucial importance in the democratisation process for they would lead to the democratisation of state institutions by fostering the development and spread of democratic values. By emphasising the demands for equality and democracy that numerous social groups have, the DTP's discourse challenged the elitist and exclusionary nature of the political system in Turkey and sought to build a coalition of democratic forces to bring about the much needed democratic change. Similar to its predecessors and the PKK's democratic discourse, the political logics of *difference* predominated since the primary aim was to put into motion Turkey's internal dynamics in order to achieve democratic change. The signifiers 'equality' and 'democracy' functioned as the 'empty signifiers' in the DTP's discourse that articulated popular demands for equality and democracy as part of Kurdish national demands for the recognition of their identity and culture in order to construct a broad democratic movement to contest political power. As was the case with the previous pro-Kurdish political parties, the proposals for comprehensive constitutional reforms were put forward to replace the 'homogenised' and 'delimited' conception of citizenship and national identity in Turkey with an inclusive common national identity (*Türkiyelilik*) based on a civic pluralist model of citizenship that respected and recognised various ethnic, cultural and religious differences.[85] Hence, the recognition and granting of Kurdish cultural rights such as education in the Kurdish language are the main Kurdish demands that the DTP articulated in its democratic discourse. It argued that, above all, the new constitution needed to 'guarantee':

> the Kurds' and other cultural identities' right, within the unity of the country, to freely express their identities, to develop their culture, to speak in their mother tongue, to develop it and to use it in education and in visual and auditory media.[86]

The democratisation of the state and society would provide a permanent and systematic solution to the Kurdish question that rejected both 'denial' and 'separation' and conceived of a solution on the basis of equality and freedom and 'the historical unity and relations of fraternity of Turks and Kurds'.[87] Moreover, to ensure societal peace 'the principle of pluralism based upon multiculturalism and the equal, free and balanced development of differences and distinctions that exist in the society must be accepted'.[88] Additionally, the DTP's programme incorporated women's emancipation and gender equality as unequivocal features of democratisation and accorded a significant role for them. Similarly, ecological

170 *Pro-Kurdish political parties in Turkey*

sustainability and environmental protection and conservation were important contours of its discourse.

On 22 July 2007 Kurdish representation in parliament returned with the elections of the 22 DTP MPs as independent candidates (*Bin Umut Bağımsız Adayları*). In Western Turkey, the DTP supported Turkish pro-democratic socialist candidates mainly from the EMEP (*Emek Partisi*, Labour Party) and the ÖDP (Freedom and Solidarity Party). One DTP MP, Sebahat Tuncel, was elected in the city of Istanbul. Another of its Istanbul candidates and its candidate in the province of Mersin lost narrowly.[89] The election success resulted in the return of the pro-Kurdish parliamentary opposition in Turkey at the July 2007 national parliamentary elections. The election of the DTP into the parliament – after 13 years of absence – restored the pro-Kurdish parliamentary opposition in Turkey and brought a new momentum to Kurdish political activism there. It also placed the DTP in the centre stage of Kurdish politics in Turkey. In the municipal elections held on 29 March 2009, the DTP consolidated its position as the leading party of the Kurdish regions winning more than 50 per cent of the votes in many towns and cities and a respectable 2,339,729 votes nationally. In total, it won 99 Councils including the Municipalities of Diyarbakir, Van, Batman, Tunceli, Iğdır, Şırnak, Siirt and Hakkari.[90] The election of the DTP MPs and the success it achieved in the municipal elections was viewed as a chance to build bridges between the different political groups to foster greater understanding. Crucially, having parliamentary representation provided the DTP with a legal democratic platform where Kurdish rights and demands could be raised.

Being represented in the national assembly and having the experience of running many of the local authorities in the Kurdish regions enabled the DTP to establish a strong regional and national presence. This allowed for the establishment and sustenance of links and associations with various other social and political groups in Turkey, which fostered exchange of views and better understanding. Having an institutional base also enabled the DTP to intensify its efforts to campaign for a democratic and peaceful solution to the Kurdish question in Turkey. In particular, being represented in the National Assembly gave the DTP MPs a chance to discuss a range of concerning issues and had major implications for the Kurds and the Kurdish question in Turkey. These ranged from issues that the Kurds in a particular locality faced – for example the education problems in the town of Hakkari[91] – to more regional issues that were directly connected to the conflict, such as the fate of the people who disappeared under detention,[92] the continual use of torture in police custody,[93] the discrimination that the Kurds continue to be subjected to in Turkey[94] and the solution to the Kurdish question.[95] On 13 March 2008, Pervin Buldan, the DTP MP for Kars, demanded that a parliamentary commission be established to investigate the extrajudicial murders which occurred during the 1990s.[96]

Additionally, having parliamentary representation allowed the DTP to disseminate its discourse nationally through the national press to the whole population of Turkey. In numerous interviews that the DTP MPs had with the Turkish media, they stressed the urgency of the political solution to the Kurdish question

Pro-Kurdish political parties in Turkey 171

and provided their alternative representation by uncoupling it from violence and from being seen as a security issue.[97] In this alternative representation, as argued by Aysel Tuğluk the MP for Diyarbakir, not resolving the Kurdish question creates security problems and conflict.[98] Such media statements are used by the DTP MPs to disseminate their proposal for political reconciliation and democratic solution of the Kurdish question:

> The solution of the Kurdish question is possible by the widest interpretation of the Copenhagen Criteria and its application to the new constitution. The solution to the Kurdish question in the end will be constitutional. As long as the constitutional guarantees are not met, the fears and suspicions of the Kurds will rightly continue. A new definition of citizenship in the constitution and arrangements to provide linguistic and cultural freedoms are the primary steps that need to be taken to solve the question.[99]

Furthermore, as an alternative framework to the unitary and highly centralised political structure in Turkey, the DTP formulated the 'Democratic Autonomy' proposal – which proposed the decentralisation of political power and envisioned the establishment of regional bodies as a framework that could be used to provide better governance and could be developed to solve the Kurdish question.[100] Since the development and deepening of democracy in Turkey is strongly linked to the EU accession process, the DTP also tried to build links with European political parties to support the development of internal dynamics for change and enhancing civilian rule in Turkey.

Despite representation in the National Assembly and running many towns and cities in the predominantly Kurdish regions, the DTP was unable to be seen as part of the political system and be accepted as a legitimate political party. In fact, the issue of the continual non-acceptance of Kurdish identity demands as being fully legitimate that has blighted the previous pro-Kurdish parties' attempts to contest democracy and pluralism in Turkey continued to be a significant barrier for the DTP. The similarity between the DTP's political demands and the PKK's demands again raised the issue of the link between the two. This presumed link that the DTP had with the PKK and the intensification of violence periodically after the end of the PKK's ceasefire in 2005 created problems for its acceptance. The link to the PKK was used extensively by the current government and the Turkish army to marginalise the DTP. Specifically, the DTP was treated as the political wing of the PKK and as separatists. Furthermore, the recent waves of arrests of leading DTP members which started on 14 April 2009 for their alleged links to the PKK following the local elections is yet another incident that shows how the alleged link to the PKK is used to exclude and repress pro-Kurdish democratic politics.[101] Such actions were interpreted by the DTP as evidence for the AKP government's unwillingness to change its policy concerning the Kurdish question and initiate measures to develop political reconciliation.

Additionally, during the campaign for the local election in 2009, the AKP government persistently attempted to undermine the validity and legitimacy of

172   *Pro-Kurdish political parties in Turkey*

the DTP's articulation of Kurdish demands by characterising the DTP as representing *solely* the Kurdish interests and as being the proponent of 'ethnic' Kurdish nationalism. The accusation of ethnic nationalism was used to undermine the DTP's claim to be a 'party of Turkey' as opposed to representing specifically Kurds or engaging in 'identity politics' as opposed to the AKP's 'politics of service'.[102] Although such claims and counterclaims can be seen as part of the overall struggle between the AKP and the DTP to be the representative of the Kurds, the rejection of the DTP and the Kurdish claims by the AKP clearly illustrates the problems Turkey experiences in accepting political pluralism. The Prime Minister's insistence that he would 'ignore' all of the DTP MPs unless the DTP publicly declared the PKK to be a 'terrorist' organisation created a stalemate during the preceding four years. The issue of describing the PKK as a terrorist organisation was constructed as the 'Litmus Test' of the DTP's claim to be a 'party of Turkey' and its commitment to democracy. On this issue, the co-chair of the DTP, Emine Ayna, stated: 'We are at the same point in terms of the definition of the problem and its solution. Concerning the Kurdish question, the difference we have with the PKK is that they are conducting an armed campaign and we are conducting a political struggle.'[103]

Furthermore, the connection with the PKK had been used on 16 November 2007 by Turkey's Chief Prosecutor, Abdurrahman Yalçınkaya, to prepare a case to close the DTP down and impose 'political bans' on the 221 leading members of the party. The DTP was seen to be the continuation of the previous pro-Kurdish parties, which in turn was used as evidence of the alleged link to the PKK. In the indictment to the Constitutional Court it was stated that the DTP was 'steered' by the PKK's jailed leader Öcalan, had become the focal point of 'separatist activities' and created the danger of 'dragging' Turkey towards a civil war.[104] The DTP's refusal to publicly declare the PKK as a 'terror' organisation was used in the indictment as proof of the link between the two organisations. The case was finally concluded by the Constitutional Court on 12 December 2009. It resulted in the closure of the DTP and a ban for the 37 founding members from taking an active role in politics, including the MPs Ahmet Türk and Aysel Tuğluk. The Court argued that the DTP became the 'focal point of activities against the indivisible unity of the state, the country and the nation'.[105] Consequently, the remaining DTP MPs have joined the BDP – the new pro-Kurdish political party – to continue their activities in the parliament.

The representation of the pro-Kurdish movement as being proponents of separatism and violence, which serve the aim of exclusion and marginalisation, was widely disseminated through popular media outlets from 1990 onwards and thus became the hegemonic discourse. This continues to create significant difficulties for the pro-Kurdish democratic movement to establish itself as a 'party of Turkey'. Consequently, attempts to legitimise Kurdish identity claims by dissociating them from terrorism and violence have failed to convince the Turkish population which continues to view the pro-Kurdish political parties with suspicion if not hostility. The problems and difficulties that the previous pro-Kurdish political parties have faced continued to affect the DTP's challenge to build and

Pro-Kurdish political parties in Turkey 173

organise a wider pro-democratic and counter-hegemonic block. This shows the difficulty of conceiving of Kurdish demands as part of democratic demands in Turkey and of transcending the current environment characterised by violence and antagonisms.

However, in the more recent period, the tense atmosphere experienced during municipal elections started to dissipate with both President Abdullah Gül and Prime Minister R.T. Erdoğan indicating a change of attitude and their willingness to strengthen the democratic standards to solve the Kurdish question.[106] This move was supported by the PKK, who offered a ceasefire until September 2009 to facilitate such efforts. The change in attitude was reflected in the establishment of the predominantly Kurdish language TV channel as part of the TRT network. Additionally, the recent discussion about the possibility of establishing Kurdish language and literature departments in Turkish universities seems to be part of a longer term project to improve education facilities in the Kurdish language. Furthermore, the government's 'Democratic Initiative' – which started with the 'brain-storming' meeting that the Interior Minister, Beşir Atalay, held with numerous journalists about the possible steps that could be taken to find a solution to the Kurdish question and continued with the meeting held on 5 August 2009 between the DTP chairman Ahmet Türk and the AKP chairman, Prime Minister Erdoğan and some of his ministers – has been interpreted as the start of a process that may result in finding a peaceful political solution to the conflict, the formal recognition of Kurdish identity and comprehensive reforms to grant cultural and linguistic rights to the Kurds. However, the strong reaction and criticism of the meeting between the AKP and the DTP from the oppositional nationalist parties shows the lack of a national consensus in Turkey for the peaceful and democratic solution of the Kurdish question.[107]

Since the closure of the DTP in December 2009, the BDP has been the main vehicle for Kurdish political activism in Turkey, and with the support of the independent socialist MP, Ufuk Uras, it managed to maintain a parliamentary group. Similar to its predecessors, the BDP's political programme contains proposals for drafting a new constitution and articulates popular and broad democratic demands such as respect for fundamental rights and freedoms. In addition, proposals for political reconciliation to end the conflict and more specific Kurdish identity demands, such as constitutional recognition of Kurdish identity and collective rights, especially the provision of education in the Kurdish language, are articulated.[108] Within a civic pluralist model of citizenship, Kurdish identity demands can be accommodated in Turkey without leading to separation. More specifically, similar to the DTP, the BDP also accepted the 'democratic autonomy' proposal as its preferred alternative to the centralised political structure in Turkey and as an effective institutional arrangement to resolve the conflict and accommodate Kurdish demands.[109]

As well as representing the Kurds in the parliament and using formal institutions to raise the Kurdish demands, the BDP activists have also taken part in protest activities in the majority Kurdish regions. On 23 March 2011, the BDP announced that it would be supporting a wave of civil disobedience protests

174 *Pro-Kurdish political parties in Turkey*

against the government's perceived lack of interest in resolving the conflict. In numerous cities in the majority Kurdish areas and Western Turkey, the protestors set up 'democratic solution tents' to draw attention to the need to generate a political solution to the ongoing conflict. These protestors demanded, as measures to reduce the tension and pave the way for political reconciliation, the Kurds' right to be educated in their mother tongue to be granted, the election threshold to be removed, military operations to be ceased and the political prisoners to be released.[110] Such activities highlight continuity in the range of activities that the pro-Kurdish political parties have organised in their struggle to obtain recognition of Kurdish identity and to campaign for peaceful resolution of the conflict. However, on 25 April the protest tents were raided by the police on the basis that they constituted a threat to 'public security', and many of the activists were arrested.[111] These protests and the actions taken by the police are highly reflective of the dilemmas faced by the pro-Kurdish movement and the lack of space it is given to articulate what are widely seen as legitimate Kurdish democratic demands.

In April 2011, the BDP formed an alliance with 17 other political parties and non-governmental organisations forming the pro-democracy 'the Labour, Peace and Democracy Block' (*Emek, Demokrasi ve Özgürlük Bloku*), and similar to the DTP's strategy for the 2007 general elections it has agreed to support independent candidates in the general elections scheduled for 12 June 2011. In addition to the leading members of the pro-Kurdish BDP, independent socialist and pro-democracy candidates are also included in the list, including the film director and columnist Sırrı Süreyya Önder for Istanbul, the leader of the EMEP Levent Tüzel for Istanbul, and the socialist activist and journalist Ertuğrul Kürkçü for Mersin.[112] Broad democratic demands, such as gender equality, better working conditions, comprehensive constitutional reform and political reconciliation are the key demands articulated in the election campaigns.[113]

Conclusion

This chapter has focused on the emergence and evolution of the pro-Kurdish democratic movement in Turkey since 1990. By analysing the pro-Kurdish democratic discourse, it has focused on the articulation of Kurdish rights and demands by the pro-Kurdish political parties and reflected upon the difficulties that they have encountered in this process. Specifically, their attempts to create space for representing Kurdish demands for political reconciliation and democratic change in Turkey were assessed. In addition, the analysis focused on the conception of democracy that emerged in their discourse and their attempts to build a wider pro-democracy movement. These attempts proved ultimately unsuccessful as the antagonistic state of affairs in Turkey prevented the emergence and growth of such a movement into a mass-based democratic movement in Turkey. Consequently, many of the pro-Kurdish political parties were closed down by the Constitutional Court, and the Kurdish parliamentarians were stripped of their legal immunity to face trial, which sentenced four of them to terms of imprisonment.

The urgency of raising popular Kurdish demands for the recognition of their identity and culture as well as formulating a political solution to the conflict have became the focal points in their discourse and have overshadowed their broader democratic demands. Therefore, from early on the pro-Kurdish political parties have found it difficult to balance articulating Kurdish national demands with being a party that represents a cross section of the numerous political groups in Turkey. In particular, their emphasis on the need for a democratic and political solution to the conflict has been interpreted as support for the PKK and Kurdish separatism. This limited their attempts to engage wider Turkish society and build a pro-democracy movement in Turkey. Moreover, throughout their existence they have been treated as outsiders and continue to find it difficult to be seen as legitimate political actors in Turkey. In total, the pro-Kurdish political parties paid a heavy price for their activities as many of their supporters and members faced persecution for their membership and support and many were murdered extrajudicially. The initial problems that they have faced continue to exist and they are still finding it difficult to be included in the political system in Turkey as legitimate actors while representing popular Kurdish demands through legitimate political channels.

The election of the DTP MPs in the general elections in 2007 and the return of the pro-Kurdish parliamentary opposition brought a new momentum to Kurdish politics in Turkey. The DTP's consolidation of its position as the leading party in the Kurdish regions in the last municipal elections created opportunities for the pro-Kurdish democratic movement to strengthen its position to campaign for change and institutionalisation of the pro-Kurdish political movement in Turkey. The EU accession process additionally creates possibilities for reconciliation and the deepening of democracy in Turkey. However, the closure of the DTP in December 2009 seems to have been a major halt to the positive developments that resulted in the minor recognition of Kurdish identity and rights. Overall however, the pro-Kurdish movement has succeeded in providing representation to the Kurds at the local as well as national level and has been a main outlet for Kurdish political participation in Turkey. Having an institutional base has significantly strengthened their position to raise popular Kurdish political and cultural demands and the awareness of the issues that the Kurds face in Turkey. Crucially, having such a local base and being represented in national assembly creates opportunities to *legitimately* raise Kurdish political demands and claims through democratic channels. That is, the expression of political demands and claims by democratically elected representatives, as opposed to a prohibited organisation, has been enhancing the authority and legitimacy of the pro-Kurdish political parties and makes their acceptance in Turkey as a legitimate political actor more likely.

Conclusion

Democracy, pluralism and Kurdish subjectivity in (post)national Turkey

Instituting a democratic pluralist political framework that would recognise cultural and national diversity and satisfy Kurdish political and cultural demands has been a difficult task for Turkey to accomplish. The PKK's insurgency from 1984 posed the most serious and sustained challenge to Turkey's authority and state sovereignty, and overall the conflict caused significant loss of life and widespread human tragedies in the region. Following the extensive developments that took place after the capture and subsequent imprisonment of the PKK leader Abdullah Öcalan in 1999, the violence in the region significantly reduced. Such developments have coincided with the ongoing political reforms successive governments in Turkey have been carrying out in the past decade to raise the standard of Turkish democracy and to meet the EU membership criteria. These reforms have resulted in the limited recognition of Kurdish identity and cultural rights. In the current environment, the Kurdish question in Turkey manifests itself as part of a broader problem of pluralism and public recognition of cultural identity and difference. Therefore, a study of this nature offers interesting conclusions concerning democracy, pluralism and political reconciliation in societies characterised by ethno-nationalist conflicts. Specifically, the issues concerning 'particularity' and 'universality', 'identity' and 'difference' and the debate surrounding post-nationalism, multiculturalism and the recognition of cultural identity and difference find a new interpretation in a society such as Turkey, and this study offers insights that enhance our understanding of these contemporary issues that also affect many other societies around the world.

Moreover, the period from the 1960s onward has witnessed a major transformation in the political culture of the Kurds in Turkey, and a detailed account that focuses on the re-emergence and evolution of the Kurdish national movement in Turkey and its mobilisation of the Kurds, as has been carried out in this book, offers interesting insights into the processes of mobilisation and the making and re-making of political identities in general and national identities in particular. By drawing on discourse theory and the discourse analysis framework, my research deploys a holistic approach to analyse an extensive amount of primary sources that the Kurdish activists, political groups and parties in Turkey have published since the 1960s. As I summarise below, by raising the issues and questions relating to Kurdish political identity and highlighting the ideological

Conclusion 177

specificity, diversity and the transformation of Kurdish nationalism, this approach enables me to make a significant contribution by developing a new empirical dimension to the study of the Kurds and the Kurdish national movement in Turkey. Furthermore, the theoretical framework and concepts that I have utilised in my study enable me to make analytical contributions that exceed the boundaries of the case study itself. The conclusions that I reach enrich the existing literature on conflict analysis, democracy and nationalism, social movements, resistance and protest movements, nationalism and nationalist interpellations, political mobilisation and the emergence and sustenance of democratic subjectivities.

Summary of findings: beyond essentialism

As discussed in detail in Chapter 1, the existing literature on Kurdish nationalism and the Kurdish movement in Turkey focuses on offering a causal explanation and descriptive account of the rise of Kurdish nationalism and the conflict during the 1980s and 1990s. The existing literature does not offer any rigorous analysis of Kurdish nationalism as an ideology and the emergence and individuation of the two hegemonic discourses, namely the 'national liberation' and the 'democratic' discourses, which have articulated Kurdish identity and national demands during the past 30 years. The cultural and linguistic pluralism prevalent in Kurdish society has often been emphasised by some scholars to question the Kurds' claim to be a separate nation. At the other end of the spectrum, scholars treat the existence of a Kurdish nation as a given. Consequently, neither of these two dominant approaches examines the characterisation of Kurdish national identity within the discourses of the Kurdish national movement and what processes have played a key role in its transformation. Similarly, the antagonistic state of relations in Turkey is also treated as a given, and the Kurds' own interpretation of their experience as oppression and the construction of the relations of oppression and antagonism, especially in the national liberation discourse, has not been examined in detail. Consequently, the ideological nature of Kurdish nationalism, its peculiarity, specificity and diversity, the construction of the relations of oppression and antagonisms, and the articulation of Kurdish identity and national demands within the two hegemonic discourses are not explored or highlighted in the current literature. As an attempt to fill this void and provide a fuller account of Kurdish identity formation, my research conducted an interpretive and critical analysis of Kurdish identity, nationalism and national movement in Turkey. This has enabled me to develop an informed account of the discursive constitution of Kurdish national identity, political subjectivity and the relations of difference and equivalence, showing the importance of the institution of political frontiers that shape and stabilise identity, the nature of the national demands and claims that Kurdish nationalist discourse articulates, and the processes and conditions that influence the course of ideological change and transformation that the Kurdish national movement has been experiencing. Additionally, this approach has enabled me to provide an account of the organisational growth and

178   *Conclusion*

evolution of the Kurdish national movement, including the political parties and groups that have been active in the period.

A closer examination of the Kurdish national liberation and the democratic discourses offers an account of the ideological diversity and specificity of Kurdish nationalism in Turkey. Focusing on the specific demands articulated by the Kurdish national movement enables me to study Kurdish nationalism on a specific level. My analysis of the discourses of the Kurdish 'organic intellectuals' during the 1960s and of the political groups and parties that have contested Kurdish identity in Turkey since the 1970s has focused on the articulation of numerous elements within each discourse to draw out the specific political demands they have been raising in the period under discussion. Moreover, the account of the organisational growth and evolution of the Kurdish movement in Turkey that I offer provides a more complete picture that raises the pertinent issue of contestation over strategy that numerous Kurdish political parties in Turkey took part in and the PKK's subsequent hegemony. The issue of contestation over Kurdish identity in the late 1970s was analysed via an examination of the institution of political frontiers and the construction of the relations of equivalence and difference in discourses of the political parties and groups that contested the representation of Kurdish identity.

A case study focusing on the Kurdish movement in Turkey offers us interesting conclusions for the broader issues connected to the institution of hegemony and why and how a particular group or practice becomes hegemonic. The PKK's discourse constructed the relations of equivalence on the basis of nation and class and proposed to 'liberate' Kurdistan from national and feudal oppression as well as capitalist exploitation. The PKK's hegemony over the Kurdish movement meant that 'liberation' emerged as the 'empty signifier' representing Kurdish national demands in Turkey. My explanation of the PKK's hegemony over the Kurdish resistance movement and its mass mobilisation of the Kurds during the 1980s and 1990s paid attention to the PKK's reactivation of the myth of *Newroz* to construct and deploy a contemporary myth of resistance that centred on the resistance practices of its leading members in Diyarbakir Prison and its general struggle. It was argued that the contemporary myth played a significant role in the mobilisation process and the sedimentation of the PKK's national liberation discourse in practice. It added force to its discourse and enabled it to construct and represent its struggle as the embodiment of the Kurd's long struggle for freedom and independence. Additionally, we are able to draw inference concerning the nationalist interpellation of the national subjects and why such an interpellation is affective and successful in mobilising the masses. In fact, the analysis of the PKK's construction of a contemporary myth of resistance highlights an interesting dimension of the nationalist discourses and shows the importance of the symbolic resources such as myths that the nationalist movements use in its interpellation of the national subject. My analysis also highlighted the importance of the PKK's reinvigoration of Kurdish culture and music, which also played a significant role in the sedimentation of its national liberation discourse in practice. The analysis of culture and music reveals the

Conclusion   179

complexities involved in a political movement's mobilisation of the masses, including the processes involved in the sedimentation of a discourse in practice, and provides an interesting dimension to how political movements in general and nationalist movements in particular represent their struggle to their target groups.

The ideological and discursive transformation that the Kurdish national movement has been experiencing since the early 1990s constituted an important aspect of this book and the analysis offers interesting insights that enhances our understanding of the process of discursive and ideological transformation that resistance and protest movements in general experience. My analysis focused on the factors that led to the fragmentation of the Kurdish national liberation discourse and the difficulties it created for the PKK. Specifically, it emphasised the role of the numerous dislocations that the PKK as a movement experienced, such as military losses, and the collapse of communism in 1989. It argued that these dislocations reduced the appeal of its national liberation discourse and threatened the PKK's hegemony over Kurdish resistance in Turkey. Hence, they played a major role in bringing about new political practices, including the PKK's attempts to find a peaceful solution to the conflict through ceasefires and the strategic transformation and discursive changes towards democracy in the past decade. In order to highlight the current demands that the PKK has been raising since its discursive transformation and to show how the Kurdish question has been rearticulated within its democratic discourse, my analysis focused on the construction and representation of Kurdish identity and difference, the articulation of Kurdish demands and the political project that the PKK seeks to construct in Turkey. A significant development has been that Kurdish national demands are articulated as part of broader democratic demands, including environmental protection, women's rights, civil society, and decentralisation of the state and the establishment of federal and confederal regional entities. This *differential* rearticulation of Kurdish identity in fact calls for the institution of a new common identity in Turkey based on a territorial definition and civic and pluralist model of citizenship to transcend the antagonistic state of affairs in Turkey and to recognise the cultural differences of the numerous minorities.

Although, as stated in Chapter 7, the democratic transformation of the PKK lessened the antagonistic state of affairs, a political solution that will end the era of political violence and conflict and accommodate Kurdish demands within Turkey is still in the making. Moreover, the PKK's democratic transformation and political and organisational renewal that such a significant transformation aims to generate has not been swift and has been marred by various difficulties. Particularly, it has found it difficult to dissociate itself from political violence and gain recognition as a 'legitimate' political actor in the region. In fact, such difficulties are shared by the pro-Kurdish democratic movement in Turkey, and the experience of a series of pro-Kurdish political parties shows the difficulties that are associated with the emergence of a new Kurdish democratic subjectivity. The hegemonic representation of the Kurdish question as strictly a case of 'security' and 'terrorism' and the institutional and legal barriers has significantly

180 *Conclusion*

weakened the Kurdish democratic movement and its ability to construct a wider democratic movement for change. This is one of the main difficulties that implicate the democratisation process and the deepening of democracy in Turkey, and the Kurdish experience highlights the difficulties associated with the building of counter-hegemonic blocks and democratic subjectivities that are central to the process of political change and democratic transformation.

The acceptance and promotion of cultural and political pluralism and the recognition of cultural difference is central to the consolidation of a democratic regime in Turkey. The successful construction of a pluralist and participatory democratic society in Turkey depends on the successful constitution of new post-national and democratic subjectivities that will mobilise wider sections of the society. The analysis that I provided of the Kurdish democratic movement has highlighted the need for the development of a new institutional framework and/or new ethos of pluralism that could accommodate Kurdish demands in Turkey. The process of democratic change and reconciliation through democratisation has been particularly difficult and slow. The repression of cultural and linguistic diversity and difference in Turkey and the challenge by various counter-hegemonic opposition movements have resulted in an environment characterised by political polarisation.

Opportunities, difficulties and challenges for the Kurdish national movement in Turkey

Since 1990, a number of pro-Kurdish political parties have been active in Turkey, and despite the oppressive and delimited political environment within which they have found themselves conducting their activities, they have succeeded in providing a platform for Kurdish representation and political engagement. Similarly, the PKK's withdrawal of its guerrillas and declaration of a permanent ceasefire in 1999 have brought about a significant reduction in political violence in the region. The occasional eruption of violence in the past decade has neither been continuous nor so severe as to indicate that the previous intensity of the conflict is to return. Consequently, political reconciliation and a solution to the Kurdish question via democratisation is closer than it has ever been; the political reforms in the past decade, the government's 'Democratic Initiative' to generate national consensus and political proposals to find a lasting solution seem to indicate that a new era may be dawning. The PKK's discursive transformations coincide with Turkey's EU integration process and the political reforms she has undertaken to satisfy the membership criteria. The prospect of EU membership and the accession process has so far been a major motivating factor in raising the country's democratic standards and recognition of cultural pluralism, which has resulted in the limited recognition of Kurdish identity and demands. Without a doubt, the EU accession process offers new opportunities for Turkey to develop a new policy to manage diversity and cultural difference, which in turn can open-up opportunities for the constitution of new democratic subjectivities. The democratisation of state institutions and of society and the

Conclusion 181

growth of norms and values commensurate with a democratic regime and politics – such as political freedoms and the practice of compromise and deliberation – can have a significant impact on the sustenance of Kurdish democratic politics and also the democratic values taking root in both Turkish and Kurdish societies. During the past five years, the AKP's initial enthusiasm for EU membership seems to have been replaced by a complacent attitude. Also, given that there is widespread opposition to Turkey's membership within the EU member states, most notably in Germany and France, Turkey's internal political dynamics take more centrality in the push for democratisation.

So far, the Kurds' demands for the recognition of their identity as a national community in Turkey and the congruent cultural and linguistic rights have been challenged by the mainstream and nationalist political parties on the basis that such rights in Turkey can only be enjoyed by the Turkish nation. Although a limited recognition of Kurdish linguistic rights has been granted, demands for the provision of education in the Kurdish language have been ignored. Hence, the space of the universal subject is only accorded to the Turkish nation and non other, which does not rule out the recognition of Kurdish identity and linguistic rights, but does so only within the restricted realm of minority ethnic rights. Moreover, this issue highlights the polarisation in opinion concerning the characterisation of Kurdish identity and the level of public recognition that it is expected to enjoy in Turkey. Whereas the nationalist Republican People's Party (*Cumhuriyet Halk Partisi,* CHP) and the ultra-nationalist Nationalist Action Party (*Milliyetçi Hareket Partisi,* MHP) – the two main opposition parties in Turkey – have been strongly opposing the recognition of Kurdish identity, the government's proposal for cultural recognition describes Kurdish identity as an ethnic identity and does not recognise the Kurds as a separate national community, which is one of the main demands that the Kurdish national movement is raising. The election of Kemal Kılıçdaroğlu to the leadership of the CHP in May 2010, who is seen as a moderate and reformer, has raised hopes that this will lead to the party adopting a more flexible policy concerning the Kurdish question. However, so far there has not been a significant discursive shift or any clear and new policy proposal from the CHP concerning the Kurdish question and the recognition of Kurdish identity.

Additionally, as my analysis revealed, the positive environment is yet to cultivate a lasting solution to the conflict and the gradual recognition of Kurdish identity and demands have been occurring at a time when the attempt to marginalise the Kurdish movement has been continuing. In particular, the continued association in the media and the state discourse of the Kurds with 'terrorism' in Turkey has been, and continues to be, used to significant effect to marginalise and exclude Kurdish demands for cultural rights and political reconciliation. The persistent attempt to blame the PKK – despite the lack of any evidence and the PKK's denial of involvement – for the explosions in the *Güngören* district of Istanbul in July 2008 shows the state's vehemence to exclude the Kurds in the public sphere and prevent the PKK from transforming itself into a democratic movement. Additionally, international developments in the past decade, in

182   Conclusion

particular the 'war on terror', have also placed huge barriers in front of the PKK's attempts to transform itself into a democratic movement and transcend the antagonistic state of affairs. The continued threat that the PKK guerrillas pose and the PKK's sporadic attacks against the Turkish security forces enhance the association in the popular Turkish mind between Kurdish demands and 'separatism' and 'terrorism'. Such a representation plays a significant role in representing the Kurdish demands as 'illegitimate', which has been a major barrier preventing the development of a process of political reconciliation and recognition of Kurdish identity in Turkey. In particular, its significance is that the pro-Kurdish democratic movement has been unable to extend its appeal to the broad masses of Turkey. The assumed link between the pro-Kurdish political parties and the PKK and the attempts to show one to be the extension of the other has been given as the reason to close a number of pro-Kurdish political parties in the past, most recently the DTP.

In fact, the marginalisation and associated difficulties that the pro-Kurdish democratic movement currently experiences have been ongoing since the early 1990s. As discussed in Chapter 8, numerous pro-Kurdish political parties have sought to overcome such difficulties by putting forward political proposals to end the conflict and bring about wide-ranging constitutional reforms that would widen the political space, provide recognition of Kurdish identity and satisfy Kurdish rights and demands. As discussed in Chapter 7, in the PKK's democratic discourse Kurdish identity and demands are rearticulated as part of a chain of democratic demands for equality, which have led to pluralisation in the demands that it articulates and have enabled it to construct a more condensed democratic discourse that could appeal to a broader section of the Turkish and Kurdish societies. Additionally, this rearticulation has resulted in the pluralisation of Kurdish politics and the emergence of numerous civil society organisations. In recent years, such civil society organisations have flourished, and these currently include various organisations advocating political reconciliation such as the Peace Council of Turkey (*Türkiye Barış Meclisi*), the Peace Mothers (*Barış Anneleri*), the Kurdish language pressure group *TZP Kurdi* as well as numerous human rights and women rights organisations that campaign on diverse issues. The pluralisation of Kurdish politics has extended the logic of equality to wider social spheres and creates opportunities to forge new links with various other civil society organisations in Turkey as well as in Europe.

Overall, the Kurdish movement in Turkey is putting forward a radical democratic alternative to the current stalemate; however, so far it has not been successful in breaking the antagonistic state of relations in Turkey. Therefore, the PKK's and pro-Kurdish democratic movement's efforts of constructing a pro-democratic movement in Turkey for change and democratisation and the challenges it has been facing raises interesting questions concerning the links between democracy and nationalism. Not only do violence and insurgency need to end before democracy can take root in society, but the political stalemate and polarisation in Turkey needs to be overcome, and the demands of various sections of society need to be accommodated. Although the rearticulation of

Conclusion 183

Kurdish demands within the democratic discourse emphasises the democratic nature of Kurdish demands, the limitations that the Kurdish movement has been facing in articulating wider democratic demands are starkly visible. For example, as my analysis in Chapter 7 revealed, the articulation of gender equality within the PKK's democratic discourse has led to internalisation of the women's movement and not to the emergence of an autonomous Kurdish feminist movement that is able to problematise the numerous practices of gender inequality within the Kurdish society and form links with other feminist organisations in Turkey and Europe. This raises an important question about the ability of the PKK's democratic discourse to represent the demands for gender equality that women in Turkish and Kurdish societies have. Also, as the results of the municipal elections held in March 2009 suggest, the pro-Kurdish DTP did not make much progress in terms of appealing to voters in areas outside the majority Kurdish regions. The BDP's choice of independent candidates in the general election scheduled for 12 June 2011 includes numerous Turkish left-wing politicians, such as Levent Tüzel, Sırrı Süreyya Önder and Ertuğrul Kürkçü, and despite the difficulties and setbacks, such a choice is in line with the pro-Kurdish political parties' attempts to represent a cross section of Turkish society.

The differential articulation of Kurdish identity as part of an equivalential chain of demands for democracy and equality in Turkey has brought about a major shift in the way Kurdish identity claims are articulated. Whereas the articulation of Kurdish identity within democratic discourse opens up the possibility to adapt a critical line in relation to the essentialist claims articulated by nationalists, and the homogenising tendency that nationalisms harbour, balancing the articulation of 'particularistic' national demands with the more 'universal' democratic demands is of paramount importance. The important issue to consider is the limitations that this tension places on a national movement to deviate from making national claims by placing universal democratic demands at the centre of its political discourse. The Kurds' attempts to form a wider democratic movement in Turkey clearly highlight the tension between 'particularity' and 'universality'. Articulating 'particular' Kurdish demands differentially within the universal democratic discourse attempts to construct a new universality. The relation between particularity and universality was highlighted in the brief discussion offered in Chapter 2 of Laclau and Mouffe's theorisation of radical democracy. In Turkey, universal claims have been articulated by Turkish nationalism, and the way citizenship and national identity have been defined places 'Turkishness' at the centre of the political power and above all, identifications. The Kurds' demands for constitutional recognition of their identity have been rejected on the basis that such recognition will endanger the indivisible unity of the Turkish nation and state. This characterisation has been used to reject Kurdish national demands and claims as 'illegitimate' and 'particularistic'.

In contrast, the Kurdish movement has been contesting the Kurds' national demands and rights on the basis of reformulating the conception of national identity and citizenship in Turkey to institute a territorial, civic and pluralist conception of citizenship that recognises national and cultural pluralism there. This

184 *Conclusion*

reformulation seeks to transform the republic into a 'democratic republic' to transcend the narrow Turkish nationalist interpretation of citizenship in Turkey, which denies cultural pluralism by imposing a homogenous national identity on the Kurds and other minorities. Hence, the extent to which the 'particularistic' Kurdish demands delimit the universal rights and claims articulated by the PKK or the pro-Kurdish democratic movement is of significance. It is highly difficult to envision in this environment whether the current limitations in front of the Kurdish movement to claim the space of the universal subject or to compete to fill its place can be totally surmounted, which is necessary if they are to contest democracy and pluralism in Turkey. Additionally, the possibilities offered by the politics of recognition and the difficulties involved in the institution of a post-national society in Turkey are also of huge significance. The limitations that such a state of affairs places on the success of a process of political reconciliation have become quite visible in the difficulties the government has experienced in reaching out to the main opposition parties in the parliament to generate a national consensus for a political solution. This clearly shows that there are major barriers preventing the emergence of a political will and consensus that are needed to carry out widespread reforms. The ensuing public debate and the Turkish nationalist's unequivocal rejection of any move towards peace and the recognition of Kurdish identity show the strength and appeal of Turkish nationalism and its hegemonic representation of the Kurdish question as strictly a 'security concern' and 'terrorism'.

Although political violence has not been totally eliminated, the demands raised by the PKK and the pro-Kurdish democratic movement can be satisfied without endangering Turkey's territorial integrity. Hence, an institutional framework that can facilitate coexistence within the same polity and transform antagonisms – and the conditions that gave rise to political violence in the first place – is possible. Whereas some attempts to recognise Kurdish identity and demands in Turkey have been made in the past decade, their scope has been limited, and so far the main political groups representing the Kurds have been excluded from the process. The exclusion and denial of Kurdish identity in the past have not caused the desired outcome of assimilation. In fact, the inflexible attitude that the successive governments maintained vis-à-vis the Kurdish demands has resulted in exacerbation of, rather than containment of, violence. Open dialogue and a participatory framework that includes Kurdish representation and engages with Kurdish demands and concerns can unlock the current stalemate. Additionally, as a practical step and as demanded by numerous political groups in Turkey, drafting a new constitution, which embeds a new notion of citizenship that respects pluralism and cultural identity and difference, is also of significance. Such a process of comprehensive political reform needs to be complemented with a daring attempt to address, in particular, the human tragedies of the Kurdish conflict and its ongoing ramifications. In fact, the reconciliation process needs to address past instances of the use of state violence against the Kurds, most notably during the suppression of the Dersim uprising in 1938; it also needs to be broader and include the traumas inflicted on the wider Turkish society in

Conclusion 185

the period following the military coup in 1980. As the democratisation experience elsewhere shows, in particular the important role that the Truth of Reconciliation Commission played in South Africa's transition to democracy and in its re-foundation as a democratic plural society, comprehensive political reforms need to be complemented with the establishment of a neutral platform where the past horrors of the conflict can be expressed and the process of political reconciliation can begin.

Notes

Introduction: the Kurdish question in Turkey

1 For a general discussion on internal displacement see: Ayşe Betül Çelik, 'Transnationalisation of Human Right Norms and Its Impact on Internally Displaced Kurds', *Human Rights Quarterly* 27 (2005); Bilgin Ayata and Deniz Yükseker, 'A Belated Awakening: National and International Responses to Internal Displacement of Kurds in Turkey', *New Perspectives on Turkey*, No. 32 (2005); Joost Jongerden 'Resettlement and Reconstruction of Identity: The Case of Kurds in Turkey', *Ethnopolitics*, Vol. 1, No. 1 (September 2001).

2 In addition, significant Kurdish communities exist in Iraq, Iran, Syria and Lebenon, and in the Caucasus and Central Asia. Their population is estimated to be between 25 and 35 million. See, Mehrdad Izady, *The Kurds: A Concise Handbook*, (Washington DC: Taylor & Francis, 1992), p. 118; David McDowall, *A Modern History of Kurds*, (2nd edn) (London: I.B. Tauris, 2000), vi.

3 M. Şükrü Hanioğlu, *A Brief History of the Late Ottoman Empire*, (Princeton and Oxford: Princeton University Press, 2008), 106.

4 For an extensive discussion of the Tanzimat Era of Ottoman History see: Hanioğlu, *A Brief History of the Late Ottoman Empire*, 72–108; and, Stanford J. Shaw and Ezel Kural Shaw, *History of the Ottoman Empire and Modern Turkey. Volume II: Reform, Revolution and Republic: The Rise of Modern Turkey, 1808–1975*, (Cambridge: Cambridge University Press, 1977), 55–171.

5 Hanioğlu, *A Brief History of the Late Ottoman Empire*, 145.

6 Ibid., 150.

7 See, Shaw and Shaw, *History of the Ottoman Empire and Modern Turkey*, 123–8.

8 Named after the founder and the first President of the Republic, Mustafa Kemal, who was given the surname 'Atatürk' – 'Father of the Turks' – on 21 June 1934 (Shaw and Shaw, *History of the Ottoman Empire and Modern Turkey*, 386).

9 For an excellent and comprehensive discussion of the management of ethnocultural diversity in the legal system during the late Ottoman and the Republican era in Turkey and the Turkish nationalist framing of the 'problem' of cultural pluralism, see D. Bayır, 'Negating Diversity: Minorities and Nationalism in Turkish Law', (PhD Diss., University of London, 2010).

10 By 1923, only 120,000 Greeks and 100,000 Armeninans were left of the pre-war populations of 1.8 million and 1.3 million (Shaw and Shaw, *History of the Ottoman Empire and Modern Turkey*, 373).

11 Necmi Erdoğan and Fahriye Üstüner, 'Quest for Hegemony: Discourses on Democracy', in *The Politics of Permanent Crises: Class, Ideology and State in Turkey*, Neşecan Balkan and Sungur Savran (eds), (New York: Nova Science Publishers, 2002, 196). See also, Metin Sever and Cem Dizdar, *2. Cumhuriyet Tartışmaları* (The Second Republic Discussions), (Ankara: Başak Publications, 1993).

Notes 187

12 Ernesto Laclau and Chantal Mouffe, *Hegemony and Socialist Strategy: Towards a Radical Democratic Politics*, (London: Verso, 1985); Ernesto Laclau, *On Populist Reason*, (London and New York: Verso, 2005); Ernesto Laclau eds., *The Making of Political Identities*, (London: Verso, 1994); Aletta J Norval, 'Thinking Identities: Against a Theory of Ethnicity', in *The Politics of Difference: Ethnic Premises in a World of Power*, ed. Edwin N. Wilmsen and Patrick McAlister, (London and Chicago: University of Chicago Press, 1996); Aletta J Norval, 'Frontiers in Question', *Filozofski Vestnik*, XVIII (2/1997); Katherine Verdery, 'Wither "Nation" and "Nationalism"?', in *Mapping the Nation*, ed. Gopal Balakrishnan (London: Verso, 1996); Alan Finlayson, 'Ideology, Discourse and Nationalism', *Journal of Political Ideologies*, Vol. 3 No. 1 (1998); Claire Sutherland, 'Nation Building Through Discourse Theory', *Nations and Nationalism*, Vol. 11, No 2, (2005).
13 Amir Hassanpour, 'The Making of Kurdish Identity: Pre-20th Century Historical and Literary Discourse', in *Essays on the Origins of Kurdish Nationalism*, ed. Abbas Vali, (California: Mazda Publishers, Inc., 2003); Izady, *The Kurds*.
14 Kemal Kirişci and Gareth M. Winrow, *The Kurdish Question and Turkey: An example of Trans-state Ethnic Conflict*, (London: Frank Cass, 1997); Paul White, *Primitive Rebels or Revolutionary Modernizers? The Kurdish National Movement in Turkey*, (London: Zed Books, 2000).
15 Stuart Hall, 'Introduction: Who Needs "Identity"?', in *Questions of Cultural Identity*, ed. Stuart Hall and Paul du Gay, (London: Sage Publications, 1996), 3.

1 Deconstructing Kurdish identity and nationalism in academic discourses

1 The French language study by Basile Nikitine, *Les Kurdes: Etude Sociologique et Historique*, (published in Paris 1956) and Vladimir Minorsky's subject entries for 'Kurds' 'Kurdish' and 'Kurdistan' in the *Encyclopaedia of Islam*, which were translated into Turkish and made available to a greater number of Kurds in Turkey, constituted the main sources on Kurds and Kurdish history in the 1960s and 1970s.
2 The following studies are good examples of such literature: Şükrü Mehmet Sekban, *La Question Kurde: des Problémes des Minorités*, (Published in 1933 in Paris); M. Şerif Fırat, *Doğu İlleri ve Varto Tarihi* (Eastern Provinces and the History of Varto), (published in 1945 in Turkey).
3 On Turkey's framing of the Kurdish issue as reactionary politics and separatism, see M. Yeğen, 'The Archaeology of Republican Turkish State Discourse', (PhD diss., University of Essex, 1994).
4 Turkish Sociologist İsmail Beşikci lost his job as an Assistant Professor at the Atatürk University in Erzurum after publishing *Doğu Anadolunun Düzeni* (The Order of East Anatolia) in 1969. Subsequently, he was prevented from taking any employment at Turkey's state universities and continued his researches as an independent scholar. In total he spent 17 years in prison for charges brought against him as a result of his research on the Kurds. See Martin Van Bruinessen 'İsmail Beşikçi: Turkish sociologist, critic of Kemalism, and kurdologist' for a fuller account of Beşikçi's work and prosecution, www.hum.uu.nl/medewerkers/m.vanbruinessen/publications/ismail_besikci.htm. As a more recent example of suppression of academic freedom, Nesrin Uçarlar was prevented by Marmara University from submitting her doctoral thesis on Kurdish language rights in Turkey because it was seen as promoting the division of Turkey's territorial unity ('Akademik Çalışmaya Bölücülük Suçlaması' *Taraf*, 7 July 2009). She subsequently submitted and defended her thesis at the Department of Political Science, Lund University in Sweden in September 2009.
5 See, for example: DDKO, *Sen Faşist Savcı İyi Dinle! Dünyada Kürt Vardır (DDKO'nun Savunması)*, (Uppsala: Behoz, 1973).
6 These include: İsmail Beşikci, *Doğu Mitinglerinin Analizi*, (Originally published in

188 *Notes*

1967 and republished in Ankara: Yurt Kitap Yayın, 1992) and İsmail Beşikci, *Doğu'da Değişim ve Yapısal Sorunlar: Göcebe Alikan Aşireti*, (Istanbul: E Yayınları, 1969 (reprinted Ankara: Yurt Kitap Yayın, 1992).

7 Martin van Bruinessen, *Agha, Shaikh and State: The Social and Political Structures of Kurdistan*, (London: Zed Books, 1992); Robert Olson, *The Emergence of Kurdish Nationalism and the Sheikh Said Rebellion, 1880–1925*, (Austin: University of Texas Press, 1989); Gerard Chaliand, ed., *People Without a Country: Kurds and Kurdistan*, (new and revised edition translated by Michael Pallis) (London: Zed Books, 1993); Nader Entessar *Kurdish Ethnonationalism*, (London: Lynne Rienner Publishing, 1992); Martin Van Bruinessen, *Kurdish Ethno-nationalism Versus Nation-Building States: Collected Articles*, (Istanbul: Isis, 2000); Abbas Vali, eds., *Essays on the Origins of Kurdish Nationalism*, (California: Mazda Publishers, 2003); Denise Natali, *The Kurds and the State: Evolving National Identity in Iraq, Turkey and Iran*, (New York: Syracuse University Press, 2005); McDowall, *A Modern History of the Kurds*; Hussein Tahiri, *The Structure of the Kurdish Society and the Struggle for a Kurdish State*, (California: Mazda Press, 2007).

8 Omer Taspinar, *Kurdish Nationalism and Political Islam in Turkey: Kemalist Identity in Transition*, (London and New York: Routledge, 2005); Farhad Ibrahim and Gülistan Gürbey, eds, *The Kurdish Conflict in Turkey: Obstacles and Chances for Peace and Democracy*, (Germany: Lit Verlag, 2000); Robert Olson, ed., *The Kurdish Nationalist Movement in the 1990s: Its Impact on Turkey and the Middle East*, (Lexington: University of Kentucky Press, 1996); Martin Van Bruinessen, 'Shifting National and Ethnic Identities: The Kurds in Turkey and the European Diaspora', *Journal of Muslim Minority Affairs*, Vol. 18, No. 1 (Apr 1998); White, *Primitive Rebels or Revolutionary Modernizers?*; Henri J. Barkey, and Graham E. Fuller, *Turkey's Kurdish Question*, (New York: Rowman and Littlefield Publishers, 1998); Kirişci and Winrow, *The Kurdish Question and Turkey*; Michael Gunter, *The Kurds in Turkey*, (Oxford: Westview Press, 1990); Michael Gunter, *The Kurds Ascending: The Evolving Solution to the Kurdish Problem in Iraq and Turkey*, (Basingstoke: Palgrave Macmillan, 2008); Mohammed M.A. Ahmed and Michael Gunter, eds, *The Evolution of Kurdish Nationalism*, (Costa Mesa: Mazda Publishers, 2007); and, Kerim Yıldız and Mark Muller, *The European Union and Turkish Accession: Human Rights and the Kurds*, (London and Ann Arbor, MI: Pluto Press, 2008).

9 Ali Kemal Özcan, *Turkey's Kurds: A Theoretical analysis of the PKK and Abdullah Öcalan*, (London and New York: Routledge, 2006); David Romano, *The Kurdish Nationalist Movement: Opportunity, Mobilisation and Identity*, (Cambridge: Cambridge University Press, 2006); Aliza Marcus, *Blood and Belief: The PKK and the Kurdish Fight for Independence*, (New York and London: New York University Press, 2007).

10 In her discussion of Kurdish political activism in the 1960s Watts examines the public debate concerning the Kurdish issue. She does not, however, offer an exclusive account of the Kurdish activists' discourses in the period. See Nicole F. Watts, 'Silence and Voice: Turkish Policies and Kurdish Resistance in the mid-20th century', in *The Evolution of Kurdish Nationalism*, ed., Mohammed M.A. Ahmed and Michael Gunter, (CA: Mazda Publishers, 2007).

11 Van Bruinessen, 'Shifting National and Ethnic Identities', 44.

12 Taspinar, *Kurdish Nationalism*, 97.

13 Barkey and Fuller, *Turkey's Kurdish Question*, 30.

14 Hamit Bozarslan, '"Why the Armed Struggle" Understanding Violence in Kurdistan of Turkey', in *The Kurdish Conflict in Turkey: Obstacles and Chances for Peace and Democracy*, ed. Farhad Ibrahim and Gülistan Gürbey, (Germany: Lit Verlag, 2000), 18.

15 Laclau and Mouffe, *Hegemony and Socialist Strategy*, 124. They argue 'The usual description of antagonism in the sociological or historical literature confirms this

Notes 189

impression: They explain the *conditions* which made antagonism possible but not the antagonism as such' (ibid.).
16 Barkey and Fuller, *Turkey's Kurdish Question*, 23.
17 Ibid., 24 emphasis mine.
18 Ibid.
19 White, *Primitive Rebels or Revolutionary Modernizers?*, 136.
20 Ibid., 142.
21 Izady, *The Kurds*, 185.
22 Hassanpour, 'The Making of Kurdish Identity', 108–9.
23 See Kirişci and Winrow, *The Kurdish Question and Turkey*, 5–11 for a discussion on the criteria to define a nation and ethnic groups.
24 Kirişci and Winrow, *The Kurdish Question and Turkey*, 24.
25 White, *Primitive Rebels or Revolutionary Modernizers?*, 14–29.
26 Ibid., 43.
27 Ibid.
28 Ibid., 48.
29 Abbas Vali, 'Genealogies of the Kurds: Constructions of Nation and National Identity in Kurdish Historical Writing', in *Essays on the Origins of Kurdish Nationalism* ed. Abbas Vali, (California: Mazda Publishers, 2003).
30 Maria T. O'Shea, *Trapped Between the Map and Reality: Geography and Perceptions of Kurdistan*, (London and New York: Routledge, 2004).
31 Konrad Hirschler, 'Defining the Nation: Kurdish Historiography in Turkey in the 1990s', *Middle East Studies*, Vol. 37, No 3 (July 2001):145–66.
32 Van Bruinessen, 'Shifting National and Ethnic Identities', 42–6.
33 N. Uçarlar, 'Between Majority Power and Minority Resistance: Kurdish Linguistic Rights in Turkey', (PhD diss., Lund University, 2009).
34 Nicole F. Watts, 'Institutionalizing Virtual Kurdistan West: Transnational Networks and Ethnic Contention in International Affairs,' in *Bounderies and Belonging: States and Societies in the Struggle to Shape Identities and Local Practices*, ed. Joel Migdal, (Cambridge: Cambridge University Press, 2004).
35 Gürdal Aksoy, *Bir Söylence Bir Tarih: Newroz*, (Yurt Yayınları: Ankara, 1998).
36 D. Aydın, 'Mobilizing the Kurds in Turkey: *Newroz* as a Myth', (Masters diss., Middle East Technical University, 2005).
37 Handan Çağlayan, *Analar, Yoldaşlar, Tanrıcalar: Kürt Hareketinde Kadınlar ve Kadın Kimliğinin Oluşumu* (Mothers, Comrades, Goddesses: Women in the Kurdish Movement and the Constitution of Women's Identity), (Istanbul: İletişim, 2007).
38 Cemil Gündoğan, *Kawa Davası Savunması ve Kürtlerde Siyasi Savunma Geleneği*, (Istanbul: Vate Yayınları, 2007).
39 Osman Ölmez, *Türkiye Siyasetinde DEP Depremi* (The DEP Earthquake in Turkish Politics), (Ankara: Doruk Yayınları, 1995); Eyyüp Demir, *Yasal Kürtler* (The Legal Kurds), (Istanbul: Tevn Yayınları, 2005); Mahmut Alınak, *HEP, DEP ve Devlet: Parlamento'dan 9. Koğuşa* (HEP, DEP and the State: From the Parliament to the 9th Prison Ward), (Istanbul: Kaynak Yayınları, 1996). Aside from the above the following articles are concerned with Kurdish democratic politics: Nicole F. Watts, 'Activists in Office: Pro-Kurdish Contentious Politics in Turkey', *Ethnopolitics*, Vol. 5, No. 2 (June 2006); Nicole F. Watts, 'Allies and Enemies: Pro-Kurdish Parties in Turkish Politics, 1990–94', *International Journal of Middle East Studies*, Vol. 31, No. 4 (November 1999); Aylin Güney, 'The Peoples Democracy Party', *Turkish Studies*, Vol. 3 (1) (2002); Henri J. Barkey, 'The People's Democracy Party (HADEP): The Travails of a Legal Kurdish Party in Turkey', *Journal of Muslim Minority Affairs*, Vol. 18, No. 1 (April 1998).
40 Watts, 'Allies and Enemies', 650.
41 Watts, 'Activists in Office', 126.
42 Ibid., 130–1.

190 Notes

43 Ibid., 137.
44 This section will not include a review of Aliza Marcus, *Blood and Belief*. This is because it is based exclusively on her interviews with the dissident PKK members and her study seems to be concerned only with the harsh treatment the PKK's internal critics received as opposed to understanding the PKK as a movement. Although the personal accounts provided in the interviews are informative, she does not at all attempt to verify the claims made by the dissidents and she does not engage with any questions related to mobilisation, identity and ideology as raised in my research.
45 Romano, *The Kurdish Nationalist Movement*, 2.
46 Ibid., 41.
47 Ibid., 43.
48 Ibid., 42.
49 Ibid., 47.
50 Ibid., 48.
51 Ibid., 72–4.
52 Ibid., 73.
53 Ibid., 92.
54 Özcan, *Turkey's Kurds*, 156.
55 Ibid., 180.
56 Ibid., 1.
57 Ibid., 20.
58 Ibid., 101.
59 Ibid., 104.
60 Ibid., 121.
61 Ibid., 124.
62 Ibid., 121.
63 Romano, *The Kurdish Nationalist Movement*, 101.
64 Ibid., 129.
65 Ibid., 131.
66 Ibid.
67 Ibid., 145.
68 Ibid., 99.
69 Ibid., 101.
70 Ibid., 102–8.
71 Ibid., 172.

2 Understanding Kurdish identity and nationalism in Turkey

1 Finlayson, 'Ideology, Discourse and Nationalism', 99.
2 Verdery, 'Wither "Nation" and "Nationalism"?', 227.
3 Finlayson, 'Ideology, Discourse and Nationalism', 100.
4 Ibid., 103.
5 Ibid.
6 Ibid., 105.
7 Ibid., 109.
8 Ibid. 105.
9 Michael Freeden, 'Is Nationalism a Distinct Ideology?', *Political Studies*, Vol. 46, No. 4 (1998).
10 Ibid., 751.
11 Ibid., 751.
12 Verdery, 'Wither "Nation" and "Nationalism"?', 230.
13 Ibid., 227.
14 Ibid.
15 Ibid.

Notes 191

16 David Howarth and Yannis Stavrakakis, 'Introducing Discourse Theory and Political Analysis', in *Discourse Theory and Political Analysis: Identities, Hegemonies, and Social Change*, ed. David Howarth, Aletta Norval and Yannis Stavrakakis, (Manchester: Manchester University Press, 2000), 7.
17 Ibid., 2.
18 Ernesto Laclau, *New Reflections on the Revolution of Our Time*, (London: Verso, 1990), 27.
19 Laclau and Mouffe, *Hegemony and Socialist Strategy*, 98.
20 Laclau, *New Reflections*, 20–1.
21 Ibid., 38.
22 Norval, 'Thinking Identities', 65.
23 Laclau, *New Reflections*, 21.
24 Ibid., 17. Emphasis original. Laclau borrows the term 'constitutive outside' from Henry Staten who used it in relation to Derrida's discussion of the 'metaphysics of presence'. See Henry Staten, *Wittgenstein and Derrida*, (Oxford: Blackwell, 1985), 20.
25 Laclau, *New Reflections*, 17–18; Also, Laclau and Mouffe, *Hegemony and Socialist Strategy*, 122–7.
26 Norval, 'Thinking Identities', 64.
27 Howarth and Stavrakakis, 'Introducing Discourse Theory', 7.
28 Ibid., 8.
29 Norval, 'Frontiers in Question', 60. Emphasis original.
30 Laclau and Mouffe, *Hegemony and Socialist Strategy*, 105; Also Howarth and Stavrakakis, 'Introducing Discourse Theory', 8.
31 Laclau and Mouffe, *Hegemony and Socialist Strategy*, 105.
32 Howarth and Stavrakakis, 'Introducing Discourse Theory', 3.
33 Ibid., 3–4, 13.
34 Ibid., 13.
35 Jason Glynos and David Howarth, *Logics of Critical Explanation in Social and Political Theory*, (Abingdon and New York: Routledge, 2007), 110.
36 Laclau, *New Reflections*, 40.
37 Howarth and Stavrakakis, 'Introducing Discourse Theory', 3–4.
38 Aletta J. Norval, 'Trajectories of Future Research in Discourse Theory', in *Discourse Theory and Political Analysis: Identities, Hegemonies, and Social Change*, eds. David Howarth, Aletta Norval and Yannis Stavrakakis, (Manchester: Manchester University Press, 2000), 220.
39 Norval, 'Thinking Identities', 64–5.
40 Laclau and Mouffe, *Hegemony and Socialist Strategy*, 130.
41 Glynos and Howarth, *Logics of Critical Explanation*, 106.
42 Laclau and Mouffe, *Hegemony and Socialist Strategy*, 130.
43 Norval, 'Trajectories of Future Research in Discourse Theory', 220.
44 Norval, 'Frontiers in Question', 57.
45 Ibid., 67.
46 Ibid., 68.
47 Laclau, *On Populist Reason*; Ernesto Laclau, 'Populism: What's in a Name?,' in *Populism and the Mirror of Democracy*, ed. Fransisco Panizza, (London and New York: Verso, 2005).
48 Laclau, *On Populist Reason*, 73.
49 Laclau, 'Populism: What's in a Name?', 37.
50 Laclau, *On Populist Reason*, 73–4.
51 Ernesto Laclau, 'Why do Empty Signifiers Matter to Politics?', in *Emancipation(s)*, Ernesto Laclau, (London and New York: Verso, 1996).
52 Ibid., 42.
53 Ibid.

192   *Notes*

54   Laclau, 'Populism: What's in a Name?', 39; For a further elaboration of this see also Laclau, *On Populist Reason*, 93–100.
55   Aletta J. Norval, *Aversive Democracy: Inheritance and Originality in the Democratic Tradition*, (Cambridge: Cambridge University Press, 2007), 46.
56   Antonio Gramsci, *Selections from the Prison Notebooks*, edited and translated by Quintin Hoare and Geoffry Nowell Smith, (London: Lawrence and Wishart, 1971), 12, 57–8.
57   Laclau and Mouffe, *Hegemony and Socialist Strategy*, 136. Emphasis original.
58   Norval, *Aversive Democracy*, 46.
59   David Howarth, *Discourse*. (Buckingham: Open University Press, 2000), 109.
60   Laclau and Mouffe, *Hegemony and Socialist Strategy*, 134.
61   Ibid., 135–6.
62   Ibid., 137.
63   Laclau, *New Reflections*, 61.
64   Ibid., 64.
65   Ibid., 67 and 61.
66   Ibid., 34.
67   Ibid., 64.
68   Ibid., 65.
69   Laclau and Mouffe, *Hegemony and Socialist Strategy*, pp. 149–95; Chantal Mouffe, *Democratic Paradox*, (London and New York: Verso, 2000); Norval, *Aversive Democracy*.
70   Laclau and Mouffe, *Hegemony and Socialist Strategy*, 166.
71   Ernesto Laclau, 'Democracy and the Question of Power', *Constellations*, Vol. 8, Issue 1 (2001), 4. Emphasis original.
72   Ibid.
73   Ibid.
74   Laclau, *On Populist Reason*, 166.
75   Glynos and Howarth, *Logics of Critical Explanation*; Howarth, *Discourse*; David Howarth, 'Applying Discourse Theory', in *Discourse Theory in European Politics*, ed. David Howarth and Jacob Torfing, (London: Palgrave, 2005); Howarth and Stavrakakis, 'Introducing Discourse Theory'.
76   Howarth, 'Applying Discourse Theory', 318.
77   Ibid.; Also, Glynos and Howarth, *Logics of Critical Explanation*, 167. For an extensive description of Foucault's archaeological and genealogical methods of analysis see Howarth, *Discourse*, 48–85.
78   Howarth, 'Applying Discourse Theory', 318.
79   Regime refers to an entity that 'structures practices' and also regimes are entities that are 'produced by practices' (125). See Glynos and Howarth, *Logics of Critical Explanation*, 120–7 for a fuller account of their discussion of regimes.
80   Glynos and Howarth, *Logics of Critical Explanation*, 104.
81   Ibid., 105.
82   Ibid.
83   Ibid., 136. Emphasis original.
84   Ibid., 106.
85   Ibid., 133.
86   Ibid., 134.
87   Ibid., 108, emphasis original.
88   Ibid., 106.
89   Ibid., 137 and 106.
90   Ibid., 138.
91   Ibid., 137.
92   Ibid., 106. Emphasis original.
93   Ibid., 141.

Notes 193

94 Howarth and Stavrakakis, 'Introducing Discourse Theory', 13.
95 Ibid., 145.
96 Glynos and Howarth, *Logics of Critical Explanation*, 107.
97 Ibid., 107 and 117.
98 Yannis Stavrakakis, *The Lacanian Left: Psychoanalysis, Theory, Politics*, (Edinburgh: Edinburgh University Press, 2007).
99 Ibid., 190–2. Fantasy plays an important function in this process because it creates and maintains desire in the 'subject': 'In Lacan, the emergence of desire is primarily related to the process of symbolic castration: desire presupposes the sacrifice of a pre-symbolic *jouissance qua fullness*, which is prohibited upon entering the social world of linguistic representation. It is only by sacrificing its pre-symbolic enjoyment that the social subject can develop desire (including the desire to identify with particular political projects, ideologies and discourses)' (Stavrakakis, *The Lacanian Left*, 196). Hence, it is the subject's desire to obtain their lost/impossible pre-symbolic *juissance* that 'provides, above all, the fantasy support for many of our political projects and choices' (ibid.).
100 Ibid., 196.
101 M. Emin Bozarslan, *Doğu'nun Sorunları*, (Safak Kitapevi: Diyarbakır, 1966) Reprint (Avesta Yayınları: Istanbul, 2002); Ismet Chériff Vanly, *Survey of the National Question of Turkish Kurdistan With Historical Background*, (Rome: Hevra Organisation of the Revolutionary Kurds of Turkey in Europe, 1971); İsmail Beşikci, *Doğu Mitinglerinin Analizi*.
102 *PSK Bulten*, 'Kemal Burkay'ın kısaca yaşam öyküsü ve eserleri', http://www.kurdistan.nu/psk/psk_bulten/burkay_yasam.htm.
103 Mazlum Doğan, *Toplu Yazıları* (Collected Writings), (Cologne: Weşanên Serxwebûn, 1982).

3 The organic intellectuals and the re-emergence of Kurdish political activism in the 1960s

1 Antonio Gramsci uses the term to describe intellectuals of rural and traditional backgrounds who still maintained a strong link with the countryside or the peasant masses and to highlight the important role that they play in political movements: 'Every social group, coming into existence on the original terrain of an essential function in the world of economic production, creates together with itself, organically, one or more strata of intellectuals which give it homogeneity and an awareness of its own function not only in the economic but also in the social and political fields' (Gramsci, *Prison Notebooks*, 4).
2 Musa Anter, *Hatıralarım* (My Memoirs), (Istanbul: Avesta Yayınları, 1999), 63 and 112.
3 Furthermore, Musa Anter describes his involvement in the establishment in the mid 1940s of the Society for the Rescue of the Kurds (*Kürtleri Kurtarma Cemiyeti*) which aimed at raising Kurds' national consciousness and awareness among the Kurdish students of their language, culture and status in Turkey (Anter, *Hatıralarım*, 61–8; Naci Kutlay, *49'lar Dosyası*, (Istanbul: Fırat Yayınları, 1994), 234).
4 Feroz Ahmad, *The Turkish Experiment in Democracy, 1950–1975*, (London: C Hurst, 1977), 129.
5 Anter, *Hatıralarım*, 143; Ayşe Hür '"Kımıl" olayından 49'lar Davası'na', *Taraf*, 13 July 2008.
6 Anter, *Hatıralarım*, 143–4.
7 Ayşe Hür, 'Kürtleri imha etmek" fikri kime aitti?', Taraf, 3 August 2008.
8 Kutlay, *49'lar Dosyası*, 7 and 11.
9 Ibid., *49'lar Dosyası*, 217.
10 Yaşar Karadoğan, 'Kürd Demokratik Mücadelesinde Bir Kilometre Taşı: 1967–1969

194 Notes

Doğu Mitingleri ve Kürd Uyanışı', in *Bîr: Kovara Lêgerîn û Lêkolîn*, No. 5 (Summer 2006): 256–8.

11 Yaşar Kaya, *23 Kürt Aydını*, (Cologne: Mezopotamya Yayınları, 1998), 47.

12 See the party programme: Yeni Türkiye Partisi (YTP), *Tüzüğü ve Programı 1961*, (Ankara: Nebioğlu Yayınevi, 1961); Yeni Türkiye Partisi (YTP), *Tüzüğü ve Programı 1963*, (Ankara, 1963) (Publisher not stated).

13 www.belgenet.net/ayrinti.php?yil_id=4 Accessed 12 April 2008.

14 Kendal Nezan, 'Kurdistan in Turkey', in *People Without a Country: Kurds and Kurdistan*, ed. Gerard Chaliand, (Zed Books: London, 1992), 66–7.

15 Yeni Türkiye Partisi, *1969 Seçim Bildirisi* (1969 Election Leaflet), (Date and Place of publication not stated), 6.

16 See Kendal Nezan 'Kurdistan in Turkey', 66–8; Karadoğan, 'Kürd Demokratik Mücadelesinde Bir Kilometre Taşı', 258–9.

17 Hamit Bozarslan, 'Some Remarks on the Kurdish Historiographical Discourse in Turkey (1919–1980)', in *Essays on the Origins of Kurdish Nationalism*, ed. Abbas Vali, (California: Mazda Publishers, 2003), 37.

18 Edip Karahan, 'Niçin Çıkıyoruz', *Dicle-Fırat*, October 1962, 4.

19 'Kürtlerin Menşei' (Origins of the Kurds), *Dicle-Fırat*, October 1962, 3.

20 'Aryan' in the Middle Eastern context refers to the pre-Islamic culture of the region and does not have a racist and anti-Semitic connotation as in Europe. Also, it is used to differentiate Indo-European languages of the region (Persian, Kurdish, Dari, etc.) from Arabic and other Semitic languages.

21 In an article on the five year development plans, Yaşar Kaya criticised the state policies for solely focusing on economic sectors and ignoring regions. He argued that the existing development plans needed to be supplemented with a regional development plan that addressed the issues specific to the Eastern and South-Eastern regions (Yaşar Kaya, 'Bölge Planlaması ve Beş Yıllık Plan', *Dicle-Fırat*, February 1963, 6).

22 Edip Karahan, 'Niçin Çıkıyoruz', *Dicle-Fırat*, October 1962, 4.

23 Edip Karahan, 'Doğu Kalkınması ve Yanlış Görüşler', *Dicle-Fırat*, November 1962, 4.

24 Ibid.

25 Ibid.

26 *Milli Yol*, 20 April 1962; Edip Karahan, 'Hukuk Devleti', *Dicle-Fırat*, December 1962, 4; Sait Elci, 'Irkçıların Doğu Düşmanlığı', *Dicle-Fırat*, January 1963, 2.

27 Gümüşpala quoted in Sait Kırmızıtoprak 'Doğunun Baş Düşmanı Faşizm I', *Dicle-Fırat*, December 1962, 2.

28 Edip Karahan, 'Doğu Kalkınması', *Dicle-Fırat*, November 1962, 4.

29 Edip Karahan, 'Birlik Ve Beraberliğe Dair' (Concerning Unity and Togetherness), *Dicle-Fırat*, January 1963, 1.

30 Literature on nationalism often makes the distinction between 'civic nationalism' and 'ethnocultural nationalism'. In the case of the former, nation is defined 'in terms of a shared commitment to, and pride in, the public institutions of state and civil society, which connect the people to the territory that they occupy. The nation is thus depicted as united by a common public culture, a way of life, a national character, which is shared by all citizens irrespective of ethnic origins'. In the case of the latter, it is used to denote the nation 'as a community united by its ethnocultural sameness, which stems from the common ancestry of its members' (David Brown, *Contemporary Nationalism: Civic, Ethnocultural and Multicultural Politics*, (London and New York: Routledge, 2000) 34–5).

31 Kırmızıtoprak, 'Doğunun Baş Düşmanı Faşizm I', 2; Also, Edip Karahan, 'Demokratik Cephe', *Dicle-Fırat*, April 1963, 1.

32 Sait Kırmızıtoprak, 'Doğunun Baş Düşmanı Faşizm II', *Dicle-Fırat*, January 1963, 2.

33 Şakir Epözdemir, *Türkiye Kürdistan Demokrat Partisi: 1968/235 Antalya Davası Savunması*, (Istanbul: Peri Yayınları, 2005), 102–3.

Notes 195

34 Ibid., 26.
35 Ibid., 18.
36 Ibid., 26. Emphasis mine.
37 Ibid., 19.
38 Sadun Aren, *TİP Olayı 1961–1971*, (Istanbul: Cem Yayınevi, 1993), 31.
39 Anter, *Hatıralarım*, 210–1.
40 Aren, *TİP Olayı*, 70–1.
41 Mehmet Ali Aybar quoted in Ismet Chériff Vanly, *Survey of the National Question*, 50.
42 Aybar quoted in Vanly, *Survey of the National Question*, 52.
43 Igor P. Lipovsky, *The Socialist Movement in Turkey 1960–1980*, (Leiden: Brill, 1992), 103.
44 Ibid., 109.
45 Vanly, *Survey of the National Question*, 53; For the full text of the resolution, see Vanly, *Survey of the National Question*, 53–4; and also *Aren, TİP Dosyası*, 71–2. In fact, this resolution was used as the pretext for closing down the party in 1971.
46 For a more thorough account of the 'Eastern Meetings' see A. Z. Gündoğan, 'The Kurdish Political Mobilization in the 1960s: The Case of "The Eastern Meetings"', (Masters diss., Middle East Technical University, 2005).
47 DDKO, *Sen Faşist Savcı*, 182. Conflicting information is given of the dates of the meetings in İsmail Beşikci, *Doğu Mitinglerinin Analizi*, 15.
48 Ali Beyköylü, 'Koma Azadixwazên Kurdistan: Hodri Meydan', in *Bîr: Kovara Lêgerîn û Lêkolîn*, No. 5 (Summer 2006): 199).
49 Beşikci, *Doğu Mitinglerinin Analizi*, 33.
50 Ibid., 260–1, 65; Vanly, *Survey of the National Question*, 43.
51 Atsız quoted in Karadoğan, 'Kürd Demokratik Mücadelesinde Bir Kilometre Taşı', 265.
52 Atsız quoted in Vanly, *Survey of the National Question*, 44.
53 Beyköylü, 'Hodri Meydan', 199. The title in Turkish was: 'Kim kimi kovuyor: Hodrimeydan'. It is claimed by a Kurdish activist Ali Beyköylü that this statement was prepared by the Koma Azadixwazen Kurdistan, distributed publicly in Istanbul, Izmir, Ankara, Diyarbakir as well as other places and it received ample media interest.
54 Quoted in Nezir Şemmikanlı, 'Geçmiş Olmadan Gelecek Olamaz', in *Bîr: Kovara Lêgerîn û Lêkolîn*, No. 5 (Summer 2006), 80.
55 Quoted in Vanly, *Survey of the National Question*, 46.
56 Diyarbakır Sıkıyönetim Komutanlığı 1 Numaralı Askeri Mahkemesi, *DDKO Dava Dosyası (Ankara ve İstanbul Devrimci Doğu Ocakları'na Ait Davanın Gerekçeli Kararı* (DDKO Court File) (Date, place and publisher not stated), 199–220); Karadoğan, 'Kürd Demokratik Mücadelesinde Bir Kilometre Taşı', 279.
57 Diyarbakır Sıkıyönetim Komutanlığı 1 Numaralı Askeri Mahkemesi, *DDKO Dava Dosyası*, 202.
58 Ibid., 208.

4 The emergence of the Kurdish socialist movement

1 Lipovsky, *The Socialist Movement in Turkey*, 78.
2 Kemal Burkay, *Anılar Belgeler: Cilt 1*, (Stockholm: Roja Nû Yayınları, 2001), 277–8.
3 Anter, *Hatıralarım*, 210.
4 Naci Kutlay, 'Devrimci Doğu Kültür Ocakları ve Öncesi', in *Bîr: Kovara Lêgerîn û Lêkolîn*, No. 5 (Summer 2006): 163). Also, another activist Ümit Fırat states 'Among the Kurds in this conjuncture – and as a result of the development of the national feelings – the opinion that not all of the problems could be solved by a revolution and

196   *Notes*

that it was not enough for them to invest so much expectation in a future revolution, which may not even happen, began to develop. These developments, of course brought with themselves a new understanding for a new type of organisation and consequently, for the first time in republican history, the Kurds began their search for a legal organisation' (Ümit Fırat, 'Ümit Fırat ile DDKO Söyleşisi' (A conversation on the DDKO with Ümit Fırat), in *Bîr: Kovara Lêgerîn û Lêkolîn*, No. 5 (Summer 2006): 177–8).

5 Mümtaz Kotan, 'Tarihin Karartılması Eylemi Üzerine Somut Bir Örnek: DDKO', in *Bîr: Kovara Lêgerîn û Lêkolîn*, No. 6 (Winter 2007): 45).

6 Ali Buran, 'DDKO İlk Ulusalcı, Demokratik ve Ayrı Örgütlenmeyi Hedefleyen Kürt Demokratik Gençlik Örgütüydü', in *Bîr: Kovara Lêgerîn û Lêkolîn*, No. 6 (Winter 2007): 103).

7 Diyarbakır Sıkıyönetim Komutanlığı 1 Numaralı Askeri Mahkemesi, *DDKO Dava Dosyası*, 175.

8 Ibid., 186.

9 Kotan, 'Tarihin Karartılması', 48.

10 Diyarbakır Sıkıyönetim Komutanlığı 1 Numaralı Askeri Mahkemesi, *DDKO Dava Dosyası*, 3.

11 DDKO, *Sen Faşist Savcı*, 52–6.

12 Ibid., 58–9.

13 Ibid., 52.

14 Ibid., 77–88.

15 Ibid., pp. 108–30.

16 Ibid., 88–9.

17 Ibid., 100.

18 Ibid., 136–7.

19 Ibid., 134.

20 Hıdır Murat, *Türkiye Şartlarında Kürt Halkının Kurtuluş Mücadelesi* (The Liberation Struggle of Kurdish people in Turkey's Conditions), (Zurich: Ronahi Yayınları, (2nd Edition 1977)); Hevra: Devrimci Türkiye Kürtleri Örgütü, *Türkiye Şartlarına Ters Düşen Bir Tez: Milli Demokratik Devrim* (National Democratic Revolution: A Thesis that is Contrary to Turkey's Conditions), (Zurich: Ronahi Yayınları, 1974).

21 Hevra, *Milli Demokratik Devrim*, 14.

22 Ibid., 20; A similar argument is made in Hıdır Murat, *Kürt Halkının Kurtuluş Mücadelesi*, 43.

23 Hevra, *Milli Demokratik Devrim*, 19.

24 Ibid., 28.

25 Ibid., 29.

26 Ibid., 84.

27 Ibid., 85.

28 Ibid., 86.

29 Ibid., 182–3.

30 Hevra, *Milli Demokratik Devrim*, 44.

31 TİİKP, *Türkiye İhtilalci İşçi Köylü Partisi Dava Dosyası* (Case File of TİİKP), (Ankara: Töre Devlet Yayınları, 1973), 433.

32 Furthermore, during the early 1990s the Aydınlık group (seen as the continuation of the TİİKP) seemed sympathetic to Kurdish demands. However, from the late 1990s onwards it began to incorporate many elements from Kemalism to become one of the most nationalist Turkish left-wing groups. See Mesut Yeğen, *Müstakbel Türk'ten Sözde Vatandaşa: Cumhuriyet ve Kürtler*, (Istanbul: İletişim Yayınları, 2006), 145–94, for an extended discussion of the representation of the Kurdish question within the Turkish Left discourse.

33 *Rizgarî*, March 1976, 18–19.

34 *Rizgarî*, March 1976, 10.

Notes 197

35 *Rizgarî*, June 1978, 10; Also two articles critical of the position of the Communist Party of Turkey (TKP) appeared in *Özgürlük Yolu*, October 1977, Issue 29; and *Özgürlük Yolu*, November 1977, Issue 30; Articles critical of the position of Devrimci Yol (Revolutionary Path) appeared in *Özgürlük Yolu*, August 1978, Issue 39; *Özgürlük Yolu*, September 1978, Issue 40; and *Özgürlük Yolu*, November 1978, Issue 42. Similarly the PKK argued: 'Despite all the contradictions that exist amongst them, these groups – from the TKP to the TIKP [the Revolutionary Communist Party of Turkey] – are mainly social chauvinist because they do not go beyond applying a thin version of Kemalism' (PKK, *Kurulus Bildirisi* (The Founding Declaration), (Date and the place of the publication not stated), 43.

36 It is generally accepted that *Newroz* has been celebrated for nearly 3,000 years in the Near and Middle East. It has a strong connection with Zoroastrianism, and Persian mythology; however, there are various other ancient festivals celebrated by the ancient societies, including the Hittites and the Babylonians to which its origins are also traced (Aydın, 'Mobilizing The Kurds', 46; Gurdal Aksoy, *Bir Soylence*, 21–3).

37 Aydın, 'Mobilizing the Kurds', 46.

38 Ibid., 71. Furthermore, Aydın offers an extended discussion of the construction of *Newroz* as a myth of origin. She draws attention to the various discussions in the Kurdish journal *Jîn* during 1918–1919, which highlighted the lack of a national holiday for Kurds and it was within this framework that the legend of Kawa was constructed as a Kurdish national figure (60). However, initially the celebration of a national holiday was proposed for 31 August as opposed to 21 March. Further attempts were made in the 1930s to construct the legend of Kawa as the myth of origin by the leader of the Ararat Rebellion, Ihsan Nuri. Nuri associated the legend of Kawa with the festival of Tolhildan rather than *Newroz* because *Newroz* had already acquired a national character in Iran and was strongly associated with the Persian legend of Jamshid (Ibid., 66–8).

39 For the 'family tree' of the Kurdish political groups, see Rafet Ballı, *Kürt Dosyası*, (Istanbul: Cem Yayınları, 1991), 48–9.

40 Ballı, *Kürt Dosyası*, 334–5.

41 Ibid., 82–3. See also the brochure: *Ala Rizgarî, Kürdistan Devriminde Genel Olarak Örgütlenme ve Proleteryanın Örgütü*, (Date, place and publisher not stated).

42 Ballı, *Kürt Dosyası*, 146, 163.

43 Ibid., 48–9.

44 Abdullah Öcalan, *İlk Konuşmalar*, (*Weşanên Serxwebûn*, 1999) (Date and Place not stated).

45 *Serxwebûn* Özel Sayı (Special Issue), December 2008, 33. Also the following DVD *Dîroka Ji Agir/Ateşten Tarih*, (Cologne: Mir Production, 2008) contains extensive footage of interviews with the PKK's leading members about the movement's early years.

46 UDG, *Kürdistan Ulusal Demokratik Güçbirliği (UDG Deklerasyonu)*, (Van: Jîna Nû Yayınları, 1980).

47 See Welat Zeydanlıoğlu, 'Torture and Turkification in the Diyarbakır Military Prison', in *Rights, Citizenship & Torture: Perspectives on Evil, Law and the State*, edited by John T. Parry and Welat Zeydanlıoğlu, (Oxford: Inter-Disciplinary Press, 2009).

5 The Kurdish national liberation discourse

1 Ulrike Meinhof – German Left-Wing Militant.

2 Guy Fawkes (1570–1606).

3 Hıdır Murat, *Kürt Halkının Kurtuluş Mücadelesi*, 28.

4 See TKSP, *Program* (Party Programme), (TKSP Yayınları, 1985 (Place of publication not stated), 1; Abdullah Öcalan, *Kürdistan Devriminin Yolu (Manifesto)*, (Cologne: Weşanên Serxwebûn, 1992, 4th Edition), 99–100.

198   *Notes*

5   *Rizgarî*, March 1976, 20.
6   *Rizgarî*, March 1976, 20–1.
7   Gündoğan, *Kawa Savunması*, 403.
8   *Rizgarî*, March 1976,19.
9   Öcalan, *Manifesto*, 100.
10 *Özgürlük Yolu*, November 1978, 24.
11 Öcalan, *Manifesto*, 142.
12 Ibid., 166.
13 PKK, *Kürdistan Ulusal Kurtuluş Problemi ve Çözüm Yolu* (Kurdistan's National Liberation Problem and Its Solution), (Cologne: *Weşanên Serxwebûn*, 1992, 2nd edition), 39.
14 *Özgürlük Yolu*, September 1977, 19.
15 Öcalan, *Manifesto*, 169.
16 *Özgürlük Yolu*, August 1975, 41.
17 *Rizgarî*, March 1976, 8–9.
18 *Özgürlük Yolu*, November 1978, 55.
19 *Özgürlük Yolu*, August 1975, 45.
20 Gündoğan, *Kawa Savunması*, 509.
21 Öcalan, *Manifesto*, 190.
22 *Özgürlük Yolu*, November 1978, 33. Emphasise mine.
23 Öcalan, *Manifesto*, 192.
24 *Rizgarî*, March 1976, 25.
25 PKK, *Politik Rapor: Merkez Komitesi Tarafından PKK 1. Konferansına Sunulmuştur* (Political Report of the Central Committee Submitted to the PKK's 1st Congress), (Cologne: *Weşanên Serxwebûn*, 1982), 86–7.
26 Ibid., 87.
27 Gündoğan, *Kawa Savunması*, 430.
28 Öcalan, *Manifesto*, 186.
29 Ibid., 200–1.
30 TKSP, *Program*, 17.
31 Ibid., 22.
32 PKK, *Politik Rapor*, 87.
33 Öcalan, *Manifesto*, 202.
34 They established HEVKARI in 1981 and the Tevgera Rizgariya Kurdistan in June 1988 (Kurdistan Liberation Movement, TEVGER). However, both of these attempts also failed to overcome the fragmentation of the Kurdish movement. There were eight organisations – including *Ala Rizgarî*, the KUK and the TKSP – which took part in the foundation of the TEVGER (Tevger, *Program: Tevgera Rizgariya Kurdistan*, (Weşanên Tevger, 1988), 34 (place of publication not stated)).
35 Gündoğan, *Kawa Savunması*, 40.
36 Öcalan, *Manifesto*, 196.
37 Öcalan, *Manifesto*, 198.
38 PKK, *Kürdistan'da Zorun Rolü (Ulusal Kurtuluş Savaşı – Ulusal Kurtuluş Siyaseti)*, (Cologne: *Weşanên Serxwebûn*, 1983); PKK, *Kürdistan Ulusal Kurtuluş Problemi ve Çözüm Yolu: Kürdistan Ulusal Kurtuluş Cephesi Program Taslağı*, (Cologne: *Weşanên Serxwebûn*, 1984, 2nd Edition).
39 PKK, *Politik Rapor*, 96.
40 Ibid., 162; Also PKK, *Çalışma Raporu: PKK II. Kongresine Sunulan PKK-MK* (The Activities Report Submitted by the Central Committee to the PKK's Second Congress), (Cologne: *Weşanên Serxwebûn*, 1984), 57–8).
41 Öcalan, *Manifesto*, 198; PKK, *Kürdistan Ulusal Kurtulus Problemi ve Çözüm Yolu*, 153.
42 TKSP, *Program*, 18.
43 Ibid., 20.

Notes 199

44 This changed after 1993 when socialism was seen as a long-term achievement of the revolution (PSK, *Program*, (PSK Yayınları, 1993 (place of publication not stated), 13).
45 TKSP, *Program*, 10.
46 Ibid., 19. The need to construct an anti-imperialist and anti-fascist united front was also emphasised in *Özgürlük Yolu*, November 1978, 56.
47 *Jîna Nû*, November 1979, 45–8.
48 PKK, *Faşizme ve Ulusal Baskı Sistemine Karşı Ortak Mücadelenin Sorunları* (The Problems of Common Struggle Against Fascism and the System of National Oppression), (Cologne: *Weşanên Serxwebûn*, 1984); PKK, *Faşizme Karşı Mücadelede Birleşik Cephe Üzerine* (Concerning the United Front in the Struggle Against Fascism), (Cologne: *Weşanên Serxwebûn*, 1982).
49 *Rizgarî*, July 1977 (Special Issue: 'Özgürlük Yolu Oportunizmine İstediği Bir Cevap' (An answer to Opportunism of *Özgürlük Yolu*); *Rizgarî*, November 1978.
50 See 'Rizgarî Dergisinin Siyaseti Üzerine' (On the Politics of *Rizgarî* Magazine), *Özgürlük Yolu*, August 1977 and September 1977.
51 PKK, *Örgütlenme Üzerine* (Concerning Organisation), (Cologne: *Weşanên Serxwebûn*, 1983), 166–82; PKK *Devrimcilerdeki Kafa Karısıklığı'mı, yoksa bir Küçük-burjuva reformistin iflah olmazlığı mı?* (Confusion Among Revolutionaries or the Impossibility of the Rehabilitation of a Petty Bourgeois Reformist), (Cologne: *Weşanên Serxwebûn*, 1984).
52 Kemal Burkay, *Devrimcilik mi Terörizm mi? PKK Üzerine* (Revolutionism or Terrorism? Concerning the PKK), (Özgürlük Yolu Yayınları, 1983, Place of publication not stated), 5–8.
53 *Jîna Nû*, November 1979; and, *Jîna Nû*, January–February 1980.
54 Öcalan, *Manifesto*, 45.
55 Ibid., 45–6.
56 *Rizgarî*, March, 1976, 16.
57 *Özgürlük Yolu*, April 1977. See also Aydın, 'Mobilizing the Kurds', 72–83 for a discussion of the appropriation of the *Newroz* myth into Kurdish socialist discourse.
58 Kemal Burkay, *Devrimcilik mi Terörizm mi?*, 24–7.
59 Öcalan, *Manifesto*, 32. Locating the origins of the nation in the distant past is further strengthened by tracing the origin of the word Kurd: 'In this period the Greek Scholars used the names "Kurdo" and "Kurdienne"' (ibid., 102).
60 Without providing much detail, Gündoğan also makes a similar point about the 'golden age' of the nation (Gündoğan, *Kawa Savunması*, 268–9).
61 Ibid., 368.
62 Ibid., 323.
63 Öcalan, *Manifesto*, 170. Moreover, two main leaders of the PKK were of Turkish origin and the PKK cadres identified themselves as 'Patriots of Kurdistan' (*Kürdistan Yurtseverleri*) as opposed to Kurdish nationalists.
64 Mazlum Doğan, *Toplu Yazıları* (Collected Writings), (Cologne: *Weşanên Serxwebûn*, 1982), 113. Poignant accounts of the PKK's resistance in Diyarbakir Military Prison are provided in: Hüseyin Yıldırım, *Kürdistan Halkının Diriliş Mücadelesi: Diyarbakır Zindanı*, (Cologne: *Weşanên Serxwebûn*, 1985) and, M. Selim Çürükkaya, *12 Eylül Karanlığında Diyarbakır Şafağı*, (Cologne: Ağrı Yayınları, 1990).
65 Human Rights Foundation of Turkey, *File of Torture: Deaths in Detention Places or Prisons (12 September 1980–12 September 1994)*, (HRFT Publications: Ankara, 1994), 41 and 51. In the *File of Torture* the date on which the self-immolation of the four prisoners occurred is given as 17 March 1982.
66 The PKK members captured by the state were put on common trials that began in early 1981 and were concluded in 1983. The biggest trial of PKK members and sympathisers was held in Diyarbakir and started on 13 April 1981 and was concluded on 25 May 1983 (*Serxwebûn*, June 1983, 1). Separate trials were held in Ağrı, Kars,

200   *Notes*

Urfa-Birecik, Elazığ, Siirt-Batman and G.Antep. The defence of Kemal Pir was serialised in the March, April and May 1982 issues of *Serxwebûn*; of Mazlum Doğan in the May, June and July 1982 issues of *Serxwebûn*; of Mehmet Hayri Durmuş in the August and September 1982 issues of *Serxwebûn*. They were published in Yıldırım, *Kürdistan Halkının Diriliş Mücadelesi*, 59–136. Furthermore, a comprehensive overview of the PKK inmates' resistance at the Diyarbakir Military Prison, including their defence at the courts is provided on the following website: www.diyarbakirzindani.com/.

67 Extensive coverage of the trials was provided in the early issues of *Serxwebûn*. See *Serxwebûn*, March 1982, 1; *Serxwebûn*, June 1982, 1; *Serxwebûn*, December 1982, 1; and *Serxwebûn*, June 1983, 1.

68 Marcus, *Blood and Belief*, 67.

69 According to Gündoğan, only the PKK and *Kawa* members presented a political defence of their organisations (Gündoğan, *Kawa Davası Savunması*, 213–14).

70 PKK, *Politik Rapor*, 136–7.

71 See, Abdullah Öcalan, *Kürdistan'da İşbirlikcilik-İhanet ve Devrimci Direniş* (Collaboration, Betrayal and Revolutionary Resistance in Kurdistan), (Cologne: *Weşanên Serxwebûn*, 1993) for the text of the agreement (447–9).

72 Furthermore, a protocol expressing similar measures was signed by the PKK and the Patriotic Union of Kurdistan (PUK) in May 1988, calling for fostering of better relations between the two parties.

6 'Becoming a Kurd': the 'national liberation' war and mass mobilisation

1 The Kurdish translation '*Ji bo Serxwebûn û Azadiye bi rumettir tiştek nine*' of Ho Chi Minh's sentence is quoted in the headline of the PKK's monthly magazine *Serxwebûn*.

2 Popular Kurdish mantra meaning 'Resistance is life'.

3 Laclau, *New Reflections*, 34.

4 Norval, *Aversive Democracy*, 46.

5 PKK, *Politik Rapor*, 142.

6 PKK, *Kürdistan Ulusal Kurtuluş Problemi ve Çözüm Yolu: Kürdistan Ulusal Kurtuluş Cephesi Program Taslağı*, (Cologne: *Weşanên Serxwebûn*, 1984, 2nd Edition). First edition published in 1982.

7 Ibid., 193.

8 Abdullah Öcalan, *3. Kongre Konuşmalari* (3rd Congress Speeches), (Cologne: *Weşanên Serxwebûn*, 1993), 152.

9 PKK, *Bağımsız Kürdistan Yolunda*, (Cologne: *Weşanên Serxwebûn*, 1987).

10 Human Rights Foundation of Turkey, *Örneklerle Türkiye İnsan Hakları Raporu 1991* (Human Rights Report of Turkey 1991), (Ankara: TİHV Yayınları, 1992), 155.

11 Öcalan, *3. Kongre Konuşmaları*, 145.

12 Ibid., 143–4.

13 *Berxwedan*, March 1987, 2–4.

14 *Berxwedan*, April 1987, 2.

15 *Berxwedan*, May 1987, 3.

16 *Berxwedan*, August 1987, 2.

17 *Berxwedan*, 15 August 1990, 5.

18 *Berxwedan*, 1 March 1991, 3; *Berxwedan*, 30 April 1991, 3–7; *Berxwedan*, 15 July 1991, 4–6; *Berxwedan*, 30 September 1991, 4–8.

19 Doğu Perinçek, *Abdullah Öcalan ile Görüşme* (Interview with Abdullah Öcalan), (Istanbul: Kaynak Yayınları, 1990), 44.

20 Abdullah Öcalan, *Kürdistan'da Halk Savaşı ve Gerrilla* (People's War and Guerrilla in Kurdistan), (Cologne: *Weşanên Serxwebûn*, 1991), 301–22.

Notes 201

21 The agreement with the KDP was abrogated by KDP leader Massoud Barzani, and the relations between the PKK and KDP started to deteriorate during the late 1980s. To compensate for the loss of the alliance with the KDP, the PKK signed a similar agreement with the PUK (Patriotic Union of Kurdistan) in 1988 that promoted closer cooperation between the two parties but also sought to promote the construction of a wider Kurdish national front. However, in practice this did not bring about the development of a pan-Kurdist movement (McDowall, *A Modern History of the Kurds*, 426).

22 Ibid., 361. The food poisoning was deliberately done to pressure the refugees to return back to Iraqi Kurdistan. The refugee crisis in 1991 was much bigger in scale and nearly 1.5 million people abandoned their homes in search of safety in Iran and Turkey (Ibid., 373).

23 *Serxwebûn*, September 1991, 1–2. Behdinan is the area south of the Turkish border in Iraqi Kurdistan where many of the PKK's forces were based.

24 Türkiye İnsan Hakları Vakfı, *1992 Türkiye İnsan Hakları Raporu*, (Ankara: TİHV Yayınları, 1993), 73.

25 Human Rights Foundation of Turkey, *1993 Turkey Human Rights Report*, (Ankara: HRTF Publications, 1994), 72.

26 Marcus, *Blood and Belief*, 82.

27 Öcalan, *3. Kongre Konuşmaları*, 151.

28 Ibid., 155.

29 PKK, *Politik Rapor*, 155–6.

30 Although the present population of Kurds in Europe is unknown, the Kurdish organisations estimate it to be nearly 2 million.

31 *Berxwedan*, September 1987, 12.

32 PKK, *Çalışma Raporu*, 61.

33 *Berxwedan* (Special Edition), 27 March 1990, 6.

34 *Berxwedan*, 31 March 1988, 1. The week of national heroism was celebrated annually from 1987. Numerous articles published in the PKK's official magazines stressed the significance of the resistance shown by the leading members during the early years of the movement and called upon the PKK members and sympathisers to recreate the spirit of their resistance.

35 *Berxwedan* 15 July 1990, 1.

36 *Serxwebûn*, July 1991, 4.

37 TİHV, *Türkiye İnsan Hakları Raporu 1991*, (Ankara: TİHV Yayınları, 1992), 51

38 TİHV, *Türkiye İnsan Hakları Raporu 1992*, (Ankara: TİHV Yayınları, 1993), 22

39 Ibid.

40 See www.mkmbakur.com for an overview of cultural activities (Music, Dance, Cinema, Theatre, Literature) that the MKM coordinates in its main office in Istanbul, branches in other Turkish cities and the main towns and cities in the Kurdish region. Accessed 8 November 2009.

41 See Uçarlar, 'Between Majority Power and Minority Resistance', especially Chapters 7 and 8 (191–266), for a discussion of the activities of the exiled Kurdish writers and intellectuals and the cultural organisations in Europe.

42 See Kurdish Academy of Language (www.kurdishacademy.org) for a detailed overview of written and linguistic standardisation of Kurmanci Kurdish and the broader issues concerning the Kurdish Language. Additionally, the Kurds in the Soviet Union have also made significant contributions to the study of Kurdish history, language and literature. However, the Kurdish works published in the Soviet Union used the Cyrillic alphabet.

43 Since the early 2000s, Kurdish film festivals started to be organised in many western cities (London, Paris, Montreal, Hamburg, Cologne, Frankfurt, Berlin and Melbourne) on a regular basis making a significant contribution to Kurdish cultural life in the Diaspora. See www.kurdishcinema.com/Festivals.html for more details.

44 ROJ TV, 'Dillere Göre Rapor' (Report on language use), 22 December 2007.

202 Notes

45 ROJ TV, 'Broadcasting Committee – Minutes of the weekly meeting', 09/06/2008.
46 *Serxwebûn*, June 1982, 10–11. Headline 'Diyarbakir Cezaevinde Katliam' was used by *Serxwebûn* to announce the death of Dogan.
47 *Serxwebûn*, March 1983, 9.
48 *Serxwebûn*, December 1982, 4. Emphasis mine.
49 *Berxwedan*, Special Issue, June 1994.
50 *Serxwebûn*, April 1994, 16–22.
51 *Serxwebûn*, September 1990, Special Issue.
52 Numerous articles on the guerrilla war and numerous obituaries of guerrillas described them as 'heroes of national resistance' (*Ulusal Direniş Kahramanları*) and 'Martyrs of Resistance' (*Direniş Şehitleri*) (*Serxwebûn*, Mart 1988, 4).
53 *Berxwedan* (Special *Newroz* Edition), March 1992, 13; *Berxwedan* (Special Issue), March 1994, 15–18; *Serxwebûn*, April 1994, 18–19.
54 www.hpg-online.com/tr/ekim_sehitleri/4.html Accessed 7 September 2009.
55 Norval, *Aversive Democracy*, 194.
56 Ibid., 204.
57 Ibid., 179.
58 *Berxwedan*, March 1994 (Special Issue).
59 The poem was first published in *Serxwebûn*, May 1982, 9. Since then, it has been reproduced in numerous texts. See www.antoloji.com/siir/siir/siir_SQL.asp?siir_id=29582 for the text of the poem.
60 *Dilan* can also refer to a call for struggle, with struggle seen as a joyful activity.
61 http://www.rojaciwan.com/haber-34815.html Accessed 1 April 2008.
62 For a more comprehensive study of the Kurdish women's role in the national movement and their participation and identity see Çağlayan, *Analar, Yoldaşlar*; According to Marcus, in 1993 'women comprised about a third of the PKK's armed forces' (Marcus, *Blood and Belief*, 173).
63 Norval uses Wittgenstein's discussion of 'aspect dawning' and 'aspect change' to provide an account of the way political grammars are challenged and for the changes that take place in them: 'Aspect dawning and change occurs when one realizes that a new kind of characterization of an object or situation may be given, and we see it in those terms' (Norval, *Aversive Democracy*, 113).
64 Cağlayan, *Analar, Yoldaşlar*, 106.
65 Ibid., 107.
66 Ibid., 206–8.
67 'Dağların Tek Kollu Kızı' Firat News Agency, 26 September 2009 www.firatnews.com/index.php?rupel=nuce&nuceID=14324 Accessed 27 November 2009.
68 Marcus, *Blood and Belief*, 172.
69 Aydın, 'Mobilizing the Kurds', 90; Lerna K. Yanik, '"Nevruz" or "Newroz"? Deconstructing the "Invention" of a Contested Tradition in Contemporary Turkey', *Middle Eastern Studies*, Vol. 42, No. 2, March 2006, 285.
70 In his influential study Anderson states, 'In an anthropological spirit, then, I propose the following definition of the nation: it is an imagined political community – and imagined as both inherently limited and sovereign' Benedict Anderson, *Imagined Communities* (London: Verso, 1983), 15.

7 Dislocations and the PKK's turn to democracy (1992–present)

1 Laclau, *New Reflections*, 39.
2 Howarth and Stavrakakis, 'Introducing Discourse Theory', 13.
3 Andrew Schaap, *Political Reconciliation*, (London and New York: Routledge, 2005), 11).
4 Abdullah Öcalan, *Sosyalizm ve Devrim Sorunları* (Socialism and the Problems of Revolution), (Cologne: Weşanên Serxwebûn, 1992), 283.

Notes 203

5 Ibid., 284.
6 Ibid., 305–7.
7 Abdullah Öcalan, *Kürt Hümanizmi ve Yeni İnsan* (Kurdish Humanism and the New Human), (Istanbul: Mem Yayınları, 2001), 182–3.
8 Ibid., 183; See also Özcan, *Turkey's Kurds*, pp. 115–23 for a discussion of Öcalan's new socialist theorisation.
9 Perinçek. *Abdullah Öcalan ile Görüşme*, 91.
10 'Uygunsa Türk Parlementosunada Girerim, Türk Genel Kurmayı'na da', *Özgür Gündem*, 8 June 1992.
11 Oral Çalışlar, *Öcalan ve Burkayla Kürt Sorunu*, (Istanbul: Pencere Yayınları, 1993), 17–18.
12 See, Watts, 'Institutionalizing Virtual Kurdistan West', for a fuller account of the activities of Kurdish political and cultural organisations in Europe. In her assessment of the Kurdish transnational advocacy networks in Europe, she states: 'I argue here that key to the emergence of Virtual Kurdistan West was the institutionalization of a distinctive set of pro-Kurdish norms and practices within nongovernmental and governmental arenas in Europe. This institutionalization provided Kurdish activists with a concrete array of legal, material, political, and ideational resources with which to sustain their agenda' (Watts, 'Institutionalizing Virtual Kurdistan West', 124). Furthermore, concerning the impact the Kurdish transnational advocacy networks had on Kurdish political practices in general, she argues that they 'provided a space for the emergence of new expectations about "appropriate" behavior among Kurds and new legal, cultural, and political practices that collectively came to constitute *national* practices' (ibid., 125).
13 *Berxwedan*, 15 February 1994, 16–17.
14 See http://belgenet.net/ayrinti.php?yil_id=12 for a list of the MPs elected to represent each province of Turkey after the General Election held on 24 December 1995.
15 Fulya Atacan, 'A Kurdish Islamist Group in Modern Turkey: Shifting Identities', *Middle Eastern Studies*, Vol. 37, No. 3, July 2001, pp. 111–44; Bulent Aras and Gokhan Bacik, 'The Mystery of Turkish Hizballah' *Middle East Policy*, Vol. IX, No. 2, June 2002.
16 The conflict between the Hizbullah and the PKK initially flared in 1991 in Batman, with the Hizbullah (İlim Group) attacking the pro-PKK businesses. From then on the Hizbullah was involved in many of the murders of pro-PKK individuals by unknown assailants. Other high-profile murders committed by the Hizbullah include the Feminist writer Konca Kuriç in 1998. The assassination of the head of security in Diyarbakir province Gaffar Okkan on 24 January 2001 is also attributed to the organisation. The connection between the state and Hizbullah has been especially emphasised by the PKK. The connection between the Hizbullah and the state has been also made by İsmail Beşikci, who argues that Hizbullah was established by the state to mobilise the religious Kurds against the PKK (İsmail Beşikci, *Hayali Kürdistan'ın Dirilişi*, (Istanbul: Aram Yayınları, 1998), 66). However, according to the official information provided by the state, the origins of the Hizbullah are traced to the early 1980s, and attention is drawn to its early links to Iran and other Jihadist/ Islamist organisations such as the Muslim Brotherhood. The division between the Menzil Group and İlim Group during the mid 1990s and the conflict between the two groups seems to further complicate the story. The crack down on Hizbullah activities at the beginning of the 2000s and the death of its leader Huseyin Velioglu on 17 January 2000 has weakened the organisation significantly and seems to suggest the end of tolerance shown by the security forces for its activities. Even if it is impossible to establish a clear link between the state and the Hizbullah, it is generally assumed that Hizbullah was used in the counter-insurgency operations against the PKK (Ruşen Çakır, *Derin Hizbullah: İslami Şiddetin Geleceği*, (Istanbul:

204 *Notes*

Siyah Beyaz Metis Güncel, 2001), 76). Furthermore, the fact that during the 1990s Hizbullah did not carry out any attacks against the Turkish security forces seems to strengthen the link.

17 *Berxwedan*, 15 March 1994, 20–1.
18 TİHV, *Türkiye İnsan Hakları Raporu 1992*, 90; McDowall, *A Modern History of the Kurds*, 436.
19 TİHV, *Türkiye İnsan Hakları Raporu 1991*, 156. Most importantly, the law restricted the prosecution of security forces who committed crimes against Kurdish civilians.
20 'Forced Evictions and Destruction of Villages in Turkish Kurdistan', *Middle East Report* 199 (April–June 1996) 8; Metin Can, Hasan Kaya, Kemal Kılıç, Cemal Akar, Mehmet Sincar and Sevket Epözdemir, *Yıkılan Köylerden bir Kesit*, (Ankara: İnsan Hakları Derneği Yayınları, 1994), 227–42.
21 TİHV, *Türkiye İnsan Hakları Raporu 1994*, (Ankara: TİHV Yayınları, 1995), 74.
22 TİHV, *Türkiye İnsan Hakları Raporu 1992*, 20–7.
23 The pro-Kurdish newspaper *Özgür Gündem* described the attack on Şırnak as a 'massacre'. Özgür Gündem, 21 August 1992.
24 TİHV, *Türkiye İnsan Hakları Raporu 1992*, 28.
25 HRFT, *Turkey Human Rights Report 1993*, 61–2.
26 According to the Human Rights Foundation of Turkey, in the year 1992 alone 297 people were killed by the Hizbullah in the Kurdish regions (TİHV, *Türkiye İnsan Hakları Raporu 1992*, 63–70). The information that is becoming available in the course of the trial of the *Ergenekon* organisation is that numerous high ranking Turkish army personnel and JITEM members had been closely involved with the murder of Kurdish civilians by unidentified assailants.
27 TİHV, *Türkiye İnsan Hakları Raporu 1994*, (Ankara: TİHV Yayınları, 1995), 121–2, 125.
28 TİHV, *Türkiye İnsan Hakları Raporu 1992*, 63–72.
29 For an extensive account see the Human Rights Foundation of Turkey, *Turkey Human Rights Report 1993*, 143–58 and Human Rights Foundation of Turkey, *Türkiye İnsan Hakları Raporu 1994*, 115–38.
30 TİHV, *Türkiye İnsan Hakları Raporu 1992*, 93.
31 According to the Human Rights Foundation of Turkey, the numbers of those killed as a result of raids on houses or businesses, during demonstrations and those who did not obey 'stop' warning were as follows: 98 in 1991, 192 in 1992, 186 in 1993 and 129 in 1993 (TİHV, *Türkiye İnsan Hakları Raporu 1994*, 140).
32 Human Rights Foundation of Turkey, *Turkey Human Rights Report 1995*, (Ankara: HRFT Publications, 1997), 294–6.
33 Ibid., 277.
34 *Berxwedan*, 15 June 1994, 1; PKK, *5. Kongre Kararları* (The Decisions of 5th Congress), (Cologne: *Weşanên Serxwebûn*, 1995), 37.
35 TİHV, *Türkiye İnsan Hakları Raporu 1996*, (Ankara: TİHV Yayınları, 1998), 147.
36 'Britons Hurt in Turkish Bomb Blasts', *Independent*, 23 June 1994.
37 TİHV, *Turkey Human Rights Report 1993*, 80–2.
38 A Kadir Konuk, *PKK'nin Tek Taraflı ilan Ettiği Ateşkes ve Yankıları* (The PKK's Unilateral Ceasefire and its Consequences), (Cologne: Agrı Yayınları, 1993), 34.
39 TİHV, *Türkiye İnsan Hakları Raporu 1996*, 58.
40 Suspicions have been raised about the events leading to the attack. The PKK described the attack on unarmed soldiers as a provocation and initially refused responsibility stating that the attack was carried out without the knowledge and initiative of the PKK leadership. Later on, the PKK blamed Şemdin Sakık the commander in charge of the units which carried out the attack. Whilst in prison, Abdullah Öcalan claimed that the PKK units that carried out the attack were wrongly informed that the soldiers were preparing an attack, and in fact the Turkish government was prepared to take steps to respond to the PKK's unilateral ceasefire. The

Notes 205

attacks, however, ended any hope of a peaceful solution to the conflict (See 'Çözüm Olmasın diye 33 Askeri Öldürttüler', *Taraf*, 8 November 2008).

41 TİHV, *Türkiye İnsan Hakları Raporu 1996*, 54.

42 TİHV, *Türkiye İnsan Hakları Raporu 1996*, 55. Additionally, similar meetings were held in numerous European cities.

43 Ibid., 60.

44 Ibid., 61.

45 Ibid., 61.

46 'Fugitive on the Run: Öcalan's Mystery Tour' http://news.bbc.co.uk/1/hi/world/europe/280473.stm. Accessed 30 July 2009.

47 One of the deadliest of such attacks was carried out in a shopping centre in Göztepe District of Istanbul on 13 March 1999. The fire that the petrol bomb caused resulted in the death of 13 civilians ('İşte Eseriniz: 13 Ölü', *Hurriyet*, 14 March 1999).

48 In November 2009, Öcalan was transferred to a newly built prison on Imrali Island, which houses 5 other inmates.

49 As part of the Terrorism Act 2000, the UK included the PKK among the proscribed organisations. This coincides with the period when the PKK ceased its military operations, withdrew its force and called a permanent ceasefire. However, between 1984 and 1998 when the PKK was fighting the Turkish army and the state security forces it was not formally outlawed in the UK. In Germany, following large-scale unrest in 1993 and in France the PKK was declared a 'terrorist organisation' and its activities banned. In May 2002 the PKK was added to the list of terrorist organisations as were the organisations that the PKK would subsequently form. However, this decision was overturned by the European Court of First Instance in April 2008 on 'procedural grounds' (See 'EU Court Annuls PKK Terror Ruling' http://news.bbc.co.uk/1/hi/world/europe/7328238.stm). Accessed 25 August 2009.

50 Abdullah Öcalan, *Savunma: Kürt Sorununda Demokratik Çözüm Bildirgesi*, (Istanbul: Mem Yayınları, 1999); Abdullah Öcalan, *Ek Savunma: Kürt Sorununda Çözüm ve Çözümsuzluk Ikilemi*, (Istanbul: Mem Yayınları, 1999); Abdullah Öcalan, *AİHM Savunmaları (Cilt 1): Sümer Rahip Develtinden Demokratik Cumhuriyete* (ECHR Defence Volume 1: From Sumerian Monk State to Democratic Republic), (Cologne: Mezopotamya Yayınları, 2001); Abdullah Öcalan, *AİHM Savunmaları (Cilt 2): Sümer Rahip Develtinden Demokratik Cumhuriyete* (ECHR Defence Volume 2: From Sumerian Monk State to Democratic Republic), (Cologne: Mezopotamya Yayınları, 2001); Abdullah Öcalan, *Bir Halkı Savunmak*, (Cologne: Weşanên Serxwebûn, 2004); Abdullah Öcalan, *Demokratik Toplum Manifestosu*, (Cologne: Mezopotamya Yayınları, 2009).

51 Klaus Happel, 'Introduction', in Abdullah Öcalan, *Prison Writings: The Roots of Civilisation* (Translated by Klaus Happel) (Pluto Press: London and Ann Arbor, 2006), xv.

52 Happel 'Introduction', xv.

53 Öcalan, *Savunma*, 111.

54 Ibid., 32; Also pp. 17–18 and 111–12 discusses the suitability of the democratic solution in greater detail.

55 Öcalan, *Savunma*, 34–7.

56 Öcalan, *AİHM Savunmaları* (Volume 2), 170.

57 Öcalan, *Savunma*, 10.

58 Ibid., 38–50.

59 Ibid., 75–108 and 122–39.

60 PKK, *Dönüşüm Süreci ve Görevlerimiz (PKK 7. Olağanüstü Kongresine MK Raporu)* (The Transformation Process and our Duties – The Central Committee Report Submitted to the 7th Congress of the PKK), (*Weşanên Serxwebûn*, 2000 (place of publication not stated)), 181–8.

61 Ibid., 190–1.

206 Notes

62 Ibid., 14.
63 Ibid., 21–2.
64 Ibid., 163–4.
65 PKK, *PKK VI. Ulusal Konferansına Sunulan Politik-Örgütsel Rapor* (The Political-Organisational Report Submitted to the PKK's 6th National Conference), (*Weşanên Serxwebûn*, 2001 (Place of publication not stated)), 33–4.
66 PKK, *Dönüşüm Süreci Ve Görevlerimiz*, 166.
67 In fact the new discourse establishes a series of complicated adversarial relations with a number of states, including the USA, UK, Israel and Greece for taking part in an 'international conspiracy' against the PKK leader that ended in his arrest and imprisonment and that aims at the ultimate destruction of the PKK as a movement. The changes that are introduced are partly to thwart the impending danger created by the 'international conspiracy'.
68 PKK, *Dönüşüm Süreci Ve Görevlerimiz*, 180.
69 Ibid., 168.
70 Ibid., 166.
71 Ibid., 190.
72 Mahsum Şafak, *KADEK Kuruluş Kongresi (PKK VIII Kongresi Belgeleri)* (The Foundation Congress of KADEK – Documents of the PKK 8th Congress), (Istanbul: Mem Yayınları, 2002), 16–19.
73 Ibid., 208.
74 Ibid., 212–13.
75 Ibid., 179.
76 Ibid., 210.
77 Ibid., 179, 198.
78 Kongra Gelê Kurdistan (*Kongra-Gel*), *Program, Tüzük ve Kararları* (The Program, Regulations and Decisions of the People's Congress of Kurdistan), (*Weşanên Serxwebûn*, 2004) (Place of publication not stated), 25.
79 PKK, *Program ve Tüzüğü*, (Cologne: *Weşanên Serxwebûn*, 2005), 11–12.
80 Ibid., 13.
81 Şafak, *KADEK Kuruluş Kongresi*, 208–9.
82 Ibid., 213.
83 Ibid., 218.
84 Kongra-Gel, Program, Tüzük ve Kararları, 112.
85 Ibid., 103–4.
86 PKK, *Program ve Tüzüğü*, 93.
87 Ibid., 95.
88 'KCK'den Çözüm Deklerasyonu', *Yeni Özgur Politika*, 3 December 2007.
89 'PKK 10. Kongresi Sonuç Bildirisi Açıklandı' www.firatnews.com/index.php?rupel =arsiv&anf=nuce2&nuceID=2576 Accessed 14 September 2009.
90 Kongra-Gel, Program, Tüzük ve Kararları, 184–9; Şafak, *KADEK Kuruluş Kongresi*, 218, 240–4.
91 Ibid., 191.
92 However, the desire and effort to form strong links between the Kurdish women's movement and the wider feminist movement and to promote solidarity among women from the Middle East and Europe is apparent in the establishment of the 'International Free Women's Foundation' (www.freewomensfoundation.org/index. htm) in Amsterdam in 2001.
93 Şafak, *KADEK Kuruluş Kongresi*, 218.
94 Ibid., 224; *Kongra-Gel, Program, Tüzük ve Kararları*, 240–1.
95 Şafak, *KADEK Kuruluş Kongresi*, 217.
96 A book by a leading member of the PKK, Mustafa Karasu, makes the link explicit and is in fact titled 'Radikal Demokrasi' (Mustafa Karasu, *Radikal Demokrasi*, (Mezopotamya Yayınları: Neuss, 2009)).

Notes 207

97 Abdullah Öcalan, *Demokratik Toplum Manifestosu*, (Cologne: Mezopotamya Yayınları, 2009).
98 ?Kani Yılmaz Kuzey Irak da Öldürüldü', *Radikal*, 12 February 2006.
99 Schaap, *Political Reconciliation*, 11.
100 Ephraim Nimni, 'Introduction: The National Cultural Autonomy Model Revisited', in *National Cultural Autonomy and Its Contemporary Critics*, ed. Ephraim Nimni, (London and New York: Routledge, 2005).
101 The 'National Cultural Autonomy' model was first developed by Karl Renner as an alternative to separation and the nation-state model and was designed 'to manage ethno-national conflicts and prevent secession by offering national and ethnic minorities constitutionally guaranteed collective rights, wide cultural autonomy and non-territorial self-determination' (Nimni, 'Introduction', 1). In elucidating the rights and responsibilities that different nations had within the common polity, Renner distinguished the 'personality principle' from the 'territorial principle' and argued: 'the personality rather than the territorial principle should form the basis of regulation; the nations should be constituted not as territorial entities but as personal associations, not as states but as peoples, not according to age-old constitutional laws, but according to living national laws. Of course, no people exist without territory, and internal reconstruction cannot be independent of the geographical stratification of the population. If the personality principle forms the constitutive principle which brings about the separation of the nationalities and the union of individuals, then the territorial principle will have a significant role to play as an organisational principle.' (Karl Renner, 'State and Nation' in *National Cultural Autonomy and Its Contemporary Critics*, ed. Ephraim Nimni, (London and New York: Routledge, 2005), 29).
102 www.tbmm.gov.tr/tutanak/donem21/yil4/bas/b115m.htm.
103 AK Parti Tanıtım ve Medya Başkanlığı, *Soruları ve Cevaplarıyla Demokratik Açılım Süreci: Milli Birlik ve Kardeşlik Projesi*, (Place and publisher not stated, January 2010), 16–17.
104 Ibid., 20–1.
105 'Kandil Dağı ve Mahmur'dan gelen 10 kişi tutuklandı', *Radikal*, 18 June 2010.
106 'Mass Trial of Kurdish Activists Starts in Turkey', www.bbc.co.uk/news/world-europe-11565813 Accessed 20 April 2011.
107 AK Parti, *Demokratik Açılım Süreci*, 26.
108 'Kimyasalla Katledildiler', *Yeni Özgür Politika*, 27 March 2006.
109 'Children of Repression', *Guardian*, 5 June 2006.
110 'Kurdish Rebel Leader Calls for a ceasefire', *Guardian*, 28 September 2006.
111 'Dünyanın gözü sınırda', *Radikal*, 18 October 2007.
112 '12 askeri şehit eden PKK'lıların 32'si öldürüldü Irak'ta sıcak takip', *Radikal*, 22 October 2007. Subsequently, during the course of the 'Ergenekon investigation', it was claimed that the commander of the battalion which came under the HPG attack passed crucial security information to a member of the Ergenekon organisation, Ayse Asuman Özdemir (See 'Damaging Evidence Leads to Doubts over Daglica Ambush', *Today's Zaman* (www.todayszaman.com/tz-web/detaylar.do?load=detay &link=150921) accessed 10 September 2009. Moreover, *Taraf* newspaper published crucial intelligence evidence the Army disregarded that suggested the attack was about to happen ('Dağlıca Baskını Biliniyordu', *Taraf*, 24 June 2008).
113 'Eight Hostage Soldiers Released' http://bianet.org/english/crisis/102694-eight-hostage-soldiers-released Accessed 10 September 2009.
114 'KCK'den Çözüm Deklerasyonu', *Yeni Özgür Politika*, 3 December 2007.
115 'Turkey Must End Iraq Raid – Bush' http://news.bbc.co.uk/1/hi/world/europe/7268345.stm Accessed 10 September 2009.
116 'Turkish Troops Pull Out of Iraq', http://news.bbc.co.uk/1/hi/world/europe/7270566.stm Accessed 10 September 2009.

208 *Notes*

117 'TSK'nin 25. Operasyonuda Fiyasko', Firat News Agency, 29 February 2008 http://www.akintiya-karsi.org/koxuz/node/616 Accessed 10 September 2009.
118 'BBG Evinde Kanlı Saldırı Çıktı', *Radikal*, 5 October 2008.
119 'Turkish air force chief attacked for directing anti-insurgency operation from golf course', *The Guardian*, 10 October 2008. The *Taraf* newspaper published the evidence that substantiated the claim that the Turkish Army had prior knowledge of the attack and failed to increase the security in the military post despite such information ('Artık İtiraf Edin bu "İkinci Dağlıca"', *Taraf*, 8 October 2008).
120 'PKK Leader offers Turkey an Olive Branch to end the War', *The Times*, 26 May 2009.
121 'HPG Tokat Eylemini Üstlendi' www.firatnews.com/index.php?rupel=nuce&nuceID=18349 Accessed 17 December 2009.
122 'Şemdinli'de Kan. Ankarada Kavga', *Radikal*, 20 June 2010; 'Turkey's PM Erdogan vows to annihilate PKK rebels' www.bbc.co.uk/news/10359237 Accessed 20 April 2011.
123 'Shadowy Kurdish Group's Unclear Aims' http://news.bbc.co.uk/1/hi/world/europe/5297182.stm Accessed 13 September 2009.
124 'PKK Behind Turkey Resort Bomb' http://news.bbc.co.uk/1/hi/world/europe/4690181.stm Accessed 13 September 2009.
125 'Turkey Police Hunt Blast Suspects' http://news.bbc.co.uk/1/hi/world/europe/5294160.stm Accessed 13 September 2009.
126 'State Disciplines Kurdish Children in Prison', http://bianet.org/english/english/115044-state-disciplines-kurdish-children-in-prison Accessed 7 September 2009.

8 Contesting democracy and pluralism: the pro-Kurdish political parties in Turkey

1 The closing speech of Leyla Zana – the HEP and the DEP MP for Diyarbakir from 1991 to 1994 – to the State Security Court in Ankara (Retrieved from the documentary 'Leyla Zana' by Kudret Güneş 2002).
2 www.chris-kutschera.com/A/mehdi_zana.htm.
3 Norval, *Aversive Democracy*, 1.
4 Norval's discussion of decontestation is drawn from Freeden's analysis of political ideology and it involves a morphological analysis that highlights the core, adjacent and peripheral concepts (Michael Freeden, *Ideologies and Political Theory: A Conceptual Approach*, (Oxford: Oxford University Press, 1996), 77).
5 Chantal Mouffe, 'Decision, Deliberation, and Democratic Ethos', *Philosophy Today* (Spring 1997), 26.
6 Ibid.
7 For a more general discussion of the exclusion of Kurdish identity in the state discourse see: Mesut Yeğen, 'Turkish Nationalism and the Kurdish Question', *Ethnic and Racial Studies*, Vol. 30, No. 1 (January 2007), 119–51; Mesut Yeğen, '"Jewish Kurds" or the new frontiers of Turkishness', *Patterns of Prejudice*, Vol. 41, No. 1 (2007), 1–20; Mesut Yeğen, *Müstakbel Türk'ten Sözde Vatandaşa*; Mesut Yeğen, 'The Turkish State Discourse and the Exclusion of Kurdish Identity', *Middle Eastern Studies* 32, (April 1996), 216–29.
8 See www.belgenet.net for a list of the MPs elected to the parliament in the 1987 national election.
9 Ölmez, *DEP Depremi*, 60; Demir, *Yasal Kürtler*, 61.
10 Ölmez, *DEP Depremi*, 73–4.
11 Ibid., 60, 79.
12 Ibid., 88–9.
13 'Siyasi Niyetler Bildirisi' (Notice of Political Intensions) in Ölmez, *DEP Depremi*, 88–90.

Notes 209

14 Ölmez, *DEP Depremi*, 92; Demir, *Yasal Kürtler*, 86.
15 Demir, *Yasal Kürtler*, 92–3; Ölmez, *DEP Depremi*, 87.
16 Ölmez, *DEP Depremi*, 96–7; Ahmet Türk, *DEP Savunması* (Ankara: Matsa Basimevi, 1994), 7. Many others left the movement including Murat Belge, Kemal Anadol, Hüsnü Okcuoğlu and Mehmet Kahraman.
17 Halkın Emek Partisi (HEP), *Tüzük* (HEP Regulations), (Date and place of publications not mentioned), 5; Halkın Emek Partisi (HEP), *Program*, (Date and place of publications not mentioned), 11.
18 HEP, *Program*, 10.
19 Ibid., 17.
20 Ibid.
21 Ibid., 18.
22 Ibid., 18–19, 29.
23 Ibid., 29.
24 Ibid., 60.
25 Ibid., 22.
26 Ibid., 64.
27 Fehmi Işıklar quoted in Demir, *Yasal Kürtler*, 117–18.
28 Demir, *Yasal Kürter*, 116.
29 '1991 Yılı Genel Seçim Sonuçları' (The Results of the 1991 General Elections) www.belgenet.net/ayrinti.php?yil_id=11 Accessed 20 April 2011.
30 The SHP's Kurdish MPs drawn from the HEP list were seen as representatives of the HEP even though formally they remained within the SHP until May 1992.
31 Ölmez, *DEP Depremi*, 162.
32 Ibid., 163; Demir, *Yasal Kürtler*, 134.
33 Ölmez, *DEP Depremi*, 160.
34 Ibid., 161.
35 Sosyaldemokrat Halkçı Parti (SHP), *Sosyaldemokrat Halkçı Parti'nin Doğu ve Güneydoğu sorunlarına bakışı ve çözüm önerileri*, (Ankara: SHP, 1990).
36 Article three reads: 'The state of Turkey, with its territory and nation, is an indivisible entity. Its language is Turkish' www.anayasa.gen.tr/1982ay.htm Accessed 1 August 2009.
37 Ölmez, *DEP Depremi*, 169–70.
38 Ibid., 178.
39 Ibid., 194. The transfer to the HEP was through the Party of Freedom and Equality (ÖZEP – Özgürlük Ve Eşitlik Partisi) as the MPs were prevented from joining directly (*Özgür Gündem*, 18 June 1992 and 23 June 1992; Demir, *Yasal Kürtler*, 165–7).
40 Ölmez, *DEP Depremi*, 198.
41 HEP file http://www.anayasa.gov.tr/index.php?l=manage_karar&ref=show&action=karar&id=2154&content= Accessed 31 July 2007.
42 Demir, *Yasal Kürtler*, 173–82; Ölmez, *DEP Depremi*, 202–10.
43 'Merkezi Parlemento Çözüm Üretemiyor', *Özgür Gündem*, 16 June 1992.
44 Halkın Emek Partisi (HEP), *1992 Program*, (Place and date of publication not stated), 17–18.
45 Mahmut Kılınç, '1992 Yılı Değerlendirmesi', *Halkın Emek Partisi Parti Bülteni (Merkez Yayın Organı)*, Year 2 No. 5 (January–February 1993).
46 Public statement 'Türkiye ve Dünya Kamuoyuna', *Halkın Emek Partisi Parti Bülteni (Merkez Yayın Organı*, Year 2 No. 5 (January–February 1993).
47 Ölmez, *DEP Depremi*, 119.
48 Demokrasi Partisi (DEP), *Program*, (Date and place of publication not stated), 9.
49 DEP, 'Demokrasi Partisinin Barış Çağrısıdır' (The Democracy Party's Peace Call), (Place and date of leaflet not stated).
50 Demir, *Yasal Kürtler*, 192; Ölmez, *DEP Depremi*, 213.

210 *Notes*

51 Ölmez, *DEP Depremi*, 233; Demir, *Yasal Kürtler*, 218.
52 Ölmez, *DEP Depremi*, 465; Demir, *Yasal Kürtler*, 552–5.
53 'DEP Genel Merkezi'ne Bomba: 1 Ölü', *Cumhuriyet*, 19 February 1994.
54 'Başbakandan Hainlik Suçlama'sı', *Cumhuriyet*, 23 February 1994.
55 'Güreş'den DEP'lilere Suçlama', *Cumhuriyet*, 29 February 1994.
56 'DEP Seçimleri Boykot Ediyor', *Cumhuriyet*, 25 February 1994; 'DEP Seçim'den Çekiliyor', 26 February 1994.
57 Ölmez, *DEP Depremi*, 423; Demir, *Yasal Kürtler*, 314.
58 Demir, *Yasal Kürtler*, 544; Ölmez, *DEP Depremi*, 374.
59 Ölmez, *DEP Depremi*, 430; See Also 'Anayasa Mahkemesi Kararları (Decisions of the Constitutional Court)' (http://www.anayasa.gov.tr/index.php?l=manage_karar&r ef=show&action=karar&id=2158&content=) Accessed 1 July 2007.
60 Halkın Demokrasi Partisi (HADEP), *Program 1995*, (Date and place of publication not stated), 6–8.
61 HADEP, *4. Olağan Büyük Kongre Faaliyet Raporu* (Activities Report of the People's Democracy Party Submitted to the 4th Congress), (Ankara, 2000), 60.
62 HADEP, *Program 1995*, 9.
63 Ibid.
64 Ibid., 8.
65 'Election Leaflet' *Emek, Barış ve Özgürlük Bloku* (Date and place of the leaflet not stated); Also, www.belgenet.net.
66 Demir, *Yasal Kürtler*, 382.
67 *Hürriyet*, 20 November 1998; *Turkish Daily News*, 20 November 1998. Detention of HADEP members continued throughout November and December and during February when Öcalan was captured in Kenya and brought to Turkey. In total according to Turkish Daily News over 2,000 HADEP members were arrested (*Turkish Daily News*, 30 January 1999).
68 *Turkish Daily News*, 30 January 1999.
69 *Hürriyet*, 26 February 1999; *Turkish Daily News*, 9 March 1999.
70 'Türkiye Seçimleri (Turkish Elections): www.belgenet.net. Accessed 3 September 2009.
71 Demir, *Yasal Kürtler*, 456–7; *Hürriyet*, 20 February 2000 and 24 February 2000.
72 *Turkish Daily News*, 29 February 2000.
73 *Hürriyet*, 24 February 2000.
74 For the list of the HADEP members murdered see Demir, *Yasal Kürtler*, 555–7.
75 The HADEP was closed on 13 March 2003 for becoming the centre of threats 'against the unity of the state and nation' and engaging in 'unconstitutional activities'.
76 www.belgenet.net. Accessed 3 August 2009.
77 *Evrensel*, 17 September 2002.
78 'Kahvaltı Ettiler Valiye Gittiler', *Hürriyet*, 19 June 2004.
79 'Eski Deplilerden Demokratik Toplum Hareketi', *Hürriyet*, 22 October 2004.
80 'Demokratik Toplum Partisi Resmen Kuruldu', *Hürriyet*, 9 November 2005.
81 Demokratik Toplum Partisi (DTP), *Program ve Tüzüğü* (Programme and Regulations), (Date and place of publication not mentioned), 4.
82 HADEP, *4. Kongre*, 107–9.
83 'Yargı 'çok dilli belediye'yi fesh etti', *Radikal*, 15 June 2007.
84 DTP, *Program*, 3.
85 Ibid., 37–8.
86 Ibid., 38.
87 Ibid., 38.
88 Ibid., 31.
89 In Mersin the pro-Kurdish candidate lost by only 309 votes ('Bağımsızlar barajı yıktı', *Radikal*, 23 July 2007).

Notes 211

90 See the website (in Turkish) of High Election Committee (Yüksek Seçim Kurulu) for the details of the local elections held on 29 March 2009. www.ysk.gov.tr/ysk/index.html.
91 MP for Hakkari Hamit Geylani's speech in the parliament on 16 July 2008, www.tbmm.gov.tr/tutanak/donem23/yil2/bas/b131m.htm. Accessed 1 May 2009.
92 MP for Muş Sırrı Sakık's speech on 8 July 2008, www.tbmm.gov.tr/tutanak/donem23/yil2/bas/b127m.htm. Accessed 1 May 2009.
93 MP for Diyarbakir Akin Birdal's speech in the parliament on 12 June 2008, www.tbmm.gov.tr/tutanak/donem23/yil2/bas/b117m.htm. Accessed 1 May 2009.
94 MP for Şırnak-Sevahir Bayındır's speech in the National Assembly on 30 July 2008. www.tbmm.gov.tr/tutanak/donem23/yil2/bas/b137m.htm. Accessed 1 May 2009.
95 MP for Muş Sırrı Sakık's speech in the National Assembly on 27 May 2008, www.tbmm.gov.tr/tutanak/donem23/yil2/bas/b109m.htm. Accessed 1 May 2009.
96 www.tbmm.gov.tr/tutanak/donem23/yil2/bas/b077m.htm.
97 Aysel Tuğluk, 'Kürt Sorununun Geleceği', *Radikal*, 28 October 2007; Aysel Tuğluk, 'Positif Milliyetcilik', *Radikal*, 26 December 2007; *Evrensel*, 12 October 2006; 'DTP Kürtlere yönelik oyunları bozuyor', *Yeni Özgürpolitika*, 11 February 2008.
98 Aysel Tuğluk, 'Kürt Sorununun Geleceği', *Radikal 2*, 28 October 2007.
99 Ibid.
100 'DTP Kongresi'nden "20–25 Özerk Bölge" Önerisi', http://bianet.org/bianet/bianet/102605-dtp-kongresinden-20–25-ozerk-bolge-onerisi. Accessed 25 April 2011.
101 'DTP Operasyona Tepkili: AKP Seçimleri Hazmedemedi', http://bianet.org/bianet/siyaset/113816-dtp-operasyona-tepkili-akp-secimleri-hazmedemedi. Accessed 25 April 2011.
102 Zafer Yörük 'The AKP and the Kurds: Lessons of Elections' in Kurdish Globe www.kurdishglobe.net/displayArticle.jsp?id=4F515299955721090664F8A4FE7949 DE. Accessed 2 May 2009.
103 'DTP: Farkımız silahtır', *Yeni Özgür Politika*, 3 January 2008.
104 'Kapatınca bitecek mi?', *Radikal*, 17 November 2007.
105 'Turkish Court Bans Pro-Kurd Party', http://news.bbc.co.uk/1/hi/world/europe/8408903.stm. Accessed 11 December 2009.
106 'Is Turkey Preparing for Peace', *Guardian*, 28 July 2009.
107 The leader of the Republican People's Party (CHP) Deniz Baykal and the far-right Nationalist Action Party (MHP) Devlet Bahçeli have both condemned the meeting and interpreted it as being equal to starting a dialogue with the PKK ('Erdoğan'ın muhatabı PKK ve Öcalan'dır', *Radikal*, 6 August 2009).
108 Barış ve Demokrasi Partisi (BDP), *Program*, (2008, place not stated).
109 'Türk: Demokratik Özerklik Devlet Tanırsa Olur', http://bianet.org/bianet/azinliklar/122961-turk-demokratik-ozerklik-devlet-tanirsa-olur. Accessed 24 April 2011.
110 'BDP ve DTK: Sivil İtaatsizlik Yarın Diyarbakır'da Başlıyor', http://bianet.org/bianet/siyaset/128810-bdp-ve-dtk-sivil-itaatsizlik-yarin-diyarbakirda-basliyor. Accessed 24 April 2011.
111 'Çadırları da "Gözaltına" Aldılar, Emniyet'e Götürdüler', http://bianet.org/bianet/insan-haklari/129547-cadirlari-da-gozaltina-aldilar-emniyete-goturduler. Accessed 28 April 2011.
112 'BDP adaylarını açıkladı', *Radikal*, 11 April 2011.
113 'Emek, Demokrasi ve Özgürlük Bloku Genişleyerek Sürmeli', http://bianet.org/bianet/siyaset/129187-emek-demokrasi-ve-ozgurluk-bloku-genisleyerek-surmeli. Accessed 25 April 2011.

Bibliography

Kurdish weekly or monthly political magazines

Dicle-Fırat (Tigris-Euphrates) (1962–1963)
Deng (Voice) (1963)
Özgürlük Yolu (The Path of Freedom) (1974–1979)
Rizgarî (Liberation) (1975–1979)
Jîna Nû (The New Life) (1979–1980)
Serxwebûn (Independence) (1982–present)
Berxwedan (Resistance) (1985–1995)

The dates above represent the dates of the issues used during the research for this book. This matches the duration of publication except for the following which continued to be distributed after the years stated in brackets above: *Özgürlük Yolu, Rizgarî, Jîna Nû*.

Daily newspapers

Cumhuriyet
Evrensel
Guardian
Hürriyet
Kurdish Globe
Milliyet
Özgür Gündem (1992–1993)
Radikal
Taraf
Turkish Daily News
Yeni Özgür Politika

News and other websites cited

www.anayasa.gov.tr
www.anayasa.gen.tr/1982ay.htm
www.bbc.co.uk
www.belgenet.net/
www.bianet.org/
www.chris-kutschera.com/A/mehdi_zana.htm

Bibliography 213

www.diyarbakirzindani.com/
www.kurdishacademy.org

Discography

Koma Berxwedan (The Group of Resistance) – *Berxwedan Jiyana* (1983)
Koma Berxwedan – *Dayê* (1983)
Koma Berxwedan – *Marşen Netewi* (1984)
Koma Berxwedan – *Dilan* (1985)
Koma Berxwedan – *Botan* (1987)
Koma Berxwedan – *Gula Cihane* (1987)
Koma Berxwedan – *Kaniya Welat* (1987)
Koma Berxwedan – *Pesmerge* (1988)
Koma Berxwedan – *Newroz* (1989)
Koma Berxwedan – *Sad Bibe Welate Min* (1990)
Koma Berxwedan – *Amed* (1991)
Koma Berxwedan – *Ey Ferat* (1992)
Koma Berxwedan – *Meşa Azadi* (1992)
Koma Berxwedan – *15ê Têbax* (1993)
Koma Berxwedan – *Name Mi Mezopotamiya* (1995)
Şivan Perwer – *Kîne Em* (1979)
Şivan Perwer – *Gelê Min Rabe* (1981)
Şivan Perwer – *Helepçe* (1988)
Dirok li Agir (DVD) 2008
'*Leyla Zana*' (DVD) Documentary by Kudret Güneş 2002

Primary and secondary literature

Adamson, Fiona B. and Madeleine Demetriou. 'Remapping the Boundaries of "State" and "National Identity": Incorporating Diasporas into IR Theorizing', *European Journal of International Relations*, Vol. 13, No. 4 (2007), 489–526.

Ahmad, Feroz. *The Turkish Experiment in Democracy, 1950–1975*, London: Hurst, 1977.

Ahmed, Mohammed and Michael Gunter. *The Evolution of Kurdish Nationalism*, eds., Costa Mesa, California: Mazda Publishers, 2007.

AK Parti Tanıtım ve Medya Başkanlığı. *Soruları ve Cevaplarıyla Demokratik Açılım Süreci: Milli Birlik ve Kardeşlik Projesi* (Questions and Answers on the Democratic Initiative Process: The National Oneness and Brotherhood Project), Place and publisher not stated, January 2010.

Akdoğan, Yalçın. *AK Parti ve Muhafazakar Demokrasi* (The AK Party and Conservative Democracy), Istanbul: Alfa Yayınları, 2004.

Aksoy, Gürdal. *Bir Söylence Bir Tarih: Newroz* (Legend and History: *Newroz*), Ankara: Yurt Yayınları, 1998.

Al-Ali, Nadje and Khalid Koser, eds. *New Approaches to Migration: Transnational Communities and the Transformation of Home*, London and New York: Routledge, 2002.

Ala Rizgarî. *Kürdistan Devriminde Genel Olarak Örgütlenme ve Proleteryanın Örgütü* (The General Question of Organisation and the Proletarian Organisation in Kurdistan's Revolution), (Date, place and publisher not stated).

Alınak, Mahmut. *HEP, DEP ve Devlet: Parlemento'dan 9. Koğusa* (The HEP, DEP and

214 Bibliography

the State: From the Parliament to the 9th Prison Ward), Istanbul: Kaynak Yayınları, 1996.

Althusser, Louis. 'Ideology and Ideological State Apparatus (Notes Towards an Investigation)', in *Mapping Ideology*, Slovoj Zizek, ed., London: Verso, 1994, 100–40.

Anderson, Benedict. *Imagined Communities*, London: Verso, 1983.

Anter, Musa. *Hatıralarım* (My Memoirs), Istanbul: Avesta Yayınları, 1999.

Aras, Bülent and Gökhan Bacık. 'The Mystery of Turkish Hizballah', *Middle East Policy*, Vol. IX, No. 2 (June 2002), 147–60.

Aren, Sadun. *TİP Olayı 1961–1971* (The TIP Event 1961–1971), Istanbul: Cem Yayın Evi, 1993.

Argun, Betigul Ercan. 'Point and Counterpoint – Universal Citizenship Rights and Turkey's Kurdish Question', *Journal of Muslim Minority Affairs*, Vol. 19, No. 1 (April 1999), 85–104.

Armstrong, John. *Nations before Nationalism*, Chapel Hill: University of North Carolina Press, 1982.

Arslan, Müjde, ed. *Kürt Sineması: Yurtsuzluk, Sınır ve Ölüm* (Kurdish Cinema: Statelessness, Borders and Death), Istanbul: Agora Kitaplığı, 2009.

Atacan, Fulya. 'A Kurdish Islamist Group in Modern Turkey: Shifting Identities', *Middle Eastern Studies*, Vol. 37, No. 3 (July 2001), 111–44.

Ayata, Bilgin and Deniz Yükseker. 'A Belated Awakening: National and International Responses to Internal Displacement of Kurds in Turkey', *New Perspectives on Turkey*, No. 32 (2005), 5–42.

Aybar, Mehmet Ali. *TİP (Türkiye İşçi Partisi) Tarihi 3* (The Workers Party of Turkey – History 3), Turkey: BDS Yayınları, 1988.

Aydın, D. 'Mobilizing the Kurds in Turkey: *Newroz* as a Myth', Masters diss., Middle East Technical University, 2005.

Aydın, Zülküf. 'Uncompromising Nationalism: The Kurdish Question in Turkey', in *The Politics of Permanent Crises: Class, Ideology and State in Turkey*, Neşecan Balkan and Sungur Savran, eds., New York: Nova Publishers, 2002, 85–105.

Balibar, Etienne. 'The Nation Form: History and Ideology', in *Race, Nation, Class: Ambiguous Identities*, Etienne Balibar and Immanuel Wallerstein, eds, London and New York: Verso, 1991, 86–106.

Ballı, Rafet. *Kürt Dosyası* (The Kurdish File), Istanbul: Cem Yayınları, 1991.

Barkey, Henri J. 'The People's Democracy Party (HADEP): The Travails of a Legal Kurdish Party in Turkey', *Journal of Muslim Minority Affairs*, Vol. 18, No. 1 (Apr 1998), 129–38.

Barkey, Henri J. and Graham E. Fuller. *Turkey's Kurdish Question*, New York: Rowman and Littlefield Publishers, 1998.

Barış ve Demokrasi Partisi. *Program* (Programme), (place of publication not stated, 2008).

Başkaya, Fikret. *Paradigmanın İflası: Resmi İdeolojinin Eleştirisine Giriş* (The Bankruptcy of the Paradigm: An Introduction to the Critique of the Official Ideology), Ankara Özgür Üniversite, 2007.

Bayır, D. 'Negating Diversity: Minorities and Nationalism in Turkish Law', PhD Diss., University of London, 2010.

Bayrak, Mehmet. *Köy Enstitüleri ve Köy Edebiyatı* (The Village Institutes and Village Literature), Ankara: Özge Yayınları, 2000.

Bayrak, Mehmet. *Geçmişten Günümüze Kürt Kadını* (Kurdish Women: From the Past to the Present), Ankara: Özge Yayınları, 2000.

Bibliography 215

Beşikci, İsmail. *International Colony Kurdistan*, Reading: Taderon Press, 2004.

Beşikci, İsmail. *Hayali Kürdistan'ın Dirilişi* (The Resurrection of the Imaginary Kurdistan), Istanbul: Aram Yayınları, 1998.

Beşikci, İsmail. *Bilincin Yükselişi* (The Rise of Consciousness), Ankara: Yurt Kitap Yayın, 1993.

Beşikci, İsmail. *Kendini Keşfeden Ulus Kürtler* (The Kurds: A Nation Discovering Itself), Ankara: Yurt Kitap Yayın, 1993.

İsmail Beşikci. *Doğu'da Değişim ve Yapısal Sorunlar: Göcebe Alikan Aşireti*, Istanbul: E Yayınları, 1969 (reprinted Ankara: Yurt Kitap Yayın, 1992).

Beşikci, İsmail. *PKK Üzerine Düsünceler: Özgürlüğün Bedeli* (Thoughts on the PKK: The Value of Freedom), Istanbul: Melsa Yayınları, 1992.

Beşikci, İsmail. *Dogu Mitinglerinin Analizi* (The Analysis of the Eastern Meetings), Ankara: Yurt Kitap Yayın, 1992.

Beşikci, İsmail. *Doğu Anadolunun Düzeni: Sosyo-Ekonomik and Etnik Temeller* (The Order of Eastern Anatolia: Socio-Economic and Ethnic Foundations), Istanbul: E Yayınları, 1969.

Beyköylü, Ali. 'Koma Azadixwazên Kurdistan: Hodri Meydan' (The Freedom Wishers of Kurdistan: The Arena), *Bîr: Kovara Lêgerîn û Lêkolîn*, No. 5 (Summer 2006), 197–204.

Billig, Michael. *Banal Nationalism*, London: Sage, 1995.

Bozarslan, Hamit. 'Some Remarks on the Kurdish Historiographical Discourse in Turkey (1919–1980)', in *Essays on the Origins of Kurdish Nationalism*, Abbas Vali ed., California: Mazda Publishers, 2003, 14–39.

Bozarslan, Hamit. 'Kurdish Nationalism in Turkey: From Tacit Contract to Rebellion (1919–1925)', in *Essays on the Origins of Kurdish Nationalism*, Abbas Vali, ed., Costa Mesa, California: Mazda Publishers, 2003, 163–90.

Bozarslan, Hamit. '"Why the Armed Struggle": Understanding Violence in Kurdistan of Turkey', in *The Kurdish Conflict in Turkey: Obstacles and Chances for Peace and Democracy*, Farhad Ibrahim and Gülistan Gürbey, eds., Germany: Lit Verlag, 2000, 17–30.

Bozarslan, Hamit. 'Political Crises and the Kurdish Issue in Turkey', in *The Kurdish Nationalist Movement in the 1990s: Its Impact on Turkey and the Middle East*, Robert Olson, ed., Lexington: University of Kentucky Press, 1996, 135–53.

Bozarslan, Hamit. 'Political aspects of the Kurdish Problem in Turkey', in *The Kurds: A Contemporary Overview*, Philip G. Kreyenbroek and Stefan Sperl, eds., London and New York: Routledge, 1992, 95–104.

Bozarslan, M. Emin. *Doğu'nun Sorunları*, Safak Kitapevi: Diyarbakır, 1966. Reprint Avesta Yayınları: Istanbul, 2002.

Brown, David. *Contemporary Nationalism: Civic, Ethnocultural and Multicultural Politics*, London and New York: Routledge, 2000.

Brubaker, Rogers. *Nationalism Reframed*, Cambridge: Cambridge University Press, 1996.

Bruinessen, Martin Van. 'Ehmadî Xanî's Mem û Zîn and Its role in the Emergence of Kurdish National Awareness', in *Essays on the Origins of Kurdish Nationalism*, Abbas Vali, ed., California: Mazda Publishers, 2003, 40–57.

Bruinessen, Martin Van. *Kurdish Ethno-nationalism Versus Nation-Building States: Collected Articles*, Istanbul: Isis Press, 2000.

Bruinessen, Martin Van. *Mullas, Sufis and Heretics: The Role of Religion in Kurdish Society (Collected Articles)*, Istanbul: Isis Press, 1999.

216 Bibliography

Bruinessen, Martin Van. 'Shifting National and Ethnic Identities: The Kurds in Turkey and the European Diaspora', *Journal of Muslim Minority Affairs*. Vol. 18, No. 1 (April 1998), 39–52.

Bruinessen, Martin Van. 'Ismail Beşikçi: Turkish sociologist, critic of Kemalism, and kurdologist', published on the University of Ultrecht's website:http://www.hum.uu.nl/medewerkers/m.vanbruinessen/publications/ismail_besikci.htm, 1997.

Bruinessen, Martin Van. *Agha, Shaikh and State: Social and Political Structures of Kurdistan*, London: Zed Books, 1992.

Bulut, Faik. *Türk Basınında Kürtler* (The Kurds in Turkish Press), Istanbul: Evrensel Basım Yayın, 2005.

Buran, Ali. 'DDKO İlk Ulusalcı, Demokratik ve Ayrı Örgütlenmeyi Hedefleyen Kürt Demokratik Gençlik Örgütüydü' (The DDKO was the First Kurdish Democratic Youth Organisation that was Nationalist, Democratic and to have Advocated Separate Organisation), *Bîr: Kovara Lêgerîn û Lêkolîn*, No. 6 (Winter 2007), 85–103.

Burkay, Kemal. *Sorular Cevaplarla PSK ne diyor? Ne istiyor?* (With Questions and Answers: What Does the PSK Say and Want?), Sweden: Weşanên Roja Nû, 2003.

Burkay, Kemal. *Anılar Belgeler: Cilt 1* (Memoirs and Documents: Volume 1), Stockholm: Roja Nu Yayınları, 2001.

Burkay, Kemal. *TKSP Yurt Dışı Konferansı Tezleri* (The Thesis of TKSP's Conference in Abroad), TKSP Yayınları, 1989 (place of publication not stated).

Burkay, Kemal. *Devrimcilik mi Terörizm mi? PKK Üzerine* (Revolutionism or Terrorism? Concerning the PKK), Özgürlük Yolu Yayınları, 1983 (Place of publication not stated).

Calhoun, Craig. *Nationalism*, Buckingham: Open University Press, 1997.

Campbell, David. *National Deconstruction: Violence, Identity and Justice in Bosnia*, Minneapolis and London: Minneapolis University Press, 1998.

Can, Metin, Hasan Kaya, Kemal Kılıç, Cemal Akar, Mehmet Sincar and Sevket Epözdemir, *Yıkılan Köylerden bir Kesit* (A Section from the Destroyed Villages), Ankara: İnsan Hakları Derneği Yayınları, 1994.

Celîl, Ordîxanê. *Cegerxwîn'in Yaşamı ve Şiir Anlayışı* (The Life of Cegerxwîn and his Understanding of Poetry), Istanbul: Evrensel Basım Yayın, 2004.

Chaliand, Gerard ed., *People Without a Country: Kurds and Kurdistan*, (new and revised edition translated by Michael Pallis), London: Zed Books, 1993.

Connolly, William E. *Identity\Difference: Democratic negotiations of Political Paradox*, Ithaca and London: Cornell University Press, 1991.

Cox, Robert W. 'Gramsci, Hegemony and International Relations: An Essay in Method', *Millenium: Journal of International Studies*, Vol. 12, No. 2 (1983), 162–75.

Çağlayan, Handan. *Analar, Yoldaslar, Tanrıçalar: Kürt Hareketinde Kadınlar ve Kadın Kimliğinin Oluşumu* (Mothers, Comrades, Goddesses: Women in the Kurdish Movement and the Constitution of Women's Identity), Istanbul: İletişim, 2007.

Çakır, Ruşen. *Derin Hizbullah: İslami Şiddetin Geleceği* (The Deep Hizbullah: The Future of Islamic Violence), Istanbul: Siyah Beyaz Metis Güncel, 2001.

Çalışlar, Oral. *Öcalan ve Burkay'la Kürt Sorunu* (The Kurdish Question with Öcalan and Burkay), Istanbul: Pencere Yayınları, 1993.

Çamlıbel, Yavuz. *49'lar Davası: Bir Garip Ülkenin İdamlık Kürtleri* (The Case of 49'ers: The Kurds of a Strange Country Condemned to Death), Ankara: Algıyayın, 2007.

Çelik, Ayşe B. 'Transnationalisation of Human Right Norms and Its Impact on Internally Displaced Kurds', *Human Rights Quarterly*, 27 (2005), 969–97.

Çelik, N.B. 'Kemalist Hegemony from its Constitution to its Dissolution', PhD diss., University of Essex, 1996.

Bibliography 217

Çürükkaya, M. Selim. *12 Eylül Karanlığında Diyarbakir Şafağı* (The Dawn of Diyarbakir in the Darkness of 12 September), Cologne: Ağrı Yayınları, 1990.

DDKO. *Sen Faşist Savcı İyi Dinle! Dünyada Kürt Vardır: DDKO'nun Savunması* (You the Fascist Prosecutor Listen Carefully! Kurds Exist in the World: The Defence of DDKO), Uppsala: Bahoz, 1973.

Demir, Eyyüp. *Yasal Kürtler* (The Legal Kurds), İstanbul: Tevn Yayınları, 2005.

Demokrasi Partisi. *'Demokrasi Partisinin Barış Çağrısıdır'* (The Democracy Party's Peace Call – Leaflet), (Date and place of leaflet not stated).

Demokrasi Partisi. *Program* (Programme), Date and place of publication not stated.

Demokratik Toplum Partisi. *Program ve Tüzüğü* (Programme and Regulations), (Date and place of publication not stated).

Dersimî, Nuri. *Kürdistan Tarihinde Dersim* (Dersim in the History of Kurdistan), Mezopotamya Yayınları, 1999 (Place of Publication not stated).

Dicleli, Ali. *Kürt Sorunu Barış Demokrasi Yazılar* (The Kurdish Question – Writings on Peace and Democracy), Istanbul: Deng Yayınları, 1995.

Diyarbakir Sıkıyönetim Komutanlığı 1 Numaralı Askeri Mahkemesi. *DDKO Dava Dosyası (Ankara ve İstanbul Devrimci Doğu Ocakları'na ait Davanın Gerekçeli Kararı* (DDKO Court File), Place, Date and publisher not stated.

Doğan, Mazlum. *Toplu Yazıları* (Collected Writings), Cologne: *Weşanên Serxwebûn*, 1982.

Ekinci, Tarık Ziya. *Türkiye'de Demokrasi ve İnsan Hakları Sorunları* (Democracy and Human Rights Problems in Turkey), Istanbul: Cem Yayınları, 2004.

Ekinci, Tarık Ziya. *Türkiye'nin Kürt Siyasetine Eleştirel Yaklaşımlar* (Critical Approaches to Kurdish Politics in Turkey), Istanbul: Cem Yayınları, 2004.

Entessar, Nader. *Kurdish Ethnonationalism*, London: Lynne Rienner Publishing, 1992.

Epözdemir, Şakir. *Türkiye Kürdistan Demokrat Partisi: 1968/235 Antalya Davası Savunması* (The Kurdistan Democrat Party of Turkey: The Defence of 1968/235 Antalya Trial), Istanbul: Peri Yayınları, 2005.

Erbay, Vecdi. *Türkiye Barışını Arıyor: Ya Gerçek Demokrasi Ya Hiç!* (Turkey in Search of its Peace: Either Real Democracy or Nothing), Istanbul: Aram Yayıncılık, 2007.

Erdoğan, Necmi and Fahriye Üstüner. 'Quest for Hegemony: Discourses on Democracy', in *The Politics of Permanent Crises: Class, Ideology and State in Turkey*, Neşecan Balkan and Sungur Savran, eds, New York: Nova Science Publishers, 2002, 195–213.

Ergil, Doğu. *Kürt Raporu: Güvenlik Politikalarından Kimlik Siyasetine* (The Kurdish Report: From Security Policies to Identity Politics), Istanbul: Timas Yayınları, 2009.

Ergil, Doğu. 'The Kurdish Question in Turkey', *Journal of Democracy*, Vol. 11, No. 3 (July 2000), 122–35.

Finlayson, Alan. 'Ideology, Discourse and Nationalism', *Journal of Political Ideologies*, Vol. 3, No.1 (1998), 99–119.

Fırat, Ümit, 'Ümit Fırat ile DDKO Söyleşisi' (A conversation on the DDKO with Ümit Fırat), in *Bîr: Kovara Lêgerîn û Lêkolîn*, No. 5 (Summer 2006): 177–8

Foucault, Michel. *The Archaeology of Knowledge*, London and New York: Routledge, 2002.

Foucault, Michel. 'Politics and the study of Discourse', in *The Foucault Effect: Studies in Governmentality*, Graham Burchell, Colin Gordon and Peter Miller, eds, Chicago: University of Chicago Press, 1991, 53–72.

Foucault, Michel. 'Questions of Method', in *The Foucault Effect: Studies in Governmentality*, Graham Burchell, Colin Gordon and Peter Miller, eds, Chicago: University of Chicago Press, 1991, 73–86.

218 Bibliography

Foucault, Michel. 'Governmentality', in *The Foucault Effect: Studies in Governmentality*, Graham Burchell, Colin Gordon and Peter Miller, eds, Chicago: University of Chicago Press, 1991, 87–104.

Foucault, Michel. 'Nietzsche, Genealogy and History', in *The Foucault Reader*, Paul Rabinow, ed., Harmondsworth: Penguin Books, 1984, 76–100.

Freeden, Michael. 'Is Nationalism a Distinct Ideology?', *Political Studies*, Vol. 46, No. 4 (1998), 748–65.

Freeden, Michael. *Ideologies and Political Theory: A Conceptual Approach*, Oxford: Oxford University Press, 1996.

Gellner, Ernest. *Nations and Nationalism*, Oxford: Blackwell, 2006.

Gellner, Ernest. *Thought and Change*, London: Weidenfeld and Nicolson, 1964.

Glynos, Jason. 'The Grip of Ideology: A Lacanian Approach to the Theory of Ideology', *Journal of Political Ideologies*, Vol. 6, Issue 2 (2001), 191–214.

Glynos, Jason and David Howarth. *Logics of Critical Explanation in Social and Political Theory*, Abingdon and New York: Routledge, 2007.

Gramsci, Antonio. *Selections from the Prison Notebooks*, edited and translated by Quintin Hoare and Geoffry Nowell Smith, London: Lawrence and Wishart, 1971.

Guibernau, Montserrat. *Catalan Nationalism: Francoism, Transition and Democracy*, New York and London: Routledge, 2004.

Guibernau, Montserrat. *Nations without States*, Cambridge: Polity Press, 1999.

Gunaratnum, Yasmin. *Researching 'Race' and Ethnicity: Methods, Knowledge and Power*, London: Sage Publications, 2003.

Gunes, Cengiz. 'Kurdish Politics in Turkey: Ideology, Identity and Transformations', *Ethnopolitics*, Vol. 8, No. 2 (June 2009), 255–62.

Gunes, Cengiz. 'Kurdish Politics in Turkey: A question of Identity', *International Journal of Kurdish Studies*, Vol. 21, Nos 1&2 (2007), 17–36.

Gunter, Michael. *The Kurds Ascending: The Evolving Solution to the Kurdish Problem in Iraq and Turkey*, Basingstoke: Palgrave Macmillan, 2008.

Gunter, Michael. 'The Kurdish Question and International Law', in *The Kurdish Conflict in Turkey: Obstacles and Chances for Peace and Democracy*, Farhad Ibrahim and Gülistan Gürbey, eds, Germany: Lit Verlag, 2000, 31–56.

Gunter, Michael. 'Kurdish Infighting: The PKK-KDP Conflict', in *The Kurdish Nationalist Movement in the 1990s: Its Impact on Turkey and the Middle East*, Robert Olson, ed., Lexington: The University Press of Kentucky, 1996, 50–62.

Gunter, Michael. *The Kurds in Turkey*, Oxford: Westview Press, 1990.

Gündoğan, Cemil. *Kawa Davası Savunması ve Kürtlerde Siyasi Savunma Geleneği* (The Defence in Kawa Trial and The Tradition of Political Defence Among the Kurds), Istanbul: Vate Yayınları, 2007.

Gündoğan, A.Z. 'The Kurdish Political Mobilization in the 1960s: The Case of "The Eastern Meetings"', Masters diss., Middle East Technical University, 2005.

Güney, Aylin. 'The People's Democracy Party', *Turkish Studies*, Vol. 3 (1) (2002), 122–37.

Gürbey, Gülistan. 'Peaceful Settlement of Turkey's Kurdish Conflict through Autonomy', in *The Kurdish Conflict in Turkey: Obstacles and Chances for Peace and Democracy*, Farhad Ibrahim and Gülistan Gürbey, eds, Germany: Lit Verlag, 2000, 57–91.

Gürbey, Gülistan. 'The Development of Kurdish Nationalist Movement in Turkey since 1980s', in *The Kurdish Nationalist Movement in the 1990s: Its Impact on Turkey and the Middle East*, Robert Olson, ed., Lexington: University of Kentucky Press, 1996, 9–38.

Bibliography 219

Halkın Demokrasi Partisi. *Program* (Programme), Date and place of publication not stated.

Halkın Demokrasi Partisi. *Halkın Demokrasi Partisi 4. Olağan Büyük Kongre Faaliyet Raporu* (Activities Report Of the People's Democracy Party Submitted to the 4th Congress), Ankara 2000.

Halkın Demokrasi Partisi. 1995 *Program* (1995 Programme), Date and place of publication not stated.

Halkın Emek Partisi. *Halkın Emek Partisi Tüzük* (HEP Regulations), Date and place of publication not stated.

Halkın Emek Partisi. *Halkın Emek Partisi Parti Bülteni (Merkez Yayın Organı)* (The Party Bulletin (Central Publication Organ), Year 2, No. 5 (January–February 1993).

Halkın Emek Partisi (HEP). *1992 Program* (1992 Programme), Date and place of publication not stated.

Halkın Emek Partisi (HEP). *Program 1990* (Programme 1990), Date and place of publication not stated.

Hall, Stuart and Paul du Gay, eds. *Questions of Cultural Identity*, London: Sage Publications, 1996.

Hanioğlu, M. Şükrü. *A Brief History of the Late Ottoman Empire*, Princeton and Oxford: Princeton University Press, 2008.

Hanioğlu, M. Şükrü. *Preparation for a Revolution: The Young Turks, 1902–1908*, Oxford: Oxford University Press, 2001.

Hanioğlu, M. Şükrü. *The Young Turks in Opposition*, New York and Oxford: Oxford University Press, 1995.

Happel, Klaus. 'Introduction', in Abdullah Öcalan, *Prison Writings: The Roots of Civilisation* (Translated by Klaus Happel) (Pluto Press: London and Ann Arbor, 2006).

Hasretyan, M.A. *Türkiye'de Kürt Sorunu (1918–1940) Cilt I* (The Kurdish Question in Turkey (1918–1940) Volume I), Berlin: Weşanên Înstîtuya Kurdî, 1990.

Hasretyan, M.A. *Türkiye'de Kürt Sorunu (1945–1990) Cilt II* (The Kurdish Question in Turkey (1945–1990) Volume II), Berlin: Weşanên Înstîtuya Kurdî, 1990.

Hassanpour, Amir. 'The Making of Kurdish Identity: Pre-20th Century Historical and Literary Discourse', in *Essays on the Origins of Kurdish Nationalism*, Abbas Vali, ed., Costa Mesa, California: Mazda Publishers, 2003, 106–62.

Hassanpour, Amir. 'Satellite Footprints as National Borders: Med TV and the Extraterritoriality of State Sovereignty', *Journal of Muslim Minority Affairs*, Vol. 18, No. 1 (April 1998), 53–72.

Hassanpour, Amir. 'The Creation of Kurdish Media Culture', in *Kurdish Culture and Identity*, Philip G. Kreyenbroek and Christine Allison, eds, London and New Jersey: Zed Books, 1996, 48–84.

Hevra: Devrimci Türkiye Kürtleri Örgütü. *Türkiye Şartlarına Ters Düşen Bir Tez: Milli Demokratik Devrim* (National Democratic Revolution: A Thesis that is Contrary to Turkey's Conditions), Zurich: Ronahi Yayınları, 1974.

Hirschler, Konrad. 'Defining the Nation: Kurdish Historiography in Turkey in the 1990s', *Middle East Studies*, Vol. 37, No. 3 (July 2001), 145–66.

Hobsbawm, Eric. *Nations and Nationalism since 1780: Programme, Myth, Reality*, Cambridge: Cambridge University Press, 1990.

Hobsbawm, Eric. 'Introduction: Inventing Traditions', in *The Invention of Tradition*, Eric Hobsbawm and Terence Ranger, eds, Cambridge: Cambridge University Press, 1983, 1–14.

220 Bibliography

Houston, Christopher. *Islam Kurds and the Turkish Nation State*, Oxford and New York: Berg, 2001.

Houston, Christopher. 'Islamic Solutions to the Kurdish Problem: Late Rendezvous or Illegitimate Shortcut?', *New Perspectives on Turkey*, 16 (Spring 1997), 1–22.

Howarth, David. *Discourse*, Buckingham: Open University Press, 2000.

Howarth, David. 'Complexities of identity/difference: Black Consciousness ideology in South Africa', *Journal of Political Ideologies*, Vol. 2, Issue 1 (1997), 51–78.

Howarth, David. 'Applying Discourse Theory', in *Discourse Theory in European Politics*, David Howarth and Jacob Torfing, eds, London: Palgrave, 2005, 316–49.

Howarth, David and Aletta Norval. 'Subjectivity and Strategy in South African Resistance Politics: Prospects for a New Imaginary', University of Essex, Colchester: Essex Papers in Politics and Government: Sub Series in Ideology and Discourse Analysis (85), May 1992.

Howarth, David and Yannis Stavrakakis. 'Introducing Discourse Theory and Political Analysis', in *Discourse Theory and Political Analysis: Identities, Hegemonies, and Social Change*, David Howarth, Aletta J. Norval and Yannis Stavrakkakis, eds, Manchester: Manchester University Press, 2000, 1–23.

Human Rights Foundation of Turkey (HRFT). *Torture and Impunity*, Ankara: HRFT Publications, 2004.

Human Rights Foundation of Turkey (HRFT), *Turkey Human Rights Report 1995*, Ankara: HRFT Publications, 1997.

Human Rights Foundation of Turkey (HRFT). *Turkey Human Rights Report 1993*, Ankara: HRFT Publications, 1994.

Human Rights Foundation of Turkey (HRFT). *File of Torture: Deaths in Detention Places or Prisons (12 September 1980–12 September 1994)*, Ankara: HRFT Publications, 1994.

Hutchinson, John. *Modern Nationalism*, London: Fontana, 2004.

Ibrahim, Farhad. 'The "Foreign policy" of the PKK: Regional Enemies and Allies', in *The Kurdish Conflict in Turkey: Obstacles and Chances for Peace and Democracy*, Farhad Ibrahim and Gülistan Gürbey, eds, Germany: Lit Verlag, 2000, 103–18.

Ichijo, Atsuka and Gordana Uzelac. eds. *When is the Nation?: Towards an Understanding of Theories of Nationalism*, London: Routledge, 2005.

Izady, Mehrdad R. *The Kurds: A Concise Handbook*, Washington DC: Taylor & Francis, 1992.

Jabri, Vivienne. *Discourses of Violence: Conflict Analysis Reconsidered*, Manchester and New York: Manchester University Press, 1996.

Jongerden, Joost. 'Resettlement and Reconstruction of Identity: The Case of Kurds in Turkey', *Ethnopolitics*, Vol. 1, No. 1 (September 2001), 80–6.

Kalkan, Duran. *Kürdistanda Demokratik Siyasetin Rolü Üzerine* (Concerning the Role of Democratic Politics in Kurdistan), *Weşanên Serxwebûn*, 2006 (Place of Publication not stated).

Karadoğan, Yaşar. 'Kürd Demokratik Mücadelesinde Bir Kilometre Taşı: 1967–1969 Doğu Mitingleri ve Kürd Uyanışı' (A Mile Stone in Kurdish Democratic Politics: The 1967–1969 Eastern Meetings and Kurdish Awakening), *Bîr: Kovara Lêgerîn û Lêkolîn*, No. 5 (Summer 2006), 255–84.

Karahan, Edip. *Bir Kürt Devrimcisi. Edip Karahan Anısına* (A Kurdish Revolutionary: In Memory of Edip Karahan), Istanbul: Elma Yayınları, 2005.

Karasu, Mustafa. *Radikal Demokrasi* (Radical Democracy), Mezopotamya Yayınları: Neuss, 2009.

Bibliography 221

Kaya, Yaşar. *23 Kürt Aydını* (23 Kurdish Intellectuals), Cologne: Mezopotamya Yayınları, 1998.

Keating, Michael. *Nations against the State: The New Politics of Nationalism in Quebec, Catalonia and Scotland*, 2nd Edition. Baginstoke: Palgrave, 2001.

Keating, Michael. *Plurinational Democracy: Stateless Nation in a Post-Sovereign Era*, Oxford: Oxford University Press, 2001.

Keck Margaret E. and Kathryn Sikkink. *Activists Beyond Borders: Advocacy Networks in International Politics*, New York and London: Cornell University Press, 1998.

Kieser, Hans-Lukas, eds. *Turkey Beyond Nationalism: Towards Post-Nationalist Identities*, London and New York: I.B.Tauris, 2006.

Kirişci, Kemal and Gareth M Winrow. *The Kurdish Question and Turkey: An example of Trans-state Ethnic Conflict*, London: Frank Cass, 1997.

KİP/DDKD. *KİP/DDKD Davası: Kesinleşmiş Karar* (KİP/DDKD Trial: The Final Decision), Ankara: Jina Nû Yayınları, Ankara 2006.

Klein, Janet. 'Kurdish Nationalists and Non-Nationalist Kurdists: Rethinking Minority Nationalism and the Dissolution of the Ottoman Empire, 1908–1909', *Nations and Nationalism*, Vol. 13, Issue 1 (January 2007), 135–53.

Koğacıoğlu, Dicle. 'Progress, Unity, and Democracy: Dissolving Political Parties in Turkey', *Law & Society Review*, Vol. 38, No. 3 (2004), 433–62.

Kongra Gelê Kurdistan (*Kongra-Gel*). *Program, Tüzük ve Kararları* (The Program, Regulations and Decisions of the People's Congress of Kurdistan), *Weşanên Serxwebûn*, 2004 (Place of publication not stated).

Konuk, A. Kadir. *PKK'nin Tek Taraflı ilan Ettiği Ateşkes ve Yankıları*, (The PKK's Unilateral Ceasefire and its Consequences), Cologne: Ağrı Yayınları, 1993.

Kotan, Mümtaz. 'Tarihin Karartılması Eylemi Üzerine Somut Bir Örnek: DDKO' (A Concrete Example of Action to Darken History: DDKO), *Bîr: Kovara Lêgerîn û Lêkolîn*, No. 6 (Winter 2007), 25–84.

Kreyenbroek, Phillip G and Stefan Sperl, eds. *The Kurds: A Contemporary Overview*, London and New York: Routledge, 1992.

Kurdish Human Rights Project. *The Status of Internally Displaced Kurds in Turkey and Compensation Rights*, London, 2005.

Kutlay, Naci. 'Devrimci Doğu Kültür Ocakları ve Öncesi' (The Revolutionary Cultural Hearths of the East and Before), in *Bîr: Kovara Lêgerîn û Lêkolîn*, No. 5 (Summer 2006), 158–73.

Kutlay, Naci. *49'lar Dosyası* (The 49'ers Trial), Istanbul: Fırat Yayınları, 1994.

Laciner, Sedat and İhsan Bal. 'The Ideological and Historical Roots of the Kurdist Movements in Turkey: Ethnicity, Demography, and Politics', *Nationalism and Ethnic Politics*, 10 (2004), 473–504.

Laclau, Ernesto. *On Populist Reason*, London and New York: Verso, 2005.

Laclau, Ernesto. 'Populism: What's in a Name?', in *Populism and the Mirror of Democracy*, Fransisco Panizza, ed., London and New York: Verso, 2005, 32–49.

Laclau, Ernesto. 'Glimpsing the Future', in *Laclau: A Critical Reader*, Simon Critchley and Oliver Marchart, eds., London: Routledge, 2004, 279–328.

Laclau, Ernesto. 'Democracy and the Question of Power', *Constellations*, Vol. 8, No. 1 (2001), 3–14.

Laclau, Ernesto. *Emancipation(s)*, London and New York: Verso, 1996.

Laclau, Ernesto. 'Why do Empty Signifiers Matter to Politics?', in *Emancipation(s)*, Ernesto Laclau, London and New York: Verso, 1996, 36–46.

222   Bibliography

Laclau, Ernesto. 'Introduction', in *The Making of Political Identities*, Ernesto Laclau, ed., London: Verso, 1994, 1–8.

Laclau, Ernesto. *New Reflections on the Revolution of Our Time*, London: Verso, 1990.

Laclau, Ernesto and Chantal Mouffe. 'Post-Marxism Without Apologies', *New Left Review* 166 (November–December 1987), 79–106.

Laclau, Ernesto and Chantal Mouffe. *Hegemony and Socialist Strategy: Towards a Radical Democratic Politics*, London: Verso, 1985.

Lenin, Vladimir Ilyich. *The National Liberation Movement in the East*, Moscow: Progress Publishers, 1952.

Lipovsky, Igor P. *The Socialist Movement in Turkey 1960–1980*, Leiden, New York and Köln: E.J. Brill, 1992.

Maraşlı, Recep. *Yasaklı Yazılar* (The Prohibited Writings), Istanbul: Komal, 1996.

Marcus, Aliza. *Blood and Belief: The PKK and the Kurdish Fight for Independence*, New York and London: New York University Press, 2007.

Mater, Nadire. *Voices from the Front: Turkish Soldiers on the War with the Kurdish Guerrillas*, Basingstoke: Palgrave Macmillan, 2005.

McDowall, David. *A Modern History of the Kurds*, 2nd Edition, London: I.B. Tauris, 2000.

Minority Rights Group International (MRG) and Foundation for Society and Legal Studies (TOHAV). *The Problem of Turkey's Displaced Persons: An Action Plan for their Return and Compensation*, London, 2006.

Mojab, Shahrzad, ed. *Women of a Non-State Nation: The Kurds*, Costa Mesa, California: Mazda Publishers, 2001.

Mouffe, Chantal. *Democratic Paradox*, London and New York: Verso, 2000.

Mouffe, Chantal. 'Decision, Deliberation, and Democratic Ethos', *Philosophy Today* (Spring 1997), 24–30.

Mouffe, Chantal. 'Hegemony and Ideology in Gramsci', in *Gramsci and Marxist Theory*, Chantal Mouffe, ed., London: Routledge & Kegan Paul, 1979, 168–204.

Muller, Mark. 'Nationalism and the Rule of Law in Turkey: The Elimination of Kurdish Representation during the 1990s', in *The Kurdish Nationalist Movement in the 1990s: Its Impact on Turkey and the Middle East*, Robert Olson, ed., Lexington: University of Kentucky Press, 1996, 173–99.

Murat, Hıdır (Kemal Burkay). *Türkiye Şartlarında Kürt Halkının Kurtuluş Mücadelesi* (The Liberation Struggle of Kurdish People in Turkey's Conditions), Zurich: Ronahi Yayınları, 1977.

Natali, Denise. *The Kurds and the State: Evolving National Identity in Iraq, Turkey and Iran*, New York: Syracuse University Press, 2005.

Nezan, Kendal. 'Kurdistan in Turkey', in *People Without a Country: Kurds and Kurdistan*, Gerard Chaliand ed., (translated by Michael Pallis), London: Zed Books, 1992, 38–94.

Nimni, Ephraim. *National Cultural Autonomy and its Contemporary Critics*, London: Routledge, 2005.

Nimni, Ephraim. *Marxism and Nationalism: Theoretical Origins of a Political Crisis*, London: Pluto Press, 1991.

Norval, Aletta J. *Aversive Democracy: Inheritance and Originality in the Democratic Tradition*, Cambridge: Cambridge University Press, 2007.

Norval, Aletta J. 'Trajectories of Future Research in Discourse Theory', in *Discourse Theory and Political Analysis: Identities, Hegemonies, and Social Change*, David Howarth, Aletta Norval and Yannis Stavrakakis, eds, Manchester: Manchester University Press, 2000, 219–36.

Bibliography 223

Norval, Aletta J. 'Frontiers in Question', *Filozofski Vestnik*, XVIII (2/1997), 51–76.

Norval, Aletta J. 'Thinking Identities: Against a Theory of Ethnicity', in *The Politics of Difference: Ethnic Premises in a World of Power*, Edwin Wilmsen and Patrick McAlister, ed., London and Chicago: University of Chicago Press, 1996, 59–70.

Nuri, İhsan. *Ağrı Dağı İsyanı* (The Uprising of Mount Ararat), Istanbul: Med Yayınları, 1996.

Odabaşı, Yılmaz. *Eylül Defterleri* (The September Notebooks), Ankara: Doruk Yayınları, 1991.

Olson, Robert, ed. *The Kurdish Nationalist Movement in the 1990s: Its Impact on Turkey and the Middle East*, Lexington: University of Kentucky Press, 1996.

Olson, Robert. *The Emergence of Kurdish Nationalism and the Sheikh Said Rebellion, 1880–1925*, Austin: University of Texas Press, 1989.

Oran, Baskın. *Atatürk Milliyetçiliği: Resmi İdeoloji Dışı Bir Araştırma* (Ataturk Nationalism: A Study Outside the Official Ideology), Ankara: Bilgi Yayınevi, 1990.

O'Shea, Maria T. *Trapped Between the Map and Reality: Geography and Perceptions of Kurdistan*, London and New York: Routledge, 2004.

Öcalan, Abdullah. *Demokratik Toplum Manifestosu* (The Manifesto of Democratic Society), Mezopotamya Yayınları: Cologne, 2009.

Öcalan, Abdullah. *Prison Writings: The Roots of Civilisation*, (Translated by Klaus Happel), London and Ann Arbor: Pluto Press, 2007.

Öcalan, Abdullah. *PKK Yeniden İnşa Kongresi: Politik Rapor* (Political Report: The PKK's Re-Building Congress), *Weşanên Serxwebûn*, 2005 (place of publication not stated).

Öcalan, Abdullah. *Bir Halkı Savunmak* (Defending A Nation), Cologne: *Weşanên Serxwebûn*, 2004.

Öcalan, Abdullah. *Özgür İnsan Savunması* (Defence of the Free Human Race), Cologne: Mezapotamya Yayınları, 2003.

Öcalan, Abdullah. *AIHM Savunmaları (Cilt 1): Sümer Rahip Develtinden Demokratik Cumhuriyete* (ECHR Defence Volume 1: From Sumerian Monk State to Democratic Republic), Cologne: Mezopotamya Yayınları, 2001.

Öcalan, Abdullah. *AIHM Savunmaları (Cilt 2): Sümer Rahip Develtinden Demokratik Cumhuriyete* (ECHR Defence Volume 2: From Sumerian Monk State to Democratic Republic), Cologne: Mezopotamya Yayınları, 2001.

Öcalan, Abdullah. *Kürt Hümanizmi ve Yeni İnsan* (Kurdish Humanism and the New Human), Istanbul: Mem Yayınları, 2001.

Öcalan, Abdullah. *Savunma: Kürt Sorununda Demokratik Çözüm Bildirgesi* (Defence: The Democratic Solution Report for the Kurdish Question), Istanbul: Mem Yayınları, 1999.

Öcalan, Abdullah. *Ek Savunma: Kürt Sorununda Çözüm ve Çözümsüzlük İkilemi* (Additional Defence: The Dilemma of Solution and Impasse in the Kurdish Question), Istanbul: Mem Yayınları, 1999.

Öcalan, Abdullah. *İlk Konuşmalar* (Early Speeches), *Weşanên Serxwebûn*, 1999 (Place of publication not stated).

Öcalan, Abdullah. *Mektuplar* (Letters), *Weşanên Serxwebûn*, 1998 (Place of publication not stated).

Öcalan, Abdullah. *Diriliş Tamamlandı Sıra Kurtuluşta* (Revival is Completed; Time for Liberation – Interview with Ertuğrul Kürkçü and Ragıp Duran), Istanbul: Güneş Ülkesi Yayıncılık, 1995.

Öcalan, Abdullah. *PKK 5. Kongresi'ne Sunulan Politik Rapor* (The Political Report Submitted to the PKK's 5th Congress), Istanbul: Güneş Ülkesi Yayıncılık, 1995.

224   Bibliography

Öcalan, Abdullah. *PKK Zindan Direniş Konferansı Konuşmaları* (The Speeches During the PKK's Prison Resistance Conference), Cologne: *Weşanên Serxwebûn*, 1994.

Öcalan, Abdullah. *Kürdistan'da İşbirlikcilik-İhanet ve Devrimci Direniş* (Collaboration, Betrayal and Revolutionary Resistance in Kurdistan), Cologne: *Weşanên Serxwebûn*, 1993.

Öcalan, Abdullah. *3. Kongre Konuşmaları* (3rd Congress Speeches), Cologne: *Weşanên Serxwebûn*, 1993.

Öcalan, Abdullah. *Sosyalizm ve Devrim Sorunları* (Socialism and the Problems of Revolution), Cologne: *Weşanên Serxwebûn*, 1992.

Öcalan, Abdullah. *Kürdistan Devriminin Yolu (Manifesto)* (The Path of Kurdistan Revolution (Manifesto), Cologne: *Weşanên Serxwebûn*, 1992.

Öcalan, Abdullah. *PKK IV Ulusal Kongresi'ne Sunulan Politik Rapor* (The Political Report Submitted to the PKK's IV National Congress), Cologne: *Weşanên Serxwebûn*, 1992.

Öcalan, Abdullah. *Kadın ve Aile Sorunu* (Women and the Family Problem), Istanbul: Melsa Yayınları, 1992.

Öcalan, Abdullah. *Kürdistan'da Halk Savaşı ve Gerrilla* (People's War and Guerrilla in Kurdistan), Cologne: *Weşanên Serxwebûn*, 1991.

Öcalan, Abdullah. *Seçme Yazıları IV* (Collected Articles IV), Cologne: *Weşanên Serxwebûn*, 1989.

Öcalan, Abdullah. *Seçme Yazıları III* (Collected Articles III), Cologne: *Weşanên Serxwebûn*, 1988.

Öcalan, Abdullah. *Seçme Yazıları II* (Collected Articles II), Cologne: *Weşanên Serxwebûn*, 1986.

Öcalan, Abdullah. *Seçme Yazıları I* (Collected Articles I), Cologne: *Weşanên Serxwebûn*, 1986.

Ölmez, Osman. *Türkiye Siyasetinde DEP Depremi* (The DEP Earthquake in Turkish Politics), Ankara: Doruk Yayınları, 1995.

Özcan, Ali Kemal. *Turkey's Kurds: A Theoretical Analysis of the PKK and Abdullah Öcalan*, London and New York: Routledge, 2006.

Özkırımlı, Umut. *Contemporary Debates in Nationalism: A Critical Engagement*, Basingstoke: Pelgrave Macmillan, 2005.

Özkırımlı, Umut. *Theories of Nationalism: A Critical Introduction*, London: Macmillan Press, 2000.

Partiya Karkerên Kurdistan (PKK). *PKK 10. Kongre Belgeleri: Program ve Tüzüğü* (The Documents of the PKK's 10th Congress: Programme and Regulations), *Weşanên Serxwebûn*, 2009 (Place of Publication not stated).

Partiya Karkerên Kurdistan (PKK). *Program ve Tüzüğü* (Programme and Regulations), Cologne: *Weşanên Serxwebûn*, 2005.

Partiya Karkerên Kurdistan (PKK). *21. Yüzyılın Mücadele Çizgisi Olarak Meşru Savunma Stratejisi* (Legitimate Defence Strategy as the Principle of Struggle for the 21st Century), *Weşanên Serxwebûn*, 2004 (place of publication not stated).

Partiya Karkerên Kurdistan (PKK). *PKK VI. Ulusal Konferansına Sunulan Politik-Örgütsel Rapor* (The Political-Organisational Report Submitted to the PKK's 6th National Conference), *Weşanên Serxwebûn*, 2001 (Place of publication not stated).

Partiya Karkerên Kurdistan (PKK). *1. Halk Hareketı Konferansı Belgeleri* (The Documents of the 1st People's Movement Conference), *Weşanên Serxwebûn*, 2001 (place of publication not stated).

Partiya Karkerên Kurdistan (PKK). *Demokratik Kurtuluş Mücadelesinde Halk Hareketi:*

Bibliography 225

Serhildan (The People's Movement in the Democratic Liberation Struggle: *Serhildan* (Uprising)), *Weşanên Serxwebûn*, 2001 (place of publication not stated).

Partiya Karkerên Kurdistan (PKK). *Dönüşüm Süreci ve Görevlerimiz (PKK 7. Olağanüstü Kongresine MK Raporu)* (The Transformation Process and Our Duties – The Central Committee Report Submitted to the 7th Congress of the PKK), *Weşanên Serxwebûn* 101: 2000 (place of publication not stated).

Partiya Karkerên Kurdistan (PKK). *Kürdistanda Önderliksel Gelişme Ve Uluslararası Komplo* (The Development of the Leadership in Kurdistan and the International Conspiracy), Cologne: *Weşanên Serxwebûn*, 1999.

Partiya Karkerên Kurdistan (PKK). *5. Kongre Kararları* (The Decisions of 5th Congress), Cologne: *Weşanên Serxwebûn*, 1995.

Partiya Karkerên Kurdistan (PKK). *Program ve Tüzüğü* (The Programme and Regulations), *Weşanên Serxwebûn*, 1995 (Place of publication not stated).

Partiya Karkerên Kurdistan (PKK). *Bağımsız Kürdistan Yolunda* (On the Path of Independent Kurdistan), Cologne: *Weşanên Serxwebûn*, 1987.

Partiya Karkerên Kurdistan (PKK). *İdeoloji ve Politika Nedir Nasıl Ortaya Çıkmıştır* (What is Ideology and Politics and How Have They Come About?), Cologne: *Weşanên Serxwebûn*, 1986.

Partiya Karkerên Kurdistan (PKK). *Kürdistanda Darağaçları, Kışla Kültürü ve Devrimci İntikam Üzerine* (Concerning Gallows, Military Culture and Revolutionary Revenge in Kurdistan), Cologne: *Weşanên Serxwebûn*, 1985.

Partiya Karkerên Kurdistan (PKK). *Bağımsızlık ve Özgürlük Mücadelesinde PKK 4. Yılını Yaşıyor* (The PKK is in its 4th Year in its Struggle for Independence and Freedom), Cologne: *Weşanên Serxwebûn*, 1984.

Partiya Karkerên Kurdistan (PKK). *PKK II Kongresine Sunulan PKK-MK Çalışma Raporu* (The Activities Report Submitted by the Central Committee to the PKK's Second Congress), Cologne: *Waşenên Serxwebûn*, 1984.

Partiya Karkerên Kurdistan (PKK). *Kürdistan Ulusal Kurtuluş Problemi ve Çözüm Yolu: Kürdistan Ulusal Kurtuluş Cephesi Program Taslağı* (Kurdistan's National Liberation Problem and Its Solution: The Draft Programme of Kurdistan's National Liberation Front), Cologne: *Weşanên Serxwebûn*, 1992, 2nd edition.

Partiya Karkerên Kurdistan (PKK). *Devrimcilerdeki Kafa Karışıklığı'mı, yoksa bir Küçük-burjuva reformistin iflah olmazlığı mı?* (Confusion Among Revolutionaries or the Impossibility of the Rehabilitation of a Petty Bourgeois Reformist), Cologne: *Weşanên Serxwebûn*, 1984.

Partiya Karkerên Kurdistan (PKK). *12 Eylül Faşist Rejimi Dördüncü Yılına Girerken Genel Durum, Sorunlar ve Görevlerimiz* (The General Conditions, Problems and Our Duties in the 4th Year of the Fascist Regime of 12 September), Cologne: *Weşanên Serxwebûn*, 1984.

Partiya Karkerên Kurdistan (PKK). *Faşizme ve Ulusal Baskı Sistemine Karşı Ortak Mücadelenin Sorunları* (The Problems of Common Struggle Against Fascism and the System of National Oppression), Cologne: *Weşanên Serxwebûn*, 1984.

Partiya Karkerên Kurdistan (PKK). *Devrimci Mücadelede Küçük Burjuvazi ve Küçük Burjuvazinin Kürdistandaki Rolü Üzerine* (Concerning the Petty Bourgeois in Revolutionary Struggle and the Role of Petty Bourgeois in Kurdistan), Cologne: *Weşanên Serxwebûn*, 1984.

Partiya Karkerên Kurdistan (PKK). *Örgütlenme Üzerine* (Concerning Organisation), Cologne: *Weşanên Serxwebûn*, 1983.

Partiya Karkerên Kurdistan (PKK). *Kürdistan'da Zorun Rolü (Ulusal Kurtuluş Savaşı*

226   Bibliography

– *Ulusal Kurtuluş Siyaseti)* (The Role of Force (The National Liberation War – The Politics of National Liberation), Cologne: *Weşanên Serxwebûn*, 1983.

Partiya Karkerên Kurdistan (PKK). *Politik Rapor: Merkez Komitesi Tarafından PKK 1. Konferansina Sunulmuştur* (Political Report of the Central Committee Submitted to the PKK's 1st Congress), Cologne: *Weşanên Serxwebûn*, 1982.

Partiya Karkerên Kurdistan (PKK). *Faşizme Karşı Mücadelede Birleşik Cephe Üzerine* (Concerning the United Front in the Struggle against Fascism), Cologne: *Weşanên Serxwebûn*, 1982.

Partiya Karkerên Kurdistan (PKK). *Kuruluş Bildirisi* (The Foundation Declaration), Place, date or publisher not stated.

Partiya Sosyalist a Kurdistana Tirkiye (PSKT). *Kongra 2* (Second Congress), Weşanên PSKT, 1986 (place of publication not stated).

Peach, Norman. 'International Law and Kurdish Struggle for Freedom', in *The Kurdish Conflict in Turkey: Obstacles and Chances for Peace and Democracy*, Farhad Ibrahim and Gülistan Gürbey, eds, Germany: Lit Verlag, 2000, 159–80.

Perinçek, Doğu. *Abdullah Öcalan ile Görüşme* (Interview with Abdullah Öcalan), Istanbul: Kaynak Yayınları, 1990.

PSK (Kurdistan Sosyalist Partisi). *İlkeli, Kararlı, Direngen ve Onurlu Bir Mücadele: PSK 30 Yaşında* (A Principled, Determined, Resolute and Honourable Struggle: The PSK is 30 Years Old), Cologne: PSK Yayınları, 2004.

PSK (Kurdistan Sosyalist Partisi). *Program* (Programme), PSK Yayınları, 1993 (place of publication not stated).

PSK (Kurdistan Sosyalist Partisi). *3. Kongre Belgeleri* (The Third Congress Documents), PSK Yayınları, 1992 (place of publication not stated).

Rabinow, Paul, ed. *The Foucault Reader*, London: Penguin Books, 1984.

Rancière, Jacques. *Disagreement. Politics and Philosophy*, trans. Julie Rose, Minneapolis and London: University of Minnesota Press, 1999.

Renner, Karl. 'State and Nation', in *National Cultural Autonomy and Its Contemporary Critics*, Ephraim Nimni, ed., London and New York: Routledge, 2005, 15–47.

Robins, Kevin. 'Interrupting Identities: Turkey/Europe', in *Questions of Cultural Identity*, Stuart Hall and Paul du Gay, eds, London: Sage Publications, 1996, 61–86.

Romano, David. *The Kurdish Nationalist Movement: Opportunity, Mobilisation and Identity*, Cambridge: Cambridge University Press, 2006.

Sakallıoğlu, Umit Cizre. 'Kurdish Nationalism From an Islamist Perspective: The Discourses of the Turkish Islamist Writers', *Journal of Muslim Minority Affairs*, Vol. 18, No. 1, (1998), 73–89.

Sakallıoğlu, Umit Cizre. 'Historicizing the Present and Problematizing the Future of the Kurdish Problem: A critique of the TOBB Report on the Eastern Question', *New Perspectives on Turkey*, 14 (Spring 1996), 1–22.

Sayari, Sabri and Yılmaz Esmer, eds. *Politics, Parties and Elections in Turkey*, Boulder and London: Lynne Reinner Publishers, 2002.

Scalbert-Yücel, Clémence and Marie Le Ray. 'Knowledge, Ideology and Power: Deconstructing Kurdish Studies', *European Journal of Turkish Studies*, Thematic Issue 5, No. 5 (2007), www.ejts.org/document777.html.

Schaap, Andrew. *Political Reconciliation*, London and New York: Routledge, 2005.

Seufert, Gunter. 'Between Religion and Ethnicity: A Kurdish Alevi Tribe in Globalising Istanbul', in *Space, Culture and Power: New Identities in Globalising Cities*, Ayse Öncü and Petra Weyland, eds, London: Zed Books, 1997, 157–76.

Bibliography 227

Sever, Metin and Cem Dizdar. *2. Cumhuriyet Tartışmaları* (The Second Republic Discussions), Ankara: Başak Publications, 1993.

Shaw, Stanford J. and Ezel Kural Shaw. *History of the Ottoman Empire and Modern Turkey. Volume II: Reform, Revolution and Republic: The Rise of Modern Turkey, 1808–1975*, Cambridge: Cambridge University Press, 1977.

Sosyaldemokrat Halkçı Parti (SHP). *Sosyaldemokrat Halkçı Parti'nin Doğu ve Güneydoğu sorunlarına bakışı ve çözüm önerileri* (The Social Democrat Populist Party's Views and Proposals for Solution for the Eastern and South-Eastern Problems), Ankara: SHP, 1990.

Staten, Henry. *Wittgenstein and Derrida*, Oxford: Blackwell, 1985.

Stavrakakis, Yannis. *The Lacanian Left: Psychoanalysis, Theory, Politics*, Edinburgh: Edinburgh University Press, 2007.

Stavrakakis, Yannis. *Lacan and the Political*, London: Routledge, 1999.

Sutherland, Claire. 'Nation Building Through Discourse Theory', *Nations and Nationalism*, Vol. 11, No. 2 (2005), 185–202.

Şafak, Mahsum. *KADEK Kuruluş Kongresi (PKK VIII Kongresi Belgeleri)* (The Foundation Congress of KADEK – Documents of the PKK's 8th Congress), Istanbul: Mem Yayınları, 2002.

Şemmikanlı, Nezir. 'Geçmiş Olmadan Gelecek Olamaz' (Without the Past There Can Be No future), *Bîr: Kovara Lêgerîn û Lêkolîn*, No. 5 (Summer 2006), 72–98.

Tahiri, Hussein. *The Structure of the Kurdish Society and the Struggle for a Kurdish State*, Costa Mesa, California: Mazda Press, 2007.

Taspinar, Omer. *Kurdish Nationalism and Political Islam in Turkey: Kemalist Identity in Transition*, London and New York: Routledge, 2005.

Tevger. *Program: Tevgera Rizgariya Kurdistan* (Programme: The Movement for Kurdistan's Liberation), Weşanên Tevger, 1988 (place of publication not stated).

TİİKP. *Türkiye İhtilalci İşçi Köylü Partisi Dava Dosyası* (Case File of the Revolutionary Party of Workers and Peasants of Turkey), Ankara: Tore Devlet Yayınları: Ankara, 1973.

Türk, Ahmet. *DEP Savunması* (The DEP Defence), Ankara: Matsa Basımevi, 1994.

Türkiye Kürdistanı Sosyalist Partisi (TKSP). *Program* (Party Programme), TKSP Yayınları, 1985 (Place of publication not stated).

Türkiye Kürdistanı Sosyalist Partisi (TKSP). *Devrimci Demokratlar Üzerine: UDG Neden Hayata Geçmedi* (Concerning the Revolutionary Democrats: Why Didn't the National Democratic Unity of Forces Manage to Survive), Özgürlük Yolu Yayınları, 1981 (place of publication not stated).

Türkiye İnsan Hakları Vakfı. *Türkiye İnsan Hakları Raporu 1996* (Human Rights Report of Turkey 1996), Ankara: TİHV Yayınları, 1998.

Türkiye İnsan Hakları Vakfı. *Türkiye İnsan Hakları Raporu 1994* (Human Rights Report of Turkey 1994), Ankara: TİHV Yayınları, 1995.

Türkiye İnsan Hakları Vakfı. *Türkiye İnsan Hakları Raporu 1992* (Human Rights Report of Turkey 1992), Ankara: TİHV Yayınları, 1993.

Türkiye İnsan Hakları Vakfı. *Örneklerle Türkiye İnsan Hakları Raporu 1991* (Human Rights Report of Turkey 1991), Ankara: TIHV Yayınları, 1992.

Türkiye Sanayi ve İşadamları Derneği (Turkish Industrialists' and Businessmen's Association (TUSIAD). *Türk Demokrasisi'nde 130 Yıl (1876–2006)* (130 Years of Turkish Democracy (1876–2006)), Istanbul, 2006.

Türkiye Sanayi ve İşadamları Derneği (Turkish Industrialists' and Businessmen's Association (TUSIAD). *Türkiyede Demokratikleşme Perspektivleri* (The Democratisation Perspectives in Turkey), Istanbul, 1997.

228 Bibliography

Uçarlar, N. 'Between Majority Power and Minority Resistance: Kurdish Linguistic Rights in Turkey', PhD diss., Lund University, 2009.

UDG, *Kürdistan Ulusal Demokratik Güçbirliği (UDG Deklerasyonu)* (Kurdistan National Democratic Unity of Forces (Declaration), Van: Jîna Nû Yayınları, 1980.

Vali, Abbas. 'Genealogies of the Kurds: Constructions of Nation and National Identity in Kurdish Historical Writing', in *Essays on the Origins of Kurdish Nationalism*, Abbas Vali, ed., Costa Mesa, California: Mazda Publishers, 2003, 58–105.

Vali, Abbas. 'Kurds and their "Others": Fragmented Identity and Fragmented Politics', *Comparative Studies of South Asia, Africa and the Middle East*, Vol. XVIII, No. 2 (1998), 82–95.

Vanly, Ismet Chériff. *Survey of the National Question of Turkish Kurdistan With Historical Background*, Rome: Hevra Organisation of the Revolutionary Kurds of Turkey in Europe, 1971.

Verdery, Katherine. 'Wither "Nation" and "Nationalism"?', in *Mapping the Nation*, Gopal Balakrishnan, ed., London: Verso, 1996, 226–34.

Verdery, Katherine. *National Ideology under Socialism: Identity and Cultural Politics in Ceauşescu's Romania*, Berkeley, Los Angeles and Oxford: University of California Press, 1991.

Watts, Nicole F. 'Silence and Voice: Turkish Policies and Kurdish Resistance in the mid-20th century', in *The Evolution of Kurdish Nationalism*, Mohammed Ahmed and Michael Gunter, eds, Costa Mesa, California: Mazda Publishers, 2007, 52–77.

Watts, Nicole F. 'Activists in Office: Pro-Kurdish Contentious Politics in Turkey', *Ethnopolitics* Vol. 5, No. 2 (June 2006), 125–44.

Watts, Nicole F. 'Institutionalizing Virtual Kurdistan West: Transnational Networks and Ethnic Contention in International Affairs', in *Boundaries and Belonging: States and Societies in the Struggle to Shape Identities and Local Practices*, Joel Migdal, ed., Cambridge: Cambridge University Press, 2004, 121–47.

Watts, Nicole F. 'Allies and Enemies: Pro-Kurdish Parties in Turkish Politics, 1990–94', *International Journal of Middle East Studies*, Vol. 31, No. 4 (Nov. 1999), 631–56.

White, Paul. *Primitive Rebels or Revolutionary Modernizers? The Kurdish National Movement in Turkey*, London: Zed Books, 2000.

White, Paul and Joost Jongerden, eds. *Turkey's Alevi Enigma: A comprehensive Overview*, Leiden and Boston: Brill, 2003.

Xemgin, E. *Kürdistan'da İnsan Hakları* (Human Rights in Kurdistan), Cologne: Agri Verlag, 1989.

Yanik, Lerna K. ' "*Nevruz*" or "*Newroz*"? Deconstructing the "Invention" of a Contested Tradition in Contemporary Turkey', *Middle Eastern Studies*, Vol. 42, No. 2 (March 2006), 285–302.

Yavuz, M. Hakan. 'Five Stages of the Construction of Kurdish Nationalism in Turkey', *Nationalism & Ethnic Politics*, Vol. 7, No. 3 (Autumn 2001), 1–24.

Yavuz, M. Hakan. 'A Preamble to the Kurdish Question: The Politics of Kurdish Identity', *Journal of Muslim Minority Affairs*, Vol. 18, No. 1 (1998), 9–18.

Yeğen, Mesut. 'Turkish Nationalism and the Kurdish Question', *Ethnic and Racial Studies*, Vol. 30, No. 1 (January 2007), 119–51.

Yeğen, Mesut. ' "Jewish Kurds" or the new frontiers of Turkishness', *Patterns of Prejudice*, Vol. 41, No. 1 (2007), 1–20.

Yeğen, Mesut. *Müstakbel Türk'ten Sözde Vatandaşa: Cumhuriyet ve Kürtler* (From Future Turk to So-called Citizen: The Republic and the Kurds), Istanbul: İletişim Yayınları, 2006.

Bibliography 229

Yeğen, Mesut. 'The Turkish State Discourse and the Exclusion of Kurdish Identity', *Middle Eastern Studies* 32, (April 1996), 216–29.

Yeğen, M. 'The Archaeology of republican Turkish State Discourse', PhD diss., University of Essex, 1994.

Yeni Türkiye Partisi (YTP). *1969 Seçim Bildirisi* (1969 Election Leaflet), (Date and Place of publication not stated).

Yeni Türkiye Partisi (YTP). *Tüzüğü ve Programı 1963* (Regulations and Programme 1963), Ankara, 1963) (Publisher not stated).

Yeni Türkiye Partisi (YTP). *Tüzüğü ve Programı 1961* (Regulations and Programme 1961), Ankara: Nebioğlu Yayınevi, 1961.

Yıldırım, Ali. *Belgelerle FKF, Dev Genç 2: Dev Genç, 1969–1971* (With Documents – the Federation of Thought Clubs, The Revolutionary Youth 2: the Revolutionary Youth, 1969–1971), Ankara: Yurt Kitap Yayın, 1990.

Yıldırım, Ali. *Belgelerle FKF, Dev Genç 1:FKF, 1965–1971* (With Documents the Federation of Thought Clubs, The Revolutionary Youth 1: the Federation of Thought Clubs, 1965–1971), Ankara: Yurt Kitap Yayın, 1988.

Yıldırım, Hüseyin. *Kürdistan Halkının Diriliş Mücadelesi: Diyarbakır Zindanı* (The Revival Struggle of the Kurdish People: the Diyarbakir Prison), Cologne: *Weşanên Serxwebûn*, 1985.

Yıldız, Kerim and Mark Muller. *The European Union and Turkish Accession: Human Rights and the Kurds*, London and Ann Arbor, MI: Pluto Press, 2008.

Yoruk, Z.F. 'Identity Crisis in Turkey: A Genealogical Inquiry into the Exclusion of the Others (1985–2004)', PhD diss., University of Essex, 2006.

Yücel, Müslüm. *Türk Sinemasında Kürtler* (The Kurds in Turkish Cinema), Istanbul: Agora Kitaplığı, 2008.

Zana, Leyla. *Writings from Prison*, Watertown, Massachusetts: Blue Crane Books, 1999.

Zana, Mehdi. *Prison No. 5: 11 Years in Turkish Jails*, Watertown, Massachusetts: Blue Crane Books, 1997.

Zeydanlıoğlu, Welat. 'Torture and Turkification in the Diyarbakır Military Prison', in *Rights, Citizenship & Torture: Perspectives on Evil, Law and the State*, John T. Parry and Welat Zeydanlıoğlu, eds., Oxford: Inter-Disciplinary Press, 2009, 73–92.

Zeydanlıoğlu, Welat. 'The White Turkish Man's Burden': Orientalism, Kemalism and the Kurds in Turkey', in *Neo-colonial Mentalities in Contemporary Europe? Language and Discourse in the Construction of Identities*, Guido Rings and Anne Ife, eds, Newcastle upon Tyne: Cambridge Scholars Publishing, 2008, 155–74.

Zizek, Slavoj. 'Eastern Europe's Republics of Gilead', *New Left Review*, 183 (September–October 1990), 50–62.

Zürcher, Eric J. *Turkey: A Modern History*, London: I.B. Tauris, 2004.

Index

agency 29; *see also* democratic
   subjectivity; political subjectivity
agonism 154
AKP (Justice and Development Party) 3,
   171–3
Aksoy, İbrahim 156
Aksoy, Gürdal 34
Aksu, Sezen 168
Ala Rizgarî 45, 33, 78, 82, 91–3
Alevi Community 156, 167
Alevi Kurds 13, 107, 110, 115
Alkan, Zekiye 117–18
Anatolia 1, 13, 61, 70
Anderson, Benedict 202n70
Ankara 50, 61, 65, 68, 78–9, 163, 166,
   188n6, 195n53, 208n1, 208n122
antagonism 27–9, 32–3, 35, 39, 188n15
antagonistic 27, 29–30, 32, 62, 83, 107,
   101, 154
antagonistic relations 40; discursive
   construction of 30, 63, 82–3, 88–9, 91,
   96, 100, 102; political frontiers and 82,
   100; transformation in 30, 35, 132–4,
   137, 142, 150, 174
Anter, Musa 17, 42–3, 50–3, 59, 67, 131,
   193n3
anti-imperialism 94
Anti-Terror Law 130, 150
Anyık, Eşref 98
Aren, Sadun 60
ARGK (Kurdistan People's Liberation
   Army): activities 104–6, 110, 138;
   women in 119–20; *see also* HPG; HRK
Armenians 3
articulation 9, 12, 20, 28–9, 31–2, 36, 41,
   153; differential 49–50, 57–9;
   equivalential 65–6, 80, 139, 154; of
   Kurdish rights and demands 14, 18, 32,
   41, 44, 48, 60, 64, 94

artistic representation 102
aspect change 120, 123, 153–4, 202n63
assimilation 3, 8, 18, 39, 56, 80, 85, 137
Assyrians 13, 77, 96, 115, 168
Atatürk, Mustafa Kemal 144, 186n8; *see
   also* Kemalism; Turkish nationalism
Atsız, Hüseyin Nihal 62
attacks on tourists 132
authoritarian 30, 144
Aydar, Zübeyir 141
Aydın, Vedat 111
Aydın, Delal 14, 47, 197n38, 199n57
Aydınlık 196n32
Ayna, Emine 172
Azizoğlu, Yusuf 50

Ballı, Rafet 197n39
Barış Anneleri 182
Barkey and Fuller 9–11
Barzani, Massoud 201n21
Barzani, Mustafa 75
Basque Country 128
Bayır, Derya 186n9
BDP (Peace and Democracy Party) 164,
   169, 172–4
Bedirxan, Celadet Ali 113–14
Belli, Mihri 72
Beritan (Gülnaz Karataş) 117
Berxwedan 46, 105–6, 108, 110, 118, 128
Beşikci, İsmail 8, 43, 61, 78, 187n4,
   195n47, 203n16
Beş Parçacılar 78
Bildirici, Hasan 127
Boran, Behice 60
Botan Behdinan War Government 108
Botan province 106
Bookchin, Murray 136
boundaries 37, 139–41
Boycott Turkish Tourism campaign 132

Index   231

Bozarslan, Hamit 10
Bozarslan, Mehmet Emin 43, 50–1, 53
Bruinessen, Martin Van 9–10, 14, 187n4
Bucak, Faik 50, 58
Bucak tribe 79
Buldan, Pervin 170
Burkay, Kemal 42–4, 51, 61, 66–7, 71–3,
    75, 83, 96; *see also* TKSP

capitalism 11, 29, 34, 39, 73, 75, 84–5, 87,
    90
Cegerxwîn 114
citizenship: civic plural model of 142, 169,
    173; in Turkey 16, 24, 36, 42, 47, 153,
    171; of Turkey 140, 169
civic friendship 125, 145
civic nationalism 56, 194n30
Cizre 106, 111, 131
CHP (Republican People's Party) 181
colonialism 18, 75; in Kurdistan 74, 81,
    83–5, 88, 90
commemoration: practices 112, 118–9;
    events 118
Committee for Union and Progress 2
communism 90
comprador classes 88
Constitutional Court 161, 164, 166–7, 172,
    174
constitutive outside 27
contestation 23, 33, 42, 47, 82, 91, 121,
    153–4, 178
contingency 27–9, 32–3, 39, 82, 102, 125
counter-insurgency 131–3
counter-guerrillas 108, 131
counter-hegemony 39, 173, 154
Çağlayan, Handan 14–15, 47
Çakır, Ruşen 203n16
Çalışlar, Oral 127
Çicek, Ali 98
Çiller, Tansu 134

Dailamites 13
DDKO (Revolutionary Cultural Hearths of
    the East) 6, 66–9, 77–8; defences 69–71,
    77, 98
death fast 98, 116; *see also* hunger strike
death under detention 132
DEP (Democracy Party) 155, 162–4
DGM (State Security Court) 46–7, 161,
    163–4
decontestation 153
Dehak 77
DEHAP (Democratic People's Party)
    164–5, 167–8

Demir, Eyyüp 14, 48
democratic autonomy 171, 173
democratic discourse 5, 21, 41, 153–5,
    169, 174; *see also* radical democracy
Democratic Initiative 146–7, 173, 180
democratic opening 16, 161; *see also*
    National Oneness and Togetherness
    Project
democratic subjectivity 35, 153–4, 157
Democratic Unity Thesis 136–7
Denge Kawa 44–5, 74, 78
Denmark 114
Derrida, Jacque 30
Dersim rebellion 52, 184
Devrimci Yol 197n35
Dicle-Fırat 42, 51, 53, 56
Dicle, Hatip 160–1, 163–4
Dicle Talebe Yurdu 50
disappearances 132, 165, 170
dislocations 21, 28–9, 32–4, 39, 49, 82,
    124–6, 150
discourse: construction 41, 57; definition
    28; force of 39–40, 129; fragmentation
    34; identity and 23, 27–31, 82;
    ideological condensation of 41, 74, 81,
    87; ideological transformation of 41;
    nationalist 41; *see also* Laclau; Foucault
discourse analysis 4, 41–2
discourse producers 41–8
discourse theory 4, 22, 27, 39
Diyarbakir 61, 68, 78, 106–7, 111, 117, 123,
    129, 131, 133–4, 146, 148, 160, 163, 166,
    168, 171; Newroz in 34; municipality
    167–8, 170; mayors of 78, 152
Diyarbakir Prison 34, 80, 96, 98, 100, 102,
    104, 116–19, 123
Doğan, Mazlum 98, 111, 116, 118
Doğan, Orhan 164
Doğu Mitingleri; *see* Meetings of the East
DP (Democrat Party) 52
DTP (Democratic Society Party) 164,
    171–5, 182–3
Durmuş, Mehmet Hayri 98

East 38, 43, 50, 61–3, 69
Eastern Question 43, 49–57, 64, 68
Easterners 38, 62
Eastist movement 51, 64–5, 68, 76, 78
ECHR (European Court of Human Rights)
    46–7, 141
Ekinci, Tarık Ziya 51, 60–1
Elçi, Sait 50, 56–7, 61
empty signifiers 31, 33, 36, 65, 94, 154,
    169, 178

232 Index

Enstîtuya Kurdî 113
Epözdemir, Şakir 58
Erdoğan, Recep Tayyip 173
Ergenekon 204n26
ERNK (National Liberation Front of
  Kurdistan) 102, 109–13, 118, 129; *see
  also* PKK mobilisation
essentialism 4, 27
ethnic identity 22
ethnic 22, 60, 65, 158, 161, 169; demands
  147; minorities 36, 144, 153–4;
  nationalism 172; origins 63
ethos of pluralism 180
Eruh 101, 105
Europe 14, 29, 34–5, 43, 45–6, 71, 75, 91,
  132; Eastern 126; Kurdish political
  activism in 19, 51, 99–102, 107–14,
  118, 122, 128; Turkey and 9, 146, 156,
  171, 175, 180
EU (European Union) 146, 171, 175, 180
exemplars 34, 115, 117–18, 120, 123
Ey Reqip (Kurdish National Anthem)
  115

Federation of Thought Clubs (FKF)
  67–8
feminism 136, 143
feminist critique of nationalism 143
feudal classes and elites 30, 42, 72, 82–3,
  85, 87–9, 91, 95, 100, 102, 107
feudalism 30, 37, 70, 73, 84, 86, 93; *see
  also* Kurdish feudal practices
Finlayson, Alan 26
flags 111, 115, 122, 127, 132, 166
folk dancing 112–13, 119, 122; *see also*
  Mîhrîcan 113
folk music 113, 119
forced migration 134, 150
Forty-niners (49'ers) 52
Foucault, Michel 37
France 84, 112
Freeden, Michael 26

gendarme stations 62, 105–6
gendarmeries 62, 110
gender equality 15, 36, 125, 141, 143, 169,
  174, 183
gender politics 47, 138, 143
Germany 99, 105, 110, 112, 117
Glynos, Jason 37, 39, 192n79
Gramsci, Antonio 31–2, 102, 193n1
Grand National Assembly 47
Greece 135, 206n67
Greek Migration 3

Greeks 2, 3
Gunter, Michael 9
Gül, Abdullah 173
Gül, Aydın 79
Gündoğan, Azat Zana 195n46
Gündoğan, Cemil 14, 45, 47, 199n60,
  200n69
Güney, Yılmaz 114
Gürbey, Gülistan 9–10

HADEP (People's Democracy Party)
  164–8
Hakkari 104, 106–7, 131, 146, 148, 166–7,
  170, 211n91
Halkın Kurtuluşu 78–9
Hanioğlu, M. Şükrü 186n4
Hassanpour, Amir 4
hegemony 26, 31–4, 102, 126, 138;
  Gramsci 31; institution 102; Laclau and
  Mouffe 32, 34
hegemonic: articulation of identity 32,
  102; discourse 11, 20, 26, 31, 41–2, 172,
  81; order and regimes 39; representation
  of the Kurds 6, 35, 82, 146, 149, 154,
  172
Hegemony and Socialist Strategy (Laclau
  and Mouffe) viii, 28–9, 31
Helwe camp 99
HEP (People's Labour Party) 15, 111, 131,
  153, 155–63, 165
Hilvan 63, 79, 119
Hirschler, Konrad 14
Hizbullah 129, 131, 203n16, 204n26; *see
  also* murders by unknown assailants
Howarth, David 37, 39, 192n79
HPG (People's Defence Forces) 138, 143,
  148; *see also* ARGK; HRK
HRFT (Human Rights Foundation of
  Turkey); *see* TİHV (Türkiye İnsan
  Hakları Vakfı)
HRK (Kurdistan's Liberation Forces) 104,
  111; *see also* ARGK; HPG
human rights 36, 94, 98, 111, 122, 149,
  156–8, 160, 165, 182; abuses 21, 156,
  160; discourse of 22; organisations 30,
  35, 108, 110, 121, 134; reports 47
hunger strikes 98, 109, 162–3, 166

identity: academic discussions of Kurdish
  4, 9, 11–14, 20–3; articulation of
  Kurdish 6, 26, 41, 57–8, 64, 67, 81, 87,
  139, 153, 177, 179, 183; common 3,
  29, 50, 140, 142, 153, 167, 169, 179,
  183; contestation of Kurdish 33, 66,

Index 233

82, 178; denial of Kurdish 50, 70, 80, 83, 142, 160, 171, 184; discursive construction of 15–16, 27–31, 40, 82, 177, 179; ethnic conception of Kurdish 4, 7, 33, 66, 97, 100, 115; exclusion of Kurdish 2, 38, 208n7; individuation and delimitation of 28, 82; Kurdish political 16, 21, 23, 25, 29, 41, 107, 168; nationalism and 25–7; political frontiers and 29–31, 177; popular expression of Kurdish 110–11, 104; recognition of Kurdish 1, 3, 15, 36, 58, 133, 142–8, 152–5, 160–1, 165, 169, 173–6, 180–3; relations of difference and 4–5, 77, 96; representation of 4, 7, 20, 33, 41, 95–8, 115, 122, 178–9; stabilisation of Kurdish 21; Turkish 1–2, 16; women and 15, 120, 143, 202n62

ideology 2, 1–2, 18–22, 31, 43, 46, 75–6, 86; grip of 39–40; Kurdish nationalist 10, 19, 25, 35, 41, 43, 45, 176–8; nationalism 9, 25–7, 72–3, 78; *see also* Marxism-Leninism

ideological 20, 70, 74, 81–2, 94, 99, 104, 139; condensation 22, 81, 87; dimension 71; dogmatism 136; impasse 125; orientation 127; specificity 10, 176–8; transformation 12, 177, 179

İHD (Human Rights Association) 134
imaginaries 27, 41, 153
imagined community 122, 202n70
İmralı prison 135
Indo-European 13, 54, 70, 97
İnönü, Erdal 160
Institute Kurde 113
internal displacement 1, 147, 186n1
interpellation 39, 177; nationalist; 177–8
Iran 11–12, 16, 50, 77, 140
Iran-Iraq War 107
Iraq 11–12, 15–16, 50, 57, 76, 84, 133, 140, 148
Iraq–Turkey border 101, 105, 201n23
Iraqi Kurds 52, 75–7, 80, 108, 117, 130
Iraqi Kurdistan 15, 51, 58, 77, 84, 99, 107–8, 114, 124, 130, 132, 134, 145
Islam 3, 110, 128–9
Islamist 3, 10–11, 129, 203n16
Israel 206n67
Istanbul 50, 65, 68, 78, 99, 113, 134, 162, 166, 170, 174, 181, 195n53, 201n40, 205n47
Izady, Mehrdad 4, 12, 186n2

Izmir 59, 117, 195n53

Jacobinism 36
JİTEM (Gendarmerie Intelligence and Counter-Terrorism Organisation) 131
Jongerden, Joost 186n1
Justice Party 55
Justice and Development Party; *see* AKP

KADEK (Kurdistan Freedom and Democracy Congress) 124, 135, 140–4
Kandal, Salih 79
Karahan, Edip 42–3, 50–3, 55–6, 61
Karasu, Mustafa 206n96
Karer, Haki 79, 119
Kartal, Remzi 164
Kawa the Blacksmith 33, 66, 77, 80, 83, 96
Kawa Movement 33, 44–5, 74, 77–8, 81–2, 84, 88–93, 97, 99
Kaya, Yaşar 52, 194n21
Kaytan, Ali Haydar 118
KCK (Council of Communities of Kurdistan) 141–2, 147–8
KDP (Kurdistan Democrat Party) 57, 76, 89, 99, 117, 130, 134, 201n21
Kemalism 2, 40, 89; *see also* Atatürk, Mustafa Kemal; Turkish nationalism
KİP (Kurdistan Workers' Party) 74, 77–9, 82, 91, 94–5, 99
Kirişci and Winrow 4
Kılınç, Mahmut 162
KNK (Kurdistan National Congress) 128
Koma Berxwedan 46, 112–14, 119; *see also* resistance music
Kongra Gel (People's Congress of Kurdistan)
Korkmaz, Mahsun 111, 118
Kotan, Mumtaz 43, 45
KUK (National Liberationists of Kurdistan) 77–9, 95, 99; conflict with the PKK 95
Kutay, Ferhat 98
Kutlay, Naci 61, 67
Kurds: description of 12–15; fragmentation of 13, 35, 38, 83–7, 97, 100, 103, 110; migration and 9, 16 ; origins of 9, 33, 54, 66, 69–70, 115; unity of 14, 20, 40, 80, 83, 96–7, 103, 115, 121, 125; *see also* Alevi Kurds; Iraqi Kurds; Yezidi Kurds; Zaza Kurds
Kurdish: cultural festivals 15, 109, 113, 115; difference 9, 21, 36, 41–2, 55–6, 70, 77, 96, 122, 137, 144, 153; feudal practices 18, 37–8, 40, 86–9; historiography 13–14, 23; language 13-4, 51, 53–6, 58, 69–71,

234 Index

Kurdish *continued*
  88, 97, 112–15, 119, 122, 140, 142–3,
  146–7, 149–50, 160, 163, 168–9, 173,
  181–2; national demands 11–12, 14, 18,
  20, 22, 33, 40–1, 43, 61, 66–7, 75, 81, 89,
  94, 97, 100, 142, 146–7, 159, 161, 169,
  175, 177–9, 183; people 80
Kurdish national movement 9–11, 13–17,
  19, 22, 25, 27, 31, 33–4, 38, 40–2, 49,
  66, 73–4, 82, 86, 91–4, 99, 103, 115,
  119, 125, 143, 147, 161; fragmentation
  of 43–4, 73–7, 79; in Iraq 51, 57, 75–6,
  77, 80, 89–90
Kurdish nationalism: appeal and affect of
  10, 13, 19, 24–5, 34–5, 39–42, 78,
  100–3, 107, 112, 120–2, 127, 129, 141,
  146, 154, 158–9, 166, 178–9, 182, 184;
  ideological diversity of 4, 11, 40–1,
  177–8; origins of 8, 76, 81; pluralism
  and 143, 145, 150; transformation of 11,
  16, 21–2, 24, 35, 41, 45, 137–45
Kurdism 52, 62, 71
Kurdistan 14, 50, 72, 80, 82, 142, 187n1;
  geography and maps 14, 115; division
  7, 40, 66, 71, 83–8; independent 12, 20,
  37; history of 12, 116; liberation of 18,
  30, 61, 81, 83, 103–8, 127, 178;
  minorities in 36, 97–8, 144; parliament
  in exile 108, 128; representation 47,
  114–15, 122; revolution in 19, 75–6,
  83, 88–91; underdevelopment of 50,
  53–7, 60, 62, 64, 72–3; unity of 30,
  83–4, 90, 142
Kürkçu, Ertuğrul 174, 183

Lacan, Jacque 39, 193n99
Laclau, Ernesto 27, 29, 31–2, 34–6, 49,
  102, 125, 153, 183, 191n24; *see also*
  articulation; discourse; dislocation;
  empty signifiers; hegemony; myth;
  nodal point; sedimentation
Laclau and Mouffe 4, 26, 28–32, 34–5,
  188n15; *see also* discourse theory;
  hegemony; logics of equivalence; logics
  of difference; radical democracy
Lenin, Vlademir 60
linguistic: diversity in Kurdish society 13,
  25, 35, 40, 55, 74, 112, 129; oppression
  1, 55, 70, 83, 85; rights 14, 137, 142,
  147, 153, 171, 173
logic of equality 36, 153, 182
logics: definition 37; fantasmatic 37, 39,
  40, 121, 193n99; political 29–30, 37, 39,
  42, 82; social 37–8; *see also* logics of

difference; logics of equivalence; logics
  of difference 29–30, 33, 91, 153, 169;
  logics of equivalence 29–31, 33, 82, 91,
  102, 125, 128, 139, 153, 162

Manifesto (The Path of Kurdistan
  Revolution) 88, 92, 95–6
maps of Kurdistan 115, 122
Marcus, Aliza 120, 190n44
martyrs 109, 117–19, 121, 202n52
Marxism 6, 9, 20, 26, 31–2, 68, 71, 102,
  136; appropriation of 57, 65–6, 69, 76,
  80; articulation of Kurdish national
  demands and 6, 22, 65–6, 80, 89, 100;
  Leninism 11–12, 21–2, 76, 127
McDowall, David 9
Med TV 114
Medya TV 114
Meetings of the East 6, 49, 57, 59, 61–4
Mem–û–Zîn 51, 53
Mersin 131, 170, 174, 210n89
MGK (National Security Council) 157
MHP (Nationalist Action Party) 181
Middle East 2, 8–11, 74, 77, 81, 83–4, 96,
  108, 114, 128, 136, 140–4
migration 1, 9, 16; to western Turkey 39;
  to western Europe; *see also* counter-
  insurgency; forced migration; internal
  displacement; village evacuations
Mîhrîcan 113
military coups 45, 52, 69, 78–80, 82, 91,
  94, 156
millet system 2
minority rights 22, 142
Misak-ı-Milli 30
MKM (Mesopotamian Cultural Centre)
  113, 201n40
mobilisation 16–19, 26, 34, 39, 42, 64, 101,
  122, 150, 176, 178–9; of Kurds in Europe
  103–11, 122, 143; of Kurds in Turkey 14,
  23, 25, 31, 109–11, 139; of women 15,
  120; *see also* ERNK; insurgency and
  PKK; Serhildan Mouffe, Chantal 154;
  see also Laclau and Mouffe
Mountain Turks 8
myth 13, 31–4; *see also* Newroz

national cultural autonomy 145–6,
  207n101
national liberation discourse 4–5, 7, 42–4,
  86; articulation of Kurdish national
  demands in 41, 76, 81; constitution of 6,
  76, 81–2; fragmentation of 34–5,
  126–30; feudalism and 86–7; force of

Index 235

121–2, 125; hegemony of 20, 80–1, 87; transformation of 35, 135–45; suitability of 76–7, 80
National Oneness and Togetherness Project 147
nationalism 25–6; Arab 73, 100; civic and ethnic distinction 194n30; Turkish 2, 15, 35, 38, 56, 83, 85, 100, 125, 133, 138, 146; Persian 73, 100
nationalist historiography 22
neo-Ottomanism 3
Newroz: as a myth of Kurdish origin 7, 19, 21, 23, 47, 66, 77, 80, 95–7; as a myth of Kurdish resistance 20, 34, 40, 46, 83, 97–100, 115–17, 119, 121, 178; celebrations 109–11, 115; contestation of 121; PKK and reactivation of 19, 96, 102, 115–19, 178; *see also* myth
Nietzsche, Friedrich 117
Nimni, Ephraim 145, 207n101
nodal point 28, 32–3, 80, 81, 97, 139
Norval, Aletta 30, 32, 117–18, 153, 202n63, 208n4

OHAL 104
oligarchy 139
oppression 1, 7, 18, 21, 36, 39–41, 52, 57, 64, 69–70, 72, 116–18, 129–30, 139, 157–8, 160, 163, 165–7; discursive construction of relations of 10, 23, 42, 47, 50, 136, 143; national oppression 60–1, 63, 66, 68, 73–7, 80–3, 85, 87–9, 95–6, 100
organic intellectuals 6, 42, 50, 54, 58; Edip Karahan Ottomanism 2; *see also* Musa Anter
Öcalan, Abdullah 46, 98, 106, 114, 127–8, 133–4, 148, 163, 172, 176; cult of personality 19–21; detention and trial 35, 124, 126, 135, 149–50, 166; legal defences 21, 47, 136–7, 141, 144
Öcalan, Osman 130, 145
Ölmez, Osman 14, 48
Önder, Sırrı Süreyya 174
Öner, Necmi 98
Ötüken 61
Özal, Turgut 3
Özcan, Ali Kemal 16, 19–21, 203n8
Özgür Halk 111, 114
Özgür Gündem 114, 127
Özgürlük Yolu 74, 77, 95–6

PAJK (Freedom Party of Women of Kurdistan) 141

Palestinian movement 99
pan-Kurdism 108
particularity 31, 176, 183; nationalism and 25; Turkish 153
party closures 162–5, 167, 172–3, 175
patriotism 90, 93
PÇDK (Kurdistan Democratic Solution Party) 141
peasants 18, 30, 33–4, 38, 42, 51, 60, 73, 77, 80, 90, 105, 109, 139, 193n1
Perinçek, Doğu 127
Persians 62
Perwer, Şivan 113
Pêshmerge forces 130
Pir, Kemal 98
PJA (Party of Free Women) 143
PJAK (Party of Free Life in Kurdistan) 141
PKK (Kurdistan Workers' Party): articulation of Kurdish demands 12, 18–20, 102; ceasefires 1, 133–5, 148–50; civil disobedience and legitimate defence 138–9; collapse of communism and 107, 125–7; congresses and conferences 79, 92, 99, 103–5, 108–9, 111, 132, 137–8, 140, 143; contemporary myth of resistance 115–22; establishment of 78–9; hegemony of 5, 10, 16, 19, 23, 40, 82, 91, 101–2, 107, 125–7; ideological and organisational transformation 129, 137–42, 144, 150; insurgency and 1, 101–9, 121, 124, 126; mobilisation of women 109–10, 117, 119–21, 143; organisational development 79, 91, 99, 101–2, 109; relations with Iraqi Kurds 89, 99, 117, 130, 134, 201n21; revolutionary strategy 91–5; Syria and 99, 134–5, 140; Turkish left and 80, 82, 91, 93–5, 100, 107; *see also* national liberation discourse; democratic discourse mobilisation
pluralism 1–3, 5, 16, 27, 36, 42; pro-Kurdish political parties and 153–5, 165, 167–9, 171–2
political frontiers 29–31; *see also* boundaries
political reconciliation 30, 125–7, 132, 138; PKK and 145–8, 150; pro-Kurdish political parties and 7, 152, 154–6, 159, 165, 167–8, 171, 173–4
political subjectivity 28
post-Marxism 4, 26–7

236 *Index*

post-nationalism 176, 180, 184
poststructuralism 26
pro-democracy election block 165, 167, 173–4
pro-Kurdish political parties: and pluralism and democracy in Turkey 153–4, 157–65–7, 169, 171, 176, 180, 184; and solution to the Kurdish conflict 158–62, 165–77; difficulties and challenges of 153–5, 158, 160, 168–9, 172, 180–5; and elections 152, 156, 159, 163, 166–8, 170–1, 173, 173–5, 183, 211n90; organisational development 164, 167; parliamentary representation 159–62, 164, 166–7, 170, 173, 175; party congresses 155, 159–61, 166; *see also* party closures, BDP, DEHAP, DEP, DTP, HADEP
psychoanalysis 26–7, 39–40
PUK (Patriotic Union of Kurdistan) 130, 133, 200n72, 201n21
PWD (Patriotic Democratic Party) 145

Qandil Mountain 148
Qimil 51

radical democracy 3, 5, 31, 35–6, 136, 144, 182–3
refugees 1, 108, 201n22; *see also* internal displacement
religious minorities 13, 102, 110, 115, 128–9, 144, 154; *see also* Alevi Kurds; Yezidis
representation of Kurdish question in Turkey 146–8
republicanism in Turkey 2–3
republican era 54, 58, 63, 84, 137
resistance 5, 10, 43; practices 34, 79, 91–2, 98; representation of 7, 80, 96–7, 115–22, 199n64, 200n66, 201n34, 202n52; movements 100, 177–9; *see also* Newroz; PKK
resistance music 112–14, 118–9; *see also* Koma Berxwedan
Revolutionary Democrats 78
Rizgarî 33, 44–5, 74–5, 78, 81–4, 87, 89–90, 95–6, 99
ROJ TV 114–15
Romano, David 16–19, 21–3
Russia 128, 135

secular 3, 38, 129
secularisation 38
sedimentation 32–4, 40, 47, 101–3, 112, 119–21, 123

self-immolation 98, 116–18, 199n65
separatism 3, 8, 64, 50, 55, 58, 62–3, 127, 144, 148, 182, 187n3
Şemdinli 101, 149, 208n122
Serhildan 102, 104, 109–10, 116, 118–9; Diyarbakir 111, 119; Nusaybin 110
Serxwebûn 46, 105, 110, 118
Silvan 61–2, 68, 131
Siirt 104, 106, 110, 166–7, 170, 200n66
Siverek 61, 63, 79
Şırnak 104, 106, 110–11, 130–1, 146, 167, 170, 204n23
SHP (Social Democratic Populist Party) 152
socialism 11, 16, 20–1, 59–60, 67–8, 74, 81, 87, 94, 127; collapse of 126; experienced 127
scientific 127
socialist revolution 20, 60, 73, 94; in Kurdistan 73, 98; *see also* national liberation
Solmaz, Edip 152
Stalin, Joseph 60
Stalinism 12
Staten, Henry 191n24
Stavrakakis, Yannis 37, 39, 193n99
strategy 82; revolutionary strategy
strategic transformation 124–5, 135, 137–42
Süleymanlar Tribe 79
Syria 11–12, 50, 84, 140

TAK (Teyrêbazên Azadiya Kurdistan) 149
Tak, Cuma 79
Talabani, Jalal 133
Taş, Nizamettin 145
Tevger 78, 198n34
TİHV (Türkiye İnsan Hakları Vakfı) 47, 108
TİP (Workers' Party of Turkey) 6, 43, 50–1, 57, 59–60, 65, 69, 77; and articulation of Kurdish demands 60, 64, 67; the Eastern Meetings 61–4
TKDP (Kurdistan Democrat Party of Turkey) 6, 42, 50–1, 57–8, 61, 64, 76–8, 80, 95; *see also* Faik Bucak; Sait Kırmızıtoprak
TKSP (Socialist Party of Turkish Kurdistan) 33, 79, 81–4, 87, 90–5, 99; critique of the PKK 95–7; divisions 78; establishment 44, 77; Turkish socialists and 67, 86–8, 94; *see also* Özgürlük Yolu, national liberation discourse, Kemal Burkay

Index 237

TKİİP 74
Tori, Sabri 145
trade unions 30, 59, 67, 134, 166, 168
tribal 88, 103, 110; leaders 52, 103
tribes 10, 13, 22, 38, 40, 97
TRT Şeş 146
Tuğluk, Aysel 171–2
Tunceli 61, 79, 104, 106, 117, 132, 146, 170
Turkey: EU accession 171, 175, 180; incursions into Iraq 130, 148; political polarisation 3, 121, 133, 166; security discourse 121, 133, 147–8; terrorism 8, 95, 121, 131, 133, 147–9, 161, 164, 172, 179, 181–2, 184, 205n49
Turkish: nationalism 2–3, 15, 35, 38, 56, 70, 73, 83, 85, 125, 133, 138, 146; security forces 8, 18, 80, 101–6, 111, 129, 131–2, 147–8, 150, 158, 182; socialists 17, 23, 33, 43, 50, 61, 65–8, 71, 73–6, 80, 82, 91, 93–5, 100, 107, 153, 156
Türk, Ahmet 172–3, 156, 163–4
Türkiyelilik 164
Türkiye Barış Meclisi 182
TZP Kurdî 149, 182

Uçarlar, Nesrin 34, 187n4
UDG (Union of National Democratic Forces) 79
underdevelopment 9, 11, 59, 65, 68–71
United Kingdom 205n49
unity of the nation 52, 54–6, 59, 62, 74, 137
universal rights and values 153, 156, 158, 165
universality 35–6
Uzun, Mehmet 114

Vanly, Ismet Serif 43
Vali, Abbas 13
Verdery, Katherine 26
village guards 101, 104–6, 108, 119, 130, 160
village evacuations 130, 132, 150, 160; *see also* internal displacement
violence: against civilians 111, 147; by state security forces 10, 59, 64, 69, 131, 133, 164; justifications of 82, 91–3, 137–8, 144; political violence 1, 9, 91, 95, 101, 103, 106, 122, 126, 135, 138, 142–5, 148–9, 171–3, 152, 176, 179–80, 184

Watts, Nicole 14–15, 34, 188n10
westernisation 38
Weşanên Serxwebûn 110
Wittgenstein, Ludwig 30
White, Paul 4, 12–13
World Peace Day 134, 163

Xanî, Ehmadi; *see* Mem–û–Zîn

Yeğen, Mesut 187n3, 196n32, 208n7
Yezidis 110, 115
Yıldıran, Esat Oktay 98–9
Yılmaz, Akif 98
Yılmaz, Kani 145
YTP (New Turkey Party) 52–3

Zana, Mehdi 43, 61, 63, 152
Zana, Leyla 160–1, 164, 208n1
Zaza: Kurds 13; language 115
Zengin, Mahmut 98
Zilan (Zeynep Kınacı) 117, 132

Taylor & Francis eBooks
FOR LIBRARIES

ORDER YOUR FREE 30 DAY INSTITUTIONAL TRIAL TODAY!

Over 23,000 eBook titles in the Humanities, Social Sciences, STM and Law from some of the world's leading imprints.

Choose from a range of subject packages or create your own!

- Free MARC records
- COUNTER-compliant usage statistics
- Flexible purchase and pricing options

- Off-site, anytime access via Athens or referring URL
- Print or copy pages or chapters
- Full content search
- Bookmark, highlight and annotate text
- Access to thousands of pages of quality research at the click of a button

For more information, pricing enquiries or to order a free trial, contact your local online sales team.

UK and Rest of World: **online.sales@tandf.co.uk**
US, Canada and Latin America:
e-reference@taylorandfrancis.com

www.ebooksubscriptions.com

A flexible and dynamic resource for teaching, learning and research.

CPSIA information can be obtained
at www.ICGtesting.com
Printed in the USA
JSHW011319201219
3107JS00002B/25